The Animal Mind

D0713965

The study of animal cognition raises profound questions about the minds of animals and philosophy of mind itself. Aristotle argued that humans are the only animal to laugh, but recent experiments suggest that rats laugh too. In other experiments, dogs have been shown to respond appropriately to over 200 words in human language.

In this introduction to the philosophy of animal minds Kristin Andrews introduces and assesses the essential topics, problems, and debates as they cut across animal cognition and philosophy of mind. She addresses the following key topics:

- what is cognition, and what is it to have a mind? What questions should we ask to determine whether behavior has a cognitive basis?
- the science of animal minds explained: Classical ethology, behaviorist psychology, and cognitive ethology
- rationality in animals
- animal consciousness: what does research into pain and the emotions reveal? What can empirical evidence about animal behavior tell us about philosophical theories of consciousness?
- does animal cognition involve belief and concepts; do animals have a "Language of Thought"?
- animal communication
- other minds: do animals attribute "mindedness" to other creatures?
- moral reasoning and ethical behaviour in animals
- animal cognition and memory

Extensive use of empirical examples and case studies is made throughout the book. These include Cheney and Seyfarth's vervet monkey research, Thorndike's cat puzzle boxes, Jensen's research into humans and chimpanzees and the ultimatum game, Pankseep and Burgdorf's research on rat laughter, and Clayton and Emery's research on memory in scrub jays.

Additional features such as chapter summaries, annotated further reading, and a glossary make this an indispensable introduction to those teaching philosophy of mind and animal cognition. It will also be an excellent resource for those in fields such as ethology, biology, animal studies, and psychology.

Kristin Andrews is Associate Professor in the Department of Philosophy and Director of the Cognitive Science Program at York University, Canada. She is the author of *Do Apes Read Minds? Toward a New Folk Psychology* (2012), and co-editor of the forthcoming *Routledge Handbook of Animal Cognition*.

The Animal Mind

An Introduction to the Philosophy of
Animal Cognition

Kristin Andrews

Routledge
Taylor & Francis Group

LONDON AND NEW YORK

First published 2015
by Routledge
2 Park Square, Milton Park, Abingdon, Oxon OX14 4RN

Simultaneously published in the USA and Canada
by Routledge
711 Third Avenue, New York, NY 10017

Routledge is an imprint of the Taylor & Francis Group, an informa business

British Library Cataloguing in Publication Data
A catalogue record for this book is available from the British Library

Library of Congress Cataloging in Publication Data
Andrews, Kristin, 1971-
The animal mind : an introduction to the philosophy of animal cognition / Kristin Andrews.
pages cm
Includes bibliographical references and index.
1. Cognition in animals. 2. Animal behavior. 3. Cognition–Philosophy. I. Title.
QL785.A69 2015
591.5'13–dc23
2014021202

ISBN13: 978-0-415-80957-3 (hbk)
ISBN13: 978-0-415-80960-3 (pbk)
ISBN13: 978-1-315-77189-2 (ebk)

Typeset in Franklin Gothic
by Saxon Graphics Ltd, Derby

Printed and bound in the United States of America by Edwards Brothers
Malloy on sustainably sourced paper.

Contents

Acknowledgments

I've been teaching the Philosophy of Animal Minds at York University for over ten years, and I've learned much about how to present this material from all the students who have passed through my classroom. Some of them read draft chapters of this book, some of them saw slides that I turned into text, but they all helped shape the book you are looking at now. First thanks to all of them.

I wasn't planning on turning my class into a textbook but one day Tony Bruce from Routledge showed up in my office and asked me to write *The Animal Mind*. It sounded like a great idea. During the next two years I was lucky enough to have lots of eyes on drafts. In particular, I'd like to thank those who gave me comments on part or all of the manuscript: Laura Adams, Jacob Beck, Rachel Brown, Devin Curry, Grant Goodrich, Bryce Huebner, Brian Huss, Imola Ilyes, Georgia Mason, Irina Meketa, Edward Minar, Anne Russon, Sara Shettleworth, Elliott Sober, Olivia Sultanescu, and anonymous reviewers for Routledge. I'd also like to thank members of the GTA Animal Cognition Group for helpful discussions about many of these issues. Olivia Sultanescu and Brian Huss deserve extra thanks for their work proofreading, and thank you Olivia for drafting the glossary, and for cleaning up and putting together the pieces that make up this book.

I am lucky to have had experiences working directly with animal cognition researchers. I have to thank Adam Pack and Lou Herman of the Kewalo Basin Marine Mammal Laboratory for accepting my application to work with the dolphins as an intern back in 1992. More recently I was given the opportunity to observe cognition research on rehabilitant orangutans by accepting an invitation to visit Samboja Lestari Reintroduction Project by the Borneo Orangutan Survival Foundation in Indonesia. I greatly thank BOS, and Anne Russon for facilitating the invitation. Seeing the differences between lab and field cognition research played an important part in how I now think about the best way to study animal minds.

Thanks to Brian and Poppy, and to Huxley and Mono, for putting up with me working on yet another book project, and all the time and distraction that goes along with that. Thanks to John and the crew at Annex Montessori for teaching Poppy while I worked, and to the cafés in Kensington Market and Bloordale for offering me good places to work. Much of this was written listening to The Smiths at Café Pamenar and Ethiopian jazz at Holy Oak. Thanks to my faculty organization YUFA for giving me the course release needed to write, and thanks to SSHRC for funding the materials and support I needed to put it all together.

I also want to thank all the animals who were used in the research discussed in this book. Many of these individuals died in captivity, including some I had personal relationships with. I appreciate their forced sacrifice.

Introduction

Kinds of minds

"Rico, get the tyrex." Rico ambles into the next room, picks up the blue dinosaur from among a jumble of stuffed toys, and carries it back with him. "Rico, get the ball ... the Santa Claus ... the sock, the white bunny ..." Again, and again, Rico leaves the room, and returns with the named object. Rico's performance would be pretty good for a small child. For a border collie, it is astounding.

Rico has been taught 200 labels by his owners, who show Rico a new object—say, a rubber chicken—and then repeat the name of the object—"chicken, chicken, chicken"—two or three times. Then Rico gets to play with the toy, and not before long he is able to retrieve the chicken from his collection of objects when asked. In a formal study of Rico's word learning ability, researchers found that Rico can also fast map new words via a learning-by-exclusion mechanism—he is able to deduce the referent of an unfamiliar word by realizing, for example, that the word has to refer to one of eight objects, and that it can't refer to the seven familiar objects. So, if Rico is asked to retrieve the dax, and the other objects are the familiar ball, Santa Claus, sock, white bunny, etc., he is able to infer that the unfamiliar object must be the dax. In a video of this test that is posted online, you can see Rico nosing the various objects in the room before finally choosing the correct one (Kaminski et al. 2004).

How do toddlers and border collies infer that the novel object is the target, when they are asked to pick up a "dax"? How does fast mapping work? Developmental psychologists think that children rely on operating principles in their language learning, and that even toddlers understand that words refer to objects. Rico's ability to fast map is taken as evidence that he shares some of the operating principles—he knows that objects can have names—and he possesses a learning-by-exclusion mechanism that allows him to deduce the referent of the unfamiliar word. For example, when asked, "Where is the dax?" Rico realizes that the word has to refer to one of the eight objects in the array, and since he knows the name of seven objects, "dax" cannot refer to any of them. In order to make this inference, he needs to either believe that objects can only have one name, or believe something about his owners' intentions.

Rico's fascinating abilities raise a number of questions about how to interpret his behavior, as well as about the mechanisms involved. Does Rico understand that words refer? Does he grasp the intention of speakers who utter an unfamiliar word? Is his word learning similar to that of human children? Or does he take the word "sock" to be a command to fetch the sock, and is his "word learning" just a result of obedience training; is it like teaching a dog to sit or come?

We may have different intuitions about these questions. Some dog lovers might think that Rico really does understand words. But for others, the intuition goes the other way, and they may explain Rico's success as a matter of forming simple associations between objects and utterances. However, neither intuition goes very far as a meaningful or justified answer to the questions. The dog owner may be biased by her relationship with her own dog, and more likely to *anthropomorphize*—or attribute human qualities—to dogs and other familiar animals, and she may not have thought carefully about what it means to know something as a *word*. The skeptic may be biased in the other direction, being inclined to *anthropectomy*—or denying human qualities to other animals—and she may not realize that training and understanding often go hand in hand for humans as well as dogs, as in the cases of learning to play the violin, or to speak a second language.

In order to provide justified answers to the questions raised by Rico's feats, we need to turn to both science and philosophy. Questions about animal minds are addressed across academic disciplines, with psychologists, biologists, anthropologists, ecologists, ethologists, primatologists, and philosophers—among others—engaged in answering overlapping sets of questions using different methods. The scientific methods are in place to minimize bias and to develop and test hypotheses. The philosophical methods are in place to clarify the questions, as well as the answers. As in any interdisciplinary endeavor, it can be difficult for a person from one discipline to make herself understood to someone from the other disciplines because, along with different methods, there are often different vocabularies. However, the possibility of increasing overall understanding certainly makes it worth the extra effort. And a growing number of researchers have been dual-trained in more than one of these disciplines; for example, Juliane Kaminski, the lead researcher on the Rico study, was trained in biology and psychology, and she has worked with a number of different species, including humans, other great apes, and goats.

The scientific research on the cognitive abilities of animals comes from many different disciplines and involves many different methodological approaches. In laboratories, zoos, or other captive settings, psychologists ask questions about the cognitive mechanisms involved in perception, memory classification, spatial cognition, numerical abilities, learning, future planning, social intelligence, communication, and so forth. In the field, psychologists, biologists, ethologists, ecologists, and anthropologists are interested in documenting what different species do, examining similarities and differences between individuals and groups, and conducting experiments to learn something about the causes of behavior and the contents of animal minds. These and other biological approaches to studying animals take seriously animals' evolved nature, and aim to answer questions about the evolutionary function of the observed behaviors, as well as the reproductive benefits that the behavior offers. In front of the computer, some psychologists and ecologists seek to answer questions about animal minds by developing and manipulating functional models of animal behavior based on the interaction between individuals and the environment. And, in the neuroscience lab, scientists are engaged in studying the brains of animals as they process different kinds of information. But for all these sciences, there arise fundamental issues about the concepts used in the investigation, and the usefulness of the methods implemented to address the questions and interpret the data.

To see why taking all these different perspectives into account is productive in animal cognition research, consider again the questions we asked about Rico's behavior. While scientists can ask the empirical question of whether Rico will respond by fetching a new object when he is commanded to fetch the dax, philosophers are more focused on how we should best interpret Rico's behavior. Philosophers may investigate whether Rico understands words that refer, appealing to some account of reference, naming, or understanding. In addition, philosophers may investigate the nature of reference, naming, and understanding, using Rico's behavior as additional evidence for developing new theories of these notions. The philosopher's analysis of concepts is first fed by what she sees in the world, and then again by how the world behaves once it is seen through the theoretical lens. For example, suppose we understand consciousness as necessarily involving the ability to feel pain, and evidence of feeling pain comes from observing irritant responses, such as shrinking back from a pinprick or a hot stove. We can use this simple account to investigate the distribution of consciousness, and find that a meditating monk doesn't react to a pinprick, and a mimosa plant will close its leaves when brushed—but doesn't respond after being given an anesthetic that eliminates pain responses in humans. Given other reasons we have for thinking that the monk is conscious (say, her verbal report), and other reasons for thinking that plants don't experience pain (say, our identification of pain as being caused by neural structures that are absent in plants), we can modify our understanding of consciousness slightly, and use the new understanding to investigate the world again, which may lead to a further revision of the concept. This constant calibration of concepts and observations means that no simple answer is going to be available to any of the questions asked in this book. We will be investigating the nature of animal consciousness, rationality, belief, communication, social understanding, and morality, while at the same time looking at what animal behavior can help teach us about these concepts. The hope is that by looking at a wide range of behaviors displayed by a variety of minded creatures, we will gain a greater understanding of the various aspects of the biological mind, which will help us better understand the human animal as well as our nonhuman relatives.

1 Getting to know other minds

Close your eyes, and reach for an object in front of you. Now open your eyes, and try to identify which object you touched. Easy, right? For human adults, cross modal perception between the visual and tactile senses is natural. It's even easy for human infants, who at one month old can select a picture of a pacifier after having blindly sucked on one. Chimpanzees, too, can also easily match what they see and what they feel; even when they touch an oddly shaped object they've never seen before, they can pick the object out of an array once they open their eyes. Dolphins, however, don't appear to use their tactile modality to recognize objects (though it is very important to their social interactions), and so we shouldn't expect dolphins to have such an easy time with this kind of cross modal perception. Should we conclude that dolphins lack cross modal perception? That would be hasty! Dolphins are different from humans and chimpanzees in interesting ways. For one, they use echolocation, a kind of sonar, to perceive the physical world in the water (dolphin echolocation doesn't work in the air). Scientists have found that dolphins who echolocate on a strange shape hidden behind a screen under water will select that object from an array when they can see it in the air (Pack and Herman 1995).

Animals clearly think and feel—after all, we are animals, and we think and feel. Members of the human species have human minds, and if members of other species have minds, they will have species-specific minds of their own. Despite the title of this book, there is no such thing as *the* animal mind. Different animal species have different biological, environmental, social and morphological features, and all of these differences could have cognitive impact. Octopuses with neurons in their tentacles might have minds that are more distributed and embodied than the minds of some other animals (though the human "gut brain"—the neurons in the stomach— might lead some to make similar inferences about the human mind). The dolphin's ability to echolocate on other dolphins may allow them to observe others' physical states, including their brain states. This has led one philosopher to hypothesize that dolphin groups share a single group mind (White 2007). Thomas Nagel famously argued that we can't know what it's like to be a bat because humans are so different from bats both physically and socially, and the best we can do is to imagine what it would be like for *us* to be bat-like (Nagel 1974).

And while animals are clearly different from one another in some ways, in other ways they may be the same. Sociality is another difference between animal species that may impact their cognitive processes. Animals who live in complex social societies have complex worlds, so the idea goes, and in order to keep track of those complex worlds their cognitive capacities must have evolved in ways that allow them to handle such complexity. Consider baboon communities. Most baboon species live in troops with a largely stable female hierarchy, and a more flexible male dominance hierarchy. Because these hierarchies are linear, any change in dominance between two individuals affects the status of the other individuals in the group, and when there is a rank reversal in the female line, the relatives of the baboon who lost status are also demoted, and the entire line is revised. In order to keep track of fluid changes in social status and understand who can do what given their current standing, baboons have to handle quite a bit of information, and this suggests that baboons require more complex cognition than they would have needed if their social lives were not structured in this way.

Another way to investigate the similarities and differences between species is to examine individual development. We can examine the similarities and differences between the early development of humans and other apes, and for example, can find that infant chimpanzees will engage in neonatal imitation just as some human children do. If humans and chimpanzees engage in the same kind of social behavior early in infancy, yet diverge in social behavior later in life, we can examine intervening stages of social development in order to determine what might lead to the differences we see in adults.

Furthermore, while there are differences between species, differences between groups of species, and differences between stages of development, there can also be differences between individuals. Just as adult humans vary in our personalities, preferences, and cognitive capacities, we might expect that there are individual differences between adults of other animal species.

So while we shouldn't expect that there is any such thing as *the* animal mind, there certainly may be a variety of kinds of minds that are in some ways interestingly similar, and in other ways interestingly different from one another.

1.1 Mind and cognition

Before we get started asking questions about the nature of animal minds, however, we need to know that other species have minds, and to do that we need to know what a mind is. In one sense, we all know what is meant by mind. When we turn our attention toward our own minds, what is perhaps most evident is the phenomenal aspect—the experience of the conscious mind which can feel (itchy), taste (salty), crave (affection), and experience (stillness). When we look past the phenomenal aspects of mind—what it feels like to have a mind—we can also see that the mind permits us to do things, such as remember, analyze, form associations, think, wonder, learn, perceive, decide, and act. An amazing feature of the human mind is that it permits a reason-respecting flow of thought. Even after a long bout of daydreaming, we can retrace our thoughts to figure out how we got from there to here.

But in another sense, the mind is mysterious to us. Mind doesn't seem to be like a tree or a mountain, something whose existence we can verify with our senses. We can wonder whether the people around us really have minds, or whether they just act like they do. Furthermore, we don't always have conscious experience of our reasoning or sensory processes. We engage in automatic driving, tooth brushing, dish washing, and other habitual behaviors without always having any feeling of what is going on. We are influenced by stimuli that we are unaware of, such as subliminal images in advertising. And we are sometimes wrong about the causes of our own behaviors. We make errors. These are also things our mind does. Mind is rational and irrational, conscious and unconscious, it remembers and forgets.

The variety of properties we associate with mind makes it difficult to define, which is what we should expect given that our understanding of mind is constantly calibrated with what we observe minds doing. One way to clarify our questions about the mind is to narrow the focus to certain elements of it. This is what many cognitive scientists do in their investigation of the mind—they study cognition. Cognition is generally understood to refer to the processes that mediate between our sensory inputs and our later behavior, including things like memory, problem solving, navigation, reasoning, and language processing. The cognitive processes that make possible reliving your early childhood memories, recognizing your father's face, and judging that two lines are the same length are causes that may be described in terms of knowledge or concepts, functional parts, or neural processes in the organism. Cognitive processes cause the behavior the organism engages in given the stimuli the organism perceives.

Cognition is often described as permitting learning and flexible behavior. Having flexible behavior means that you can do different things in similar situations, and learning means that you can change your responses given experience. Some animal behaviors lack this sort of flexibility needed for learning. The greylag goose, for example, will bring a displaced egg back into her nest by reaching out with her neck and rolling it toward the nest with her beak. If you were to place a golf ball, a doorknob, or a much larger egg on the edge of her nest, she would roll those items into her nest as well.

As the ethologists Nikolaas Tinbergen and Konrad Lorenz showed us, the greylag goose's egg rolling behavior is a fixed action pattern for the species: a motor program that is initiated by anything that closely enough resembles an egg. The goose can't help but retrieve it. She doesn't have a concept of egg, or knowledge that eggs need to be kept safe in her nest, or that goslings will hatch from the egg. She can't learn to discriminate doorknobs from eggs. All she has is an invariant response to egg-like stimuli (Tinbergen 1951).

Much of human behavior, on the other hand, is quite flexible, and is mediated by concepts and knowledge that allow us to understand the situation. We can learn how to ask appropriate questions in the classroom, we learn how to use words, and how to tie shoes. We can also decide not to tie our shoes, or to use words incorrectly, in order to achieve a different response.

The idea that the cognitive aspects of mind permit learning and flexible behavior offers us an answer to the first question: we can examine mind in entities that appear to learn and behave flexibly. If other entities learn, and engage in flexible behavior, then they are also proper objects of cognition research.

1.2 Historical views

Now let's turn to the second question: what is our justification for thinking that other animals have minds? Interest in the question of animal minds has a long history in the Western philosophical tradition, and a number of figures have denied some aspect of mind to animals. St. Aquinas thought that on this planet, humans alone are rational thinking beings who are able to make decisions and choose their own actions. (The realm of God and angels is another story.) Immanuel Kant, too, denied rationality to animals due to their assumed inability to consider their reasons for action, and to will their actions. But Kant thought animals have desires (another mental property), and that they are blindly driven by their desires. However, without rationality animals lack the ability to step back and consider whether their desires ought to be fulfilled, or how best to fulfill them.

But it is perhaps René Descartes, in his *Discourse on Method*, who did the most to undermine the view that animals have rational, thinking minds, by arguing that only language users think:

> For it is rather remarkable that there are no men so dull and so stupid (excluding not even the insane), that they are incapable of arranging various words together and of composing from them a discourse by means of which they might make their thoughts understood; and that, on the other hand, there is no other animal at all, however perfect and pedigreed it may be, that does the like. This does not happen because they lack the organs, for one sees that magpies and parrots can utter words just as we can, and yet they cannot speak as we do, that is to say, by testifying to the fact that they are thinking about what they are saying; on the other hand, men born deaf and dumb, who are deprived just as much as or more than, beasts of the organs that aid others in speaking, are wont to invent for themselves various signs by means of which they make themselves understood to those who, being with them on a regular basis, have the time to learn their language. And this attests, not merely to the fact that the beasts have less reason than men but that they have none at all. For it is obvious it does not need much to know how to speak; and since we notice as much inequality among animals of the same species as among men, and that some are easier to train than others, it is unbelievable that a monkey or a parrot that is the most perfect of its species would not equal in this respect one of the most stupid children or at least a child with a disordered brain, if their soul were not of a nature entirely different from our own.
>
> (Descartes 1637/2000, 72)

For Descartes, animals are soulless machines like the automaton toys of his day—lifelike robotic figures that were able to play music, dance, or even draw pictures. Descartes claims that animal movements are the result of simple mechanisms, rather than being caused by the kinds of mental operations that result in human behavior. Because Descartes thinks the thinking capacity is not part of the material world, any behavior that can be explained mechanistically is not the result of rational mind. He argues that all animal action can be given a mechanistic explanation, but that humans, who engage in truly novel behavior, and come up with insightful solutions to problems they run across, are too complex for such explanations. Most importantly, by using language humans demonstrate a richness of behavior for which no purely mechanistic explanation can suffice.

The skeptics about animal minds were not without their critics. Voltaire thought Descartes was wrong about the complexity of animal behavior:

> What! that bird which makes its nest in a semi-circle when it is attaching it to a wall, which builds it in a quarter circle when it is in an angle, and in a circle upon a tree; that bird acts always in the same way? That hunting-dog which you have disciplined for three months, does it not know more at the end of this time than it knew before your lessons? Does the canary to which you teach a tune repeat it at once? Do you not spend a considerable time in teaching it? Have you not seen that it has made a mistake and that it corrects itself?
>
> (Voltaire 1764/1929, 21)

Voltaire's point is that other animals engage in rational behavior as well: they learn, they solve problems and correct themselves. Voltaire isn't denying Descartes' claim that these kinds of behaviors are necessary for having a mind, but rather he is disputing Descartes' empirical claims about what animals actually do. Here we see two kinds of debates about animal minds— debates about the requirements for having a mind, and debates about whether some species fulfills those requirements.

Like Voltaire, David Hume was dismissive of the idea that animals lack minds. He wrote:

> Next to the ridicule of denying an evident truth, is that of taking much pains to defend it; and no truth appears to me more evident than that beasts are endowed with thought and reason as well as man. The arguments are in this case so obvious, that they never escape the most stupid and ignorant.
>
> (Hume 1738/2000, 118)

Unlike Voltaire, Hume didn't think it necessary to give an argument for the claim that animals have minds, since anyone worth talking to should already know it! Given the number of philosophers who deny animals minds, Hume might be wrong about that last point. Let's then turn to three philosophical arguments that have been offered for the existence of animal minds, in order to see whether our initial assumption about Rico having a mind is warranted.

1.3 Arguments for other animal minds

The problem of other animal minds is a subset of the more general question of whether anything else has a mind. When the question of other minds is asked about humans, the reasoning often goes like this: our minds are private and cannot be directly observed by others, so we don't have access to minds other than our own; our belief that other humans have minds is the result of an inferential process. We *infer* the existence of other minds rather than seeing them directly, and the skeptic asks whether this inference is legitimate. A solution to the problem of other human minds requires a justification of that inferential process.

Despite the skeptic's challenge, developmentally there is really no problem at all when it comes to seeing others as minded creatures. We are not born into a world of solipsism, thinking that we are the only minded creature (despite children's notorious egoism). Rather, human infants are born into intersubjectivity and appear to understand their own mind along with the mind of their mother or other intimate caregiver. If children have a problem, it is the opposite of the skeptic's problem. Young children are quasi-animists who see mind and responsibility throughout the world. A child sees agency in the "bad" rose bush that scratches her as well as the "nice" stuffed toy she cuddles. Thus, the child's task is to *reduce* the number of individuals in the class of minded creatures. To justify the child's intuition that there are other minds, we are required to address the philosophical problem.

1.3.1 Arguments from analogy

A first attempt to solve the other minds problem can take the form of an argument style known as *the argument from analogy*. The argument from analogy for other minds follows this schema:

1   I have a mind and I have some set of properties *M*.
2   Other humans also have the set of properties *M*.
3   Therefore, other humans probably have a mind.

This isn't a valid deductive argument, but rather a very weak inductive argument, where the reference class consists of only one entity (namely, oneself). The argument can be made stronger with a complementary argument in favor of a particular reference property *M*. For example, one of my properties is that I am female. But using *female* as our *M* is extremely problematic, for there is no good reason to think that gender or sex has anything to do with having a mind. In its formulation by John Stuart Mill, the argument from analogy for other minds relies on a guiding theory that identifies as the reference property *M* the causal link between behavior and mind. The bulk of the argumentation, then, turns from the inductive argument for other minds to an argument in defense of some theory about the nature of mind. Given the weakness of the inductive inference, and the lack of a widely accepted reference property, it is fair to say that the argument from analogy for human minds is not very good. But what about the argument from analogy for animals minds?

When we turn from the traditional problem of other minds to what Colin Allen and Marc Bekoff (1997) call the *other species of mind problem*, John Searle (1994) calls the *other animals' minds problem*, and Jesse Prinz (2005) calls the *who problem*, the argument from analogy is stronger in one sense, but weaker in another. Consider this formulation of the argument:

1   All humans who have minds have some set of properties *M*.
2   Individuals of species *A* have the set of properties *M*.
3   Therefore, individuals of species *A* probably have minds.

While this argument is stronger than the argument for other minds, in the sense that it is an inductive argument with over six billion entities in its reference class, the strength of the argument also relies on the complementary argument about what should count as the reference properties M. The reference properties M might include a general capacity such as the ability to solve problems, a specific ability such as using language, a type of behavior such as hiding from predators, or even a type of brain activity.

This argument also seems to assume that there is a common set of properties M, essential for mentality, and perhaps we should not commit ourselves to such a claim at this early stage of the investigation. After all, when inquiring into the minds of other species, we don't want to rule out from the start the claim that there are different kinds of minds in nature, and the difference might go as far as there not being an essential property for mindedness. Rather than there being some necessary and sufficient condition for mindedness, creatures who have minds may resemble one another in various ways, just as family members share some physical properties but not others, and there is no one property that is shared by all.

If there were some property or set of properties required for having a mind, there would be a further problem about how to identify it. After all, identifying a reference property for the argument concerning animals may be even more difficult than identifying one for the argument concerning humans, since some species are very different from us. The octopus, for example, has a distributed nervous system that consists of a small central brain and more neurons in its legs. Dolphins use echolocation to "see" objects by receiving echoes from focused bursts of sounds aimed toward the objects. The argument from analogy focuses on similarity, but for most other species we will be able to identify more differences than similarities, thus challenging the strength of the analogy. There is a greater analogical distance between humans and other species than there is between you and other humans. And the analogical distance grows with species whose life histories, environment, evolutionary histories, and social structures are quite different from our own. Animals who live deep underwater, fly, perceive through echolocation, live for only a few hours, are solitary, or eusocial (i.e. form social groups with a division of reproductive labor and cooperative care of offspring, such as honeybee colonies with sterile worker castes) are so different from most humans that the analogy becomes dangerously weak. Thus, the argument from analogy for other animal minds on its own will not provide good justification for a belief in animal minds. However, in combination with other argument styles, analogical arguments may help to offer good reason for accepting animal minds.

1.3.2 Arguments from evolutionary parsimony

Several scholars have appealed to evolutionary parsimony to bolster the argument from analogy. On its own, the mere fact that we share property M with an animal is not enough to establish that the animal is minded. But the shared property M can be enough to attribute mind when it is supported by relevant background assumptions. Primatologist Frans de Waal and philosopher Elliott Sober have each argued that the theory of evolution provides just such adequate assumptions. In particular, they argue that the fact that we share property M with an animal is enough to establish the animal as (probably) minded if we assume: (a) that we share a common ancestor with the animal; and (b) that we should prefer the most parsimonious explanation of the emergence of property *M* (de Waal 1999; Sober 2005).

The most parsimonious explanation is the one that requires the fewest changes in the phylogenetic tree that maps out the evolutionary relation among species. In short, it is the simplest and most evolutionarily likely explanation. If we share a close common ancestor with an animal with whom we also share property *M*, then the most parsimonious explanation is that the animal is minded. The alternative explanation—that while our mindedness causes our property *M*, an entirely different nonmental mechanism causes the same property *M* in the animal—requires too much complexity of the phylogenetic tree to be probable.

While this evolutionary solution may overcome the problems raised by differences between animal species, it once again runs into worries about what should count as the reference property *M*. It is unclear, absent a complete defense of any given theory about the nature of mind, which properties of humans (if any) are linked to the existence of the human mind. The most obvious such property—full language capability—is of no use because, as far as we know, it is a property we do not share with any other species. And worse yet, some humans who we take to be minded, such as infants, lack linguistic abilities. Further problems arise when determining what counts as a close common ancestor, and how close is close enough.

1.3.3 Inference to the best explanation arguments

Another approach to arguing for animal minds is to make an *inference to the best explanation*. This kind of argument can be seen as an illustration of the scientific method, according to which the scientist identifies a particular phenomenon and then, through a process of generating hypotheses and evaluating them one by one, arrives at the most plausible explanation. Children who begin to slough off rose bushes and stuffed toys from the class of minded creatures do so around the same time they begin to understand the causal powers of mind, when they come to see that some behaviors are intentional or purposeful and others are unintentional or accidental. This argument for animal minds is based on the idea that the kinds of behaviors animals exhibit are better explained as being caused by cognitive phenomena than by simple deterministic rules that govern the movement of objects. And while we may find out that deterministic rules do explain mental phenomena, such rules would have to be much more sophisticated than the rules that govern the overt movement of those things that lack minds.

The inference to the best explanation argument for other animal minds takes this form:

1 Individuals of species *A* engage in behaviors *B*.
2 The best scientific explanation for an individual engaging in behaviors *B* is that it has a mind.
3 Therefore, it is likely that individuals of species *A* have minds.

While the inference to the best explanation argument doesn't suffer from the analogical argument's troubles with size of reference class and closeness of analogy, it does require further support. In this case, some justification must be given for premise (2). A certain behavior is best explained in terms of some mental property if that mental property provides more predictive and explanatory power than do other possible explanations. That is, by assuming the explanation, one can make better predictions about what the animal will do in future circumstances, and the explanation is coherent with other things we know about that species and mental property. For example, we might use what we know about the species' evolutionary history and defend premise (2) by appeal to the evolutionary parsimony argument discussed in the last section.

Of course, since what we mean by "better" is relative to other competing hypotheses, this argument is stronger when plausible alternative hypotheses have been formulated. If premise (2) is supported merely because the candidate explanations are either (a) the animal has a mind, or (b) the animal is a robot controlled by aliens, then discrediting the implausible hypothesis (b) does very little to support hypothesis (a). When using an inference to the best explanation argument to justify the existence of animal minds, or some particular mental property, one must be charitable and consider and reject all other plausible candidate explanations before settling on the mentalistic hypothesis.

Note that this argument can't be used to demonstrate in one go that all other species have minds, but only works on a case-by-case basis. For example, the argument for dolphin minds might refer to their behavior of using sponges to protect their rostrum (the beaky part of their face) when foraging for fish at the ocean floor, but we wouldn't refer to *that* behavior to support the claim that ants have minds, since ants don't use sponges as tools. But we can't use the lack of evidence that ants use tools as evidence that they don't have minds, either. For one, it might turn out that some ant species do use tools. But more importantly, tool use probably isn't a necessary condition for being minded; there are other behaviors that demonstrate the flexibility that is best explained by being minded. The same goes for any one behavior. So, for example, one might try to argue that ants are not minded beings because their behavior is terribly inflexible, as demonstrated by their penchant for taking live ants to the ant graveyard just because scientists have sprayed their nest mates with oleic acid, which dead ants typically excrete. However, flexibility may be found in other contexts. Current research on the ant species *Ectatomma ruidum* suggests a complex and flexible social structure. The ants spend much of their time in the nest grooming themselves and one another, like apes and monkeys. They also feed one another with the liquid food that serves as the only nourishment for adult ants:

> Droplet-laden foragers returned immediately to the nest tube and, after a few seconds of excitation behavior, either stood still or walked slowly about the nest with [their] mandibles open and mouthparts usually retracted. They were generally approached within a few seconds by unladen workers who gently antennated the clypeus, mandibles, and labium of the drop-carrier, using the tips of their antennae. The carrier then opened its mandibles wide and pulled back its antennae, while the solicitor opened its mandibles, extruded its mouthparts and began to drink. During feeding, the solicitor continued to antennate the donor, who remained motionless. Usually the solicitor also rested one or both front legs on the head or the mandibles of the donor.
>
> (Pratt 1989, 327)

Ectatomma are also sensitive to the levels of food they have in storage, and when supplies are low or merely sufficient, neighboring ants are attacked by guard ants when they attempt to enter the nest. However, when food supplies are abundant, guards allow neighboring ants inside, and food exchanges like those observed with nestmates also occur. This sort of behavior is compelling in an inference to the best explanation for ant minds if one cannot find other explanations that better account for the observed behavior (like the existence of simple heuristics that illustrate the ant behavior is actually inflexible).

There is a potential problem with all the arguments for animal minds that we have seen so far, but it is perhaps best seen in the inference to the best explanation argument for other animal minds. The problem has to do with the nature of mind. What exactly are we interested in when we ask if ants have minds? Do we want to know whether they reason—the central issue at stake in Descartes' rejection of animal minds? Do we want to know if they use memory, engage in decision making, or if they have emotions? Given that the notion of mind is still vague, instead of arguments for animal minds, we might look at arguments for more specific cognitive abilities.

For example, we can use the inference to the best explanation argument to continue investigating the questions about Rico's word learning (recall Rico is the dog who knows the names of 200 different objects). We might formulate two hypotheses about Rico's behavior: (a) he understands that words refer to objects (and thus has some aspect of human language); or (b) he has been trained to fetch particular objects when he hears a particular vocal signal (and he learns new commands via a general learning-by-exclusion mechanism). To distinguish between these two hypotheses, we need to know more about what Rico and other border collies can do. We need to know how flexible Rico's behavior is. As the psychologist Paul Bloom suggests, we can ask whether Rico can learn words for objects that are not fetchable (such as "fire hydrant") (Bloom 2004). Can he appropriately respond to requests *not* to fetch an object (e.g. to commands such as "Rico, please get anything but the sock")?

The psychologists who tested Rico report anecdotal evidence that he knows the word as a word rather than as a command, because he can do things like put the requested object in a box, or bring the requested object to a different person—he can do things with words like "sock" and "ball" other than bringing the objects back to the person who uttered the request. But critics point out that the anecdotal evidence isn't sufficient—experiments need to be run. (We'll have more to say about the role of anecdotal evidence in the next chapter.)

Though Rico died before researchers were able to take up this challenge, another group of psychologists has been teaching a border collie named Chaser to respond to over a thousand named objects. These psychologists wanted to examine Bloom's questions, and so they also taught her different verbs. In addition to "take," Chaser was taught "paw" (touch with paw) and "nose" (touch with nose). After being taught these different verbs, Chaser's ability to understand each word was formally tested. She was given compound commands she had never heard before, such as "take lamb" (pick it up in the mouth), "paw lamb" (touch with paw), and "nose lamb" (touch with nose).[1] Chaser performed perfectly on these tests (Pilley and Reid 2011). This formal study of a border collie's word learning demonstrates that the alternative hypothesis offered by Bloom—that the dogs understand noun terms as commands to fetch objects—isn't the best explanation for the behavior. The psychologists working with Chaser take her performance on these and other tests to be best explained by the hypothesis that she, like human children, learns words and knows that they refer. However, the conclusion that Chaser understands that words refer is still subject to further examination, particularly as we investigate what is involved in knowing that words refer.

1.3.4 Direct perception arguments

Direct perception arguments (also known as non-inferential arguments) for animal minds are based on the idea that when we interact with a minded creature, we simply see that the creature has a mind. There is no need to first observe behavior and then infer that there must be mind. Instead, we just see mind in others. While this sort of argument reflects the developmental account of how human children understand other minds, it also reflects a different view about the nature of minds. Whereas both arguments from analogy and inference to the best explanation take minds to be unobservable entities that must be inferred, on non-inferential views we directly perceive mindedness. Both John Searle (1994) and Dale Jamieson (1998) suggest that the problem of other minds is a vestige of an unjustified Cartesian dualism, and that once we reject mind/body dualism, we will in effect dissolve the problem of other minds. Searle argues that the existence of animal minds is a foundational or basic fact about the world that doesn't require justification, and it follows from this commitment that biological entities are the only things that can have minds (which he defends with his famous Chinese Room argument against artificial intelligence). Jamieson endorses what he takes to be Hume's praise of common sense in concluding that other animals have minds, and in thinking that we don't need "heavy philosophical or scientific artillery to prove that animals have thought and reason" (Jamieson 1998, 81). Jamieson's reasoning is that the problem of animal minds is taken to be different from the problem of other human minds without any justification. We might state the argument like this:

1   We reasonably think that some other animals are minded.
2   If we reasonably think that some other animals are minded, then we think so either because we infer that they have minds or because we directly perceive that they have minds.
3   We do not infer that other animals have minds.
4   Therefore, we reasonably think that other animals are minded because we directly perceive their minds.
5   And if (4) is true, then we know animals have minds.
6   Therefore, we know animals have minds.

The inferential arguments reject premise (3), and presume that when we see other animals, we see behaving bodies rather than minds. Jamieson objects that behaving bodies are philosophical monsters. Just as the folk—and psychologists—need not worry about skepticism when it comes to other human minds, they need not worry about other animal minds. In both cases, we directly perceive others' mental states, and the better we know the individual, their way of life, their relationships, their background, and so forth, the better we are at understanding the individual, regardless of species.

Critics will object to premise (3), but also to premise (5). A thirsty traveler might think they perceive water when walking through a desert, but thinking that we see something doesn't make it so. And humans seem to easily see mind in the natural world—we see faces in the clouds and feel sad for the old lamp who is discarded in favor of a pretty new one.[2] The critic will worry that this argument begs the question, and that it will only "convince" individuals who already believe in animal minds. But besides begging the question, the argument has another problem—it can't help to solve the other species of mind problem, because the argument doesn't allow us to draw conclusions about species we cannot get to know. Amoeba may be too small, the giant squid may be too big and elusive, and the pelican eel may be too ugly and scary. While Jamieson says that the non-inferential approach leaves open the possibility that such creatures are minded, he doesn't offer a means for overcoming the difficulties we will certainly encounter when trying to get to know some animals that are very different from ourselves. Thus, while the non-inferential approach may work with dogs and chimpanzees, it may be less useful when it comes to different taxa.

While the non-inferential method may not satisfy the critic, it, along with inference to the best explanation, makes sense of why so many people think that animals do have minds. Though the predominant view among philosophers and psychologists is that animals have some kind of mind, there is widespread disagreement about what sorts of cognitive properties they have. And this leads us to ask more specific questions about animal minds.

1.4 The calibration method

Once we've accepted that animals are the sorts of things that might have minds, then it may seem that we only have to ask more specific questions about animal minds—questions like do they have conscious experience? Do they reason? Do they communicate? However, since we are simultaneously investigating the nature of these phenomena and the nature of animal minds, there is no direct application of some well-established theory to these questions. As we examine the questions about animal minds in the following chapters, we will be using the calibration method, using animal minds to better understand the mind more generally.

The calibration method starts with describing or categorizing a behavior—for example, we might see squirrels caching nuts in the fall to eat during the winter and describe their behavior as planning. Then we begin to study the behavior in terms of the stimuli that elicit it and the mechanisms that mediate between the stimuli and the behavior. To study how squirrels cache nuts, we can examine what causes them to start burying, and what causes them to bury as many nuts as they do. We might also examine the squirrels' brain processes when they are confronted with the stimuli that cause them to start caching nuts. Once we have a good initial understanding of what causes squirrels to cache nuts, we can compare squirrel planning with what we know about human planning, or planning in other animals. Based on how similar the squirrel planning is to our prototype of planning, and how useful it would be to consider squirrels to be planning, we will decide both what we mean by planning and whether the squirrels' behavior counts. And that decision can help us to examine further questions about caching. If we decide to understand the squirrels as planning their future meals, we can also ask how well they plan, what sort of individual differences there are in planning among squirrels, and whether squirrels only plan when it comes to nut storage, or whether they plan in other domains, such as their travel routes. And this investigation may lead to another point at which we will want to revisit our notion of planning and the question of whether squirrels plan. For example, if we find that squirrels don't do anything resembling planning in any other domain, that may serve as evidence against squirrel planning in the domain of nut caching, if we are conceiving of planning as a domain general process—one that can be used in a number of different kinds of situations.

Given the calibration method, as we describe a behavior we are beginning to explain it. We make sense of the behavior by saying it is a behavior of a certain type. But it is only the beginning of an explanation, because we have further questions to ask about the mechanism involved in the behavior, and mechanistic explanations can offer additional explanatory power by showing us how the behavior is caused by the cognitive system. To better understand the calibration method, let us look at both what is involved in describing behaviors and in determining the mechanisms underlying them.

1.4.1 Describing behaviors

It might seem like an easy matter to describe behavior, but worries quickly arise. When Rico responds to a request to get the Frisbee, it may be natural for us to say that Rico understands that his human wants him to get the Frisbee, and that Rico wants to do what his human wants. We also might quite naturally understand Rico's behavior as evidence that he knows what a Frisbee is, and what it means to fetch. This initial step of describing the behavior is consistent with our *folk psychology*, or commonsense understanding of other minds. We use folk psychology when we explain why a friend quit his job and started a farm in the country by saying the friend wanted some peace and quiet, or believed that he had to escape the rat race to keep his sanity, or that he was having a mid-life crisis, or even just that he's the kind of person who makes radical changes to his life every few years.

Describing a behavior in terms of folk psychology is often seen as an act of interpretation. We take the observable behavior and then interpret its meaning much the way we take linguistic utterances and interpret the sounds as meaningful sentences. And while language and behavior might seem transparent to us—it may seem that no interpretation is required—we might be wrong. The philosopher W.V.O. Quine argued that even when we understand human linguistic behavior, we engage in an act of *radical translation*. He asks us to consider how a linguist goes about translating a newly discovered language. Once the linguist is embedded in the community, and has found collaborators among the native population, she can begin to develop hypotheses about what particular words mean. "A rabbit scurries by, the native says 'Gavagai,' and the linguist notes down the sentence 'Rabbit' (or 'Lo, a rabbit') as a tentative translation, subject to testing in further cases" (Quine 1960, 29). Quine argues that even after extensive testing of this hypothesis, the linguist's experience with the native population will not be sufficient to decide between that translation, and a variety of other consistent translations, such as "There are undetached rabbit-parts there" or "There is rabbitness there." This goes for all other utterances of the type, and Quine concludes that there can be different and equally consistent translations of a single language.

Problems with interpretation can be experienced first hand when interacting with people from different cultures. Bubbly Americans who are constantly telling others to "Have a great day!" might read the more reserved Russians as unfriendly. Talking to someone with your sunglasses on, showing your feet, or your knees, etc. signals disrespect in some cultures, though are acceptable in mainstream Western cultures. And hiding a giggle behind your hand is polite for a woman in Japan, but was seen as mean-spirited by my five-year-old Canadian-American daughter.

If we have such troubles with humans, we might expect even more troubles with interpreting animal behavior. When investigating animal minds, the initial step of describing behavior should be done with sensitivity to the worries about interpretation. It is an initial step, and not the end of the matter.

1.4.2 Explaining behaviors

Once we have initially described a behavior as a certain kind of behavior, we can start asking further questions about that behavior. Behaviors are open to different kinds of explanations. We might explain a behavior in terms of folk psychology, in terms of different mechanisms and processes that cause the behavior, or in terms of evolutionary function. And in many cases, these sorts of explanations can be broken down into further parts, both in terms of sub-behaviors and other more basic processes.

The goal of cognitive science is to provide a functional decomposition of cognition, which involves explaining behavior in terms of its parts. Once you have parts, you can then look at how each of those parts work, and thus gain different levels at which you can examine a system. The idea of levels of explanation was introduced by the psychologist David Marr as part of his analysis of how the brain processes visual information. Marr distinguished between what he called the *computational* (the goal of the system), the *algorithmic* (the function that achieves the goal), and the *implementation* (the physical organization of matter) levels of explanation (Marr 1982). In psychology, the computational level is considered a high level of explanation, and the implementation level is considered a low level of explanation.

Marr's levels of analysis have been influential in the philosophy of mind and adopted by those who take a functionalist approach to the metaphysics of mind (which is to be distinguished from talk of "function" in ethology or psychology, where the function of a behavior refers to the ultimate reproductive goal of the organism). In philosophy, functionalists such as Jerry Fodor (1975) and Hilary Putnam (1960, 1967) argue that we can understand mental states not as brain states but rather in terms of their causal role in a theory of behavior. Functionalism is the theory that what makes something a mental state is what it does—its causal role—and that the material composing a mental state is irrelevant. Thus functionalists assert the doctrine of multiple realizability: the same mental state can be implemented in organisms made of very different material, and with very different physical organization. Take for example an alarm clock. Many different programs and physical objects can serve the function of an alarm clock: an old-fashioned wind up clock, an iPhone's digital computer, or your very reliable (and hungry) dog can all serve the function of waking you up, even though they have distinct physical structures and causal organizations. For the functionalist, different kinds of systems, with very different kinds of software and hardware, can share the same function.

The move toward functionalism in the philosophy of mind was inspired by research in computation, and especially Alan Turing's work on the theoretical possibility of a Universal Turing Machine: a computer that can solve any well-defined problem. According to Turing, the Universal Turing Machine that fools a human into thinking it is also human has beliefs, reasons, and in sum, has a mind. On this view, the human mind is analogous to a computer program, and the human brain is analogous to the computer processor. What makes an entity minded depends on whether it is running the right sort of program, a program which corresponds at least generally to the human theory of folk psychology (Lewis 1972).

Given her commitment to multiple realizability, the functionalist is more interested in explaining behaviors in terms of smaller functional parts, and so looks for explanations at Marr's algorithmic level. And the functionalist approach to animal cognition is unconcerned with whether a behavior is caused by the same mechanisms; all that matters is that the behavior serves the same sort of goal within a largely similar theory of the organism's complete repertoire of behavior. Thus, the functionalist's job is to interpret behavior and build a complete theory of behavior at the algorithmic level. For example, humans and octopuses may have different biological mechanisms that are triggered by tissue damage, but if the same kinds of functional descriptions can be given for both organisms, the functionalist will conclude that both humans and octopuses can feel pain.

Neuroscientists and philosophers who identify mental processes with brain processes will focus more attention on, and offer explanations at, the implementation level. For example, to study pain on the implementation level we might note that specialized receptors in the skin called nociceptors send signals to the spinal cord in response to tissue damage. Those signals cause reflexive behavior to avoid the damage. If we want to know whether octopuses experience pain, then we can also look to see if they have nociceptors as part of their nervous system.

A scientific explanation of animal behavior and capacities might involve different levels of explanation, and it is sometimes difficult to identify which level of explanation is being invoked. The study of pain, for example, might involve explanations at all three levels. The goal of pain avoidance is to avoid tissue damage, and an irritant response such as pulling away from a heat source is a behavior that fulfills this goal. The biological organization that causes this behavior can be examined in the physical organism.

Because explanations can be given at different levels, when it appears that there are two competing explanations for an animal's behavior, it is important to first determine whether the explanations really are competitors. It is possible that two different explanations that appear to be inconsistent are really consistent explanations at two different levels. For example, suppose that we find that Rico's behavior is explainable in terms of his forming associations between sets of stimuli. Must we conclude that Rico doesn't understand the words? Not unless we have some additional reason for thinking that the two hypotheses are inconsistent with one another. For example, if children learn language by forming associations between sets of stimuli, and children also understand the meaning of words, we should suspect that the explanation in terms of forming associations is at a lower level of explanation than the explanation in terms of Rico's understanding words. When examining various explanations for behaviors, we must keep in mind that different explanations need not be competing ones, and this is especially important when dealing with inference to the best explanation arguments.

Animal cognition research is in the business of explaining animal behavior, but as we've seen, there are various ways of explaining behavior. Different scientists focus on different levels and kinds of explanations, which sometimes leads to confusion. Psychologists who work with humans are very often interested in folk psychological explanations in terms of beliefs, desires, goals, emotions, personality, and so forth. Some work in animal cognition aims to explain behavior in these terms as well. It is important to note, though, that an explanation in folk psychological terms can be consistent with explanations in algorithmic and implementation terms, just as it can be consistent with evolutionary and developmental explanations.

1.5 A case: explaining monkey alarm calls

To see the calibration method at work, we can turn to the philosopher Daniel Dennett's investigation into the meaning of monkey alarm calls. In 1983 Dennett traveled to Kenya at the invitation of primatologists Dorothy Seyfarth and Robert Cheney, a husband-and-wife research team who were then studying communicative behaviors in a community of vervet monkeys. Earlier observers had noticed that vervet monkeys give different alarm calls for different predators. When a vervet sees a snake, he stands on his hind legs and begins to make a kind of chuttering sound; when he sees an eagle he makes a very different sound, and when he sees a leopard, he makes a third sound. Each of these calls invokes a distinct behavior in the other vervets in his community. When they hear a leopard alarm call, they run up a tree. In response to the eagle alarm call, the vervets run into bushes where they can hide from the eagle, or they look up.

Cheney and Seyfarth wanted to know whether vervets understand alarm calls as referential, in the sense that the eagle alarm call means "there is an eagle around," or if the calls are more like generalized alerting systems, and mean something like "Take cover!" or express emotion like "Oh, scary!" If the calls do not refer, the difference in behaviors between the alarm calls may be due to each individual looking around in response to the alarm call, observing the predator, and then taking the appropriate predator avoidance action. In order to test between these hypotheses, Cheney and Seyfarth ran playback experiments, which involved hiding a speaker in the grass near the monkeys and playing an alarm call in the absence of a predator. What they found was that monkeys ran up trees when they heard the leopard alarm call even when there was no leopard around, and likewise responded appropriately to the recordings of the other alarm calls. This led the researchers to conclude that vervet monkeys use the alarm calls as words with referential properties (a claim which we will examine further when we discuss animal communication in Chapter 5).

Cheney and Seyfarth were identifying additional vervet vocalizations, and they were trying to determine what they meant. Dennett was intrigued by this real-life case of Quinean radical translation. Like Marr, Dennett realized the importance of identifying the kind of explanation one is after. Dennett identifies three different stances one can take in explaining behavior (Dennett 1987). The *intentional stance* involves looking at a behavior in folk psychological terms, as being caused by beliefs and desires. An observer who takes the *design stance* explains behavior in terms of what the system was designed to do (if the system is an artifact like a corkscrew or a chess-playing computer, the design stance would identify the designer's intention for the object; if the system is a biological one, then Dennett says that an evolutionary explanation is appropriate). Finally, an observer who takes the *physical stance* explains the behavior in terms of the physical instantiation of the object, just as in Marr's implementation level of analysis. For example, from the design stance a waiter's corkscrew and a Screwpull would have the same description—they open wine bottles—but on the physical stance they would have very different descriptions, as they are made of different material and do the job in different ways. Dennett's intentional systems theory states that anything whose behavior can be reliably and voluminously predicted from the perspective of the intentional stance is an intentional system—an agent whose behavior is accurately described in folk psychological terms (Dennett 2009).

When Cheney and Seyfarth claimed that we can interpret the vervet monkey alarm calls as referential signals with particular meaning, they were describing the behavior from the intentional stance. There are two possible challenges to this interpretation. One is that the intentional stance may not be the appropriate level at which to explain animal behavior. The other is that their particular intentional explanation may be incorrect. To confront the first challenge, they would need to show that vervet monkeys are the right sorts of thing to examine from the perspective of the intentional stance. Dennett suggests that when we don't get any additional predictive power from the intentional stance, then the system doesn't count as an intentional system—objects like lecterns are examples of non-intentional systems, because attributing to them the desire to stay put doesn't provide any additional predictive power over the predictions that come from the design stance or even the physical stance. If vervet monkeys are intentional systems, we can better predict their behavior from the intentional stance than from the design stance—it is just a matter of attributing the right sort of intentional state description. Dennett writes:

> My proposal, in simplest terms, was this. First, observe their behavior for a while and make a tentative catalogue of their needs—their immediate biological needs as well as their derivative, *informational* needs—what they *need to know* about the world they live in. Then adopt what I call the *intentional stance*: treat the monkeys as if they were—as they may well turn out to be—rational agents with the "right" beliefs and desires. Frame hypotheses about what they believe and desire by figuring out what they *ought* to believe and desire, given their circumstances, and then test these hypotheses by assuming that they are rational enough to do what they ought to do, given those beliefs and desires. The method yields predictions of behavior under various conditions; if the predictions are falsified,

something has to give in the set of tentative hypotheses and further tests will sift out what should give.

(Dennett 1988, 207)

Dennett takes us to apply a principle of rationality in our interpretive acts, and where animals are concerned, what they need to believe and desire is determined by their evolutionary history. The vervets need to believe that there is a leopard when they hear a leopard alarm call, because if they didn't so believe, they wouldn't live long enough to reproduce their genes. And while Dennett expresses conviction that the hypothesized translations of the three alarm cries have withstood sufficient experiment and observation in various contexts, he also thinks that his method is limited when it comes to studying nonhuman animals. It is limited because the kind of experiments we can set up are constrained by the fact that animals don't have language, and so animal cognition researchers cannot have the same flexibility in setting up scenarios as human psychologists do.

However, Dennett's conclusion may be too pessimistic. His initial suggestion was that researchers use what he calls the "Sherlock Holmes method." This method involves setting up a scenario in which you can attribute beliefs and make predictions about behavior. But even in the inspirational stories, Sherlock Holmes doesn't rely on language to set up these sorts of scenarios. For example, in the story "A Scandal in Bohemia," which is perhaps one of the best examples of the method, Holmes needs to discover where Irene Adler has hidden a compromising photograph of her with the hereditary King of Bohemia. In order to learn her hiding place, he makes a number of assumptions about her mental states. He expects that she values the photograph more so than any other of her possessions, and that she knows where it is hidden. Given those attributions, he predicts that if her home were to be aflame, and the photograph was hidden in the house, that she would do whatever she could to rescue it before fleeing. And so, of course, Holmes sets up a scenario in which her house appears to be on fire, and he observes her reaching into her hiding spot. While there were some shouts of "Fire!" the smoke bomb and general confusion alleviated the necessity to say anything to Miss Adler to set up the scenario and motivate her to action.

The Sherlock Holmes method can help us to determine whether someone acts as we think they ought to act given what we think they think. If they don't act as we predict, then we need to revisit our starting assumptions. One of Dennett's starting assumptions has to do with the nature of belief, which for him is not a mental representation that is hidden in the brain, but is a pattern of observable behavior. Such a view is at odds with a long history of thinking about belief as a mental representational state that is an intrinsic property of a believer. Whether a belief is considered to be a picture in the mind (as Aristotle or Locke would have it) or a sentence in a language of thought (as Jerry Fodor claims), the dominant view in psychology and the philosophy of mind is that belief is a representational state. As we calibrate our understanding of belief with our investigation into whether monkeys understand others' beliefs, the hope is that we will gain greater understanding of both issues.

1.6 Chapter summary

Given that there are different kinds of minds, we can examine the similarities and differences between adult human minds and the adult minds of other species. We can also look at the development of other species of minds in order to better understand the organizational structure of mind. As we study these different kinds of minds, though, we are learning both about the nature of mind and the specific mental properties we see in other species. Using the calibration method, we start with a theory about the nature of some mental property, then we use that theory to make a considered judgment about whether some animal has that property, and use that judgment to empirically investigate the property. The results of that investigation may cause us to tweak our theory, our considered judgment, or both.

Before we turn to the central questions of investigation, we will examine the methodologies used by scientists to study animal minds. In Chapter 2, we will see how the different methods can be used to ask the same questions, while providing different kinds of explanations. After considering the science of animal minds, we will be well placed to use the calibration method to examine specific issues in the philosophy of mind and psychology—the nature of consciousness; rationality, concepts, and belief; communication; social understanding; and finally, moral psychology.

Notes

1   The authors of the study have made accessible video of Chaser's behavior, which is available here http://www.youtube.com/watch?v=Kbl13nbDRRI
2   In a commercial for Ikea, available here https://www.youtube.com/watch?v=dBqhlVyfsRg.

Further reading

The book that introduced many of us to the philosophical issues about investigating animal minds is *Species of Mind: The Philosophy and Biology of Cognitive Ethology* by Colin Allen and Marc Bekoff (1989).
This collection of short essays by scientists and philosophers provide many examples of the fecundity of interdisciplinary cooperation: *The Cognitive Animal: Empirical and Theoretical Perspectives on Animal Cognition*, edited by Colin Allen, Marc Bekoff, and Gordon Burghardt (2002).
Section three of *Brainchildren: Essays on Designing Minds* by Daniel C. Dennett (1998) contains five of Dennett's essays on the study of animal minds.
There are a number of useful online resources. At *The Stanford Encyclopedia of Philosophy* (http://plato. stanford.edu) you can look up many of the issues discussed in this text. Some useful starting places include Alec Hyslop's entry "Other Minds" and my own entry "Animal Cognition." Another good resource is Robert Lurz's entry "Animal Minds" in the *Internet Encyclopedia of Philosophy* (http://www.iep.utm. edu).
For a sweet and entertaining account of how living with a wolf can change a philosopher in many different ways, I recommend Mark Rowlands' *The Philosopher and the Wolf* (2009).

2 The science of other minds

In *The Descent of Man*, Darwin tells the following story:

> Sir Andrew Smith, a zoologist whose scrupulous accuracy was known to many persons, told me the following story of which he was himself an eye-witness; at the Cape of Good Hope an officer had often plagued a certain baboon, and the animal, seeing him approaching one Sunday for parade, poured water into a hole and hastily made some thick mud, which he skillfully dashed over the officer as he passed by, to the amusement of many bystanders. For long afterwards the baboon rejoiced and triumphed whenever he saw his victim.
>
> (Darwin 1880, 69)

This story of Darwin's is compelling because we can so easily make sense of it. The baboon was tired of being tormented by the officer, and so he planned his revenge. He realized that the officer wouldn't appreciate being doused with mud, and thus a good revenge would be to muddy him. After gaining his revenge, the baboon was delighted every time he saw the officer, celebrating his success.

It is easy to interpret the story this way, because we would naturally see these sorts of motivations and causes when watching a human act in this manner. But we have a richer body of information about the causes and motivations of human behavior. We know typical human ways of being really well, because we spend lots of time with humans. And we can talk to people in order to gather confirming evidence of our interpretation. In the case of Smith's baboon story, however, we don't have that sort of additional evidence. How can we gather evidence in favor of what seems to be the most natural interpretation of this story?

That question remains when we turn to contemporary research in animal cognition. In 2009, the journal *Current Biology* published a report about a chimpanzee named Santino who, like

Smith's baboon, was known to throw objects at humans (Osvath 2009). Santino lives at the Furuvik Zoo in Sweden and he would target zoo visitors. But rather than getting them muddy, Santino liked to throw rocks. What is particularly interesting about this case is that Santino would collect the rocks and cache them in different locations near the visitors' area before the zoo opened, as though he was preparing the day's ammunition. The report describes Santino's behavior as calm and methodical while he gathered and created stone projectiles, and agitated or aggressive when he later threw the stones. Mathias Osvath, the study's author, claims that Santino's behavior demonstrates foresight and episodic memory. However, both foresight—the ability to plan for the future—and episodic memory—remembering your own past experiences—are capacities that are only controversially attributed to nonhuman species, and sometimes deemed problematically anthropomorphic.

Thus, it isn't surprising that some psychologists were critical of the claim that Santino was planning for the future. In two different papers, psychologists objected to the conclusions of the study by arguing that systematic experimental work would be required before dismissing the possibility that Santino's behavior could be explained in terms of mechanisms that don't require future planning (Shettleworth 2010a; Suddendorf and Corballis 2010). To decide, researchers should compare Santino's behavior in two conditions: when he expects visitors to come and when he doesn't (Suddendorf and Corballis 2010). If Santino is planning, he should only stockpile rocks on the days that he expects visitors. While it might seem very difficult to let Santino know that the zoo would be closed some days but not others, Santino was quite used to Furuvik Zoo's short season—open to the general public only from June through August, and open in May to educational groups. A follow-up study found that when the very first group of visitors arrived in May, Santino picked up pieces of concrete to throw at them, and later, as the visitor season continued, he again began stockpiling rocks and pieces of concrete. Osvath thinks that Santino was not only planning for the future, but also acting to deceive visitors by hiding projectiles in clumps of hay he carried to the edge of the visitors' area (Osvath and Karvonen 2012).

But the objecting psychologists were not convinced by this new evidence. As reported by Michael Balter in *Science Now*, Sara Shettleworth wonders: "Did he bring the first hay pile into the arena with the intent of using it to hide projectiles? We cannot know." Shettleworth suggests we conduct tests that involve researchers placing piles of hay into the enclosure in locations not conducive to throwing the rocks, to see if Santino would hide projectiles anyway. And Thomas Suddendorf likewise insists that, "we cannot rule out leaner interpretations [i.e., interpretations that don't involve planning] without experimental study" (Balter 2012).

How are we to adjudicate this debate and determine what evidence is enough evidence, and what kinds of evidence are required to defend different kinds of claims? And what counts as a "leaner interpretation"? What is the role for experimental examination? These questions are at the forefront of many debates about animal cognitive capacities. Questions about episodic memory, planning, and deception that were raised in the Santino studies are among the most controversial in animal cognition research.

The calibration method can be seen as the philosophical method used when answering questions about the nature of mental processes and the distribution of those processes across species. But the calibration method rests on a good empirical method of investigating whether some well-defined process is at use. The focus of this chapter is on the empirical methodologies that have been used to study animal minds. In the study of animal minds, methodological issues themselves become part of the controversy.

2.1 Anecdotal anthropomorphism

Charles Darwin and his contemporaries are often thought to have given birth to the field of animal mind research. Aristotle, however, offered similar insights and methods long before English gentlemen began their inquiries. In *The History of Animals* Aristotle writes:

> In the great majority of animals there are traces of psychical qualities which are more markedly differentiated in the case of human beings. For just as we pointed out resemblances in the physical organs, so in a number of animals we observe gentleness or fierceness, mildness or cross temper, courage or timidity, fear or confidence, high spirit or low cunning, and, with regard to intelligence, something equivalent to sagacity. Some of these qualities in man, as compared with the corresponding qualities in animals, differ only quantitatively: that is to say, a man has more of this quality, and an animal has more of some other; other qualities in man are represented by analogous qualities: for instance, just as in man we find knowledge, wisdom, and sagacity, so in certain animals there exists some other natural capacity akin to these.
>
> (Aristotle 1984, 921–922)

Darwin takes up Aristotle's commitment to the idea that there are some differences between humans and other animals that are merely differences in degree, as opposed to differences in kind, with the development of his theory of evolution by natural selection. According to Darwin's account of evolution, the emergence of new species happens gradually, over generations, during which time many very subtle changes happen that can lead to large biological differences. Creatures in different places can have different physical needs to flourish in their respective environments, and over time the differences between two groups build up enough that biologists consider them different species. Given this understanding of how evolution works, we expect that closely related species share many properties.

Closely related species look similar, they act in similar ways, and so Darwin presumes that they likely have similar psychological properties as well. This line of thinking results in Darwin's Mental Continuity Thesis: there is "no fundamental difference between man and the higher mammals in their mental faculties" (Darwin 1880, 66). Commitment to this thesis leads Darwin and his supporters to interpret animal behavior in the same sort of ways they would interpret human behavior, and they are not shy about offering explanations of animal behavior in terms of curiosity, imagination, wonder, and misery. For example, Darwin discusses how dogs may even show a rudimentary sense of religious devotion:

> [The] deep love of a dog for his master ... The behavior of a dog when returning to his master after an absence, and, as I may add, of a monkey to his beloved keeper, is widely

different from that towards their fellows. In the latter case the transports of joy appear to be somewhat less, and the sense of equality is shewn in every action. Professor Braubach goes so far as to maintain that a dog looks on his master as on a god.

(Darwin 1880, 96)

Despite his commitment to similarities between humans and other animals, Darwin also argues that humans are unique in key ways: "man ... is capable of incomparably greater and more rapid improvement than is any other animal ... and this is mainly due to his power of speaking and handing down his acquired knowledge" (Darwin 1880, 79). Darwin thinks that language and culture are what distinguish humans from other species, a claim that has been a matter of some debate.

The biologist George Romanes, who was a colleague of Darwin's, is often credited with inventing the science of comparative cognition. Following Darwin's commitment to the Mental Continuity Thesis, he developed a method for studying animals that we can term *anecdotal anthropomorphism*. It is anecdotal because the data take the form of stories about animal behavior, either observed by the author or told to the author, sometimes second- or third-hand. It is anthropomorphic in the sense that interpretations of the nonhuman animal behavior illustrated in these anecdotes usually rely on direct analogies to human behavior.

Darwin's *The Descent of Man* hints at the anecdotal anthropomorphic method. For example, consider his discussion of the sense of beauty. Darwin argues, "the nests of humming-birds, and the playing passages of bower-birds are tastefully ornamented with gaily-coloured objects; and this shews that they must receive some kind of pleasure from the sight of such things" (Darwin 1880, 92). The reasoning here seems to go like this: because we would only ornament our homes if we gained pleasure from doing so, the birds must be ornamenting their homes for the same reason. No alternative hypothesis is considered.

Since Darwin, however, we have learned a lot about bowerbird nest decoration, and we can now make sense of it without having to rely on introspection about our reasons for interior decoration. For example, we know that the male bowerbird creates his nest with larger objects in back and smaller objects in front, so as to create a forced perspective upon the female bowerbirds who view it (Endler et al. 2010). And while we don't know whether the male bowerbirds receive pleasure from the sight of the nest, we do know that males who build better bowers get more sex! The contemporary research offers an alternative hypothesis to Darwin's: female bowerbirds may have evolved to prefer mates with well-decorated bowers, regardless of male dominance status. The correlation between male dominance and bower-quality would have evolved secondarily (Borgia 1985). And by moving past the easier-for-us anthropomorphic explanation, we learn more interesting things about the bowerbirds' cognitive ability, given evidence that general cognitive performance in male bowerbirds is related to mating success (Keagy et al. 2009). The need to build elaborate nests in order to successfully reproduce was a problem the male bowerbirds needed to solve, and they may have solved it by considering how their nests appear to females.

While Romanes realizes that an unstructured and indiscriminate set of anecdotes does not a science make, he doesn't leave aside the anthropomorphism inherent in the easier-for-us to understand approach. Romanes wants to raise comparative psychology to the status of a respected science, taking comparative anatomy as a model. His goal in *Animal Intelligence* is to systematically categorize animals into different levels of intelligence by examining their behavior. There, Romanes articulates the idea behind his anecdotal anthropomorphism method:

> the external indications of mental processes which we observe in animals are trustworthy … so … we are justified in inferring particular mental states from particular bodily actions … It follows that in consistency we must everywhere apply the same criteria. For instance, if we find a dog or a monkey exhibiting marked expressions of affection, sympathy, jealousy, rage, etc., few persons are sceptical enough to doubt that the complete analogy which these expressions afford with those which are manifested by man, sufficiently prove the existence of mental states analogous to those in man of which these expressions are the outward and visible signs.
>
> (Romanes 1912, 8–9)

Romanes' method is not too different from the approach Darwin took to the bowerbirds. There are two steps in any examination of an animal's mind, according to Romanes. First, observe an animal's behavior (or accept someone's anecdote about an animal's behavior). For the second step, use introspection to categorize the behavior and determine what mental state a human engaging in that behavior would have, then use analogical reasoning to attribute that mental state to the animal.

Romanes himself recognizes that there are a number of problems with this method. He knows that moving away from collecting anecdotes is required for comparative psychology to become an accepted branch of scientific investigation. But at the same time, Romanes laments that the only method available to him requires that he classify animal psychology with reference to anecdotes in order to develop general principles of intelligence—his main interest. However, there may be more problems with Romanes' method than he himself recognizes—and different problems arise at each stage.

2.1.1 Problems with the first step in anecdotal anthropomorphism

One reason Romanes worries about his method is that people sometimes report false anecdotes. The reporter might be untrustworthy, and lie to get attention. Or the person may simply be wrong, or prone to be careless in thinking. In order to assure that the anecdotes gathered at step one of the method are truthful, Romanes introduces three criteria for accepting an anecdote:

1 The observer should ideally be a known individual who has some status (i.e. a white gentleman).
2 If the observer isn't a person with status (i.e. a colonized person, a woman, etc.), and the claim is of sufficient importance to be entertained, then consider whether there was any considerable opportunity for making a bad observation.
3 Examine whether there exist independent corroborating observations made by others.

Unfortunately, the scientific methodology of trusting upper-class white men's observations does not remove the worries about the use of anecdote in science—they can be wrong, too! In addition, anecdotes that lack context don't allow for statistical analysis about the frequency of the behavior, and hence make it much more difficult to eliminate alternative explanations for the behavior. They may leave out important details that could be used to offer alternative explanations. For example, in the early twentieth century a Russian trotting horse named Hans amazed crowds by his ability to do mathematical calculations, read German, and recognize musical notes. Hans could respond to a verbal request to, say, add two plus three by tapping his hoof on the ground five times. While the audience was convinced that Clever Hans knew how to add, the early psychologists in Germany were skeptical. Oskar Pfungst investigated Hans' behavior more closely, and found that Hans' owner was inadvertently cuing Hans to start and stop tapping his foot. Hans was clever all right, but not in the way the crowds thought. The horse didn't know how to do math, but he did know how to please his trainer.

A problem with truthful anecdotes is that while they may indeed suggest that an animal acted in an interesting way, we lack information about the contexts in which the animal doesn't act similarly. When someone tells a story involving a clever animal, we hear about the exciting things without also learning about all the boring things the animal was doing between bouts of "cleverness"; the boring things are just too boring to mention. Humans are biased to notice the unusual and to neglect the uninteresting. But the uninteresting facts are equally valuable when doing science. Thus, there is a selection bias inherent in Romanes' method because it doesn't give us means for calculating base rates—the probability that the animal would act in a certain way regardless.

In addition, in many cases reliance on anecdotes would result in our neglecting the history of the animal. A clever-looking behavior might be a response to prior training, or some other conditioning earlier in the individual's life. Taken together, these two worries about truthful anecdotes suggest the following argument against the first step in anecdotal anthropomorphism:

1   Data that ignores base rates or historical facts don't provide reliable evidence.
2   Anthropomorphic anecdotes about animal behavior tend to ignore base rates and historical facts.
3   Therefore, anthropomorphic anecdotes don't provide reliable evidence.

While the anecdotal anthropomorphic method has been largely rejected due to these worries, some ethologists and psychologists argue that we can gain valuable evidence of animal behavior from incident reports—anecdotes that don't ignore base rates or historical facts, and which recognize species-typical behavior. These scientists don't throw out the baby with the bathwater, they just develop better methods for gathering reports of animals' natural behaviors (and reject premise (2) in the above argument). But other psychologists reject any use of anecdotes or incident reports, preferring experimental psychology, which was developed in response to the problems with Romanes' methods. Experimental comparative psychology ideally allows for controllable environmental conditions, knowledge of the individual's past history, and collections of repeatable behavior that are subject to statistical analysis.

2.1.2 Problems with the second step in anecdotal anthropomorphism

There are two worries about the second step in Romanes' anecdotal anthropomorphism, which involves categorizing the observed behavior and using analogical reasoning to determine its psychological cause. First, when we categorize an action, we are already interpreting it. However, there are different ways of categorizing behaviors. The philosopher Colin Allen and biologist Marc Bekoff draw a distinction between two ways of categorizing animal behavior—we can describe an action *functionally*, in terms of its purpose, or we can describe an action *formally*, in terms of the actual movements of the body (Allen and Bekoff 1997). Allen and Bekoff illustrate this distinction with two different ways of describing a typical dog behavior—the play bow.

Formally, we would describe this posture in purely physical terms, such as: the dog's front end is lowered, and the forepaws are bent and extended while the hind end, including the tail, are up. A functional description of this behavior would categorize it as a play bow: a signal to other animals that the dog is ready to play. Play bows let other dogs know the bower is not a threat at that time, even if he is also engaged in threatening behavior such as jaw snapping or head shaking; play bows trump these other signals. As Allen and Bekoff point out, formal descriptions can miss important aspects of an animal's behavior—describing the dog's posture purely formally will not inform someone naive about dogs that there is no need to be afraid the dog will attack.

However, there are also problems with functional descriptions, insofar as they are subject to over-interpretations due to the same sorts of problems that arose in the Clever Hans case. We may be wrong about the function of the dog's behavior in a way we wouldn't be wrong when describing the dog's bodily movements in physical terms. And when we use analogy from why we would act to why an animal would act, we may be treading on thin ice. If we followed Darwin's reasoning about the bowerbirds building fancy nests for aesthetic pleasure because we build fancy houses for aesthetic pleasure, we might conclude that dogs bow in order to show respect to others, as humans do!

To give a good functional description of a behavior, we need to have a working theory of normal species behavior. Functional descriptions are quite powerful, because they allow us to categorize similar behaviors together, even if some element of the formal description is missing (e.g. the dog's tail might not be full mast, yet the other aspects of his posture and facial expression signal playfulness). Allen and Bekoff argue that the choice between a functional description and a formal one should vary depending on the context, depending on which is more useful, so long as there is also sufficient evidence in favor of the function.

In many cases, functional descriptions will be preferred because of the advantages identified by the ethologist Robert Hinde (1970). For one, behavior described functionally will result in fewer data sets, leading to more robust data analysis. In addition, descriptions in terms of function are more informative than formal ones, given that they include information about the cause of the behavior and/or its consequences. Finally, behavioral changes can be described in terms of environmental changes such that, for example, a vigilance behavior can be functionally described with reference to the movement of prey into view. This allows us to see the connections between the individual's behavior and other things currently happening in the individual's social and physical surroundings.

While problems arise with categorizing the behaviors, even bigger worries emerge when we turn to Romanes' advice that we should use analogical thinking to uncover the mental state behind the behavior. Romanes suggests that we rely on human folk psychology and introspection in order to draw conclusions about the function and cause of a behavior. The problem with this step is twofold—first, humans are humans, not other animals, and as we saw in the last chapter the argument from analogy to other minds is flawed enough to be reasonably rejected. Thus, using an analogy from human folk psychology to actual psychological processes of an individual of a different species is problematic insofar as it doesn't take into account the differences between species, but only the similarities. The problem here is not unlike the problem of generalizing from facts about Western humans to facts about all humans alive; the differences may be significant.

But the problems get worse. Neither folk psychology nor introspection can be counted on to be accurate in uncovering the causes of human behavior! The so-called "new unconscious" research coming out of social psychology challenges the principle of infallible access into the workings of our minds and the causes of our own behavior (Hassin et al. 2005; Wegner 2002; Wilson 2002). In one landmark experiment the psychologists Richard Nisbett and Timothy Wilson (1977) demonstrate that human subjects attribute to themselves judgments that they clearly never made. Under the impression that they are consumer-subjects in a market survey, subjects are presented with four identical pairs of pantyhose and are asked which they prefer. The majority of subjects strongly prefer the rightmost pantyhose. When asked to explain their choice, the subjects immediately, confidently, and wrongly declare that their chosen pantyhose are the softest, or have the nicest color. Not one subject notes that the hose they chose were displayed on the right. Instead, they declare that their choice was caused by a psychological state that, because the pantyhose were identical, could not have been the genuine cause of their behavior.

So one worry is based on how difficult it is to accurately determine the causes of our own behavior. But even when we are right about the causes of our own behavior, there are difficulties with generalizing from our own causal structure to the causal structure of other creatures. While Romanes recognizes this, and notes that the warrant for a mental attribution is only as strong as the analogy is, he also claims that we have no choice:

> Taking it for granted that the external indications of mental processes which we observe in animals are trustworthy, so that we are justified in inferring particular mental states from particular bodily action, it follows that in consistency we must everywhere apply the same criteria. For instance, if we find a dog or a monkey exhibiting marked expressions of affection, sympathy, jealousy, rage, etc., few persons are skeptical enough to doubt that the complete analogy which these expressions afford with those which are manifest by man, sufficiently prove the existence of mental states analogous to those in man of which these expressions are the outward and visible signs. But when we find an ant or a bee apparently exhibiting by its actions these same emotions, few persons are sufficiently non-sceptical not to doubt whether the outward and visible signs are here trustworthy as evidence of analogous or

corresponding inward and mental states. The whole organization of such a creature is so different from that of a man that it becomes questionable how far analogy drawn from the activities of the insect is a safe guide to the inferring of mental states—particularly in view of the fact that in many respects, such as in the great preponderance of 'instinct' over 'reason,' the psychology of an insect is demonstrably a widely different thing from that of a man. Now it is, of course, perfectly true that the less the resemblance the less is the value of any analogy built upon the resemblance, and therefore that the inference of an ant or a bee feeling sympathy or rage is not so valid as is the similar inference in the case of a dog or a monkey. Still it *is* an inference, and, so far as it goes, a valid one—being, in fact the only inference available. That is to say, if we observe an ant or a bee apparently exhibiting sympathy or rage, we must either conclude that some psychological state resembling that of sympathy or rage is present, or else refuse to think about the subject at all; from the observable facts there is no other inference open.

(Romanes 1912, 8–9)

While I may know how a jealous human acts, that isn't going to help me to identify a jealous honeybee that is "apparently exhibiting by its actions these same emotions." It is one thing for someone who knows the species well to interpret the behavior, and another thing altogether for a non-expert to engage in an act of interpretation. For example, the popular portrayal of an open-mouthed bottlenose dolphin suggests a happy and playful creature, ready to help save a sailor or swim with a tourist. The dolphin's open mouth resembles a human smile. But, as anyone who has spent a good deal of time with dolphins knows, treating it like a smile is a huge mistake; a dolphin's open mouth is an aggressive (or hungry) posture, and when you see it you should stay away.

The use of anecdotes, the role of anthropomorphism, and the appeal to folk psychology in animal cognition research are all matters of debate among scientists today. But everyone agrees that the method of anecdotal anthropomorphism as used by Darwin, Romanes, and their contemporaries is flawed. It amounts to simple interpretation, which is part of our natural, intuitive way of making sense of the behavior around us, but lacks any attempt to verify the interpretation. Seeing the bowerbird as decorating his nest to fulfill his desire for beauty, and seeing the dolphin's smile as evidence of a happy emotional state, turns out to be bad interpretation. Good interpretation allows us to accurately predict the future, and thinking that the bowerbird is a little artist will lead to false predictions. Science involves more than simple interpretation; it also requires formulating and testing hypotheses about the causes of phenomena and constructing general principles that can be used to predict and explain singular events and general patterns. For this reason, as psychology matured, methodological rigor became more and more important.

2.2 The rise of animal psychology as a science: Morgan's Canon

In order to avoid some of the problems associated with Romanes' comparative psychology, other scientists began developing principles for studying animal minds in a way that avoids the problems associated with anecdotal anthropomorphism. The British biologist and psychologist C. Lloyd Morgan, who is often credited with the rise of contemporary animal cognition methods, points out that animal behaviors that are interesting to us could be caused in various ways. Morgan is interested in what cognitive psychologists today refer to as mechanisms.

Consider Morgan's example of Tony, the fox-terrier pup who knew how to escape from the garden into the road. Tony would first snuggle his head under the latch of the gate, and then lift the latch and wait for the gate to swing open. A natural explanation of this behavior, Morgan suggests, is that Tony had a goal and knew the means for achieving that goal; in other words, he had a practical reasoning ability. But Morgan points out that there are various ways to interpret this explanation. Perhaps Tony was responding to the properties of the particular situation directly, and saw the latch as liftable without analyzing the structure of the gate or the consequences of lifting the latch. In this case the environment would have done much of the cognitive work, such that the animal was simply responding to what the psychologist J. J. Gibson would later call the affordances, or opportunities for action, provided by the environment. On the other hand, Tony might have been using general reasoning principles when opening the gate; if this is the case, he simply applied his general knowledge to this particular situation. It is only the latter interpretation that Morgan categorizes as rational. For Morgan, rational thought is conceptual thought that permits analysis via general principles.

Morgan argues that Tony's behavior ought not be interpreted as rational, given his famous canon: "in no case is an animal activity to be interpreted in terms of higher psychological processes, if it can be fairly interpreted in terms of processes which stand lower in the scale of psychological evolution and development" (Morgan 1903, 292). Morgan's Canon is an epistemic principle that advises us to explain a behavior in terms of the lowest cognitive capacity possible. Morgan thinks that reasoning in terms of sense experience is lower, and that reasoning conceptually in terms of general principles is a higher psychological process. In developing the Canon, Morgan writes, "the principle I adopt is to assume that the [animal's] inferences are perceptual, unless there seem to be well-observed facts which necessitate the analysis of this phenomena ... and therefore the employment of reason" (Morgan 1891, 362–363). While there is ample evidence that many species reason, there is no justification for concluding that Tony reasoned rationally, rather than in terms of sense experience. Morgan argues that the dog could have learned to open the gate without recourse to general principles, and hence we are not justified in concluding that Tony used rational thought in this instance.

Given Morgan's focus on the evolution of mind, he thinks we need to consider animal minds as well as human minds when doing psychology. He writes in his autobiography,

> throughout the whole investigation, from first to last, my central interest has been psychological as I understand the meaning of this word. My aim has been to get at the mind of the chick or the dog or another, and to frame generalizations with regard to mental evolution.
>
> (Morgan 1930, 249)

Chicks, dogs and humans are all minded creatures in Morgan's view, and we wouldn't be doing chick, dog, and human psychology if we didn't think so. Thus, Morgan never intended his Canon to be used in many of the ways it was later used. For example, Morgan didn't intend the Canon to support a defense of nonmentalistic explanations of animal behavior. He certainly would have rejected Coleman Griffith's description of his Canon:

> In Morgan's case, the principle amounted to this. Where there is a pattern of animal behavior which must be explained, both as to form and to origin, and in the simplest, but at the same time, most adequate way, the experimenter should appeal to factors observable in the situation in which the animal has been placed, in the behavior itself, and in the machinery by which the behavior is made possible. It is not incumbent on him to pass over these factors in order to appeal to a verbal construct, to a mind, or to any other kind of mental factor that lies outside of, behind, or within the behavior-situation.
>
> (Griffith 1943, 322)

Similarly, Morgan would have rejected Philip Harriman's version which was still being taught at the end of the twentieth century:

> *Parsimony, law of:* Lloyd Morgan's statement (1900) that animal behavior should be described in the simplest possible terms. It is an application of Occam's razor to animal psychology. Occam (1280–1349) had said that entities must not be multiplied beyond necessity; and Morgan accepted this view, indicating that anecdotes, attribution of human mental activities to animals, and projection of introspections have no place in animal psychology.
>
> (Harriman 1947, 255; quoted in Wozniak 1997)

Along with his acceptance that there is such a thing as animal psychology and animal minds, it may be surprising to some that Morgan also reluctantly accepts the need for anecdotes. What he rejects are the overly romantic interpretations given to anecdotes, and the unsystematic way in which they had been collected in Romanes' work. Morgan also advocates for the attribution of human mental activities to animals using the method of interpretation via introspection. What he cautions us against, however, is automatically thinking that behaviors that appear to be clever, *whether human or animal behaviors*, are really so. The upshot is that the Canon applies to humans as well as other species; it does not force a divide between human beings and other animals. And, since Morgan accepts the existence of animal minds, he thinks the lowest explanation possible is an explanation in terms of sensory modalities. Such an explanation, however, still requires interpretation.

Morgan accepts that interpretation must play an essential role in any science of animal minds. This is because the observation of behavior only offers what Morgan calls the "body-story" and never the "mind-story." "Mind-story is always 'imputed' [interpreted] insofar as one can put oneself in the place of another. And this 'imputation,' as I now call it, must always be hazardous" (Morgan 1930, 249). It is Morgan's worry about this hazard that led him to develop his Canon, yet it is also what led him to see introspection as a necessary part of a science of animal cognition. For Morgan, introspection is the necessary step that permits inference from behavior to mind, and if we want a science of animal minds, introspection is how to do it. But, as we will see in section 2.4, Morgan was also committed to not over-intellectualizing human cognition.

Morgan's appeal to introspection is the foundation of his belief that others have minds; I do something, I introspect what I think and how I feel, then I interpret those mental events as the cause of that behavior. The idea that introspection permits us to discover the cause of behavior, is, as we have already seen, a flawed methodology. Nonetheless, introspection was the predominant method of psychology in Europe during Morgan's time, given the influence of Wilhelm Wundt, who is considered the father of experimental psychology.

Despite the contemporary rejection of Morgan's use of introspection as a justified methodology, Morgan's Canon remains relevant for today's students of comparative psychology. But analysis of the Canon has raised serious questions about both the justification for it, and its application, as we will see later in this chapter.

2.3 Learning principles: associations and insight

In the meantime, other experimental psychologists in the United States and Russia were interested in uncovering principles of learning, with perhaps some influence from Morgan's work. In 1896, Morgan traveled to the US to give the Lowell Lectures at Harvard. In the audience was a graduate student named Edward Thorndike (1874–1949), who, in his famous research published 15 years later, adopted Morgan's experimental method but rejected its appeal to introspection. Thorndike worries that introspection is unscientific; because only the person doing the introspection can access the contents of her mind, the information is not publicly available. Due to this lack of observability, he thinks that we cannot test for the reliability or validity of introspection. Behavior, on the other hand, can be observed and quantified by numerous observers, so Thorndike retains the experiment as the method of animal psychology research.

Figure 2.1 A cat in one of Thorndike's puzzle boxes.

Experiments may be seen as superior to anecdotes, no matter how carefully collected and analyzed, because with experiments scientists ideally have repeatable conditions, a controlled environment, the ability to test a number of individuals, and the opportunity to use statistical analysis to determine typical responses. Thorndike's embrace of the experimental method had him putting animals into situations that he thought to be particularly compelling; most famously, he put hungry cats, who would be fed upon their escape, in puzzle boxes. By measuring the time it took for cats to escape the puzzle boxes, Thorndike found that after a successful escape, cats weren't able to immediately escape again after being placed back in the box. Rather, cats only gradually decreased the time it took for them to escape. From this, Thorndike concludes that cat learning is based on trial and error, rather than insight. While it takes several successful escapes to learn how to get out of the box, once cats learn how to escape the box, they can use that knowledge to generalize to another similar box.

Thorndike thinks we can use experiments to understand what humans and nonhumans do, how they do it, and what they feel while they are doing it. Based on his research on humans and other animals, Thorndike develops the following three laws of learning:

Law of effect: The association between a stimulus and a response is stronger when the response is associated with satisfaction, and weaker when the response is associated with annoyance.

Law of readiness: Satisfaction is the fulfillment of acts an individual is ready to perform, and annoyance is the inability to fulfill an act one is ready to perform, or when forced to perform an act one is not ready to perform.

Law of exercise: The association between a stimulus and a response are strengthened as they are used, and they are weakened as they are not used.

Thorndike's laws are early examples of principles of *associative learning*, which today is defined by comparative psychologists as "learning resulting from the procedures involving contingencies among events," or to put things into more cognitive terms, "the formation of some sort of mental connection between representations of two stimuli" (Shettleworth 2010b, 105). For Thorndike, associative learning involves forming connections between sensory input and behavioral output, and according to his laws, pleasant associations are stronger than unpleasant ones. From his research on humans, Thorndike found that rewards are more effective than punishment, and rewards work best when they are given just after the desired behavior is exhibited. Furthermore, he found that the frequency of the association, while important, is less important than the effect. As he points out, when we first learn to ride a bicycle, we fall off much more frequently than we stay on!

But it is the Russian physiologist Ivan Pavlov (1849–1936) who is usually credited with discovering that animals can form associations; the development of what is now called *classical conditioning* arose directly from his work. While Pavlov was studying the physiology of the gastric system in dogs in the 1890s, he noticed that just before bringing the dogs their food, they would begin to salivate. (Salivation was one variable he was measuring in his study of gastric function, and the dogs had been surgically altered so their saliva would drip into a tube at the side of their mouths.) Pavlov began to experiment, training dogs by using some stimulus—most famously a ringing bell—just before delivering their food. The dogs initially salivated with the delivery of the food, but over time the sound of the bell was enough for them to start to drool. This "conditioned response" arises as a dog learns to associate the bell (the "conditioned stimulus") with food (the "unconditioned stimulus"), which leads to the drooling. In contrast, the "unconditioned response" is the dog's innate tendency to drool at the sight of food.

Classical, or Pavlovian, conditioning (also known as stimulus learning), is a method of learning that allows human and nonhuman animals to make predictions about future events by associating events that occur prior to the predicted event with that event. We know that humans are so seized by these sorts of associations that they can be formed even when the subject is unaware of the stimulus (Raio et al. 2012). Classical conditioning is of great interest to psychologists studying learning, and there are a number of principles about how conditioning works.

For psychologists interested in cognition, classical conditioning or associative learning more generally is studied as a window into the processes of the animal's mind. They are interested not just in under what conditions animals learn, but also in how they learn. The cognitivist answer to how associative learning works has been given in terms of changing strengths of associations between mental representations (Shettleworth 2010b). However, the behaviorist is interested in classical conditioning not as a means to get at cognition, but rather as a way of studying behavior in order to predict and control what an individual does. For the behaviorists, appeal to introspection as well as any mention of mental entities should be avoided. Any use of a term that is mentalistic (such as thirst, hunger, fear or desire) has to be operationally defined in terms of measurable, observable qualities (such as time since last having eaten).

Given the hold behaviorism came to have on North American psychology in the twentieth century, much of the research associated with Morgan, Thorndike, and Pavlov came to be seen through the behaviorist lens. Psychological behaviorism is the scientific methodology introduced by John B. Watson (1878–1958) and popularized (and some say radicalized) by B.F. Skinner (1904–1990). Watson's goal, like Morgan's, was to make psychology a respectable science, famously stating that, "Psychology as the behaviorist views it is a purely objective experimental branch of natural science" (Watson 1913, 158). On Watson's view, psychology is not only supposed to be concerned with replicable and objective experiments, but the content of psychology should also be limited to observable effects, and so introspective reports, consciousness, as well as postulated entities (like mental representations) and mechanisms (like strengthening the association between mental representations) are excluded from the conversation. Folk psychology is not part of the behaviorist toolbox.

The behaviorist methodology starts with observations of behavior. The behavior, and the environment in which the behavior occurs, is then described using nonmentalistic language and interpreted as little as possible. The psychologist next has to note that certain aspects of behavior, such as the frequency or duration of behavior, correlate with certain aspects of the environment. That is, the psychologist has to postulate an association between the behavior and the environment. After developing the hypothesis, the psychologist can change one of the environmental variables in order to determine whether or not the behavior remains. Once she discovers which feature of the environment is necessary for the behavior, the psychologist can speak of the behavior as (and only as) a function of the environment, and the association is confirmed.

Thus, for the behaviorists, behavior is a function of the environmental stimulus alone. All behavior can be explained and is entirely shaped by the punishment and rewards of environment, and behavior can be studied in a lab where it is easier to control the environmental stimuli. The science of behaviorism can be conducted with any kind of organism, since there are no intrinsic properties of the organism that interact with the stimulus to help produce the behavior. Skinner famously said, "Give me a child and I'll shape him into anything," reflecting the behaviorist's focus on environment and complete lack of interest in anything like innate biological traits. This focus is also reflected on the behaviorists' choice of research subjects. Though interested primarily in human behavior (especially for Skinner, whose utopian goals led him to describe the ideal human community in his novel *Walden Two*) the behaviorists used rats and pigeons as their primary research subjects to learn about the power of reinforcers to modify behavior; again, they thought the organism studied doesn't matter.

Building on Thorndike's experimental method, Watson suggests that learning about the associations between the environmental stimuli and the behavior should be the only point of interest, allowing us to predict and control all animal behavior. Skinner goes even further, suggesting we modify Thorndike's law of effect. Since Thorndike thinks that an association is made more easily when there is satisfaction rather than annoyance about the association, the law of effect isn't something that can be embraced by a behaviorist. Skinner rejects the reference to satisfaction or annoyance, even as described in the law of readiness, since they are both unobservable mental states that are part of human folk psychology. Instead of talking about mental states, Skinner restates Thorndike's law of effect in behaviorist terms. Skinner defines another type of conditioning, called *operant conditioning* or *instrumental learning*, according to which a behavior that is followed by a reinforcer becomes more frequent, while behavior that is followed by a punishment becomes less frequent. By removing the mentalistic tinge of the talk of satisfaction and annoyance, Skinner rehabilitates Thorndike's findings for the behaviorist age.

Recall that classical conditioning involves relating a previously neutral and uninteresting stimulus, such as a tone or light, with some biologically relevant cue that produces a natural reflex, such as food or an electrical shock. The neutral stimulus becomes associated with the natural reflex, even in the absence of the cue. The discovery of instrumental learning lets us see that associations are also formed between two previously unrelated stimuli. For example, a trained response such as pushing a lever can become associated with an outcome such as the acquisition of food.

For the behaviorist, some variety of associative learning can account for all learned behavior. Because the behaviorist appeals only to associative learning, and never to mental states, in order to explain behavior, it might seem as though associative learning is a simple way for an organism to learn. This appears to be the reasoning employed when Morgan's Canon is filtered through the lens of behaviorism; it is associative learning that becomes the "lower," and hence simpler, mechanism. While Morgan himself never appeared to make that claim, today psychologists commonly read the canon in this way: "In contemporary practice 'lower' usually means associative learning, that is, classical and instrumental conditioning or untrained species-specific responses. 'Higher' is reasoning, planning, insight, in short any cognitive process other than associative learning" (Shettleworth 2010b, 17–18). The upshot is that even for the cognitivists, the learning mechanisms that permit classical and operant conditioning, along with other associative processes, are largely taken to be cognitively unsophisticated. And the "higher" learning mechanisms are not seen as fundamentally involving associative learning of any sort. Is this view warranted?

As psychology started regaining interest in cognitive mechanisms in the latter part of the twentieth century, associative learning came to be seen as a cognitive process involving representations of both the stimulus and the outcome. For example in one condition, after being taught an association, the value of the outcome is lowered, at which point the subject is less likely to engage in the response when confronted with the stimulus (Adams and Dickinson 1981). Thinking cognitively, this finding makes sense; if you know that pressing a lever will give you chocolate ice cream, and you just recently developed an aversion to chocolate ice cream, your knowledge about the association between pressing the lever and receiving the treat will cause you to avoid pressing the lever, no matter how many times you pressed the lever before developing the aversion. These findings suggest that associative learning is part of information processing, and that the behaviorist focus on association failed to shine a light on how associations result in behavior.

Other research on associations points to their complexity. While the initial models reflected Pavlov's discovery of one stimulus per response, subsequent research demonstrated that the stimulus may consist of several parts, and it can consist of the absence of some entity or event as well as the presence of it. Take one example, called occasion setting stimuli, which demonstrates the relationships between stimuli leading to an outcome. When a rat is trained that a tone indicates the delivery of food when accompanied by a light stimulus (but not when the light is absent), the light is considered a positive occasion setter (Holland 1992). If the light/tone compound stimulus results in no food, and the tone alone results in food, the light is called a negative occasion setter. In the first case, the light and the tone are each necessary conditions for the delivery of food, but are only jointly sufficient. In the second case, the light is sufficient for the non-delivery of food, and the tone is necessary for food delivery. The introduction of relatively small degrees of complexity into the association relationship points to the possibility that organisms are capable of much more complex compound associations, consisting at the same time of some positive and some negative occasion setters. Associative reasoning may not be quite so simple as sometimes thought.

The question about the relationship between so-called higher cognitive capacities such as insight and reasoning and associative learning is a complex one. Psychologists often describe insight as an "aha!" moment in reasoning; perhaps it most accurately refers to some inference that isn't made at the personal, conscious, level. The earliest theoretical analysis of insight was given by the psychologist Donald Hebb (1904–1985), who is perhaps best known for the development of Hebb's law: "Neurons that fire together wire together," which inspired much subsequent work on artificial neural networks. Hebb, thinking that insight is at the core of intelligence, describes it as involved in solving tasks that are neither so easy that they are automatically performed, nor so difficult that they can only be performed after lengthy rote learning. When working through such a task, an individual will often turn from some fruitless effort in one direction to work in a very different direction, and this switch is what Hebb describes as insight. We can understand this change in type of effort as caused by a restructuring of thought or conceptual change. Insight is the product of the weakening of an association in response to its failure to address the problem at hand, and the strengthening of another association. Hebb himself was an associationist, and he thought that some complex association between the situation and the organization of behavioral structures fundamentally accounted for the phenomenon of insight (Hebb 1949).

Gestalt psychologists understood insight as when one looks at a situation in a new way. The German scientist Wolfgang Köhler (1887–1967) took this approach in his research on insight reasoning in chimpanzees. He conducted experiments that required chimpanzees to solve a problem that required a creative solution. In the most famous condition, chimpanzees were allowed into an enclosure and saw a bunch of bananas hanging overhead but out of reach, and three boxes scattered around on the floor. The solution to this problem, which the chimpanzees were able to solve, was to stack the boxes on top of one another to form a ladder beneath the bananas. Köhler claimed that the chimpanzees could not have used associative learning to engage in this problem solving, because according to the associationist theory of the day, a solution to a problem derives from either previous experience in the same situation or trial and error behavior in a new one, neither of which described the chimpanzee behavior in these studies (Köhler 1925).

But Hebb suggests that Köhler's chimpanzees could have been using both associative reasoning and insight. Findings about devaluation of the outcome and the complexity of the stimuli in associative learning point to the complexity of some associative learning. And performance on transfer tests demonstrates that learning that occurred in one situation can be transferred to a novel situation, while being accounted for in terms of cognitive associations (Rescorla 1992). Furthermore, some psychologists argue that associative models of belief–desire reasoning can capture human folk psychology (Wit and Dickinson 2009).

While a full discussion of the current debates about the nature of associative reasoning isn't possible here, the apparent variety and complexity of associations undermines claims that associative learning is always simpler than reasoning, planning, or insight. Rather, these so-called higher cognitive mechanisms may be fancy versions of associative reasoning. As Morgan reminded us, the mere fact that we introspect fancy mechanisms for our own behavior doesn't mean that there are fancy mechanisms at work. And we should be wary of simple explanations of animal behavior, be they explanations in terms of associative learning or insight, without a fuller understanding of what exactly the mechanism at stake looks like. The worry is that such accounts do nothing more than gesture toward the existence of an explanation, rather than provide one.

2.4 Anthropomorphism, and Morgan's Canon revisited

The predominant contemporary interpretation of Morgan's Canon is as a directive to avoid anthropomorphism, or the attribution of human characteristics to other animals. While no scientist is open to the kind of anthropomorphizing we see in Disney films and children's books, rife with rhyming bears and cats that wear hats, there are substantive debates about anthropomorphism among scientists and philosophers interested in animal cognition. Some worry about using terms describing social relationships such as "friend" or "enemy," emotional state descriptions such as "happy" or "sad" or "depressed," and personality traits such as "brave" or "timid"—even if the terms are operationalized such that the scientist can observe whether the behavior meets the stated criteria. The psychologist Clive Wynne argues that investigation into such anthropomorphic properties in animals is not scientific, but rather an uncritical use of human folk psychology masquerading as scientific explanation, and that such attributions are nothing more than bad analogies (Wynne 2004). Psychologists like Wynne prefer to use neutral, non-anthropomorphic terminology, such as replacing "friends" with "affiliative relations" (Silk 2002).

Those who worry about anthropomorphizing animals can be categorized into two types: categorical skeptics who think that animal cognition research cannot be good science, and selective skeptics who think that some of the attributions made by some researchers are unjustified (Andrews and Huss 2014). Categorical skeptics, such as J.S. Kennedy, think that animal cognition research engages in unscientific investigation (Kennedy 1992). The problem arises from the very questions researchers ask, like whether animals have personality traits or a theory of mind—the ability to attribute beliefs and desires to others (also known as mindreading). For the categorical skeptics, the charge of anthropomorphism is a pre-empirical one; the argument amounts to the claim that researchers in animal cognition are making a category mistake by asking whether animals have certain properties—it's like asking what color the number two is (Allen and Bekoff 1997; Fischer 1990; Keeley 2004).

If the charge of inappropriate anthropomorphism is a pre-empirical one, the justification for it must be philosophical. Either the concepts being appealed to are defined as uniquely human, or the nature of the concepts or topics under investigation, alongside some well-established theory, entails that the features are unique to humans. While there are philosophical arguments against the existence of some human psychological properties in other animals, such as beliefs (Davidson 1982; Stich 1979) or consciousness (Carruthers 1989), we will see in subsequent chapters that these claims are quite controversial, and should not be taken as so well-established to undermine an entire research program. Further, the same arguments could be used, *mutatis mutandis*, to show that prelinguistic children do not have beliefs or consciousness, though no psychologists express concern about anthropomorphizing prelinguistic human infants. On the contrary, many of the topics under fire by the categorical skeptics are being currently investigated in human children as well. For example, psychologists are investigating whether human infants as young as three months old have a theory of mind, and can attribute false beliefs to others (Baillargeon et al. 2010), and several researchers in this field conclude that there is evidence for such an ability in infants (e.g. Onishi and Baillargeon 2005). Moreover, infant cognition researchers do not let infants' lack of language keep them from claiming that infants recognize intentional agency (Desrochers et al. 1995; Legerstee and Barillas 2003; Leslie 1984) and intentionally communicate via declarative pointing (Camaioni 1993). Given the lack of concern about investigating such cognitive capacities in infants, as well as the fecundity of such research, categorical skeptics cannot appeal to nonhuman animals' lack of language in order to justify ending research on animal cognition.

Sometimes the categorical skeptics seem particularly concerned about bias in animal cognition research—they worry that if psychologists are allowed to look for some human property in animals then they will see the animals' behavior through that lens. This worry is an old one; the biologist G.H. Lewes (1817–1878) criticized Darwin and Romanes on these grounds, writing "we are incessantly at fault in our tendency to anthropomorphize, a tendency which causes us to interpret the actions of animals according to the analogies of human nature" (Lewes 1860). The view remains with us today. Kennedy writes that "anthropomorphic thinking about animal behavior is built into us. We could not abandon it even if we wished to" (Kennedy 1992). But it is just these sorts of biases that the scientific method aims at overcoming in order to determine the best explanation for some phenomenon.

Besides worrying that the categorical skeptic is begging the question, we might also object that folk psychology is a necessary part of psychology. Human psychology is founded on folk psychology, and so we might expect that comparative psychology likewise needs to be based on a comparable folk animal psychology—the kind of expertise that humans have when they spend a lot of time interacting with another species (Andrews 2009, 2011, 2012a). Traditional farmers, zookeepers, and pet owners who pay close attention to the animals in their care often develop a folk animal psychology that they use to understand, predict, and better interact with the animals in their care.

Human adults often have the same kind of folk expertise when it comes to human infants, and this folk expertise is appealed to in formal studies of human children. In our studies of infant cognition, we appeal to our folk psychology in thinking that children look longer at surprising stimuli, and gaze at objects they are interested in. These interpretations are not justified by further research, but are natural interpretations of children's behavior given our robust knowledge of human children. Adults of our species become experts on human infants by sharing their lives with them. Just as psychologists who study humans are already folk experts about typical human behavior, comparative psychologists need to begin by developing folk expertise about the species they wish to study. And, just as folk experts who work with humans have knowledge about those humans that can be extracted using psychological instruments such as *The Child Behavior Checklist* (Achenbach and Edelbrock 1983) in order to determine which psychological properties are accurately attributable to a human child, we can develop instruments to extract the folk expertise of individuals who work with other species.

The selective skeptics are often comparative psychologists themselves who criticize other psychologists' interpretations of their empirical findings. The selective skeptic often appeals to the predominant contemporary interpretation of Morgan's Canon and shows how associative reasoning can explain the behavior in question, and hence concludes that the "higher" human explanation of the behavior should be rejected (Povinelli and Vonk 2004; Penn 2012). Again, the charge is often that human folk psychology is being uncritically applied to other species as a scientific account of behavior while "simpler" associative learning mechanisms suffice to explain that behavior.

In response to this worry, some have argued that the selective skeptic position reflects a bias in the methodology of animal cognition research, particularly the null hypothesis testing methods. This typical route to running experiments involves the following steps: first, a null hypothesis—a hypothesis that reflects what is expected to be the norm, and against which the researcher is looking for a statistically significant discrepancy—is devised. Then, data is collected and analyzed, and the results are reported and interpreted. In animal cognition research, what is taken to be the null hypothesis turns out to be of utmost importance. Usually the null is taken to be what we already know, especially in terms of prior statistical analyses of certain rates of outcomes. But when it comes to the question about whether an animal has a certain psychological property, we have no prior statistical information; the prior probability is only assumed.

This rule for formulating a null hypothesis is coupled with another methodological rule of thumb for psychologists, according to which it is better to commit to a false negative than a false positive. However, this rule is put in terms of the null hypothesis, and each error is given a bland name:

Type-I Error: Rejecting a null hypothesis when it is in fact true.

Type-II Error: Failing to reject a null hypothesis when it is in fact false.

The philosopher Elliott Sober suggests that the charge of anthropomorphism is often based on this understanding of the difference between the two kinds of error (Sober 2005). False positives seem to be associated with permissive and sentimental thinking, whereas Type-II errors, while still errors, are thought to demonstrate a kind of hard-nosed conservatism that is often seen as a virtue of the serious scientist. Sober thinks that this understanding of the errors has resulted in a different kind of bias in animal cognition research, an error I call *anthropectomy* (Andrews and Huss, 2014).

Sober says of both anthropomorphism and anthropectomy that they are:

maxims of 'default reasoning'. They say that some hypotheses should be presumed innocent until proven guilty, while others should be regarded as having precisely the opposite status. Perhaps these default principles deserve to be swept from the field and replaced by a much simpler idea—that we should not indulge in anthropomorphism *or* in anthropodenial [or anthropectomy] until we can point to observations that discriminate between these two hypotheses. It is desirable that we avoid the type-1 error of mistaken anthropomorphism, but it is also desirable that we avoid the type-2 error of mistaken anthropodenial.

(Sober 2005, 97)

Sober suggests that the methodological position of preferring Type-II errors is the position of preferring anthropectomy over anthropomorphism, and it seems the skeptic would agree with that analysis. But perhaps a greater problem arises at the point of deciding on the null hypothesis itself, because beginning an investigation of a property with a skeptical view may introduce a bias against animals having that property. When our concerns are purely epistemic, as they presumably are in the case of animal cognition, it isn't clear why either the skeptical or optimistic hypothesis should get preferential treatment from the outset. Unless there is some *prima facie*, pre-empirical reason to think that one of the hypotheses is more plausible, or there is some independent empirical evidence that the skeptical hypothesis is statistically more common, neither should be counted as a null hypothesis. To insist that one must be counted as the null hypothesis is to beg the question against the other hypothesis.

Indeed, one might start with Darwin's Mental Continuity Thesis, and expect to see similarities across species, thereby formulating the null hypothesis as there being no difference in psychological property between two closely related species. This line of thought may be seen as more parsimonious, and the Mental Continuity Thesis could form the basis of an argument from evolutionary parsimony. For example, the primatologist Frans de Waal argues that "the most parsimonious assumption concerning nonhuman primates is that if their behavior resembles human behavior the psychological and mental processes involved are *probably* similar too" (de Waal 1991, 316). And Sober argues that "If human beings and a closely related species (e.g. chimpanzees) both exhibit behavior B, and if human beings produce B by occupying mental state M, then this is *evidence* that M is also the proximate mechanism that chimpanzees deploy in producing B" (Sober 2012, 3–4). However, Sober concludes that we don't have enough information about the common ancestors to put the argument from evolutionary parsimony to any good use in doing animal cognition. Some evidence isn't always enough evidence to draw conclusions.

Despite their apparent opposition, some critics of anthropomorphism and critics of anthropectomy share the view that a problem with methodology in comparative cognition has more to do with psychologists' views about human cognition than with their views about other animals. When intelligent human behavior is left unanalyzed, or analyzed only at a folk psychological level, the cognitive or neural mechanisms required for the behavior are left unmentioned. Just as termites build beautiful mounds following simple rules, much of intelligent human behavior may also emerge from simple rules.

Though they may appear to be carefully thought out Gaudi-esque works of a brilliant architect, the arches that structure termite nests are built by a group of termites following two simple rules. The termites first roll up balls of mud, which through their efforts become infused with a chemical scent. Next, the termites pick up their respective balls, and carry them to the location where the chemical scent is the strongest. This means that the largest collection of mudballs attracts more mudballs, which leads the termites to build columns, as the scent is strongest near the top of the pile. When a termite on top of a column gets a whiff of a nearby column, the individual will place the mudball on the side of the column, which over time leads to the construction of an arch. Thus, by way of two rules, apparently sophisticated behavior emerges.

Shettleworth argues that the trend in animal cognition toward examining anthropomorphic questions such as "Do animals count?" or "Do animals have insight?" is problematic if these general questions are not deconstructed into sub-questions about sub-processes (Shettleworth 2010b). She suggests that when we are open to the idea that some of these sub-processes may be shared widely across species, and that others may be less common, we will be able to do truly *comparative* cognition research at the level of cognitive mechanism. And finding differences should be just as exciting as finding similarities—"killjoy hypotheses" that explain animal behavior in terms of sub-mechanisms rather than in anthropomorphic or folk psychological terms ought not kill anyone's joy!

Here, Shettleworth is reminding us of another, less well known, insight of Morgan's. In his autobiography, Morgan wrote: "To interpret animal behavior one must learn also to see one's own mentality at levels of development much lower than one's top-level of reflective self-consciousness. It is not easy, and savors somewhat of paradox" (Morgan 1930, 250). We can call this Morgan's Challenge, because he recognizes how difficult it is for us to follow his advice not to over-intellectualize human cognition. The error we risk by not meeting Morgan's Challenge has been recently dubbed "anthropofabulation" by the philosopher Cameron Buckner, because it involves both anthropocentricism and confabulation of our own typical abilities (Buckner 2013). While Morgan's Canon is taught to all students of comparative cognition, Morgan's Challenge is not, though meeting it is a requirement for doing good comparative work in psychology.

How do we confabulate our own mental faculties? Psychologists have discovered unconscious processing (such as priming), biases and heuristics (such as discounting the value of future rewards), and core cognitive processes (such as the implicit number system) in humans. These are all processes that we don't seem to have easy conscious access to, and may ignore when explaining our own behavior. Shettleworth's suggestion that animal cognition researchers examine such processes requires us to first realize that we are often wrong about the causes of human behavior, and that we cannot use introspections about the cause of our behavior in order to do good research on animal behavior.

The critique of anthropomorphism is the claim that a mistake is being made about the properties of the animal. But we do not yet have the full story of human cognition, much less animal cognition, and so we are not in a position to know whether or not a mistake is in fact being made. As we come to better understand the elements involved in kinds of behaviors, including problem solving, reasoning, and so forth, we will be better positioned to understand how to compare humans and other animals.

2.5 The rise of ethology and kinds of explanation

While behaviorist psychologists were focusing on uncovering learning principles via experiments on captive pigeons and rats, in Western Europe ethologists were learning about animal minds by traipsing around in fields, forests, and dunes, raising animals on research stations, and frequenting zoological parks in order to observe the behavior of a wider range of species in much more natural settings than the behaviorists' wire and glass cages. Unlike the behaviorists, the ethologists were particularly interested in differences between species. Rather than taking pigeons and rats and humans to be basically interchangeable, the ethologists focused on what they took to be the different innate properties of species. Ethology arose from biology, which at the end of the nineteenth century was focused primarily on the collection and study of specimens—dead animals that could be kept under glass in display cabinets. Biology primarily consisted of comparative anatomy until the zoologist William Morton Wheeler coined the term "ethology" in 1902, arguing for the study of animal instinct, intelligence, and habits by studying live animals throughout their life cycle. While critics worried that ethology would be a return to the subjectivist methods of the anecdotal method, the ethologists proved to be just as concerned with careful observation and experimentation as the behaviorists.

Ethology can be described as the scientific study of the behavior of animals as evolved organisms, in the context of anatomy, physiology, and the natural environment. The parents of the field put it more succinctly: Konrad Lorenz (1903–1989) describes ethology as the biological study of behavior, and, more colorfully, Nikolaas Tinbergen (1907–1988) describes ethology as the process of interviewing an animal in its own language. As a branch of biology, ethology is oriented differently from psychology's study of animal behavior in the context of human psychology. And while psychologists, with their desire to control the stimuli, primarily studied animals indoors in highly artificial settings, ethologists were interested in studying animals in more natural settings, with all the complexity that ensued.

Classical ethologists were interested in species-specific, or instinctual behavior, and in the interaction between biological inheritance and environmental influences. While studying comparative anatomy, Lorenz, an avid animal lover and raiser, decided that the methods of comparative anatomy could be applied just as well to pieces of animal behavior, given that both anatomy and behavior are the result of the process of evolution. (The biologist Oskar Heinroth and the zoologist Charles Otis Whitman had previously made the same point, unbeknownst to Lorenz.) By handrearing birds such as jackdaws, geese, and ducks, and by building tame colonies of birds, Lorenz was able to learn much about the natural behaviors of these species. Famously, Lorenz studied imprinting, which is a learning mechanism that requires only one exposure; for example, geese are predisposed to follow the individual they first see after hatching from an egg. Usually this individual is their mother, so imprinting is a useful learning mechanism to have in this context. But when Lorenz was the first large creature goslings saw after hatching, they would follow Lorenz around the fields, as if he were their mother.

Lorenz, along with Tinbergen, was interested in the cause of these sorts of behaviors, the purposes of the behaviors, how they developed, and how they were implemented in the physical organism. So, while the ethologists spoke of an interest in the innate traits of different species, they never ignored the role of environment or the importance of learning in the development of animal behaviors.

The interest in instinct, as well as the commitment to seeing the animal in its evolutionary context, led to Tinbergen's famous four questions about animal behavior, as presented in his book *The Study of Instinct* (1951):

1 What are the stimuli that cause the behavior?
2 How does the behavior develop with age, and are any early experiences necessary for the development of that behavior?
3 What is the reproductive and survival function of the behavior?
4 How might the behavior have evolved, and what other species share this behavior?

These questions were not understood as being unrelated to one another, but as ingredients of a full understanding of the biology of animal behavior. When writing his book, Tinbergen realized that most of the work in ethology was focused on uncovering the causal factors of instinctive behaviors, and as he wrote, he was hesitant to cover the topics of ontogeny, function, and evolution. The classical ethologists excelled in the identification of what they called innate behaviors—behaviors that are of particular use to the species, and which arise given an environmental trigger without any need for learning (but, as we will see, which can be honed with practice). For example, when Lorenz and Tinbergen met at Lorenz's private research station (at his home in Altenberg in lower Austria), they considered the interesting egg-rolling behavior of greylag geese discussed in Chapter 1. The nesting goose just can't help but retrieve an eggish object outside of her nest, leading her to engage in a fixed action pattern, a complex behavioral sequence that is indivisible and runs to completion whenever triggered by some external sensory stimulus. Though the term "fixed action pattern" has been largely abandoned, it points to a category of behavior that is associated with species-specific, and largely unlearned behavior. For example, a squirrel raised in a cage on a liquid diet, will, on first encounter with a nut, hold it properly and try to bite into it. The squirrel has never observed the behavior, so could not have learned it, but there is something about the biology of the squirrel and the trigger of the nut (which ethologists call a releasing stimulus) that leads to the food-processing behavior. However, this squirrel is not very good at opening nuts at first; only after time, after experience with nut-cracking, does the squirrel develop competence in the behavior (Eibl-Eibesfeldt 1975).

In order to determine what in the outside world triggers a particular behavior, ethologists conduct exquisite experiments to determine the causes of behavior. For example, herring gull nestlings will peck at their mother's beak and then gape their mouths open while the mother regurgitates food for the chicks. Tinbergen and Perdeck (1950) used models in order to understand the cause of the chicks' pecking behavior. They wanted to know in more detail the stimulus that causes the chicks to peck, so they made a model of an adult herring gull's head and presented it to the chicks. They found that by changing the color of the red spot on the adult's beak, they could make the chicks peck less frequently.

In another classic experiment in ethology, Karl Von Frisch (in the work that won him the Nobel Prize in Physiology in 1973, shared by Lorenz and Tinbergen) discovered that honeybees dance to indicate the location of nectar. To decode the bees' waggle dances, Von Frisch would lead a bee to food, allow it to return to the nest, and then turn the nest 180 degrees, or move the food to another place, or modify the desirability of the food—and then he would observe where the bees would fly when they next left the nest. This manipulation of the environment allowed him to conclude that the bees were using the signals of the dancing bee to orient themselves, rather than the actual location of the nectar.

While much of the famous work of ethologists focused on providing answers to Tinbergen's first question by examining the external stimuli that cause behavior, Tinbergen also wanted to know about the physiological mechanisms that lead to instinctive behaviors, and the causal factors associated with the mechanisms. He thought that the answers could be given in terms of hormones or some internal sensory stimuli. Today, the field of neuroethology—the evolutionary study of the nervous system across species—has the tools to experimentally examine the questions of mechanism in field settings. The biologist Robert Sapolsky, for example, studies the anxiety levels of baboons in Kenya as related to social status by examining their behavior and taking cortisol measures from feces samples. Another scientist working in neuroethology, John Wingfield, studies bird migrations by collecting endocrine samples and using hormone implants to uncover the mechanisms associated with migration and other seasonal bird behavior.

Tinbergen's second question—how does the behavior develop with age, and what early experiences are necessary for its development?—has been of central concern to biologists who take an evolutionary developmental (or evo-devo) approach and emphasize the joint importance of evolution and early environmental experiences. With the recognition that Mendelian genetics is the essential mechanism of biological evolution, scientists began to examine the genetic similarities and differences between organisms, and they found that humans share an overwhelming proportion of genetic material with other animals—we share 98.7 percent of our DNA with chimpanzees, and about 47 percent with fruit flies. The evo-devo approach is meant to explain how huge differences in species emerge despite great similarities in genetic material, and they find that extra-genetic influences, from epigenetics to environmental effects, will modify how genes are expressed in organisms. As well, the timing of such influences can be very important in development; the stage at which things happen in the life of the organism has large impacts downstream and can lead to the great differences we see between closely related species.

Tinbergen's questions about the evolution of the behavior and its reproductive and survival benefits were also taken up by classical ethologists. Ethologists interested in looking at the adaptive value of a behavior also want to know how a behavior aids in the ultimate goal. For example, after gull eggs hatch, the mother disposes of the eggshells from the nest. Why does she do this? Through experimentation, Tinbergen found that the eggshells attract the attention of predators, who quickly eat the newborn fledglings. Thus there is a certain adaptive value in disposing of the eggshells—it keeps your kids from being eaten.

The interest in the evolution of behavior is alive and well today, with many scientists and philosophers interested in questions about the evolution of various aspects of cognition, including culture and cultural innovations, the evolution of teaching, and, as will be discussed in the next section, the evolution of self-control.

Since the questions asked by ethologists and psychologists often overlap, and yet the methods vary, it isn't surprising that challenges have been raised about ethological methods. One worry has to do with the lack of control over the environment in experimental circumstances. While it might seem that running experiments in a laboratory setting would result in more rigorous science, Tinbergen disagrees, writing that "It would seem to be more efficient to try to improve the field methods than to try to keep a large colony of gulls under laboratory conditions" (Tinbergen 1958, 251).

Not all ethological research is experimental. Descriptive studies involve developing a catalog of behaviors, called an ethogram, and then using various sampling techniques to determine how frequently and in what contexts various behaviors occur. Ethograms can be used to generate quantitative data about how often certain behaviors occur in various situations. Concerns arise about how to characterize the behaviors that make up the ethogram. Recall Allen and Bekoff's distinction between formal descriptions in terms of movements of body parts and functional descriptions in terms of the behavior's ultimate or proximate function. In constructing an ethogram, we may lose the ability to categorize behaviors together with empirical descriptions if we rely on formal descriptions, and we may risk overinterpretation when using functional descriptions.

Some descriptive ethological research is also subject to criticism for not being repeatable; observations of an incident that is never repeated—at least not in the observer's presence—can be used as evidence for certain abilities or tactics on the part of the animal, but such interpretations are often brushed aside and the report is dismissed as anecdotal (and critics are fond to repeat "The plural of 'anecdote' is not 'data'").

Others defend the use of observations of rare events, such as the primatologist Richard Byrne, who writes, "careful and unbiased recording of unanticipated or rare events, followed by collation and an attempt at systematic analysis, cannot be harmful. At worst, the exercise will be superseded and made redundant by methods that give greater control; at best, the collated data may become important to theory" (Byrne 1997, 135). Byrne also points out that the gentlemanly anecdotes found in the writing of Darwin and Romanes should not be confused with the incident reports collected by ethologists who are trained in both the species and in observational methods.

Studying wild animal behavior in natural settings may be important when trying to answer Tinbergen's questions about ultimate mechanisms, given the finding that individual brains differ based on rearing environment. In the 1960s and 1970s, investigators found that the brains of wild rats differ significantly from those of domesticated rats (Kruska 1975), and that housing adult rats in a more highly complex and enriched environment can cause changes in brain structures and neurotransmitter activity (Krech et al. 1960; Bennett et al. 1964). Such findings suggest that the lab rats and pigeons of the behaviorists, living in metal and glass enclosures, are cognitively very different than their wild conspecifics.

2.6 New directions in animal cognition research

With technological advancements in the sciences, new ways of studying animal behavior have become available. While animal subjects still run mazes and push levers, they are also given computer-generated tests of memory and learning, as well as tests of other aspects of cognition such as individual recognition, uncertainty monitoring, and understanding of number. For example, in one study chimpanzees and humans play video games, and in some cases the chimpanzee performance is better than the human—Ayumu, a young chimpanzee who learned how to use a joystick from watching his mother is better able to remember the location of a sequence of numbers than are Japanese college students (Inoue and Matsuzawa 2007).[1]

Scientists use neuroimaging techniques to study animal brains, and use this research to uncover the processes behind the behaviors we can more directly observe. They can also use these techniques to discover similarities and differences between human and nonhuman cognitive processes. For example, by using fMRI to scan dog and human brains as they listened to a variety of dog vocalizations and human words, scientists found that both species share functionally analogous voice-sensitive regions in the cortex, and respond similarly to differences in emotional valence of the vocalizations (Andics et al. 2014). Imaging studies with monkeys are used to help us better understand human vision, and as we will see in the next chapter, neuroscientists rely on monkeys in their search to uncover the neural substrates of conscious experience.

In addition, some scientists use mathematical models to uncover the mechanisms involved in complex animal behaviors. For example, schooling fish appear to engage in group-decision making by considering both individual personal information and shared group information, as evidenced by the behavior of other individuals. In order to examine the role played by individual and collective information, along with other factors, scientists have examined whether models can predict the observed behaviors (e.g. Miller et al. 2013). When they do, the models illuminate the mechanisms that might be at work.

A recent development in animal cognition research is the creation of large collaborations of scientists across disciplines, and across species, studying the same phenomenon. The goal is to uncover the evolutionary history of cognition more generally by combining the methods of comparative psychology and evolutionary biology (MacLean et al. 2012). For example, a consortium of researchers has investigated the evolution of self-control by giving the same tasks to various taxa: primates, rodents, carnivores, elephants and birds (MacLean et al. 2014). Self-control in humans varies across individuals, and greater self-control in childhood has been correlated with better life outcomes as adults. In the 1970s, a landmark study on four- to six-year-old children examined their ability to refrain from eating a treat such as a marshmallow. The children were told that they could eat the treat now, or wait 15 minutes and receive two treats. While a few of the children immediately gobbled up the treat, the majority of subjects initially waited. In many cases the children tried to distract themselves by covering their eyes or turning their head and singing a song. About a third of the children were able to wait the full 15 minutes to receive the second treat, and age was a significant predictor, with the older children waiting longer (Mischel and Ebbesen 1970; Mischel et al. 1972).

While the ability to practice self-control has been studied in a number of species, the methods and designs of these studies varied across labs and species. In order to try to make general claims about the evolution of self-control, the same two tasks were given to 36 different species. The researchers found that the ability for self-control as measured by these tasks correlates with absolute brain volume as well as dietary breadth, but doesn't correlate with group size (MacLean et al. 2014).

These sorts of large-scale consortiums are recent developments in comparative cognition, and the benefits and potential problems associated with them are not unlike the benefits and problems with cross cultural research on human cognition. The move away from using only WEIRD (Western, Educated, Industrialized, Rich, and Democratic) subjects when doing human psychology is motivated by a desire to find out what may be universal in human cognition (Henrich et al. 2010). However, one might worry whether the same experiment can really be given across human cultures—do gambling tasks mean the same thing to people from capitalistic societies and collectivist societies, for example? Similarly, do tasks given to birds and elephants appear the same to each? The different size of the subjects, the different perceptual acuity, and other species-specific properties might make it difficult to determine whether the subjects are indeed engaged in the same task.

2.7 Chapter summary

The science of animal minds is perhaps more appropriately called *the sciences* of animal minds, given how many different disciplines are involved in investigating the cognitive capacities of animals. As the study of animal minds continues to change along with new technologies, old questions about interpretation and anthropomorphism, the role of folk psychology, and the nature of insight remain. Tinbergen's four questions, along with Marr's three levels of explanation discussed in Chapter 1, illustrate how we can ask various kinds of questions about a single behavior, leading to different answers. In particular, the interdisciplinary nature of the study of animal minds should cue us to look twice at explanations that appear to be at odds, for they may be merely answers to different kinds of questions about the same phenomenon.

As we move on to examine questions about consciousness, belief, communication, social cognition, and morality in other animals, we will be calibrating our concepts given what we find from the sciences, but as was pointed out in this chapter, science doesn't provide straightforward answers either. The investigation requires a delicate balance that involves tweaking our scientific questions and methods as well as our philosophical concepts. And so let us proceed!

Note

1   For very interesting videos of Ayumu's performance on this task, you can visit the Chimpanzee Ai web page.

Further reading

Read Morgan's original treatment of animal cognition in his *Animal life and intelligence* (1891) as well as his intellectual autobiography available online (http://psychclassics.yorku.ca/Morgan/murchison.htm).

Some of the same worries Morgan had can be seen in Cameron Buckner's 2013 paper "Morgan's Canon, meet Hume's Dictum: Avoiding anthropofabulation in cross-species comparisons" and in Sara Shettleworth's article "Clever animals and killjoy explanations in comparative psychology" (2010).

For an introduction to the science of comparative cognition as it is today, see Sara Shettleworth's excellent textbook *Cognition, Evolution, and Behavior* (2010). Another useful comparative psychology text is Clive Wynne and Monique Udell's *Animal Cognition: Evolution, Behavior and Cognition* (2013).

For a good review of the history of classical ethology, you can read Richard Burkhardt's *Patterns of Behavior: Konrad Lorenz, Niko Tinbergen, and the Founding of Ethology* (2005). Or go to the source and read one of Lorenz's popular books, such as *King Solomon's Ring* (1952).

Three books provide a range of views about using folk psychology in animal cognition research. Donald Griffin's *Animal Minds* (1992) is a plea for doing research on consciousness and mind in other animals, while J.S. Kennedy's *The New Anthropomorphism* (1992) is a critique of Griffin's position. A still-relevant collection of essays on the issues are found in the volume *Anthropomorphism, Anecdotes, and Animals* edited by Robert W. Mitchell, Nicholas S. Thompson, and H. Lyn Miles (1997).

3 Consciousness

In July 2012, a group of scientists gathered for the Francis Crick Memorial Conference "Consciousness in Humans and Non-human animals." After a day of lectures, the group of scientists signed The Cambridge Declaration of Consciousness in Non-human Animals, according to which:

> Convergent evidence indicates that non-human animals have the neuroanatomical, neurochemical, and neurophysiological substrates of conscious states along with the capacity to exhibit intentional behaviors. Consequently, the weight of evidence indicates that humans are not unique in possessing the neurological substrates that generate consciousness. Non-human animals, including all mammals and birds, and many other creatures, including octopuses, also possess these neurological substrates.

These scientists also pointed out that neuroscience research on consciousness uses animal subjects, and that the assumption that animals are conscious has led to great progress in the science of consciousness. Since the premise that rhesus macaques (the typical subjects for consciousness studies) are conscious has led to scientific knowledge about the brain structures involved in particular conscious experiences, the scientists infer that these animals are conscious. If they weren't, the research wouldn't have gone nearly so well.

3.1 What is consciousness?

Philosophers of mind are focused on the question of the nature of minds, and their theories of mind purport to answer that question. One goal of such theories is to offer a solution to the mind-body problem, which amounts to the question of how matter creates subjective experience. Another goal of the theories is to provide a criterion for distinguishing conscious creatures from nonconscious ones.

Philosophers often describe consciousness in terms of qualia—how things feel—or awareness. The perfumed smell of a spring garden, the warm feeling of sun on your skin, and the sharp taste of wasabi are all examples of the qualitative nature of consciousness. Frank Jackson focuses on what it is like to see color in his discussion of consciousness (Jackson 1986). Thomas Nagel discusses how we understand other minds by trying to think about "what it is like" to be someone else (Nagel 1974). But philosophers are also interested in the cognitive processes that unify our experiences, and allow us to make our way through the world of the senses. Since at least the time of Immanuel Kant, philosophers have wondered about the unity of consciousness, or the sense we each have of being a whole self with complex experiences, not merely a collection of various bits of qualitative experience (Kant 1781/1998).

So it shouldn't be surprising that there are many different ways of understanding consciousness. Ned Block (1998) draws a distinction between access consciousness—having information that is available to the rest of the cognitive system—and phenomenal consciousness—the qualitative nature of experience. One can have access consciousness about the quality of the road during a run and adjust one's body accordingly without having any phenomenal consciousness of every rut and bump on the path.

When inquiring into animal consciousness, the issue at stake is usually the question of phenomenal consciousness. When Nagel asked "What is it like to be a bat?" he was interested in the phenomenal sense of consciousness; a creature has experience if and only if there is something it is like to be that creature. Phenomenal consciousness is also contrasted with the sense of "consciousness" as being awake (awake consciousness), or as becoming aware of your political status (political consciousness). Furthermore, phenomenal consciousness is to be distinguished from self-consciousness, which refers to our ability to reflect upon our conscious experiences and thoughts. This distinction is important because it may be that one can have conscious experience without being self-conscious of that experience—individuals may experience pain without reflecting on the pain experience, as when engaged in a competitive sport, or when in deep meditation. As we will see, there is some debate about whether one can be conscious without at least the ability to reflect on one's experiences.

Once we agree that we are interested in discussing phenomenal consciousness, we can then use the calibration method in order to draw conclusions about the nature of phenomenal consciousness, and the distribution of phenomenal consciousness across animal species. There are two main trends in current philosophical theories of consciousness, representationalist theories and nonrepresentationalist theories. According to representationalist theories of consciousness, the aspect of mind shared by all conscious beings is the ability to represent, while nonrepresentationalist theories do not associate conscious experience with representational capacities. The representationalist theories come in two flavors: first order (FO) and higher order (HO). According to first order thought (FOT) views, for example, one is conscious in virtue of having a belief. Higher order thought (HOT) views require a metacognitive representational state in order for consciousness to emerge. Some HOT advocates, such as Peter Carruthers, have argued that most animals are not conscious because they lack the cognitive mechanisms necessary for metacognition, whereas others, such as Rocco Gennaro, think that HOTs are achievable by nonhuman animals.

Nonrepresentationalist theories of consciousness are most visibly represented by the neural correlates of consciousness view, according to which consciousness is seen as some set of neurophysiological states or processes. The lack of agreement over which behaviors are associated with phenomenal consciousness creates difficulty with examining the neurological processes associated with consciousness. Asserting, "I am aware" is taken as sufficient evidence of consciousness when working with human subjects, but neuroscientists have to be savvy in order to determine which nonlinguistic behaviors indicate the existence of conscious experience. As we will see, the neurological research rests heavily on analogy.

In the first chapter, we looked at arguments for animal minds, and one might think that minds and consciousness refer to the same thing. However, at least conceptually we can distinguish mind from conscious experience. Thomas Henry Huxley, a biologist who was known as Darwin's Bulldog for his heated defense of the theory of evolution, argued that animals, and humans, are conscious automata (Huxley 1874). All our bodily motion is determined by physical causes, though we also have experiences that go along with them. On his view, phenomenal consciousness has no causal power—in the jargon, consciousness is epiphenomenal. For the epiphenomenalist, there is causal independence between conscious experience and a physical mind, thus we can study everything that matters about the mind without studying consciousness.

A minded individual has intentional states that are about the world, and which are used to engage in cognitive activities such as learning, remembering, navigating, communicating, and so forth. For example, it seems we can study memory processes by running rats in mazes, and discover the cognitive structures underlying rats' memory, without making any claims about what it feels like for a rat to remember, and whether it feels like anything at all. Donald Griffin, the psychologist who brought scientists back to the question of animal minds in the 1970s, is skeptical of that approach, since he thinks that knowing what an animal feels can help us understand how they think (Griffin 1992). Nonetheless, representational theories of consciousness blur the distinction between being minded in terms of having intentional states and being conscious.

Consciousness has only recently become a topic of serious scientific investigation. And when we turn to see what scientists are doing in the context of consciousness, we see that they too are focusing on different aspects that fall under the umbrella of consciousness. Vision researchers are approaching the question of consciousness in terms of perception, and are interested in what goes on in the brain when we experience an optical illusion. For example, while investigating what the brain does when people report visual experience, neuroscientists Francis Crick and Christof Koch found that the visual cortex is not necessary for visual experience (Crick and Koch 1995). Research into dreaming, which is a type of conscious experience without perceptual input, shows that dreams can be disassociated with REM sleep, and what seems key to dreams are the visual and the audiovisual areas in the neo-cortex (Solms 2000). Perception and dreaming are two key areas of consciousness studies that have involved research on animal subjects.

It often seems mysterious how a physical event in the brain gives rise to the feelings we have in our conscious lives. But, perhaps it is no more strange that physical elements give rise to consciousness than that they can give rise to wetness—it only seems mysterious because we don't yet know how consciousness works (Hardcastle 1996). As Crick says, when he was starting out as a young scientist he was interested in two things: the mystery of life and the mystery of consciousness. He decided to solve the mystery of life first, and after his discovery of DNA felt he had his answer. He only started work on the question of how the mind arises from the brain later in life, and died confident that we would have already solved that mystery had he chosen to work on that question first! No matter who gets the credit, the hope is that with further work on the problem of consciousness, the mysteriousness of it will fade away.

3.2 Are other animals conscious?

If we adopt a naturalistic outlook, we should expect that consciousness is the sort of thing we could explain within our scientific worldview. The scientists participating in the conference memorializing Crick agree with this naturalist approach, and they accept that the right way to study consciousness is to search for neural correlates to conscious experience—a reductionist approach. They believe that we can do comparative studies by looking for similarities in neurological structure and activity between humans and other animals. While we can formulate the Cambridge Declaration as a form of argument from analogy, neuroscientists investigating consciousness really take animal consciousness as a starting assumption. The neuro-physiologists study animal brains, and then make inferences about human consciousness. Animal species are used to model humans.

One response to the Cambridge Declaration was amusement—look, scientists finally realize that your dog is conscious! Even Descartes, who argued that animals lack minds because they lack language, accepted that animals have phenomenal consciousness. In fact, it was part of his argument against animal thought:

> Yet, although all animals easily communicate to us, by voice or bodily movement, their natural impulses of anger, fear, hunger, and so on, it has never yet been observed that any brute animal reached the stage of using real speech, that is to say, of indicating by word or sign something pertaining to pure thought and not to natural impulse ... I do not deny sensation, in so far as it depends on a bodily organ
>
> (Descartes 1970)

Why was even Descartes certain that animals are conscious? Descartes argued from analogy, pointing out that humans engage in many behaviors without thought—we can eat, walk, avoid hazards, and "parry the blows aimed at us" (Descartes 1970). But, unless we are pretending, we don't shrink away from a threat without feeling frightened, or laugh out loud without feeling pleasure. And when we see other animals engaging in the same sorts of behaviors, we naturally impute the same kinds of sensations.

3.3 Non-inferential arguments for animal consciousness

There is a tradition in philosophy according to which it is good and right to start with the assumption that animals are conscious, as the neuroscientists who study macaque brains to draw inferences about consciousness do, and as Descartes appeared to do. The claim that we don't need to infer consciousness is associated with the philosopher Ludwig Wittgenstein, who thought that the mind is not hidden from view. Like the direct perception argument for other minds seen in Chapter 1, according to non-inferential views of consciousness mind is not private, but it is observable in our movements and interactions with others. No arguments are needed to prove the existence of consciousness. We see the dog's fear in his shrinking back from a blow, just as we see the pleasure or joy of a human laugh.

The non-inferential arguments for consciousness are quite similar to those for minds. Searle supports the argument by suggesting that in our daily lives, we are not constantly in some skeptical epistemic stance toward the world, making inferences about causality, the existence of an external world, or the existence of other human and nonhuman minds. We don't infer that people are conscious, Searle claims, we just *respond* to them that way. We ignore the possibility that they are zombies or machines.

And Jamieson asks us to consider what we would do if scientists were to discover that animals are not conscious (1998, 2009). He thinks we would go on attributing sensation to animals anyway, because we can't help but do so; the practices of everyday life don't require philosophical justification, and the idea of a behaving body—like a dog without consciousness— is a "philosophical monster."

The non-inferential arguments for animal consciousness are not going to be any more convincing than the non-inferential arguments for animal minds when presented to someone who isn't already inclined to see animals as conscious. The critic might respond, "Sure, people really believe that animals are conscious, and treat them as conscious, but that is no more evidence for animal consciousness than building shrines for the dead is evidence of a spirit world." People's insistence on seeing the world a certain way doesn't make the world be that way, unless what is being seen is socially constructed in the first place, like money or marriage. But Searle doesn't want to defend the claim that consciousness is socially constructed; it is a real biological phenomenon. Furthermore, while these social arguments may be used to draw conclusions about dogs, cats, chimpanzees, and dolphins, they do little to help us determine whether octopuses, fish, bees, or paramecia are conscious. When an animal isn't part of our social circle, we're not in a position to see that individual as conscious the way we are with other humans. And since for various reasons we may be unable to take some species into our social circle, on the non-inferential approach we would remain without a means for deciding whether or not such individuals are conscious.

3.4 Inferential arguments for animal consciousness

Worries about the non-inferential arguments lead us to examine the inferential arguments for animal consciousness. Griffin thinks that real arguments are needed as evidence for animal consciousness, and that the focus of such arguments should be twofold. Those interested in animal consciousness have to examine the similarities and differences of neural structure and functioning between humans and the target animals. In addition, they have to examine behavioral evidence about the flexibility of the associated behaviors, since flexibility allows an organism to modify behavior without having been preprogrammed by evolution or explicit learning. Behavioral flexibility is evidence for the sort of representational mental states Griffin thinks are necessary for consciousness (Griffin 2002).

First order representationalists have taken up the challenge of offering Griffin's second kind of evidence for consciousness in animals by focusing on the sorts of behaviors that seem to be associated with having representational mental states. For example, Michael Tye argues that the question of whether animals are phenomenally conscious is a straightforward application of his PANIC theory of consciousness (Tye 1997). The PANIC theory is described by Tye as having four main elements: Poised (available to belief-forming cognitive processes), Abstract (no concrete object needs to be involved, thus permitting hallucinations and dreams), Nonconceptual (no concepts are required, such that you can experience of analog or coarse-grained features such as the difference between different shades of red), and Intentional-Content (the content of the state is represented). Animals who demonstrate flexible behavior and the capacity to learn have the kind of representations required for conscious experience. For example, if we can identify a creature as having nonconceptual states that track features of the world, we will have identified a conscious creature.

Tye agrees with Griffin that the best evidence that an animal has intentional representational content comes from evidence of animal learning. In learning, the animal demonstrates flexibility in behavior across similar situations, which is different from giving responses explainable by appeal to fixed action patterns or stimulus-response conditioning. Because plants don't learn, don't engage in flexible behavior, and have movements that are genetically determined, Tye thinks that plants do not have representational states and hence they are not conscious (though recent research on plant physiology challenges this claim of Tye's, suggesting that some plants can learn and even remember things (Gagliano et al. 2014)). However, Tye thinks that fish do engage in behavior that depends on evaluations of their sense data. Tye gives the example of the gray snapper, who usually enjoys eating silverside fish. When researchers marked silverside fish who were injected with an unpalatable flavor, the gray-snapper learned to avoid the marked fish while eating only the unmarked ones. As we will see, fish have many sophisticated cognitive abilities, including discrimination abilities, maze solving, and so forth. This sort of evidence leads Tye to conclude that fish have a belief-forming cognitive process, and hence that they are conscious. Similarly, there is evidence that honeybees learn the location of food, use landmarks to navigate, learn abstract shapes, and make decisions based on how things look, taste, or feel (for an enjoyable overview of the research on honeybees, see Seeley 2010). Honeybees inform others where food is located using their famous waggle dance. But they can also evaluate the messages they receive, choosing to follow the dancer's instructions or to fly to a food source that they had past experience with (von Frisch 1967). Tye concludes that many species, not just vertebrates, are conscious, because they have beliefs that they use to track the world and modify their future behavior.

There are concerns about taking learning as sufficient evidence for conscious experience, because it may be that humans learn without conscious experience. If humans can unconsciously learn, then there is no reason to think that animals need to be conscious in order to learn.

One example of apparently unconscious learning comes from humans with the unusual condition of blindsight. People with blindsight are able to correctly react to their physical environment, and even to walk around obstacles in their path, all the while reporting no visual experience.[1] Blindsight occurs in individuals with significant damage to their primary visual cortex, and the first experimental studies of blindsight were conducted with monkeys whose visual cortex was surgically altered (Humphrey and Weiskrantz 1967).[2]

Critics of the claim that learning requires consciousness argue that humans with blindsight lack conscious experience about things in their visual field, and yet they can make judgments about objects in their visual field and behave flexibly toward items that are visually presented (e.g. Allen-Hermanson 2008). And when it comes to learning, it seems that blindsighted people can also be subject to conditioned effects by stimuli they cannot experience. In one study a cortically blind man was conditioned to associate a drawing of an airplane with an electric shock. Even though he reported no awareness of the drawing, the man would react with a greater startle response when the drawing was displayed (Hamm et al. 2003). However, in some other studies patients do report increased conscious experience with learning (Stoerig 2006).

Another argument against Tye's position comes from cases of implicit learning, without conscious awareness, of which grammatical learning is a paradigm example. We come to learn the grammatical rules of our language without conscious awareness of those rules or even introspective access to many of them. Other examples given of unconscious learning come from the priming literature. An example of priming comes from the studies indicating that people walk more slowly after being presented with words about the elderly (Bargh et al. 1996; for a critical overview of the data on priming, see Bower 2012). Psychologists report that though we say one thing, we move our bodies in ways that are inconsistent with our verbal claims. For example, when presented with Titchener circles we see the middle circle on the left as bigger than the middle circle on the right, when in fact they are the same size (Aglioti et al. 1995; Haffenden and Goodale 1998, 2000). However, when disks are used to form Titchener circles, we have no problems orienting our fingers to pick up the middle disk in both arrays, even though we view the circles as being different sizes (though see Pavani et al. 1999 for an alternate interpretation of these studies).

The critical question when examining cases such as blindsight and priming is whether the sorts of learning that take place in these cases are the same sorts of learning animals engage in. If it is learning of a different sort, then the argument by counterexample does not hold.

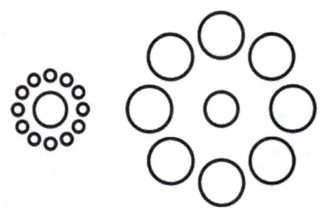

Figure 3.1 Titchener circles. While the middle circle on the left looks bigger than the middle circle on the right, the circles are actually the same size.

Even when philosophers agree with the general approach to consciousness, and about empirical data being relevant for the question, they can still disagree about the proper kind of behavioral evidence that would indicate the existence of first order representational states. The lack of agreement by FO (first-order) theorists about which species are conscious leaves some cold about the entire approach. The psychologist Cecilia Heyes thinks that the lack of agreement is a reflection of our unscientific judgments about animal consciousness, and she criticizes these arguments as based on arguments from analogy and as anthropomorphic. She suggests that when we see animals engage in a behavior like learning, we can notice that we have conscious experience when we learn, and from our own experience we might infer that animals must be having the same kind of experience when they enage in the same sort of behavior. The philosophical arguments make just that mistake—they start with an introspective judgment about whether we are conscious when we engage in a particular activity, and then rely on analogical reasoning to ascribe consciousness to animals. Heyes dismisses such arguments as "the method that we all use spontaneously in our day-to-day dealings with animals, in an attempt to understand and to anticipate their behaviour" (Heyes 2008), and argues instead that a genuine scientific investigation into animal consciousness needs to have alternative hypotheses on the table, in order to compare them and construct an inference to the best explanation argument.

3.5 A representationalist challenge to animal consciousness

Representationalist theories of consciousness have in common a focus on the intentional nature of conscious experiences—they are about the things that cause them, and so conscious states refer to, or represent, those objects or states of affairs. On representationalist views, the representational properties are what make a mental state conscious. Different answers to questions about whether we are conscious of all the things we represent have led to different versions of representational theories. There is reason to think that representation alone cannot suffice for consciousness, since photographs and maps represent what they are about, and we presume they are not conscious. According to mainstream representationalist theories, we are only conscious of those representational mental states that are also available to other systems, such as belief-forming or action-taking systems; the representations have to serve the right kind of functional role in the system. For some philosophers, that right kind of functional role is metacognitive; one must be able to have mental states like beliefs about other mental states in order to be conscious of those mental states. This leads to a major distinction between types of representational theories, namely FO theories which don't require metacognition and HO (higher-order) theories which do. Since the cognitive approach to studying animal minds assumes the existence of representations, all animal cognition researchers would simply be committed to the presence of consciousness on the FO account. Such a position is consistent with what most scientists working on animal minds seem to think: that animals are conscious, and that they use representations to navigate their world.

However, there are some worries about FO representationalist views that have to do with the fact that we seem to represent—and have available to other systems—more things than what we are conscious of. Take the example of unconscious driving. While driving over a long distance, sometimes the mind wanders. Because long drives can be tedious, we daydream, plan for the future, or otherwise focus attention on something other than the road and the other cars. After driving for some time in the daydreamy state, we might jerk back to the present, and realize that we hadn't been paying attention to the road. But, nonetheless, we were not asleep while driving, and were perfectly able to attend to the other cars, the curves on the highway, and so forth. Indeed, if you regained attention because your passenger remarked on the beautiful red barn you had just passed, you may even be able to recall the barn, even though you were not consciously aware of it when it was there. Philosophers point to these kinds of experiences—situations in which we seem to lose awareness of our automatized actions in driving, washing the dishes, brushing teeth—as prima facie evidence that we represent things that we are not conscious of, and that it takes something in addition to representation, like a focus of attention on the representation, in order to become conscious of something. Scientific evidence of unconscious processing offered by researchers working on implicit priming offers corroborating evidence that we can represent without conscious experience.

While there are many versions of HO representationalism, the one that has been most discussed in relationship to animal consciousness is the variety developed by Peter Carruthers (1989). Carruthers separates experience from consciousness—experience is what we have when we are driving without awareness, and what blindsight patients demonstrate when they sincerely claim that they can't see, yet are able to navigate across a room of obstacles, or can correctly choose a named object. The existence of unattentional driving, blindsight, priming, among other phenomena, provide evidence that humans have nonconscious experiences, and should lead us to conclude that one can have sense organs without consciousness. Sense organs are needed to gain information that allows us to experience our world, and hence to move about it in coherent ways, but they need not permit us to have consciousness of our world as well.

Carruthers thinks that even though animals have sense organs, they are not conscious, because they lack the metacognitive abilities that are required for conscious experience. According to his theory, perceptual states only become conscious when they are available to some higher-order mental system that is capable of forming beliefs about the perceptions. For example, in order to be conscious of the smell coming from a glass of wine, you have to be able to formulate a belief about the smell of the wine. If the perception is not accessible to some belief-forming system, then the perception is unconscious. When I have the conscious experience of smelling a glass of wine, I have dual content: the first order representation of the scent, along with a second-order representation of seeming to smell the wine. If animals cannot form a representation about their other representations, then animals will lack phenomenal consciousness.

One might think that if an animal is not phenomenally conscious, he does not have the capacity to suffer, and that we need not be morally concerned about causing suffering to animals. Carruthers objects that this conclusion doesn't follow. Animals may be able to suffer, which he thinks arises when an event causes harm to an individual's "ongoing mental life" (Carruthers 2004, 99). But since that mental life is entirely at a first-order level, the suffering will not become conscious. Just as a soldier hit by a bullet in the heat of battle might not be conscious of the pain until she has a moment to reflect on what happened, even though she favors the injured body part in all her actions after getting shot, animals might suffer without realizing that they do so. However, since animals may be able to represent the aversiveness of pain, and modify their behavior accordingly, they can unconsciously suffer. And if suffering is sufficient for moral concern, then we should be morally concerned about animals, even if they aren't conscious. This is why Carruthers says, "consciousness might not matter very much." Animals can have a rich mental life, full of pains and pleasures that just don't feel like anything.

Put simply, Carruthers' argument against animal consciousness can be stated as follows:

1   Animals do not have thoughts about thoughts.
2   Without having thoughts about thoughts, one cannot be conscious.
3   Therefore, animals are not conscious.

Critics have challenged both premises of this argument. Some have argued that higher order theories of consciousness are flawed, reasoning that any theory that entails animals are not conscious must be false, and so reject premise (2). But other philosophers think that (2) is false even though HO theories of consciousness are true. For example, the HO theorist Rocco Gennaro argues that the cognitive capacities required for higher order thought are not very sophisticated, and they can be had without the metacognitive concepts of *concept* or *belief* (Gennaro 2004). All that's needed is content of the form "I am in M" where the "I" can be satisfied by any number of selfhood concepts and the "M" can be satisfied by a variety of mental state concepts, without an additional concept of that concept. So, awareness of a mental token-M requires recognizing it as having some mental property, as opposed to recognizing *that* it has some mental property. It is enough to think of the entity as M *rather than* as some other state N. Animals plausibly have concepts of "looking red" or "seeing red" and since these concepts are about representations of perceived objects, and allow animals to discriminate red from green objects, such a concept would permit animals to consciously experience colors. In addition, animals plausibly have concepts such as "feeling" and "yearning" that they use to modify their other representations, thus animals could have conscious experiences of things like pains in terms of "this hurt" or "this unpleasant feeling," and these concepts would be sufficient to discriminate painful from painless experiences.

Carruthers' argument has also been challenged by those who reject the first premise. His commitment that animals lack higher order thought come from his interpretation of the empirical evidence. No nonhuman animal has passed a mindreading or metacognition task, he thinks, and so there is evidence that animals lack the ability to think about their own and other minds. We will discuss mindreading in Chapter 6, and turn to metacognition later in this chapter in the context of self-consciousness, at which point we will be better able to examine the claim that other animals lack the capacity to think about thoughts.

Others challenge premise (1) by denying that we can separate consciousness from experience. Carruthers seems to defend premise (1) in this way:

4   Humans have visual sense organs.
5   Humans have nonconscious visual experiences.
6   Therefore, it is possible for a creature to have sense organs and lack conscious experience.

This argument rests on the case of people with blindsight, as well as cases like automatic driving or dish-washing.

One problem with this argument comes from the worry that the notion of consciousness used in the premise isn't the same as the notion used in the conclusion. Carruthers aims to convince us that because humans, despite having sense organs, have experiences without being conscious of them, it is possible for an organism that has sense organs to lack *any* conscious experiences. It is here that the flaw becomes apparent. It has been pointed out that while engaged in inattentional driving, humans are not *unconscious*; rather, they are just conscious of something else (Jamieson and Bekoff 1992). Furthermore, critics point out that blindsight is a pathology that can be associated with a lack of attention to some aspect of the surroundings, but that individuals with blindsight often report some conscious experience—a feeling that something is there. The blindsight experience may not be qualitatively neutral. Jamieson and Bekoff conclude that there isn't a very close analogy between animal behavior and human blindsight behavior or automatic driving behavior. Further, there isn't any evidence that other animals are limited in the way we are when we are engaged in some automatic behaviors; we may be unable to remember some things we did when engaged in inattentional driving. If animal action were like inattentional driving, we should expect animals to lack some memory, but we don't find this to be the case.

Other challenges to the similarity argument come from those who don't share Carruthers' intuition that one is unconscious of driving when inattentionally driving. Michael Tye insists that the distracted driver is conscious of driving, because the driver responds to visual input and responds appropriately. The driver sees the road, but isn't aware that he sees it; "Things do not lose their looks to him while he is distracted. If they did, how could he keep the car on the road?" (Tye 1997, 310).

Given Carruthers' argument, it would follow that any individual who lacks the ability to have mental states subject to higher order cognitive systems would also lack consciousness. This means that humans who lack such metacognitive abilities would also lack consciousness. If human infants are not metacognitive then they would lack consciousness too. The same would go for anyone with cognitive impairments that limit metacognitive abilities, such as perhaps some people with autism. If one accepts a theory such as Carruthers', then the natural end result is to limit consciousness to a certain subclass of humans. Drawing the line to include all and only humans isn't justifiable on his account.

It's not just Carruthers' view that would exclude human infants from the class of conscious beings. Some first order representationalist theories also seem to exclude human infants, since infants would fail the behavioral tasks that are used to test for consciousness in other species. Here we have the choice of rejecting a commonsense belief in human infancy, or tweaking our theory of consciousness to accommodate human infants. If we want to retain the premise that all (mobile) living humans are conscious, then we need a theory that won't force us to reject it. Neural correlates of consciousness approaches to consciousness offer just that.

3.6 Neural correlates of consciousness arguments for animal minds

Neurofunctionalists and those looking for the neural correlates of consciousness are searching for Griffin's first set of evidence for animal consciousness. Those working to uncover physiological evidence for consciousness will focus on some particular aspects of consciousness, such as emotion or attention, and look for neurological evidence that there are brain regions in other species that can only be explained in terms of doing the same sort of work as the functionally similar human brain regions. The idea is that if we know what consciousness is for, we can determine which behaviors are associated with consciousness, and then neuroscientists can look to see if there are functionally similar neurological processes going on across species.

The philosopher Jesse Prinz argues that creatures that have both attention and working memory are conscious, because consciousness exists to deliver information to our working memory. Since attention is a selection process, it is able to choose appropriate information to be sent to outputs such as working memory for additional processing. Given that what we know about the neurophysiology of human attention and working memory comes largely from studies on monkeys and rats, we can conclude that "higher" mammals probably share both the necessary mechanism and the conscious experience (Prinz 2005). However, this thesis runs into epistemic problems when looking at other taxa, including octopuses, pigeons, bees, or slugs, because we don't know if their neural mechanisms are enough like ours to know if they are conscious, and worse, we don't have any way to know how similar is similar enough! Consider trying to find out at which neurocomputational level of abstraction we can determine that human processes of attention are the same as the octopuses' functionally similar mechanisms. We would have to try to keep the psychological state the same while varying the neural mechanisms, but so long as the replacement neural mechanisms have the same functional role, the individual will act the same, but we won't know if conscious experience is disappearing or being modified in some way. And it gets worse, because of the possibility of some creature who appears to act flexibly and learn, but who is completely unlike humans at the neurofunctional level—consider a creature with no memory or attention. While we might be justified in concluding that the "what it is like" experience of that creature is very different from our own, we wouldn't be able to conclude that it has no conscious life at all. Such epistemic worries lead to what Prinz calls "level-headed mysterianism" about the distribution of consciousness across species. But psychologists, neuroscientists, and biologists have been working on the problem of animal consciousness by looking at both neurobiological evidence as well as evidence from learning and animal behavior, and here there is promising evidence in favor of animal consciousness in a nonmammalian taxa that avoids Prinz's worry.

3.6.1 Fish pain

In a series of experiments, the biologist Victoria Braithwaite and her colleagues investigated the possibility that fish are conscious by focusing on one conscious experience—pain (for a review of their research, see Braithwaite 2010). They were interested in whether fish could feel pain for ethical reasons as well as scientific ones. Catch and release fishing is a popular sport which involves hooking fish through the lip, reeling in the fish, and then removing the hook before throwing the fish back into the water. Advocates of catch and release fishing suggest that their sport is responsible because it does no harm to individual fish or fish populations. Braithwaite and her colleagues were not so sure, and they were also concerned with the possibility that commercial fishing and aquaculture causes fish pain.

In order to address the question of whether fish feel pain—that is, whether there is something it is like to be a hooked or suffocating fish—Braithwaite first looked at the physiology of human pain. The initial stage of pain is an unconscious damage detection that is done by specialized receptors in the skin called nociceptors. The nociceptors send a signal to the spinal cord, which causes a reflex response (such as pulling one's hand away from a hot stove). The experience of pain is usually understood as an emotional response to the activation of the nociceptors, and scientists have found that the limbic system (a set of brain structures associated with emotional response) and the dopamine system (brain structures which work on dopamine, a neurotransmitter involved with motivation and reward) are associated with pain experience in humans. To find evidence of pain in fish, Braithwaite thought, we need evidence both of nociception as well as of emotional responses to nociception.

We also know that human pain experience is modified by opioids such as morphine, which works by blocking some of the signals from the nociceptors. People on morphine report that the pain is still there, but they don't mind it as much. It doesn't feel the same way. Since humans and other animals act in particular ways when they are experiencing pain, one way to test for pain in other species is to examine whether behaviors associated with tissue damage are modified when the individuals are given chemicals that work like morphine. Further, since we know that humans have difficulty learning new things when they are in pain (imagine that!), we can examine whether morphine-like chemicals will restore an individual's ability to learn.

Braithwaite and her colleagues systematically examined these issues in trout by asking three specific questions: first, do trout have nociceptors; second, are they active in response to tissue damage; finally, is trout behavior modified when nociceptors are active? Asking the next question required a yes answer to the previous one. After discovering nociceptors responding to tissue damage on the face and snout of trout, they tested the receptors using different noxious stimuli by injecting vinegar and bee venom under the skin around the mouth. They found that the fish given vinegar or bee venom breathed much more rapidly (as measured by gill beating) than fish that were injected with a saline solution, and they showed no interest in food long after the control fish began eating. Because increased heart rate and breathing as well as lack of interest in food is common among humans who are experiencing pain, Braithwaite and her colleagues took the marked difference in these two measures between the fish treated with the noxious chemical and the control subjects as evidence that fish modify their behavior in response to painful stimuli.

While this evidence was sufficient to conclude that there is nociception in fish, Braithwaite thought more data was needed to defend the claim that fish are conscious of pain. There is no reason to think that appetite cannot be suppressed unconsciously, for example. Better evidence of conscious pain would come with more complex cognitive behaviors. Since trout tend to avoid new objects that are placed in their tanks, they are able to distinguish between old and new objects. This requires attention to novelty. Braithwaite and her colleagues decided to test whether a trout would still avoid a novel object after having been injected with vinegar. They found that compared with a control group injected with saline, the vinegar-injected fish did not show the usual avoidance responses, swimming quite close to the novel object (a Lego brick). In a second experiment, as in the first, half the fish were treated with vinegar and half were given a saline injection, and all were given morphine. The difference between the two groups disappeared: the vinegar-treated fish started showing avoidance responses similar to the control fish. Braithwaite claims that these studies show the following:

> Giving the fish an injection of a noxious substance distracted its attention, but when pain relief was given, the ability to focus its attention increased again. For this to happen the fish must be cognitively aware and experiencing the negative experiences associated with pain. Being cognitively aware of tissue damage is what we mean when we talk about *feeling* pain.
> (Braithwaite 2010, 69)

While Braithwaite thinks the first set of studies offers some evidence for fish consciousness, we also need to know whether fish have any brain structure that functions like the human limbic system. Since the limbic system is where emotional processing occurs in humans, and pain is understood as an emotion, it follows by analogy that fish would also need something like a limbic system to experience pain. Because the fish brain is much simpler than most vertebrate brains, and there is no obvious neo-cortex, some biologists such as James Rose have argued that fish cannot feel pain or experience any feeling (Rose 2002, 2007). However, a group of researchers from Spain have suggested that goldfish have areas of the brain functionally equivalent to the hippocampus and amygdala, key players in the human limbic system. For example, they found that goldfish with lesions in the amygdala-like area cannot learn to avoid an electric shock, while typical goldfish can (Portavella et al. 2004; for a review of the research on goldfish see Salas et al. 2006).

While the evidence in favor of fish pain may seem surprising, this is due more to our lack of knowledge about fish behavior than to anything else. In her book, Braithwaite describes how various fish species have abilities on par with the more familiar mammals: frillfin gobies learn mazes and have sophisticated spatial abilities in natural settings (Aronson 1951, 1971), grouper and eel will join forces to hunt prey (Bshary et al. 2006), male cichlids perform transitive inference calculations on dominance relations (they can infer that if fish A is dominant over fish B, who is dominant over fish C, who is dominant over fish D, then fish B will also be dominant over fish D) (Grosenick et al. 2007), and trout, who don't like being alone, are willing to withstand an electric shock in order to be close to a conspecific (Dunlop et al. 2006). Braithwaite concludes her extended argument from analogy to the effect that fish are conscious by suggesting that they have mental representations (as evidenced by their cognitive abilities in navigation and transitive inference), as well as emotional brain regions and functioning nociceptors. With these three reference properties established, Braithwaite offers a powerful argument that combines both inference to the best explanation style argument as well as argument from analogy.

3.6.2 Evaluating animal pain

Fish are not the only animals for which we have this sort of evidence for pain experience. The philosopher Gary Varner has reviewed the huge body of research on pain in other animals. His chart is reproduced in Table 3.1.

Table 3.1 The "standard" argument by analogy.

	Invertebrates			Vertebrates			
	Earthworms	Insects	Cephalopods	Fish	Herps	Birds	Mammals
1) Nociceptors present	?	–	?	+	+	+	+
2) Brain present	–	–	+	+	+	+	+
3) Nociceptors connected to brain	–	–	+	+	?/+	?/+	+
4) Endogenous opiods present	+	+	?	+	+	+	+
5) Responses modified by known analgesics	?	?	?	+	?	+	+
6) Response to damaging stimuli analogous to that of humans	–	–	+	+	+	+	+

(Source: Table 5.2 in Varner 2012, 113)

The conclusion he draws is that vertebrates can probably all experience pain, but among the invertebrates, we only have evidence of pain experience in cephalopods (such as octopus, squid, and cuttlefish) (Varner 2012). Varner openly endorses the style of arguing by analogy, claiming that together, the reference properties of (1) nociceptors that are connected to the brain; (2) a natural opiod releasing system in the body; (3) responsiveness to analgesics; and (4) appropriate pain behavior can together establish good evidence in favor of pain in any individual that has these properties. While these features are sufficient for pain experience, they certainly are not necessary; certainly, humans with congenital insensitivity to pain are still conscious, even though they lack awareness of pain experience.

In approaching the issue of appropriate pain behaviors, recall that Braithwaite was interested in both physiological behavioral responses such as increased heart rate and reduced feeding behavior, as well as cognitive behaviors such as a lack of concern about novel stimuli. The philosopher Adam Shriver suggests that since there may be pain reflexes (like increased heart rate, reduced feeding, and even reflex withdrawal) without the experience of pain, the sorts of behaviors to focus on when looking for evidence of pain in animals would be those that indicate the existence of a sensory component (Shriver 2006). Because humans can distinguish between the sensory type of pain (throbbing, stabbing, aching) and the intensity of pain (vaguely annoying, intense, unbearable), researchers are interested to see if other animals can make similar distinctions. Working from the knowledge that humans on morphine can still sense the pain but not mind it, researchers have examined whether animals can act as if they don't mind the pain even when responding to it. One way of testing this is by using the conditioned place preference paradigm (LaGraize et al. 2004). Rats prefer dark areas to light ones, and in a cage that has a light and dark chamber, rats will spend the majority of their time on the dark side of the cage. But when researchers ligated a pain-related nerve so that rats' left paws were more sensitive to pain, they preferred the light side of the cage (where their right paws were shocked) to the dark side of the cage (where their left paws where shocked). However, once the rats were given a brain lesion in their anterior cingulate cortex, which is associated with the affective component of pain in humans, the rats preferred the dark areas again, even though they continued to be shocked in the same way, and the behavioral responses to the shocks remained the same. Shriver interprets this study as indicating that the rats felt pain (as evidenced by their withdrawal from the shocks) but didn't mind the pain (Shriver 2006). In his paper, Shriver also describes research on monkeys who were able to withstand painful stimuli longer after being given a lesion of their posterior parietal cortex, and concludes that there is evidence that monkeys and rats, like humans, have two pathways for pain, thus adding another element to the argument from analogy for pain—at least for monkeys and rats.

Varner is aware of the criticisms of arguments from analogy, and his response to those criticisms seems to capture the thinking of the scientists like Braithwaite who also use analogical arguments. Varner points out that arguments from analogy like the following are poor arguments:

1   Both turkeys (P) and cattle (Q) are animals, they are warm blooded, they have limited stereoscopic vision, and they are eaten by humans …
2   Turkeys are known to hatch from eggs …

C. So probably cattle hatch from eggs, too.
(Varner 2012, 114)

Arguments like this are bad because they ignore important disanalogies between turkeys and cattle, namely that cattle are mammals and turkeys are birds. This is a relevant disanalogy because we have a theory about the relative reproductive systems of birds and mammals; namely mammals have live births and birds hatch from eggs. Choosing the reference properties is an essential part of a useful argument from analogy, and the choice of reference property will depend on our prior theory about the issue at hand. That theory, we can add, can be itself independently justified via an inference to the best explanation argument, so that a strong argument from analogy will include both a theory that has been tested against other theories as well as an analogical aspect that lets us generalize across different taxa. Recall that Heyes criticized the representational approach to establishing animal consciousness as based on introspection and analogy, and argued that instead it should be based on inference to the best explanation arguments. However, what Varner suggests is that good analogical arguments already incorporate inference to the best explanation when we appeal to a guiding theory in choosing reference properties. The reason we look for nociceptors, endogenous opioids, responsiveness to analgesics, and pain behavior is that we have a theory of human pain that causally implicates the first element, and includes as effects the other three. Because there are causal relations between the reference properties and the property at issue according to a theory that enjoys independent justification, a good analogical argument can be scientifically grounded and as warranted as the inference to the best explanation argument that supports the choice of reference properties. Varner also points out that while arguments from analogy about animals can offer evidence *in favor* of animal consciousness, they cannot offer evidence *against* animal consciousness. Like humans with a congenital insensitivity to pain, some animals may be conscious of things other than pain.

What Varner cannot escape, however, is Heyes' worry about introspection. The pain research rests on human self reports about pain intensity and quality, and there is no getting around that. We need to examine, then, why a scientist like Heyes would be worried about using introspection in science, and it will be useful to make a distinction between introspection about sensations and introspection about mechanisms. There is a long history in philosophy of thinking that humans are infallible when it comes to introspection—if I honestly assert that I am happy or in pain, then I am happy or in pain. But the worry about introspection comes not from the introspection of sensation but from the introspection of mechanisms. Recall that social psychologists have found that we often confabulate when asked to explain why we acted as we did. There is no research that shows people are systematically mistaken about their sensations; on the contrary, there is good evidence that people's pain reports about the kind and intensity of pain are consistent (Melzack and Wall 2008). However, psychologists have also presented counterintuitive findings about how our pain experiences can be manipulated, such as by the peak-end phenomenon. For example, humans will choose to repeat what appears to be a more painful episode if it ends on a less painful note than another episode in which the level of pain remains consistently at a lower level (Kahneman et al. 1993). While there is good reason to accept Heyes' objection when it comes to introspection about mechanisms, there seems to be less reason to criticize the use of introspection in research on sensations such as pain, despite the findings of how our pain memories can be manipulated.

3.6.3 Other analogical features

While pain has been of particular interest to philosophers and scientists investigating animal consciousness, other properties have also been of interest. As we will see in Chapter 7, there has been great interest in animal emotions in the context of animal morality; many scientists have claimed that species from elephants to chimpanzees feel empathy for their conspecifics, sorrow for the dead, and that some social animals feel less pain when they are not alone. Since emotions, like pain, have a manifest conscious element for humans, the existence of emotions other than pain in animals adds to the evidence in favor of animal consciousness.

The neuroscientist Jaak Panksepp, for example, thinks emotions are the most primitive form of conscious experience, foundational to all the sophisticated conscious experience we find in modern humans (Panksepp 2005). Panksepp argues that emotions underlie the reward and punishment system of all animals, and hence they are an essential part of learning. He reports that artificial stimulation of brain regions associated with emotional systems are sufficient to cause the animal to approach or avoid a stimulus, depending on the emotion generated. He takes an evolutionary approach to the development of emotion, finding that emotions are not the brain's interpretations of signals coming from the body, nor are they primarily a function of the cortex; rather, emotions arise in subcortical circuits and are shared across species (Panksepp and Burgdorf 2003). Because emotions are primitive and conscious, Panksepp endorses focusing on some of the oldest emotions, such as the positive emotions associated with play behavior, which are found across species (Burghardt 2005). When animals such as humans, chimpanzees, and dogs play, they often engage in a panting kind of vocalization—when humans do it, we call it "laughter." While the sound is different in different species, the neurobiology and the behaviors associated with laughter may be similar. In fact, Panksepp claims to have found laughter in rats too, and he thinks that we can use rats to develop a model of the biological evolution of joy in humans (Panksepp 2005). Why think rats laugh? Panksepp found that rats vocalize in high-pitched chirps when they play, and when they are tickled "in a playful way."

The rats that Panksepp tickled become socially bonded to him, and would approach him seeking more tickles. He also found that rats who laugh a lot prefer to spend time with other rats who laugh (Panksepp and Burgdorf 2003). Here we see that Panksepp, like Braithwaite, starts with what we already know about a sensory phenomenon in humans, and then uses the theories and the typical behaviors and physiology associated with joy in humans to determine what evidence to look for when searching for rat joy. Again, it is an argument from analogy, but one that is grounded in theory about the causal relations of emotional experience in humans. And while it begins with human introspection about how human beings feel when they laugh, there is no reliance on human introspection of mechanisms, just of sensory experience.

3.6.4 Learning and consciousness revisited

While emotional experience offers one route toward making scientific arguments for consciousness, learning offers another. As we saw earlier, Tye suggests that learning offers evidence of consciousness, though there is also evidence of unconscious learning. Varner thinks we can investigate animal consciousness by examining three kinds of learning that appear to require consciousness in humans: multiple reversal trials, probability learning, and the formation of learning sets (Varner 2012). In the first kind of task, individuals are rewarded for responding one of two ways, say touching a red lever. Then, without warning, they are only rewarded for touching the green lever. It takes a while for human subjects to key into the rule change the first time the rule is reversed, but very quickly humans are able to make the switch with only one or two errors. While the speed at which other species learn to make the switch varies, Varner claims that mammals, birds, herps, and cephalopods all show progressive adjustment in response.

Probability learning paradigms reward participants for responding in a particular way only some percentage of the time. Animals solve this problem in a variety of ways, but humans, birds, and mammals will use a matching strategy, where their response depends on the stimulus that had previously been shown. Varner writes,

> To the extent that humans are consciously thinking about how to solve the problem when they exhibit the maximizing and systematic matching strategies, the fact that birds and mammals employ these strategies suggests that consciousness is also involved when they learn how to better solve probability learning problems.
>
> (Varner 2012, 129)

The final learning strategy that Varner thinks requires consciousness involves what amounts to a test of whether animals can learn the rule of disjunctive syllogism. Subjects are shown two objects, and rewarded for selecting one of the two. They are then given a set of additional trials for which the answer is the same. Next, they are given another block of trials with two different objects. After being exposed to the paradigm, the subjects who learn the rule (there is only one correct answer, and it remains correct for the entire set), individuals should be able to consistently make the correct choice starting with the second trial across a block of trials. In his discussion of the findings, Varner suggests that humans learn this paradigm faster than other great apes, who learn it faster than old world monkeys, who learn it faster than new world monkeys. Minks, ferrets, and rats also show the effect, though to a lesser degree than the primates, and corvids perform at the level of monkeys.

Of these studies, Varner writes, "It also seems plausible to say that each of these kinds of learning requires consciousness, insofar as each involves hypothesis formation and testing, and human subjects report that they do this consciously" (Varner 2012, 131). Here again Varner is relying on human introspection to get his argument off the ground, but note that in this case the humans are introspecting the method they use to solve the problems. Consider how we would gain this information about human performance on these tasks: the humans are subjects in the experiment, perform the tasks, and then later are debriefed and asked how they solved the task. Like shoppers who confabulated why they chose the right-most pantyhose, the subjects of these learning studies are trying to reconstruct why they acted as they did. While they might not be confabulating, the conscious experience of developing and testing a hypothesis need not have been the cause of their response. Additional worries about this sort of evidence for animal consciousness come from the claims about blindsight patients. Recall that perception seems to be possible without consciousness, since a blindsighted individual can navigate a hall full of obstacles while reporting seeing nothing. Normal humans who solved the task of navigating a hallway full of objects would probably report that they solved the task by plotting a course around the objects based on how close they were to other objects. But the fact that normal humans have this conscious experience of developing a rule and following it doesn't give us any reason to think that the blindsight person is wrong when she says she had no such experience. Just because it is typical for humans to have conscious experience when they perceive doesn't mean that all animals do, and, similarly, the fact that it is typical for humans to have conscious experience when they solve certain other problems doesn't seem to provide evidence that consciousness is necessary for problem solving. What is needed is further investigation into whether having this conscious experience has an effect on the response in these learning trials. A guiding theory about the role of consciousness in certain kinds of learning paradigms is necessary if we are to avoid Heyes's worry that the argument for animal consciousness is at rock bottom based on our introspection and lay opinions about animal minds.

3.7 Self-consciousness

While most philosophers and scientists are convinced that we ought to take animal consciousness as a basic assumption (in the way in which we take the existence of human consciousness for granted), there is much less consensus around the question of self-consciousness. Self-consciousness is defined as consciousness of one's own mental states (or metacognition, as philosophers like Carruthers use the notion), consciousness of one's existence as a contiguous agent who moves through the world in time, or even as awareness of one's self narrative (Varner 2012; Flannagan 1992; Schechtman 2007).

3.7.1 Mirror self-recognition

Suppose you look at yourself in a mirror, admiring (or despairing) about some feature of your face. You must be self-conscious if you are able to do that, right? At least this is the thinking that led the psychologist George Gallup to develop the mirror self-recognition task in order to examine when human children acquire a sense of self as well as whether chimpanzees ever acquire one. Gallup surreptitiously marked children's foreheads with a colored spot that the children couldn't smell or feel, and then he let them play with a mirror in the room. Gallup found that by two years old, children would more often touch the mark on their forehead when there was a mirror around than when there wasn't, and concluded that human children acquire a sense of self by that age. The same test was run on chimpanzees, who were first anesthetized before being marked. The chimpanzees, like the children, were more often observed to touch the marks when there was a mirror than when there was no mirror around, and Gallup concluded that chimpanzees also have a sense of self.

The mirror self-recognition task became a standard for researchers to run on their species; it seems easy enough to mark an animal and wait to see if they touch the mark more often in the presence of a mirror. But methodological problems arise. Some animals don't like looking into the eyes, which is something you have to do when your face is marked. For a gorilla, it seems that even one's own eyes are aversive. Elephants, who are often covered with dirt, may not care about marks on their bodies. Bottlenose dolphins lack hands that they can use to touch the mark, and some criticized the claim that dolphins recognize themselves in mirrors by pointing out the difference in behavior. Dolphins were marked on the side of their body, and instead of using a mirror, researchers used live video feedback (Reiss and Marino 2001). The dolphins were observed to spend more time in front of the mirror when they had the mark on the side, and would wiggle to position their body so that they could see the mark. Given that there are other explanations for why an animal would fail the mirror self-recognition task, it cannot be a negative test for self-consciousness; failing it is not evidence that an animal lacks self-consciousness.

And while claims have been made about some species, including elephants (Plotnik et al. 2006) and all the great apes (see Anderson and Gallup (2011) for a review) passing the mirror self recognition task, we need to ask whether passing is a positive test for self-consciousness. What is the argument that allows us to infer self-consciousness from this piece of behavioral evidence?

Gallup claims that recognizing oneself in a mirror is evidence of self-awareness because it requires that the individual become the object of her own attention, and that involves a concept of self. Gallup also thinks that having a concept of self entails being able to introspect (Gallup 1998). Gallup writes, "If you did not know who you were, how could you possibly know who it was you were confronted with when you saw yourself in a mirror?" (Gallup 1991, 122). The argument appears to go as follows:

1 If you can recognize yourself in a mirror, then you can identify the object reflected in the mirror as yourself.
2 If you can understand the object in the mirror as yourself, then you know who you are.
3 If you know who you are, you are self-conscious.
4 Therefore, if you can recognize yourself in a mirror, then you are self-conscious.

This argument is problematic, because of the various ways we could understand each of the premises. Premise (1), for example, is true if it means only that there is a matching between self and the reflection, but it may not be true if it requires that the individual have a concept of self that is activated when the individual identifies the reflection as an exemplar of the concept of self. A similar worry holds for premise (2); matching between self and the reflection may not require the existence of additional concepts describing the self. If the premise merely means that the ability to match requires some kind of knowledge or belief that the matching holds, then it is less controversial. However, this second way of understanding premise (2) makes premise (3) false; having the belief that two objects match doesn't mean that one is self-conscious, even when one of those objects is oneself.

Worries about overinterpreting the mirror self-recognition data led some to claim that mirror self recognition is a quite uninteresting phenomenon. Cecilia Heyes takes this position. In her attempt to recreate the reasoning for thinking that mirror self-recognition requires self-consciousness, she writes,

> The reasoning behind these claims has never been articulated, but it seems to be roughly as follows. 1) When I (a human) use my mirror image, I understand the image to represent

my 'self', and I understand my self to be an entity with thoughts and feelings. 2) This chimpanzee uses his mirror image. 3) Therefore this chimpanzee understands his mirror image to represent his 'self', an entity with thoughts and feelings.

(Heyes 2008, 265)

We've already seen that there are problems with these sorts of arguments, since they involve introspection about the methods we use to solve a problem, and while we can agree with Heyes that the argument, as she unpacks it, is weak, it is perhaps not the most charitable way of reconstructing Gallup's reasoning. In an earlier paper she gave a different reconstruction of the reasoning:

When a primate is confronted with a mirror it receives 'self-sensation' (Gallup 1977, page 331); it is, as a matter of fact, sensing itself. If the primate can use a mirror to inspect its own body, then this self-sensation must have given rise to 'self-perception' (Gallup 1977, page 331), or, more commonly, 'self-recognition' (e.g. Gallup 1977, page 329); the mirror image not only is, but has been perceived by the animal to be, a representation of itself. Self-recognition logically requires a pre-existing 'self-awareness' (Gallup 1977, page 330) or 'self-concept' (e.g. Gallup 1977, page 329), therefore use of a mirror for body inspection implies the possession of such a concept. The nature of a self-concept or a 'well-integrated self-concept' (Gallup 1977, page 329) is largely unspecified.

(Heyes 1994, 910)

Instead of indicating the existence of some unspecified sort of self-concept or self-consciousness, Heyes argues that passing the mirror self-recognition task only indicates that one has the ability to recognize one's own body, not one's own self. So long as an individual can recognize that some sensory inputs originate from one's own body and that others come from elsewhere, they can pass the test. Heyes claims that an animal needs that ability if it can learn that the sensory inputs originating from the reflection in the mirror correlate with the sensory inputs originating within one's own body (Heyes 1994). However, as Heyes also points out, that ability is probably widely present among vertebrates, for the ability to distinguish one's own body from the rest of the world is needed to successfully navigate in the world. Thus, Heyes fails to give us an explanation for why the great apes and dolphins pass the test, but many other species appear to fail it. Without an error theory, we don't have an explanation for success on the mirror self-recognition task.

Another suggestion is that passing the test involves the ability to generate and compare two different representations of the same thing (Bard et al. 2006; Suddendorf and Butler 2013; Perner 1991; Suddendorf and Whiten 2001). Suddendorf and Butler write, "By comparing an expectation about one's physical appearance with current perceptions of a reflection, inconsistencies, such as the mark, can be noted and motivate exploration" (Suddendorf and Butler 2013, 122). And because they think there is only good evidence for mirror self recognition among the great apes, and because they think there are no apparent fitness benefits associated with recognizing oneself in a mirror for the common ancestor of the great apes, Suddendorf and Butler conclude that self-recognition probably evolved as a spandrel, a side effect of the common ancestor's ability to compare multiple representations of the same thing—something which may have profound fitness benefits.

If mirror self-recognition abilities don't indicate self-consciousness in other animals, what else might indicate it? There are two other research areas that some think offer evidence of self-consciousness in other species, and we will turn to those now.

3.7.2 Mental monitoring

Humans can be uncertain of memories, judgments, and the truth of claims. When we are uncertain of our own mental states, we are experiencing a variety of self-consciousness. As I plan a trip to Morocco, for example, I may think that I will be able to remember the location of a hotel I enjoyed staying at ten years ago, but because I'm not certain I will also have a back-up plan in case my memory fails me once I'm on the ground in Marrakesh. Our explicit memories are available to monitoring, and so we can be more or less certain of their accuracy, while our many implicit memories allow us to function without there being any metacognitive processing. When we consider our explicit memories, we also have conscious awareness of those memories, and knowing what we remember can help us determine when we need to seek out additional information. If a student knows that she has a good command over the material, she need not spend as much time studying as she would if she thought she couldn't answer the study questions. And, if I remember explicitly that I know how to get to work, then I won't need to check a map in order to get there. An implicit memory can allow us to guess correctly, but it doesn't lead to confidence. A witness looking at people in a criminal line up might guess the correct person, but not be at all sure that the guess was correct.

If animals are conscious of their own memories and judgments, then they should demonstrate the ability to correctly indicate whether they know what they know, or not. Various uncertainty monitoring tasks have been given to birds, a dolphin, rats, and monkeys in order to determine whether any other species has a similar ability to think about the accuracy of their own thoughts. While there has never been any evidence in favor of uncertainty monitoring in pigeons, and only limited evidence in capuchin monkeys (Fujita 2009), positive evidence exists for rhesus macaques (Beran et al. 2006), a dolphin (Smith et al. 1995), and rats (Foote and Crystal 2007).

In one such study, the psychologist Robert Hampton devised a memory-monitoring paradigm that he used with macaque monkeys. Knowing that monkeys can perform a simple delayed match to sample task, Hampton added one feature—he allowed monkeys to decide whether to take the test, or to choose not to take the test. If they took the test and passed, they received a valuable treat, but if they failed the task they received nothing. However, if they decided not to take the test they were given a lesser value food reward. Thus, if monkeys could know when they would pass or fail the test, they could maximize their rewards. Hampton (2001) found that the frequency with which the monkey chose not to take the test increased with the duration of the delay since the original sample was presented.

Hampton's memory monitoring task was similar to an earlier task done with monkeys to test if they could monitor their discrimination abilities. Macaques were trained to manipulate a joystick to indicate whether or not a display was Dense (containing 2,950 pixels) or Sparse (< 2,950 pixels). Monkeys were good at easy Sparse tasks, but, like humans, they found it hard to judge as the display approached Dense. When the monkeys were given the opportunity to decline the tasks, they did so when the discrimination became too difficult (Smith et al. 1997).

Some researchers also reported distinctive behaviors around threshold conditions, when the subject was most likely to give the uncertainty response. The dolphin studied, for example, hesitated the most at the threshold problems before giving a response (Smith et al. 1995). This squares well with my own experience working with dolphins, who would respond to difficult tasks by swimming in a tight circle between the two choices before finally settling on one. I also observed Hiapo, the young male dolphin at the Kewalo Basin Marine Mammal Laboratory, to engage in this kind of uncertainty behavior when learning new tasks.

While Hampton explicity eschews drawing any conclusions about consciousness from this research (Hampton 2001), a psychologist who did some of the first tests of metacognition in animals, J. David Smith, thinks that the best explanation for the monkeys' performance is that they have "functional analogs to human consciousness" and that uncertainty monitoring research "may be opening an empirical window on animals' cognitive awareness" (Smith 2009, 389). Why? Because the data on human performance on such tasks is strikingly similar to the data on monkeys, and humans report a phenomenological experience of uncertainty when they decline a hard trial. Elsewhere Smith and colleagues claim that it is "implausible that humans would produce their highly similar graph in a qualitatively different way [from macaques]" (Smith et al. 2012, 1304). They agree with de Waal that if nonhuman primate behavior resembles human behavior then the most parsimonious conclusion is that the psychological states and processes are similar.

However, as we saw in the arguments about learning, the fact that humans have a phenomenological experience when engaging in some behavior may be epiphenomenal; the experience may play no causal role in the behavior itself, and could instead be the result of some subsequent cognitive processing. Additional evidence is needed in the human case, to show that when humans are restrained from having the phenomenological experience of uncertainty by some kind of intervention (e.g. processing demands or other distractors), their performance on the task is altered. If, on the other hand, humans can solve the tasks without experiencing uncertainty, then no degree of similarity between the macaque and human charts can provide evidence of conscious experience in the monkeys. So far as I know, no such study of human phenomenology has been carried out, though human uncertainty judgments have been tested (Smith et al. 2003).

A promising complement to the standard research on uncertainty may come from the kind of qualitative observations made by the researchers in the dolphin study. If the animal also behaves in a way that those who know the individual well characterize as displaying uncertainty, and the behavior occurs in various kinds of conditions in which the individual might be uncertain, then we would have additional evidence in favor of phenomenology. Like emotional expressions, bodily postures and movements may be expressive of an individual's feelings. Nonetheless, the evidence of an uncertain feeling may not be evidence of self-consciousness, but rather a feeling of "I don't know what to do," without knowing exactly why one's behavior doesn't flow automatically as usual.

Even if we were to successfully use these methods to defend the existence of uncertainty in other species, we may still lack evidence of metacognition. We engage in metacognitive thinking when we wonder whether we need a map to find a friend's house, but do other animals? The claims that uncertainty monitoring is evidence of metacognition in these species is a matter of some debate. After first taking the rat behavior in uncertainty tasks to be evidence of metacognition, Crystal and Foote later declared the rats may be learning how to solve the problem by forming associations between the reward and test-specific contingencies, rather than by looking inward at their mental state. They conclude that since associative processes could explain the performance, no metacognition is involved (Crystal and Foote 2009, and discussed in Meketa 2014). However, this move is only warranted if it isn't possible for the system to be both associative and metacognitive. Futher, as Meketa argues, just because a task can be solved in some way doesn't mean that the subject is actually using that method when confronted with it.

Another alternative explanation of the uncertainty monitoring performance as evidence of metacognition comes from Carruthers, who argues that animals can solve these sorts of tasks without metacognition, as long as they have beliefs and desires that come in various strengths (Carruthers 2008); moreover, they might even solve these problems in non-representational affective terms (Carruthers and Ritchie 2012). This suggestion jives with models psychologists have created to show that the strength of response traces can be used to solve problems thought to be metacognitive (Smith et al. 2008).

It is important to remember that the questions we can ask about metacognition might differ, and that answers to these questions that appear to conflict may be answers to slightly different questions, or descriptions at different levels of explanation. If we had a better understanding of all the mechanisms invovled in human metacognition, we could deconstruct the activities we label as metacognitive to see in which ways different species solve these problems.

3.7.3 Episodic memory

Another type of self-consciousness in humans is associated with a replaying of events from our past in order to re-experience them. This so-called mental time travel allows us to do more than simply know that certain things happened in the past; it allows us to recall personal experiences, such as the riot of smells, sights, and sounds of a funeral rite in Bali, or the experience of walking through the twists and turns of a casbah laneway. The psychologist who developed the notion of episodic memory, Endel Tulving, describes it as such:

> Episodic memory is a recently evolved, late developing, and early deteriorating brain/mind (neurocognitive) memory system...It makes possible mental time travel through subjective time—past, present, and future. This mental time travel allows one, as an "owner" of episodic memory ("self"), through the medium of autonoetic awareness, to remember one's own previous "thought-about" experiences, as well as to "think about" one's own possible future experiences. The operations of episodim memory require, but go beyond,

the semantic memory system...The essence of episodic memory lies in the conjunction of three concepts—self, autonoetic awareness, and subjective time.

(Tulving 2005, 9)

Autonoetic awareness is a kind of self-consciousness in which one thinks about oneself in a particular circumstance, such as a past experience or a hypothetical future one. Since autonoetic awareness is an essential aspect of episodic memory, evidence that some animal has episodic memory would be evidence of self-consciousness. Tulving suggests that the function of episodic memory is actually related to future episodic thinking; once you can replay your past, you can project yourself in the future, and by anticipating future challenges and needs one can benefit in one's present actions (Tulving 2005). Human cummulative cultural evolution and niche construction, which amount to changing the world to make us more fit to our environment, are both results of the episodic memory system according to Tulving.

Other suggestions have been that episodic memory makes it possible for an individual to return to an earlier event in her life and have a second opportunity to learn from the experience— to gain semantic memories that can be used to make decisions about what to do in the present, for example (Zentall et al. 2001).

We know that various animals have excellent memories for the location of food sources, shelters, landmarks, etc. (while this knowledge of the world is usually called by psychologists "semantic" or "declarative" memory, there is no linguistic element required for having it). However, psychologists including Tulving (1983, 2005) and Suddendorf and Corballis (1997) suggest that animals lack an episodic memory system.

While direct experimental evidence of the autonoetic consciousness that is key to human episodic memory cannot be directly tested in other species, savvy researchers have found ways to test whether other animals can access information about the *what*, *where*, and *when* aspect of their past experiences. In the first formal test of episodic-like memory in animals, researchers asked whether scrub jays, who are food storing birds of the corvid family, can remember the what, where, and when of hidden food. Scrub jays cache food for short and long term storage, but not all food decays at the same rate. Peanuts are suitable for long term storage, whereas wax worms need to be eaten relatively quickly. After training the birds to cache peanuts in one section of a sand filled ice cube tray, and wax worms in another section, the birds were allowed to uncache food after various delays. Clayton and Dickinson (1998) found that the scrub jays will uncache peanuts after a long delay, and worms after a short delay, thereby suggesting that scrub jays can recall three types of information: what was cached (worm vs. peanut), where each item type was cached, and when the worms were cached.

Nicola Clayton and colleagues subsequently tested scrub jays on a variety of versions of this task, with similar results; scrub jays are very good at finding still edible food that they had previously cached. The question, of course, is whether this ability requires the existence of autonoetic consciousness. Or, as Tulving put it, the ability to think what, when, and where may be a property of semantic/declarative memory, and doesn't require episodic memory. Episodic memory grows out of, or is an extension of semantic memory (Tulving 1983).

Clayton and Dickinson acknowledge that their study doesn't offer behavioral evidence of self-consciousness. But this isn't seen as a weakness in the experiment, because autonoetic consciousness...is probably undetectable in many species. In terms of purely behavioural criteria, however, the cache recovery pattern of scrub jays fulfils the three, 'what' 'where' and 'when' criteria for episodic recall and thus provides, to our knowledge, the first conclusive behavioural evidence of episodic-like memory in animals other than humans.

(Clayton and Dickinson 1998, 274)

However, Tulving (as well as other psychologists) think that the question of episodic memory in animals is empirically tractable. Tulving uses that position to argue that it doesn't exist in other species, whereas some animal cognition researchers use it to argue that it does exist. An empirical demonstration of episodic memory, Tulving remarks, would involve the animal behaving in an episodic memory sort of way in a situation where there existed no preferable explanation other than the existence of true episodic memory. While easy enough to say that evidence will come from an inference to the best explanation, it is more difficult to determine how to set up such a situation.

Tulving suggests a test inspired by an Estonian folk tale in which a young girl dreams that she goes to a birthday party where chocolate pudding is served. Unfortunately for the young girl, only children who brought their own spoon can eat it, and she leaves without a taste. The next night, she goes to bed with a spoon in her hand, determined not to lose out again. The "spoon test" that Tulving proposes involves determining whether an animal will plan ahead by acquiring a tool, such as a straw, which would be needed later and in another place for drinking a delicious liquid.

Recall the discussion in Chapter 2 of Santino, the chimpanzee who is living in a Swedish zoo and appears not to like visitors. His act of gathering chunks of rock and concrete and concealing them under hay seems a natural example of the spoon test, since he uses them later to throw at annoying tourists. However, the interpretation of Santino's behavior as planning for the future was criticized by psychologists who offered alternative explanations for Santino's behavior, and called for controlled experiments rather than observations. Similar questions are asked when researchers point to wild chimpanzees who carry rocks some distance to where they are needing for cracking nuts (Boesch and Boesch 1984). And, while there have been formal studies showing that apes can carry tools to leave at places they will be later needed (e.g. Mulcahy and Call 2006), non-conscious associative learning may explain why the subject carries the tool around. Rather than projecting oneself into the future and imaging the need for the tool, the individual may associate the delicious treat with the tool, and hold onto it given his past experience using the tool to get a treat.

Scrub jays seem to pass Tulving's spoon test. In one study, scrub jays were taught that they received dog kibble for breakfast in compartment A, and peanuts for breakfast in compartment C. After the jays had learned this association, a food bowl containing both kibble and peanuts was placed in compartment B, and the birds were allowed to cache either food in either compartment. The study authors suggest that a conditioning account would predict that the birds would cache food in the compartment previously associated with that food, but that a forward planning account would predict that the birds would cache in the opposite pattern, because scrub jays prefer a diversity of foods. In fact, the jays did cache in the opposite pattern, suggesting to the study authors that the birds were anticipating their future motivational states when caching the foods (Raby et al. 2007).

Other studies that try to capture aspects of episodic memory have been performed on the great apes, particularly in language trained great apes. A gorilla, King, was able to select correct photographs to report on events that he had previously witnessed (Schwartz et al. 2004; Schwartz et al. 2005). And a chimpanzee, Panzee, was able to correctly select the lexigram token for a food item that had been previously hidden in another location, return to that location with the lexigram token, and trade it for the food (Beran et al. 2012.)

If passing the spoon test or recalling past events requires autonoetic consciousness, then accepting that these studies indicate such abilities in nonhuman animals would require also accepting that these individuals have autonoetic consciousness. The question that remains, of course, is whether such conscious experience is required. As in the cognitive tasks Varner discusses, the fact that humans have consious experience while they are solving such tasks isn't sufficient to conclude that humans *must* have conscious experiences when they are solving the tasks. The corvid study, which seems to hold up against Tulving's spoon test criterion, and the ape studies, which also suggest that future planning and recall of past experiences may be had by other animals may both fall short as evidence for autonoetic consciousness. To support an inference to the best explanation that animals have self-consciousness, we will need a body of evidence that is best explained in terms of self-consciousness. However, any body of evidence suggesting that animals are self-conscious may also force us to tweak our understanding of what self-consciousness amounts to. While for many of us self-consciousness involves thinking about what will make us happy, and predicting our future hedonic states based on choices we make about education, relationships, or jobs, this aspect of self-consciousness may not be of much use for other species.

3.8 Chapter summary

The arguments for and against animal consciousness that are theory driven will not be terribly convincing for anyone who isn't already firmly committed to the theory. And theories of consciousness are widely variable. But, good arguments have been made leading to the conclusion that many other species are conscious. Some philosophers argue that we ought not argue for animal consciousness, because it is a basic fact about our world (like human consciousness) that we do accept, and should accept, as not requiring justification. Since justifications come to an end, the skeptical arguments against animal consciousness should be set aside, and we should use the existence of animal consciousness as a premise in any attempt to solve the mystery of consciousness. This is what Christof Koch does when using animal models in his research on the neural correlates of consciousness. And it is what John Searle and Dale Jamieson independently argue we ought to do. Arguing about animal consciousness may not be the best use of our philosophical resources, especially when the scientists who study animals assume consciousness in all that they do.

As we saw at the beginning of the chapter, the existence of animal consciousness in most species is taken for granted by scientists. Scientists are working with the assumption that animals like macaques and rats are conscious, and the research that results from these assumptions is well developed and continues to provide productive hypotheses and studies into the nature of consciousness. Insofar as assumptions of consciousness continue to generate good results and help to promote a well-developed science of consciousness, those assumptions should stand. That is, until there is evidence against consciousness in mammals, birds, fish, amphibians, and cephalopods, we should treat them as if they are conscious.

Notes

1   You can watch a video of a human with blindsight walk down a corridor strewn with obstacles here: http://blogs.scientificamerican.com/observations/2010/04/22/blindsight-seeing-without-knowing-it/. The patient was told that the corridor was clear, and after successfully navigating down the hall he reported no awareness that he had made any adjustments at all.
2   You can view a monkey, Helen, who was surgically altered to have blindsight navigate a room full of obstacles, here: http://www.youtube.com/watch?v=rDlsxwQHwt8

Further reading

For a comprehensive introduction to the issues raised by questions about animal consciousness, there is an excellent online resource, Colin Allen and Michael Trestman's *Stanford Encyclopedia of Philosophy* entry "Animal Consciousness" (http://plato.stanford.edu/archives/sum2014/entries/consciousness-animal/).

Daniel Dennett presents his theory of consciousness for a popular audience and discusses animal consciousness in his book *Kinds of Minds: Towards an Understanding of Consciousness*. New York: Basic Books (1996).

For a personal account of the neuroscientific study of consciousness, you can read Christof Koch's *Consciousness: Confessions of a Romantic Reductionist* (2012).

Victoria Braithwaite's *Do Fish Feel Pain?* (2010) is an enjoyable account of her research into the painful lives of fish.

4 Thinking: belief, concepts, and rationality

More than 2,000 years ago the Stoic philosopher Chrysippus gave us the following clever animal story: a dog is running nose to the ground, tracking a rabbit down a path. Arriving at a three-way crossroad, the dog quickly sniffs the first two paths, and not finding the scent in either of the first two options, immediately runs down the third path. Chrysippus' dog appears to have made a rational inference using the following deductive inference:

1 A or B or C.
2 Not A.
3 Not B.
4 Therefore, C.

If we accept the basic facts of the story, must we also accept that Chrysippus' dog is a rational thinker who has beliefs? This question has been debated for centuries, as part of a more general question about whether nonlinguistic animals can think.

Scientific research in animal cognition is largely based on the assumption that animals manipulate representations, and so have beliefs. As we saw in the last chapter, some philosophers agree that animals have beliefs, even though they disagree about whether having beliefs is sufficient for being conscious. However, there are challenges to the claim that animals have beliefs and many of these worries stem from the idea that belief requires language. Increasingly, philosophers and psychologists are drawing distinctions between kinds of thought in different species, at different stages of human development, and among different adult humans. By calibrating our starting notion of belief with the various abilities of humans and other animals, we may conclude that there exist a variety of cognitive states that might be related to our folk notion of belief, rather than taking the question of whether animals think as requiring a simple *yes* or *no* answer.

4.1 What is belief?

In common conversation, we use the term "belief" to describe a degree of uncertainty (as opposed to our use of the term "know"), as in "I believe that you need to take a left at the lights," or in contexts of faith, such as belief in a god. But when we ask whether animals have beliefs, that's not what we're interested in. Instead, we want to know something about whether animals think, and what they think. We want to know whether animals have some thoughts about things in the world.

Beliefs, as well as our other mental attitudes (such as desire, hope, or wonder), appear not to be directly observable. Like mind and conscious experience, belief is something we may have to infer. The philosopher Wilfrid Sellars argues that we do not even have direct access to our own mental states, much less the mental states of others—we have to infer the existence of belief in both ourselves and in others (Sellars 1956). To defend this position, Sellars asks us to consider the world of our Rylean ancestors—humans who used language to describe the observable things in their world, but who lacked any way to refer to mental attitudes such as beliefs and desires. With their language they could explain why they acted by talking about the world—for example, a person could explain why she was walking toward the river by saying that the tree there was fruiting.

However, a problem arose for our Rylean ancestors because explaining behavior in terms of the world doesn't work when the world isn't the way we think it is. A fruiting tree can't explain my behavior if it doesn't exist. It isn't the world that causes my behavior, then, but my *belief* about the world. The explanation is that I *think* the tree is fruiting, and this thought causes me to move toward the tree, even if I'm wrong.

Among our Rylean ancestors, so goes Sellars' origin myth, there was a genius named Jones who realized that beliefs—representations of the world—are what cause our behavior. Jones heard people speak aloud to give their reasons for action, and from that he inferred that people also must have reasons for action even when they don't state them. Jones realized that when he asked people why they did what they did, they would respond by citing reasons—*because the tree is fruiting*—and that those reasons existed for an agent even before they were uttered. Thus was born the concept of belief. From this myth we get the notion that belief is a theoretical entity, an unobservable that fills an explanatory role, and whose existence we are justified in inferring given the theories that we have. The theory that corresponds with the existence of attitudes like belief and desire is, of course, our old friend folk psychology.

Ryle's myth also emphasizes the relationship between belief and language. It seems simple to find out what people believe, because we can ask them, and so long as they aren't deceiving us we know what they believe. Also, when we consider what others might be thinking, we usually characterize their beliefs in sentence format. Though nonlinguistic comic books like *The Arrival* by Shaun Tan (2007) can tell complex stories about a person's experiences, thoughts, and feelings, typical narratives use natural language.

This focus on language and on sentences as ways of characterizing beliefs might suggest that just as sentences are built out of words, beliefs are propositions—the meanings of sentences—built out of concepts—simpler ideas. On such a view, to have a belief we would have to have concepts (though perhaps to have concepts, we need beliefs). However, philosophers disagree about the nature of belief, the relationship between belief and language, and the relationship between concepts, propositions, and belief. There are three main views about the nature of belief, which we can describe as representational, non-representational, and eliminativist.

4.1.1 Representational views

According to the Representational Theory of Mind, our beliefs are attitudes toward represented content that is seen as reflecting the way the world is (see Pitt 2013 for an introduction). Representationalism appears to be the most widely accepted account of belief, and is accepted by cognitive psychologists who are interested in explaining animal behavior in terms of representations.

There are a variety of representationalist views of thought, which differ on the nature of how our beliefs are represented—as a proposition, an image, a map, some combination of these elements, or as something else altogether. According to propositional accounts, we can reflect on another's belief in terms of a propositional attitude such as "Jimmy believes that his coffee is hot." The attitude of belief reflects a direction of fit from world to mind, whereas the attitude of desire reflects a mind to world direction of fit. When I desire that some proposition be true, I want the world to change so as to fulfill that desire, but when I believe something to be the case, I think that's how the world really is. Desire attitudes are sometimes called pro-attitudes, or conative attitudes. So-called cognitive attitudes, like believing that the world is a certain way, take the content of the attitude to be true at that time.

The propositional content of the belief, if indeed true, will represent some state of affairs in the world. On propositional accounts of belief, we use logical reasoning to connect beliefs together to infer new ones—for example, the belief that it takes five hours to fly coast-to-coast along with the belief that the flight leaves at 4 pm EST can lead you to realize that the flight should land in San Francisco at 9 pm EST. Beliefs can also connect up with desires to lead you to intentional action—for example, the belief that you will land in San Francisco at 9 pm EST and the desire to eat dinner before 9 pm EST can cause you to take an action such as packing a meal for the flight.

The philosopher Jerry Fodor is well known for developing an influential theory about the nature of representational belief in terms of the propositional attitudes. According to Fodor's language of thought hypothesis, we think in a language-like representational medium, using rules and symbols that we aren't able to introspect, but which allow us to engage in the sophisticated cognitive processing that permits rational action (Fodor 1975). Our representational abilities take a complex linguistic structure.

Other representationalists about belief argue that we can also have beliefs without propositions, in terms of images or diagrams. While images were once thought to be how we represented our ideas, worries about the generalizability and fecundity of mental representations as images as well as the lack of any logical connection between representations led to that view falling out of favor as a full account of thought. Nonetheless, mental imagery may be part of the story about how we think.

Representational belief can be understood as that which allows us to make rational inferences, to have the kind of reason-respecting flow of thought that allows us to retrace our daydreams to see where they began, or to navigate our way to the same food source year after year, even when our starting position changes. Different flavors of representational thought may permit different abilities.

4.1.2 Non-representational views

On non-representational views of belief, having a belief does not require having a mental attitude or doing a calculation. Believing isn't something that is done merely in the head. On non-representational views, we know that individuals believe by how they behave, and there is no deeper question about whether or not they *really* believe. Because non-representationalist views are not concerned with the causal mechanisms in believers, some might consider them to be non-cognitive, and not of interest to psychologists. However, some contemporary research in artificial intelligence and robotics (e.g., Brooks 1991) as well as some psychologists who accept a dynamical approach to modeling cognition (e.g. Thelen and Smith 1996) do embrace non-representationalism. The idea has also been explored by psychologists working on animal cognition. For example, Louise Barrett argues that we can make sense of animal action without appeal to complex representations and models of information processing. Following ideas associated with the psychologist J.J. Gibson, she argues that the world does the work that is usually attributed to internal representations (Barrett 2011). Scientists are interested in seeing how much can be done by entities who lack representations, and to what extent the world can serve as a substitute (for a philosophical treatment of this approach see, e.g. Clark and Toribio 1994; Thompson 2007; Van Gelder 1995).

One form of non-representationalism is dispositionalism (see Schwitzgebel 2002; Audi 1994; Marcus 1990), according to which belief is a disposition to act or feel in a certain way that corresponds to the belief. The philosopher Ruth Barcan Marcus presents a dispositional account of belief as follows: "x believes that S just in case under certain *agent-centered circumstances* including x's desires and needs as well as *external circumstances*, x is disposed to act as if S, that actual or nonactual state of affairs, obtains" (Marcus 1990, 133). For Marcus, believing is a relationship between a subject and a possible state of affairs that can be had by prelinguistic children and animals who lack language.

Another form of non-representationalism is interpretationism, according to which belief is to be understood as essentially connected to the practice of interpretation (see Davidson 1984; Dennett 1987, 1991, 2009). In Chapter 1 we saw Dennett's intentional system theory, according to which any system whose behavior can be best predicted from the intentional stance—from the perspective of folk psychology—is an intentional system who has the beliefs and desires we attribute to it. Animals have beliefs if we need to attribute beliefs to them in order to better predict and explain their behavior, and if animals demonstrate a robust pattern of behavior that is best described from the perspective of folk psychology.

The philosopher Donald Davidson has a similar view, but stresses linguistic behavior in his account of belief. Having beliefs is part of being a rational agent in a linguistic community, so that your behavior is best understood by yourself and others in terms of the beliefs that you ought to have given your behavior. We know what others believe by triangulating with another person on the objects in the world, as when we jointly look at a predator and then at each other, checking to see that the other is reacting as she should given the predator's presence. With the ability to triangulate comes an understanding that others have beliefs, that these beliefs can be mistaken, and that there is a contrast between truth and falsity (Davidson 1975). He writes:

> If the two people now note each others' reactions (in the case of language, verbal reactions), each can correlate these observed reactions with his or her stimuli from the world. The common cause can now determine the contents of an utterance and a thought. The triangle which gives content to thought and speech is complete.
>
> (Davidson 1991, 160)

Belief gains its power when people act in ways inconsistent with how the world is—e.g. when one goes to the riverside because she thinks the trees are fruiting, even though they are not. Davidson famously says, "error is what gives belief its point" (Davidson 1975, 20). But for Davidson this means that a believer has to be able to think about error, in terms of truth and falsity, and sentences in a natural language are needed to do so.

For both Davidson and Dennett, we attribute beliefs to people by thinking about what they should believe given their behavior, but there is no deeper fact of the matter about what an individual *really* thinks. Interpretationism about belief endorses a kind of indeterminacy of belief attributions, such that different sets of attributions might fit equally well, and in such a case there would be no reason to prefer one over the others.

4.1.3 Eliminativist views

A more radical account of belief is to deny its existence altogether. Eliminativists argue that there are no such things as beliefs (see Churchland 1981; Feyerabend 1963; Rorty 1965; Stich 1983); on this view, our common sense conception of human beliefs and other folk psychological categories will not map on to anything we will find as a result of future psychological and neuroscientific research. As sciences progress, we eliminate old categories and create new ones that are more compatible with the evidence. So, just as we eliminated the objects of alchemy and astrology, scientific psychology will lead us to eliminate the objects of our old folk psychology. Once we have a more complete scientific understanding of the brain we will understand that these categories refer to nothing and give them up entirely.

4.2 Requirements for having beliefs

The different starting positions about the nature of belief lead naturally to a number of different properties an animal would need were it to have beliefs, and a corresponding number of ways to test for animal belief. We will examine these different proposals in order to determine how best to confront the question of whether animals have beliefs.

4.2.1 Attributing content and concepts

Here's one kind of argument against animal belief. In order to have a belief, one has to have a perspective on the state of affairs that is being represented. That is, a believer sees some part of the world as being a certain way, for example as an expensive house, or as green grass. When we characterize our own thoughts or the thoughts of others, we necessarily include this perspectival aspect of belief. Another way of capturing this idea is to say that beliefs are opaque, and that attributions of belief do not allow for substitutions of equivalent terms without risking changing the truth-value of the sentence. For example, the sentence "Hank believes that this grass is green" may be true, while the sentence "Hank believes that this zoysia is green" is false, even though "this grass" refers to grass of the species zoysia.

When it comes to attributing belief to creatures without language, some think we are at a loss in knowing how to characterize the perspectival nature of belief. In developing a thought of Frege's, Michael Dummett discusses the dog who is routinely attacked by other dogs when traveling a particular path (Dummett 2010). Sometimes there is only one aggressor, and other times there is a pack. The dog develops different techniques for these different situations; he stands his ground when there is only one aggressor, and turns and runs if there is more than one. It is natural for us to say of the dog when he stands his ground that he *believes* there is only one dog barring his path. However, to attribute this belief to the dog requires us to attribute to the dog all the concepts in the belief, including the concept "one," which in turn requires that the dog knows what standing up against one dog, burying one bone, finding one person in the house, and so forth have in common. Dummett, like Frege, thinks that there is no possible dog behavior that would permit us to ascribe the concept of *one* to the dog. Dummett continues, "So the dog does *not* have the very thought by which we express the feature of the situation he has recognized. Conversely, we have no linguistic means of expressing just what it is he recognizes. Animals without language cannot have the very same thoughts we express in language" (Dummett 2010, 118).

Dummett's reasoning goes like this:

1   We cannot accurately ascribe belief to animals in (our) language.
2   If we cannot accurately ascribe belief to an animal in (our) language, then there is no language in which the animal's belief can be ascribed.
3   If there is no language in which the animal's belief can be ascribed, then animals do not have beliefs.
4   Therefore, animals do not have beliefs.

However, what evidence is there for premise (2)? This seems to be the issue at stake.

In making a similar argument, Stephen Stich points out that there are two ways in which we can understand the question about whether animals have beliefs (Stich 1979). In one sense, we might be inclined to say that animals have beliefs when their behaviors are consistent with our folk psychology, and when ascribing beliefs allows us to make predictions of future behavior. But, and more to the point, we should be inclined to say that animals don't have beliefs because we are not able to give folk psychological explanations of their behaviors in their own terms. For example, a dog Fido can bury a meaty bone in the backyard of his human companion's house, and retrieve it at a later time. However, we can't say of Fido that he believes there is a meaty bone buried in the backyard because he doesn't have the right kind of concepts to make this attribution true. He lacks important knowledge of bones—kinds of bones, what they are for—and he lacks important skills, such as the ability to sort real bones from synthetic ones. He also lacks important knowledge of backyards—property rights, privacy, safe places for kids to play.

Stich considers a possible reply to this worry given by David Armstrong. Armstrong suggests that we can attribute beliefs to animals by removing the perspectival aspect of the attribution, and indicating the actual states of affairs that the animals' beliefs are about. So, instead of saying something like "Fido believes that there is a meaty bone buried in the backyard" (which would require that Fido knows something about bones, skeletal structures, yards, property rights, etc.), we could correctly say that Fido believes that this thing (pointing at the bone) is there (pointing at the spot in the yard). That is, Armstrong suggests that we move from attributing an opaque *de dicto* statement to Fido—one that captures *how* Fido thinks about the meaty bone—to a transparent *de re* statement—one that refers to the objects, properties, and situations in the world. Regardless of how Fido actually represents the meaty bone in dog concepts or pictures or whatever, we can refer to the content of Fido's thought as "meaty bone in the yard." We can say, "Fido believes there is a meaty bone buried in the yard" because, though he does not have the same concept of meaty bone as we do, his belief is still directed intentionally toward the bone. While Fido doesn't believe *that* the meaty bone is buried in the yard, he does believe *of* the meaty bone and *of* the yard that the former is buried in the latter.

Stich rejects this response for two reasons. First, he is worried that characterizing beliefs *de re* will result in false inferences. One of the hallmarks of propositional attitudes is that their *de dicto* nature makes them opaque. This means that we cannot infer from "Lois believes that Clark Kent works for the paper" to "Lois believes that Superman works for the paper," even though Clark Kent and Superman are the same person, and we can't infer from "Hank believes that this grass is green" to "Hank believes that this zoysia is green" because Hank might not know that this grass is zoysia. If we were to follow Armstrong's suggestion, says Stich, we would permit ourselves to make such unwarranted inferences about animal beliefs.

But more troubling still is the worry that *de re* attributions will fail to give us any information about animal cognition. Suppose researchers accept Armstrong's proposal, and that after years of study they learn exactly which conjunction of features causes a dog to sort something into the bone category—say, *hard, white, chewable*, and *larger than 6 cm*. However, the same problem arises then, since we don't know how Fido understands *hard, white, chewable*, and *larger than 6 cm*. What is the dog correlate of *centimeters*?! Thus, Stich claims, we are *still* unable to specify the content of an animal's purported belief, because there is incommensurability all the way down. The assumption is that we will never reach a level where there are shared human and dog concepts. Stich writes that, "We are comfortable in attributing to a subject a belief with a specific content only if we can assume the subject to have a broad network of related beliefs that is largely isomorphic with our own" (Stich 1979, 22). Since neither Fido's bone beliefs nor his beliefs about the structure of bones are likely to be isomorphic with ours, Stich is not willing to attribute beliefs to Fido. And if we can't say *what* Fido believes, we can't say *that* Fido believes.

The arguments against animal beliefs based on attributing content have the following form:

1   We can't say what animals think.
2   If we can't say what animals think, then they don't have beliefs.
3   Therefore animals don't have beliefs.

Stich and Dummett both worry that because we can't know what an animal thinks, animals cannot have beliefs expressible in language. The argument against animal belief based on troubles with ascribing content are usually associated with non-representational/interpretationist and eliminativist views about beliefs. When Stich gave his argument against animal belief, he was an eliminativist, so he didn't really think anyone had beliefs. But Dummett isn't an eliminativist, and this sort of worry is expressed by representationalists and non-representationalists alike.

There have been a number of replies to the worry about ascribing content to animals, which we can examine in turn.

4.2.1.1 Reply 1: Ascribing content to language users

Arguments against animal beliefs based on problems with ascribing content seem to take for granted that we don't have parallel problems when it comes to ascribing content to humans. It may seem evident that people say what they believe, so we can easily know what humans believe. But what do children believe when they say "There is a meaty bone buried in the backyard"? The young child's concept of "bone" or "backyard" are quite different from the adult concept, and different still from the expert version of these concepts. In order for the attributions to be accurate, the concepts we ascribe to others must match our own to a degree, but our web of concepts need not be isomorphic. If it were, then everyone would share the same association between concepts, but if they did, then there would be no disagreement. To take an example, political disagreements are partially constituted by disagreements about how concepts are related to one another: Is state sanctioned killing of murderers itself murder? Is limiting gun ownership a violation of liberty? The question that arises is how close is close enough to think that we share the same concept.

Colin Allen argues that human language doesn't absolve us of worries about ascribing content (Allen 2013). Our words, he says, only approximate the content of our cognitive states that are related to those words, and those cognitive states may be constantly changing (consider thinking the sentence "I like bicycling" while sitting at a dinner party compared to thinking it while grinding up a steep hill). Because our belief attributions are made in language, they are likewise imprecise. And this goes for animals as well as for humans.

Allen argues that the imprecision in these attributions doesn't entail that the attributions shouldn't be part of scientific analysis; rather, it shows that we need a method to determine whether an attribution is similar and relevant enough to the subject's cognitive states. He suggests that such an account is forthcoming from information-theoretic approaches to "embodied and socially embedded cognitive systems" (2013, 253). Allen asks us to consider geometric objects in a three-dimensional space. These objects can be transformed into less precise or idealized objects using transformational rules, such as applying a smoothing filter that blurs the boundaries of an object, or taking a slice of the object by removing one of the dimensions. When these rules are specified precisely, the abstraction can be described in terms of properties that are commensurate with the properties of the original object, which in turn introduces a way of stating similarities between the original object and its abstraction. There is no relativity involved when saying that the abstraction is similar to the original, because of the precision of the transformation rules. Allen asks us to see an analogy between the geometry case and the attribution of propositional attitudes: cognitive systems can be taken as multi-dimensional objects, and attributing mental states to them is analogous to using a transformational rule. Two cognitive systems can think the same thing, once the original representations are abstracted from them. This is so even though the original representations may be different, may have different associations, etc. And all this will change over time and circumstances. In developing this account, Allen thinks he will be able to show both how the problem of imprecision occurs for humans and other animals, and how it can be addressed by future research on cognition. The problems are not insurmountable.

4.2.1.2 Reply 2: Ways of ascribing content to animals

In response to worries that we cannot ascribe content to creatures without language, some philosophers have developed proposals for doing just that. Mark Rowlands introduces the strategy of explaining an animal's reasons for actions in terms that the animal may not be able to entertain herself (Rowlands 2012). We can explain animal behavior in terms of *de dicto* content (p), that tracks the content the animal actually possesses ($p*$):

> (*Tracking*): Proposition p tracks proposition $p*$ if the truth of p guarantees the truth of $p*$ in virtue of the fact that there is a reliable asymmetric connection between the concepts expressed by the term occupying the subject position in p and the concept expressed by the term occupying the subject position in $p*$.

(Rowlands 2012, 58)

Tracking allows us to form the patterns of explanation we need to make accurate predictions of behavior—exactly what Stich requires for ascription of accurate content. If the human concepts "backyard" and "meaty bone" are reliably connected to the dog-context bound concepts "backyard*" and "meaty bone*," then the truth of the ascription "there is a meaty bone in the backyard" to Fido guarantees the truth of "there is a meaty bone* in the backyard*" (even if "backyard*" isn't reliably connected to "backyard," which is something we could never know, anyway. Hence the asymmetry in the relationship between p and p*.) In this way we can explain the dog's behavior in terms of content that the dog is not capable of entertaining.

In a similar proposal, José Bermúdez argues that we can attribute beliefs to animals and other mute minds via a form of success semantics, such that the content of a belief is that which would satisfy the animal's desire by causing the appropriate action (Bermúdez 2003). He thinks that researchers have in fact done a fair job in differentiating between the *de re* contents of nonverbal beliefs. For example, using the violation of expectation paradigm has allowed us to understand better how prelinguistic infants divide up the world and to realize that infants are sensitive to certain physical features from the very beginning of their lives. Bermúdez reviews the work done by Elizabeth Spelke on infant cognition (Spelke 1990; Spelke et al. 1989; Spelke and Van de Walle 1993) and suggests that what this work shows is that, "nonlinguistic creatures are perfectly capable of perceiving a structured world" (81).

Furthermore, Bermúdez thinks we have learned quite a bit about animal concepts through different sorts of experimentation. For example, rats are able to successfully recall the location of food in a cross-shaped maze. How does the rat do this? Well, the rat desires food, and has a belief about the location of the food. But what is the content of the rat's belief? Bermúdez suggests there are four possibilities (2003, 100):

(1a) Food is located at the end-point of a set of behaviors.
(1b) Food is located at coordinates (x, y) in space referenced egocentrically.
(1c) Food is located at coordinates (x', y') in space referenced by points in maze space.
(1d) Food is located at coordinates (x'', y'') in space referenced by points in the distal environmental space (e.g. wall color).

By designing and running a variety of experiments, psychologists came to realize that 1c correctly describes the rat's belief. They reasoned in the following manner: 1a and 1b are disqualified because the rat finds the food even when starting at a different place in the maze (Tolman et al. 1946), and 1d is disqualified because when the maze is shifted so that the distal environmental stimuli are different, the rat is still able to find the food (Tolman et al. 1947). Thus, careful experimentation allows us to ascribe content to an animal, which will in turn allow us to make accurate predictions of that animal's future behavior.

4.2.1.3 Reply 3: The possibility of nonconceptual content

The philosopher Jacob Beck challenges the statement "If we can't say what animals think, then animals don't have beliefs" by offering four ways to reconcile indeterminism about the content of an animal's belief with realism about animal belief (2013). It may be that indeterminism is only a momentary phenomenon, and with more time we will be better able to ascribe content to animal beliefs. It may be that animals' lack of language is simply an epistemic barrier to what they are thinking, or that they have concepts and hence contents that are unfamiliar to us, so we could not share their beliefs. Or, and this is the possibility Beck endorses, it may be that we cannot say what an animal thinks because animals think in a nonlinguistic format. This explanation takes the indeterminacy to really be about using language to express an animal's belief—we can't *say* what an animal believes, but we can share a belief with an animal when we are thinking in the same nonlinguistic format as the animal about the same thing.

What is nonlinguistic format? Beck suggests that animals may be thinking in analog format, rather than in a digital format such as language. Analog formats cannot be divided up into parts, the way language can, but like a photograph they can vary in degree of focus. Examples of analog content include pictures, images, and maps. Beck argues that we can understand some animal representations in this way, and that since we cannot translate from a picture to a sentence (he asks us to consider how to translate the *Mona Lisa* into English), we can't translate animal representations. But of course animals can still *have* representations, just as the *Mona Lisa* can still exist despite the fact that it is untranslatable.

The view Beck endorses, that animals have nonconceptual thought, is in conflict with the next property that some have taken to be necessary for having beliefs—namely having concepts. We can turn to that issue now.

4.2.2 Having concepts

According to one version of the Representational Theory of Mind, beliefs express propositions, and since propositions are made up of individual concepts, concepts are units of thoughts that make up the foundation of propositions. Concepts allow us to categorize and form generalizations about the events and objects in our world. They are implicated in cognitive processes involved with categorization, inference, memory, learning, and decision-making. On an atomistic view of concepts, animals may have concepts but lack thoughts. However, holists about concepts, such as Davidson, take the acquisition of concepts to go hand in hand with the acquisition of beliefs. For atomists like Fodor, it makes sense to investigate the existence of animal concepts without presupposing anything about animal belief.

Stich's contention that we cannot be justified in attributing concepts to animals can be supported by realist arguments against the existence of animal concepts. Nick Chater and Cecilia Heyes (1994) argue that on any of the theoretical accounts of concepts, it doesn't make sense to ask whether animals have concepts; most of those theories presuppose having a natural language, and the accounts that don't make this assumption can't be tested empirically in nonlinguistic animals. On the classical view of concepts, they are representations of necessary and sufficient conditions for class membership. Animals couldn't have a concept so understood, because one needs language to represent necessary and sufficient conditions. Any concepts used in stating necessary and sufficient conditions will be just as uncertain as the concept being defined by them. "For example, to suggest that an animal's concept WOMAN is internally defined as FEMALE, ADULT and PERSON presupposes three controversial concepts in an attempt to account for one" (Chater and Heyes 1994, 214).

On the exemplar view of concepts, a concept is a representation of a set of instances of that concept. While it might seem that the ability to sort objects into sets would be evidence of an exemplar view of concepts, other mechanisms can account for this ability. Animals can use stimulus generalization to sort objects, such that a particular sorting comes to be associated with a reward. The exemplar theory requires that the sorted set then become associated with a label—the concept—and there is no account of how animals could label these sets. They write,

> Even if animals typically showed evidence of having formed associations between stored instances, this would not be sufficient to ascribe them concepts ... stimulus generalization may be able to explain the ability to distinguish dogs from non-dogs, or furry from non-furry things, but not both at once.
>
> (Chater and Heyes 1994, 216)

And finally, on the prototype view of concepts, a concept is the ideal exemplar of the set. An object is classified as a concept C if it is similar enough to the prototype of concept C. Evidence for prototype theory comes from the psychologist Eleanor Rosch's famous work looking at the response times and order of acquisition of instances of a concept (1975). For example, when given the label *furniture* people more quickly identify sofas as fitting compared to less iconic exemplars such as sewing machine tables. Note that prototype views don't rely on linguistic formulations, but that they can be understood as clusters or vectors in some feature space that are individuated perceptually. In her field work, Rosch found that cultures that lacked words for our color concepts were still able to sort objects according to those concepts (Rosch 1973).

Chater and Heyes argue that nonetheless this view cannot be used to defend animal concepts, because associative networks alone can generate the responses that have been taken as evidence for prototypes. It is possible that the differences in response time can be explained without reference to representing an ideal prototype. They argue that it is difficult to empirically differentiate between the prototype view and the stimulus generalization, because both can make the same prediction.

The problems that Chater and Heyes raise about the attribution of concepts to nonhuman animals are part of more general questions about the accounts of concepts on the table. Problems with testing the theories and alternative explanations exist for humans as well as nonverbal creatures, and can be taken as evidence that there is more work to be done to understand the nature of concepts. For example, Chater and Heyes' conclusion must be made compatible with the existence of sorting behavior in preverbal children, and the finding that it is easier for traditional communities to learn "natural" categories rather than artificial ones, as Rosch's research demonstrates.

One approach to these criticisms is to abandon the notions of concept that psychologists have been using, and replace them with a lower-level kind of representation. The philosopher Edouard Machery suggests that we can unify what psychologists have found about so-called conceptual thought by instead talking about bodies of knowledge stored in long-term memory; he suggests that the current status of psychological research on concepts is in such disarray that the only thing to do now is abandon the notion of concept and start over (Machery 2011).

4.2.2.1 Investigating animal concepts

In the face of such concerns, one approach is to use the calibration method and start with the assumption that animals do have concepts. The assumption has been useful for research in animal cognition, and it isn't clear how a nonconceptual approach to studying animal minds could offer as much in the way of promoting the research program. From that assumption we can examine the various roles that concepts might play in order to develop a satisfactory theory. Rather than abandoning animal concepts, we might begin by assuming their existence and then asking how we can go about uncovering what they are.

Colin Allen takes this approach, pointing out that there are steep costs associated with abandoning the notion of animal concepts (Allen 1999). For one, since cognitive psychology operationalizes human cognition in terms of concepts, we would be unable to make comparisons between human and animal cognitive abilities; this would make it harder to understand the evolution of human concepts. Furthermore, since concepts are what make up beliefs and other intentional states (desires, etc.), without concepts it is hard to see how we could develop a theory of content for the intentional states of animals.

Since we don't want to give up the idea of animal concepts, and we don't yet have a good theory of concepts, we can make progress on the question by turning from the metaphysical question to the epistemic one. With the psychologist Marc Hauser, Allen argues that the attribution of a concept is justified "if there is evidence supporting the presence of a mental representation that is independent of solely perceptual information" (Allen and Hauser 1991, 231). That is, the actor has to act according to a construal of a situation, rather than an association directly from a stimulus. They give an example of how we might test for the existence of a death concept in vervet monkeys (though point out that such a test would be immoral and shouldn't ever be done!). Vervet females look toward a mother when they hear the mother's infant making a contact call, and the mother looks toward the cry. Allen and Hauser suggest that if vervets cease this behavior after the death of an infant, or engage in an agitated behavior instead, this would offer some evidence that they re-categorized the stimulus, because they understood that the infant had died. We see the work of concepts at play when someone responds differently to an identical stimulus, because the only thing that can cause the difference in the response is the conceptual change.

Even better justification for attributing a concept comes if we see that an individual can detect past errors in concept ascription, and learn from those errors. For example, if an animal categorized all nuts as food, but later learned that one type of nut was inedible and so avoided trying to eat only that kind of nut, then we would have some evidence that the animal has a *food* concept. Many species can classify objects into different categories; for example, pigeons are famously able to differentiate between pictures containing human faces and pictures lacking such faces (Herrnstein and Loveland 1964). The research on error monitoring discussed in the last chapter suggests that some species are also able to judge when they can correctly solve some task such as identifying two objects as same or different. The question remains whether individuals of a species who are able to recognize their errors come to better discriminate items as exemplars of a concept; this is a question for future research.

Psychological research into the concepts of children may help us understand the concepts of nonhuman animals. Based on her research on children, the psychologist Susan Carey draws a distinction between two types of conceptual representations: those associated with core cognition (the set of structured innate mechanisms designed to organize the world in certain ways), and those that arise as part of explicit knowledge systems (Carey 2009). The core cognition concepts are largely shared between infants and animals. The development of the concepts of knowledge systems is a cultural process, and the concepts that are held depends on the nature of one's culture. Carey argues that in order to understand the origin of concepts, we must understand how they develop in children, how they evolved, and their distribution among species. This requires doing the epistemic work Allen advocates and determining which concepts we can safely say human children and animals have. Only once we have that information can we go about forming a responsible theory of concepts.

For example, Carey argues for the existence of number representations in animals, and she thinks that by examining the nature of these representations we can come to understand something about the structure of animals' number representations. Many animals are able to keep track of number. Pigeons (Rilling and McDiarmid 1965), rats (Mechner 1958), monkeys (Hauser et al. 2003), chimpanzees (Biro and Matsuzawa 2001), orangutans (Shumaker et al. 2001), dolphins (Kilian et al. 2003), and others have demonstrated various numerical abilities. However, when testing the abilities of animals on number discrimination, it appears that animals do not represent the integers when they are performing tasks, because they find it much more difficult to discriminate between small differences in number than between large ones, which suggests that integer representation doesn't capture the ways in which animals think about quantities. This finding is robust across species, and is captured by Weber's law, which says that the ability to discriminate two magnitudes is a function of their ratio. This approximate number system allows individuals to discriminate larger from smaller sets of objects without using a precise number system to count the objects. Not only do animals demonstrate it, but so do human babies (Xu and Spelke 2000) and human adults (Barth et al. 2003). Carey argues that the correct way of understanding the concepts associated with an approximate number system is in terms of approximate number representation, so that the orangutan could correctly think there are *approximately six* grapes in an array even if there are really seven (2009).

4.2.2.2 Nonconceptual thought

It may be that Carey is too hasty in accepting that we can characterize the animals' numerosity abilities in conceptual terms. Testing alternative hypotheses about an animal's content can help us get clearer about what someone is thinking about. Following the example of the psychologists who examined how a rat is able to find food in a maze, we can consider various hypotheses about the nature of the representation of numerosity in nonverbal creatures.

This point is made by Beck (2012), who argues that we shouldn't understand the findings about numerosity as evidence of approximate number concepts, because an approximate number concept implies the existence of systematic thought, but the attributions do not obey systematicity constraints. He offers the following argument:

1   If approximate number representations have conceptual content, then approximate number representations can be expressed in sentences.
2   Approximate number representations cannot be expressed in sentences.
3   Approximate number representations have content.
4   Therefore, approximate number representations have nonconceptual content.

The key premise in this argument is the second one. The reason why Beck thinks we can't represent approximate number in sentences is that the numerosity representations (which Beck, following many psychologists, calls analog magnitude states) violate the generality constraint and hence cannot be conceptual. The generality constraint, which was introduced by Gareth Evans (1982), states that if thoughts have conceptual content then they must be systematic. For example, in order to have a concept one must be able to use that concept in various well-formed representations in which it fits—if you can understand the concept *love*, then you can understand it in the sentence "Luke loves Leia" as well as "Spock loves Kirk." Having a concept is a general ability, and possessing the concept allows its use in various contexts.

Beck argues that no translation of an analog magnitude state into language reflects the systematicity required to meet the generality constraint (Beck 2012). For example, Beck claims that the data show that pigeons can represent:

1   40 pecks are fewer than 50 pecks

and

2   38 pecks are fewer than 47 pecks.

But data shows that pigeons cannot represent

3   38 pecks are fewer than 40 pecks

or

4   47 pecks are fewer than 50 pecks.

In fact, pigeons are able to discriminate numerical values if their ratios do not exceed 9:10, which is consistent with Weber's law. But the generality constraint tells us that if someone can represent (1) and (2) they should be able to represent (3) or (4). Is there a way of reconciling these? Beck considers several ways of defending the idea that analog magnitude states can meet the generality constraint, but all of them fail. For example, in considering Carey's suggestion that we can translate the sentences into approximates, Beck claims it violates systematicity, because while the pigeon can represent that *approximately 40* pecks are fewer than *approximately 50* pecks, they can't represent *approximately 38* pecks are fewer than *approximately 40* pecks. Even worse, it may be that the representations in an approximate number system would have no fixed meaning. One might think that pigeons fail to represent (3) because *approximately 38 = approximately 40*, and so (3) is false. But we run into inequivalencies at the ends of the approximates, such that *approximately 38 = approximately 40* AND *approximately 40 = approximately 44* but *approximately 38* doesn't equal *approximately 44*.

While we normally think concepts are required to represent thoughts, the possibility of nonconceptual content offers an alternative way of thinking about animal mental content. As we saw above, Beck suggests that we can't say what animals think not because they don't think, but because they don't think in concepts. He suggests that the existence of analog magnitudes in humans shows that human cognition includes both conceptual and nonconceptual content, but that most animal content may be completely nonconceptual. What remains to be seen is whether we might positively characterize the range of nonconceptual content in order to explain the wide varieties of animal behaviors.

In contrast to Beck's argument, Carruthers (2009) argues that animals do satisfy a weakened version of the generality constraint. Even honeybees and digger wasps have belief-like and desire-like states that interact with one another, which allows them to engage in practical reasoning. These states refer to objects in their environments, such as the landmarks honeybees use in navigation. If we understand the core of the generality constraint to be that thought is compositionally structured (as opposed to the idea that a thinker must be capable of entertaining every thought possible that includes that concept), then we can state the generality constraint in the following way:

> If a creature possesses the concepts *F* and *a* (and is capable of thinking *Fa*), then for *some* other concepts *G* and *b* that the creature could possess, it is metaphysically possible for the creature to think *Ga*, and in the same sense possible for it to think *Fb*.
>
> (Carruthers 2009, 97)

Since bees use landmarks both to get from the hive to a food source, and to get from a food source back home, bees can think something like, "This tree is north of the hive" and "This tree is south of the food," thus satisfying a weakened version of the generality constraint. The way in which bees can come to have these beliefs vary too; they can acquire them as a result of direct experience, but they can also infer them from the dances of other bees who report their own experience. However, many are dissatisfied with Carruthers' version of the generality constraint. Metaphysical possibility is a very weak requirement. It is also metaphysically possible that bees think that the human use of pesticides are leading to their demise. But it's safe to say that bees don't think *that* way.

4.2.2.3 Animals and concepts?

If we have ways of understanding animal concepts that are inconsistent with any of our theories of concepts, we can use the calibration method to both tweak our understanding of concepts and use our understanding to further examine possible conceptual abilities in different species. In the context of animal concepts, we have already seen that systematicity is another property that some take as a requirement for rational thought and belief. In the next section we will examine that requirement in more detail.

4.2.3 Systematicity in propositional thought

Many species seem to store declarative information, such as the location of food sources or the dominance status of a conspecific, which may be best understood in terms of propositional representations. Many cognitive psychologists understand cognition as information processing, where the information is understood as a mental representation such as a propositional attitude. Fodor develops this insight in his language of thought hypothesis, according to which cognition's vehicle is an internal language of thought that is shared by all cognizers regardless of the natural language they may or may not have (Fodor 1975). One argument in favor of the language of thought hypothesis comes from the observation that thought, like language, is systematic—the ability to think one thought is related to the ability to think another thought using the same concepts. Our grammatical rules allow us to formulate new sentences from familiar parts in a way that obeys the rules of grammar, just as systematicity in thought allows us to construct new thoughts out of old pieces.

Fodor thinks that many species share our language of thought, as evidenced by common animal processes, including considered action, concept learning, and perceptual integration. The only way we have to explain those behaviors is by using the computational models we get from the representational theory of mind, and since many organisms lack external representations in the form of language, they must have internal representations—a language of thought (Fodor 1975, 57–59). Fodor suggests that the similarities between humans and nonverbal creatures in processing logical connectives shows that the concepts are shared between them; humans have difficulty coming to grasp disjunction, more so than their understanding of conjunction or negation, and, Fodor claims, nonhuman animals do as well. When children learn a first language they engage in a kind of hypothesis formation and testing that allows them to come to realize what information is being communicated and, at the same time, allows them to form generalizations about the extension of the symbol. All this requires the kind of thinking that allows hypothesis formation and testing, which involves propositional thought.

Psychologists such as Randy Gallistel argue that even honeybees demonstrate propositional thought in their navigation abilities (2011). Bees navigate in part using dead reckoning, which involves determining one's position in terms of velocity. For a bee to follow a dancer's instructions, the bee needs to know how fast to move in a particular direction and when to stop. While Gallistel admits that the mathematics involved in the computation are simple, he also claims that it essentially involves addition of the symbols for one's most recent change in position to the symbols that represent one's earlier judgment of position, and addition can only be done by a symbol system.

Cheney and Seyfarth give a similar argument for animal belief based on their research on baboons, claiming that there is evidence for baboons' language of thought (Cheney and Seyfarth 2007). In their book *Baboon Metaphysics*, they put forth the view that animals without language have language-like thought structures:

1 Baboon vocal communication—and, by extension, that of other primates—is very different from human language. The differences are most pronounced in call production.
2 Differences in production have been overemphasized, however, and have distracted attention from the information that primates acquire when they hear vocalizations. In perception and cognition, continuities with language are more apparent.
3 In primate groups, natural selection has favored individuals who can form mental representations of other individuals, their relationships, and their motives.
4 This social knowledge constitutes a discrete, combinatorial system of representations—a language of thought—that shares several features with human language.
5 The language of thought that has evolved in baboons and other primates is a general primate characteristic whose appearance predates the evolution of spoken language in our hominid ancestors.
6 The prior evolution of social cognition created individuals who were preadapted to develop language.
7 Several features thought to be unique to language—for example, discrete combinatorics and the encoding of propositional information—were not introduced by language. They arose, instead, because understanding social life and predicting others' behavior requires a particular style of thinking (2007, 251–252).

The baboons of Botswana's Okavango Delta communicate using vocalizations, they recognize who is making a call, and they track family relations as well as dominance relations. Female baboons have linear dominance hierarchies that are inherited from their mothers and can be stable for years, such that the dominant individual is a mother followed by her daughters, and then another mother followed by her daughters. Female kin live together throughout their lives, and enjoy very close social bonds, grooming one another for hours a day. Altercations over food or access to infants are not uncommon, but rarely lead to a change in the dominance hierarchy. When they do, Cheney and Seyfarth suggest that the baboons are able to make transitive inferences; they realize that, for example, if baboon D12 wins a fight with baboon B4, the entire D family is promoted over the B and C families in the hierarchy. See Figure 4.1.

Baboons also engage in third party reconciliation. Sometimes after an altercation between two baboons, the winner of the fight will give a grunt, which causes the loser to relax; she might stop moving away or cowering. Cheney and Seyfarth describe this as a reconciliation grunt, which signifies that the fight is over. However, even more often after the fight is over, the sister or mother of the winner will grunt, which has the same effect on the loser.

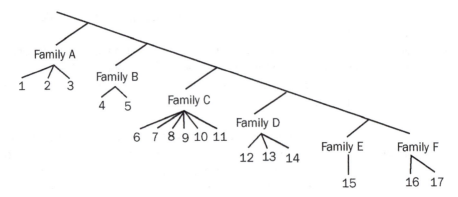

Figure 4.1 Hierarchical dominance relations in baboons. (Source: Cheney and Seyfarth 2007, 107)

Given such abilities, Cheney and Seyfarth think that baboons have a language of thought, because the inferences they make require the structure of language. By a language of thought, of course, Cheney and Seyfarth are referring to Fodor's theory.

But is language the only model we have for organizing rational inference? Fodor shares with Davidson this idea that it is only language that could preserve the reason-respecting flow of thought. But there are challenges to this claim.

For one, the philosopher Elisabeth Camp has directly responded to Cheney and Seyfarth's claim that baboon behavior can only be explained in terms of a language of thought (Camp 2009). She argues that the form of thought present in baboons might be different from that of a linguistic structure. Cheney and Seyfarth think that baboon behavior demonstrates evidence of propositional representations, but Camp argues that other representational systems can account for all the structure that is demonstrated by inferences about baboon dominance relations. The baboon representational system seems to be compositional—there are parts that can be rearranged into different orientations—and productive—the system can represent a number of different contents in virtue of different arrangement of parts. But these features are not sufficient for language, Camp points out. There exist other nonlinguistic compositional systems such as Venn diagrams or city maps. In particular, Camp claims, the hierarchical structure demonstrated by baboon dominance understanding can be accommodated by a representational system in terms of a taxonomic tree. This would make baboon cognition less general and less expressive than language, and explains the limitations of their cognitive abilities—something that is left mysterious by the language of thought hypothesis. As far as we know, baboons don't use tools, they don't make inferences about transitivity outside social relations, they don't have a theory of mind, and they don't produce structured utterances. Rather than a domain-general language of thought, Camp suggests that hierarchy understanding in baboons may be the result of a special purpose nonlinguistic module:

we get a simpler and more efficient explanation of the distinctive contours of their cognitive abilities and limitations if we hypothesize that their representational system also differs from language in at least one crucial respect: that the component of their thoughts which is hierarchically structured employs a combinatorial principle with a robust function, that of representing dominance.

(Camp 2009, 126)

Camp's arguments showing that there are alternative hypotheses to explain baboon behavior also serve to support her view about the structure of thought. Camp suggests it is a red herring to associate the existence of language with the existence of belief, because belief need not be language-like. We may be able to representationally believe things in nonlinguistic formats.

4.2.4 Logical reasoning and rationality

For those who accept the representational theory of mind, one property required for having a belief is to be able to use beliefs to engage in rational behavior. We might recall how Chrysippus' dog seemed to solve a logic problem, and Thorndike's cats learned how to escape from their puzzle boxes. We might also look at Köhler's chimpanzees who solved the problem of how to grasp out-of-reach bananas by stacking boxes.

Chrysippus' dog appeared to engage in a logical inference, but did he really use rationality to determine that the rabbit must have run down the third path? Not surprisingly, your answer to that question depends on your take on what rationality amounts to. Ruth Millikan puts it well. If one understands rationality as "the ability to make trials and errors in one's head rather than in overt behavior" (Millikan 2006, 117), then animals probably do have rationality. But if it involves "the capacity to form subject-predicate judgments sensitive to a negation transformation, hence subject to the law of non-contradiction" (Millikan 2006, 117) then humans alone may be rational. But rather than claiming that it is an *either–or* question, Millikan is suggesting that rationality comes in different styles. Here Millikan is on board with the current wide acceptance in cognitive science of the existence of two cognitive systems that underpin human cognitive operations. One way of understanding this notion is that humans have an evolutionarily old cognitive system that we share with animals, as well as a much newer cognitive system that is linguistically rich and rife with culturally based concepts. Versions of this dual process theory abound in psychology and cognitive science.

Fred Dretske has done much work to develop a deflationary account of rationality. Dretske makes plausible the idea that animals are rational by considering examples. For instance, because monarch butterflies are poisonous, it is rational for birds and mice to avoid eating them. Monarch butterflies feed on milkweed, which is toxic for most vertebrates. The predators are not born avoiding monarchs, but after eating one and vomiting, they quickly learn to avoid eating other butterflies with the monarch coloring. Dretske points out that the birds also have reason to avoid eating viceroys, who closely resemble monarchs. Both the bird's avoidance of monarchs and its avoidance of viceroys are explained by the content of the bird's thought, says Dretske, and this makes the bird a minimally rational agent (Dretske 1988, 2006).

On this view, animals like birds have beliefs, since beliefs are representational states whose contents are dependent on the processing abilities of an individual (Dretske 1983). For example, we can say that a frog believes there is a bug in front of him when he grabs a fly with his tongue, because natural selection likely selected for tongue protrusion when stimulated with the visual percepts associated with flies. Given the evolution of this reliable mechanism, it is impossible to fool the frog; a visual percept of a certain kind *just is* a visual percept of that kind, and so the frog forms a belief about the existence of a bug in front of him, due to the evolution of this reliable mechanism. Dreske argues further that the frog has knowledge that the bug is in front of him, because believing requires the capacity for knowledge:

1   To believe C, one must be exposed to information that C, and that information must be picked up and used by the learner.
2   To pick up and use information, one must have (or had) the cognitive resources for knowing C.
3   If a learner believes C, the learner has (or had) the cognitive resources for knowing C.

As Dretske puts it,

> So *if* the frog does believe that there is a bug in front of it, then it is the sort of creature capable of picking up, processing, and responding to information about bugs and, specifically, the information that there are bugs in front of it.
>
> (Dretske 1983, 12)

The accounts of minimal rationality defended by Millikan and Dretske might lead us to think that there are two kinds of thinking, a minimal nonlinguistic style of thinking and a more structured kind of thinking that comes with having language. However, there is reason to think that there are more than two degrees or styles of thought. Bermúdez advocates the existence of a middle type of thought between the minimalist accounts and the full-blown style of thought adult humans enjoy (Bermúdez 2003). Bermúdez develops Dummett's (1993) account of proto-thinking that is non-propositional and nonlinguistic, and concludes such thinking can only be imagistic and perceptual. Perceptual thought is tied to a particular context and does not permit generalizability or future planning. This style of thinking can be understood as a kind of behavioral skill rather than a structured belief; for example, using Dretske's example we can speak of the frog's thinking as knowing how to catch this fly here and now, rather than knowing that a fly is in front of his face, or having general information about how to catch a fly. The goal of proto-thinking isn't gathering information, but responding appropriately to the environment.

Bermúdez argues that minimalist conceptions of thought cannot account for all animal behavior because there are some behaviors that can only be explained in terms of propositional attitudes, informational states, or generalizations that go beyond the here and now. For example, chimpanzees naturally construct tools from vine stems by stripping off leaves and neatly biting the end before carrying it as far as 200 meters to fish for termites (Seed and Byrne 2010). And in an experimental study of chimpanzee cooperation, subjects would choose the tool needed by another chimpanzee and pass it to their partner, demonstrating that they knew which action their partner needed to perform (Melis and Tomasello 2013). And it's not just great apes that construct, carry, and use tools. New Caledonian crows manufacture two

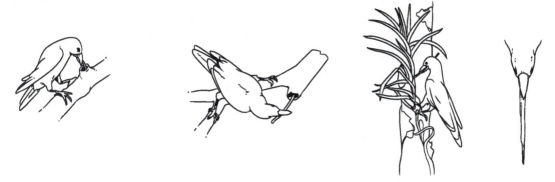

Figure 4.2 New Caledonian crows construct tools from twigs and leaves. (Source: Hunt 1996)

different kinds of hooks to catch prey (Hunt 1996). Hooked-twig tools are stripped of leaves and bark and have a hook on the wide end; stepped-cut tools are made from sturdy leafs and are cut out so that the birds can use the sharp barbs along the leaf edge.

Navigation is another example of behaviors that requires something more than minimalist rationality according to Bermúdez. If an animal can learn from experience (for example, if he can come to recognize landmarks over time) then the animal must have a more objective way of representing the environment than the minimalist account allows. Animals as diverse as bees and orangutans successfully navigate their environments, appearing to take landmarks into account as part of their navigation toolbox.

In addition, since some nonlinguistic animals can learn a symbolic communication system, these animals must have something more than minimal rationality. Bottlenose dolphins can respond to gestures representing actions, modifiers, and objects (Herman et al. 1984; Herman 2010) and chimpanzees raised in a symbolic environment can come to use lexigrams to make requests for play or food, and respond appropriately to requests to do some strange act, like to put pine needles in a microwave (Savage-Rumbaugh et al. 1993). Behaviors such as these seem hard to explain in terms of the minimalist conception.

While not minimalist, these examples of animal thought are not as robust as linguistic thought, Bermúdez claims, because they fail to show any way of thinking about thoughts, and hence they lack any logical reasoning. We will examine that argument in Chapter 6, but here let us look at how he is able to explain what looks like logical thinking in animals. He asks us to consider what looks like rational action on the part of gazelles who see a lion and then run away. This may look like a logical inference: if you see a lion, then you should run; you see a lion; therefore, you should run. However, Bermúdez claims this behavior is really causal reasoning of a sort. The material conditional can be understood causally, so the gazelle really thinks as such: lions cause me to run; lion here; therefore, I run. Causal understanding is based on sensitivity to the regularities one encounters in the environment, and while animals may not have a full understanding of causality, which would require them to make a distinction between accidental conjunctions and true causes, they have at least a proto-understanding of causality. And it is causality, not rationality, which allows the animals to engage in rational-looking behavior.

However, it isn't clear that Bermúdez's account can help us understand the behaviors that are better candidates for rational behavior. Gazelles running from lions isn't exactly the most compelling case for rational inference in animals, after all! While Bermúdez doesn't apply his account to the case of Chrysippus' dog, we can examine whether his account offers a plausible alternative. Since a disjunction is logically equivalent to a conditional with negation, and Bermúdez thinks we can account for negation in terms of contraries, he should accept that the dog's rational inference can be understood as proto-causal reasoning. Consider this:

Traditional formulation of the Chrysippus problem

1   A v B v C. (The rabbit ran down path A or the rabbit ran down path B or the rabbit ran down path C.)
2   ~ A. (The rabbit didn't run down path A.)
3   ~ B. (The rabbit didn't run down path B.)
4   Therefore C. (The rabbit ran down path C.)

Since p v q is equivalent to ~p -> q (for example, saying that either it rains or we hold a picnic is equivalent to saying that if it doesn't rain, we hold a picnic), we can rewrite the disjunction as a conditional:

Conditional version of the Chrysippus problem

1   ~ A -> (~ B -> C)
2   ~ A
3   ~ B
4   Therefore C.

Then, we convert the conditional and negations into statements of causes and contraries:

Causal version of the Chrysippus problem

1   No A causes (no B causes C).
2   No A.
3   No B.
4   C.

In plain English, the causal version of the problem shows that the dog perceived a causal relation between the lack of smells on the first two paths and the existence of the rabbit on the third, based on regularities encountered in the past. The dog thinks smells cause the existence of rabbits, or some such thing, and so he avoids the path that lacks the smell, seeking instead the path that has it.

But does this explain why the dog would have run down the third path without first sniffing? Unless that very same scenario had been learned through repeated exposures to it, Bermúdez's account can't explain why the dog thought that the absence of smell causes the absence of a rabbit. Furthermore, the first step in the causal reasoning is quite strange: no smell on A causes no smell on B which causes smell on C. It is hard to imagine what sort of experience would lead the dog to make that causal connection. It isn't clear that what looks like conditional reasoning can always be explained in terms of causal reasoning.

Even if Bermúdez's account doesn't offer a compelling explanation for the Chrysippus problem, we shouldn't jump to the conclusion that the dog did engage in logical reasoning. Again we reach the point where a conclusion cannot be justified without having tested a number of possible explanations. Our lack of creativity in coming up with theories about mechanisms for a behavior needs to be constantly checked before we can confidently accept a particular conclusion. For example, Michael Rescorla offers an alternative account of how the dog may have reasoned without propositional thought. By employing a Bayesian model lifted from robotics, he suggests that we can explain the dog's action by appeal to the dog's ability to unconsciously form and update probability formulas over mental maps given changes in perceptual information (Rescorla 2009a).

Likewise, if Bermúdez does offer a plausible alternative explanation, it wouldn't exhaust the possibilities. For example, Ronaldo Vigo and Colin Allen offer an explanation of rational-seeming behavior in nonlinguistic creatures that does follow inference rules. They show how inference rules can be understood via subsymbolic processes that compute similarity (Vigo and Allen 2009). They offer the following argument:

1   Logical connectives (conditional, biconditional, etc.) define modal similarity categories.
2   Inference is reducible to conditional categorization.
3   Hence, inference is modal similarity categorization.
4   Modal similarity categorization is a pre-linguistic process.
5   Hence, inference is a pre-linguistic process.

(Vigo and Allen 2009, 80)

Others also worry about drawing too hasty a conclusion in either direction. In his criticism of Bermúdez's argument against animal metacognition, the philosopher Robert Lurz argues that Bermúdez is approaching an empirical question by treating it as an *a priori* one, and that instead we should be asking what can the animals do in order to help us determine alternative methods for engaging in the behaviors in question. Contrary to Bermúdez's claim, we shouldn't accept that thinking about thoughts requires thinking about public language sentences (Lurz 2007). Young children are able to think about thoughts despite the fact that they are not all that great at what Bermúdez terms second-order cognitive dynamics, things like considering one's evidence for a belief, or realizing how beliefs are logically related to one another. Lurz cites the psychologist David Moshman who thinks that this sort of understanding doesn't emerge until ten years, though children are able to talk about what others believe around four years.

Whether there are two systems or two kinds of thought, and humans have both but animals only have one, or whether there are a number of gradations or varieties in thought are questions for further research. As we saw, dual systems theorists generally think that we have one quick system of cognition that is evolutionarily old, unconscious, and automatic that we share with animals (System 1), and a slow deliberate rational system that is unique to humans and may be language dependent (System 2). We saw evidence for this sort of distinction in the research on numerosity as well, where humans seem to have two systems that manipulate different kinds of content—analog magnitudes and numbers—while animals only have one.

In another version of this sort of view, Tamar Gendler suggests that animals lack representational belief, but instead have something she calls *alief* (Gendler 2008). The content of an alief is not a proposition, and it doesn't track reality in the way belief does (though it is sensitive to the environment). Alief is associative, automatic, arational, affect-laden, and action-generating. It is also conceptually prior to the other attitudes. Gendler suggests that humans have both alief and belief, while animals generally only have alief. While Gendler doesn't examine the implications of her view for research on animal cognition, it is a natural question.

Ian Apperly and Stephen Butterfill have also developed their own version of the two systems hypothesis in the context of belief reasoning. While infants and animals have a fast and inflexible system for tracking belief and belief-like states, older humans also have a more cognitively demanding theory of mind system (Apperly and Butterfill 2009). As we will see in Chapter 6, they use the existence of these two systems to explain why infants and animals pass some theory of mind tasks and fail others.

Part of the motivation of dual systems approaches to the mind comes from the desire not to overintellectualize cognition. As Morgan warned us, we must try to look at our own cognition carefully to see how fancy-seeming actions can arise out of simple mechanisms. The philosopher Susan Hurley has done much to argue for the existence of middle grounds between having full-fledged context-free concepts and arationality. In her work she argues against the traditional view of cognition as that which intervenes between perception and action. Hurley advocates a version of enaction according to which practical rationality is sufficient for acting for reasons (Hurley 2003). Having reasons for action doesn't require consciousness of those reasons, but it does involve normative constraints embodied by the individual.

Peter Carruthers suggests that we need not overintellectualize cognition while adopting a single system account of the mind. He argues that while humans and animals do demonstrate cognitive differences, there is no evidence that animals have an older System 1 and humans have a System 1 in addition to a more recent System 2 (Carruthers 2011, 2013). In part because Carruthers thinks that animals fulfill a weakened version of the generality constraint, he argues that humans and animals share a central workspace where the perceptual representations we form can be globally broadcast to various part of our cognitive system and used to make inferences and inform action. Evidence that nonhumans also have these abilities comes from studies on episodic, and other kinds of memory, as well as future planning, like those discussed in Chapter 3 as well as from evidence of insight behavior. Such studies suggest that animals can mentally rehearse representations, and manipulate them. While humans add to this ability inner speech, the difference in actions doesn't entail a difference in mental architecture or a difference in the kinds of propositions that humans and animals can entertain. There is no evidence for the existence of a special workplace, unique to humans, for abstract propositional attitudes where they enter into inferences with other propositional attitudes on some chalkboard of the brain.

4.2.5 Metacognitive capacities

In dual systems accounts of cognition, the newer System 2 has rationality, language, and metacognition, and some philosophers and psychologists will place the ability to have beliefs alongside those other capacities. Representationalists are clearly interested in the structure of cognition—and we saw in the last chapter that HO theories of consciousness may require metacognitive capacities—but even for some nonrepresentationalists, metacognitive capacities matter. For example, in a much-discussed argument against animal belief, Donald Davidson argues that rationality, language, and metacognition go hand in hand with having beliefs. Animals do not have beliefs, because having beliefs requires that we can think about our thoughts, and we can only think about our thoughts by representing them in language.

According to Davidson's version of interpretationism, we ascribe beliefs to others by adopting a principle of charity and assuming that others are rational—that their beliefs will be largely consistent. If someone's behavior doesn't meet this requirement, then she doesn't have beliefs. Beliefs exist insofar as there is a community of attributors whose behavior meets this minimal criterion. Thus, beliefs exist in a community in which the members ascribe beliefs to another. For this reason, Davidson thinks that "a creature cannot have thoughts unless it is an interpreter of the speech of another" (Davidson 1975, 9).

Davidson motivates this idea by suggesting that to have a belief one must have a concept of belief, which includes understanding that beliefs are the sorts of things that are true or false. After all, you can't believe that P without also believing that P is true, which requires having the concept of *truth*. And when you use the principle of charity, you have to consider which beliefs would be true and which would be false. Since sentences (and propositions) are the only sorts of things that can be true or false, the believers in the community must use sentences—language—and hence all believers will be language users who have the metacognitive ability to think about their own, and others', thought.

Once I have the concept of belief, I can be surprised, which means that I can realize I was wrong about a proposition I used to believe. While animals can be startled, can discriminate between stimuli in their environment, and can learn and engage in flexible behavior, Davidson says this isn't sufficient to demonstrate belief. An animal can adjust his behavior after being startled by using some associative processes, without considering that he had a belief that was false!

As we discussed earlier, Davidson thinks that an understanding of error can be arrived at only by acquiring a language, and offers what is known as the triangulation argument to defend this view. It is only with language that we can escape the tyranny of subjectivity, and realize that there are multiple ways of conceiving of the same state of affairs. The understanding of objectivity requires two individuals communicating with one another about some object in the world. It is through triangulation of this sort that the concept of truth arises.

There have been a variety of responses to Davidson's position. A central weakness of Davidson's argument is with the claim that to have a belief one needs a concept of belief. One challenge to that premise comes from the possible existence of individuals who speak yet who do not attribute beliefs. Autistic speakers, individuals who fail in metacognitive tasks yet are able to communicate using language suggest that some thinkers don't have the concept of belief (Andrews 2002; Andrews and Radenovic 2006; Glüer and Pagin 2003). The argument could go like this:

1   Some speakers, such as autistic speakers, don't attribute beliefs.
2   All speakers are thinkers.
3   Therefore, some thinkers don't attribute beliefs.

This existence of people with autism who do not attribute beliefs but who act as if they do have beliefs raises a *prima facie* worry for Davidson's position. According to Davidson's theory of meaning, all and only those who attribute beliefs have language, which would suggest that the autistic speakers don't have language, either. But since they speak, they certainly appear to have language! Davidson may bite the bullet and claim that autistic speakers do attribute beliefs, but then it isn't clear what attributing beliefs actually amounts to, given that the individuals in question speak yet fail metacognitive tasks.

Another challenge to the idea that having a belief requires having the concept of belief comes from Hans-Johann Glock (2000). Consider Davidson's argument as presented by Glock:

1   A belief is something that can be true or false.
2   To believe that p requires being able to be mistaken in believing that p.
3   To believe that p requires being able to recognize that one is mistaken.
4   To believe that p requires having the concept of a mistake.
5   Therefore, to have a belief one must have the concept of belief (because the concept of a mistake requires the concept of a belief).

Glock (2000, 54)

Glock worries about the third and fourth premises of this argument. In response to the third premise, Glock argues that the claim is too strong, and that, to be mistaken, one only needs to change one's belief and does not have to have an additional metacognitive belief about the prior false belief. As an example, Michael Tye suggests that you can come back to the lot where you had parked your car and, not seeing it, come to believe that your car has been stolen (Tye 1997). In response to that belief, you start to walk to the security office, but as you move in that direction you see your car parked on the other side of the street, and you recall that you had parked it there. So of course you change your direction and walk toward your car, without necessarily reflecting on the mistake. Tye takes this as an example of revising a belief in the face of new perceptual evidence without explicit recognition of the mistake.

The fourth premise is also problematic, thinks Glock, because we can be capable of recognizing a mistake and hence understand the possibility of being mistaken without having the concept of mistake. Instead, it is sufficient to recognize that this object that you initially thought was edible isn't edible after all, for example. Glock uses the analogy of singing in the key of C: one can be capable of singing in the key of C, and recognize that one isn't singing in the key of C, without ever having the concept key of C.

Furthermore, Glock also thinks there are examples of nonlinguistic creatures who have beliefs about the beliefs of others. He suggests that chimpanzees' ability to recognize mistaken beliefs in others, and to take advantage of others' mistaken beliefs in deception, counts as evidence of a kind of nonverbal triangulation.

Davidson's arguments also raise questions about the development of language, communication, and belief in human children. Since these capacities all require one another, and as research in developmental psychology suggests, there doesn't seem to be room for a stage-wise development of the concept of belief, much less the development of language.

4.2.6 Animal logic

If beliefs are propositions, and propositions obey logical constraints, then we should be able to examine propositional thought in animals by examining their logical reasoning abilities. At Lou Herman's dolphin cognition lab in Honolulu, four bottlenose dolphins learned to understand a gestural system of communication. The dolphins knew verbs, nouns, and modifiers such as *left* and *right*. When I was working as an intern at the dolphin lab in the early 1990s, the dolphins were being taught to add two new symbols to their communicative system: *and* and *erase*. The *and* sign was supposed to have the same function as "and" in English, and *erase* served the same function as negation. Akeakamai was taught to respond to the *and* symbol by performing two actions in a row; for example, when the trainer gestured *surfboard tailtouch and hoop under*, Akeakamai would perform each action. And when the trainer gestured *surfboard tailtouch erase*, Akeakamai would do nothing. While Akeakamai did well responding to these commands, it wasn't clear how she understood them. Because Akeakamai usually responded to the second conjunct first in the *and* gestures, perhaps she took it to be an ordering relation rather than a conjunctive one.

I was particularly interested in the introduction of what might be seen as logical connectives to the dolphins' communicative system, because with *and* and *erase* (understood as "not") we could test the dolphin's ability to recognize that two syntactically distinct symbols are semantically equivalent. For example, in the semantics as the researchers understood it, *surfboard tailtouch* is logically equivalent to *hoop under erase and surfboard tailtouch*. Because Akeakamai was also competent at marking object pairs as same or different, I thought that we could examine Akeakamai's ability to recognize that two different strings of symbols had the same meaning. Unfortunately, so far as I know, that study was never carried out.

While "language trained" animals offer particularly enticing opportunities of tests of logical reasoning abilities, researchers have also devised clever experiments to uncover whether animals can engage in different kinds of reasoning, such as transitive inference or reasoning from exclusion. While perhaps some of the best evidence of transitive inference reasoning comes from the monkeys who are able to keep track of dominance relations, and update dominance relations in a way sensitive to the transitive properties of the dominance relationship, there is a large body of research investigating whether other species can engage in transitive reasoning in controlled laboratory tasks. Rats, pigeons, pinyon jays, scrub jays, hooded crows, fish, and monkeys have been trained on versions of the 5-element transitive inference task, in which they are trained that A is rewarded over B, B is rewarded over C, C is rewarded over D, and D is rewarded over E (see Vasconcelos 2008 for a review of the findings). Once they have mastered each of these pairs, the subjects are then tested to see how they respond to a choice between B and D. Subjects reliably chose B, even though in training B was rewarded the same number of times as D was rewarded, thus suggesting that the subjects formed a representation of a transitive relationship between the elements of the set. Of course, there may be other ways of solving the task that don't require transitive inference. For example, it may be that an appeal to the kind of error-correcting rules that connectionist networks use in learning would be sufficient for solving these transitive inference tasks without needing any kind of inference reasoning (De Lillo et al. 2001). In his discussion of how best to understand transitive inference reasoning in animals, Allen suggests that the better evidence for transitive inference reasoning would come from ecological versions of the task, which wouldn't require such an elaborate training regime to begin with (Allen 2006).

Another area in which researchers have been focused on logical reasoning in animals has been in the exclusion reasoning task—which gives subjects a problem like the one Chrysippus' dog solved. Exclusion reasoning requires reasoning in terms of the disjunctive syllogism:

1   A or B.
2   Not A.
3   Therefore, B.

It turns out that dogs might be able to act in the way Chrysippus described, so long as there is no human around to challenge the dog's own epistemic authority (Erdőhegyi et al. 2007). Exclusion tests have been done on great apes, dogs, and corvids.

When food is hidden in one of two containers, apes will look in the containers when they haven't watched the baiting of the container, but won't look when they did witness the baiting or when one of the containers is transparent (Call 2004, 2006; Marsh and MacDonald 2012; Erdőhegyi et al. 2007). Furthermore, when apes don't watch the baiting, but are shown that one of two containers is empty, they won't look in the other container but instead immediately reach into it and retrieve the food they infer is there. There is evidence that monkeys, corvids, and dogs also can, in some cases, reason by exclusion. And exclusion reasoning may help to explain the fast mapping of new toy names demonstrated by the border collies discussed in Chapter 1.

Recall that Fodor thinks that humans and animals share cognitive styles in logical reasoning—for example, humans have more difficulty with disjunction than they do with conjunction or negation. However, the research on animal logic is still young, and there haven't been a lot of studies on logical abilities in other species. Comparative research that looks to compare children's developing logical abilities with the different kinds of logical abilities we see in other species can help us to come to see in what ways various species might enjoy logical reasoning ability, and if logical reasoning requires having belief, such work will offer evidence of animal belief as well.

4.3 Chapter summary

While many philosophers agree that animals have concepts, belief, or rationality, their reasoning for these conclusions takes very different forms. And what they mean by concepts, belief, or rationality likewise varies. Apparent agreement on the question "Do animals have beliefs?" may be deceptive.

While the calibration method can be used to help clarify our understanding of the nature of belief, it may also force us to distinguish different ideas that we are using the same word to describe. The kind of belief that is of interest to the representationalist is quite different from the kind of belief that the interpretationist talks about. And it is in discussions of animal belief that cross talk is pernicious. Particularly when we come to ascribe content to animals' beliefs, we run into worries about inappropriate anthropomorphism. For example, a dog owner might attribute to her dog the belief that he should protect the children, and use that attribution to explain the dog's behavior when strangers approach. That attribution might be appropriate from an interpretationist standpoint, but not correspond to any representation that the dog has (and the same disjoint can be seen in our attributions to humans). And so the worry about inappropriate anthropomorphism may be dissolved by realizing that the dog owner is using a different sense of the word "belief" than the critic is.

So, one way to answer the question "Do animals have beliefs?" is with another question— "What do you want to know?" If you want to know whether animals have representations that obey systematicity or logical constraints, you can answer this question by doing research on the structure of animal reasoning. If you want to know whether folk psychological ascriptions permit a robust predictive power that you didn't antecendently have, you can spend a lot of time with an animal and interpret its behavior in some folk- or critter-psychological terms.

This is the same point Steven Stich made in his 1979 paper against animal belief. But since the question hasn't been refined in subsequent years, it is worth noting again. Belief appears to be an umbrella concept, and without clarifying the aspect of belief that we are interested in, both empirical research and philosophical investigation into the question of animal belief will suffer.

Further reading

The *Stanford Encyclopedia of Philosophy* (http://plato.stanford.edu/) is a great online resource for learning more about the philosophical theories discussed in this chapter. In particular, see David Pitt's *Stanford* entry "Mental Representation" and Eric Schwitzgebel's entry "Belief."

The two classic arguments against animal belief by Davidson and Stich are worth going back to: "Rational animals" by Donald Davidson (1982), and "Do animals have beliefs?" by Stephen Stitch (1979).

In the chapter "Do animals have beliefs?" in his *Brainchildren: Essays on Designing Minds* (1998), Daniel Dennett gives an interpretationist argument for animal belief.

José Bermúdez offers an extended empirically informed argument that animals can think even though they are not rational in his book *Thinking Without Words* (2003).

The anthology *Rational Animals?* edited by Susan Hurley and Matthew Nudds (2006) offers an important overview of arguments about the nature of rationality in animals from philosophy and psychology.

5 Communication

Cecep walks over to Anne and sits down in front of her. He is filthy from wrestling in the dust with his buddies, dirt and twigs sticking out of his hair. Sitting across from Anne, he picks a leaf and hands it to her. Anne looks at the leaf and drops it on the ground. Cecep picks another leaf, then briefly rubs the leaf back and forth on top of his head before handing it to Anne. This time Anne uses the leaf to clean the twigs and dirt form Cecep's head.

This scenario looks like an example of communication, a case of clarifying a message in the face of misunderstanding. Cecep wanted Anne to clean him off, and he handed her a leaf to signal his desire. Because Anne often cleaned Cecep's head with a leaf, he expected her to understand what he meant. But this time she pretended that she didn't understand. So Cecep had to come up with another way of letting Anne know what he wanted; he acted it out for her. That was enough to make Anne get it, and she was able to do what he wanted her to do.

This story, and this interpretation of the story, sounds normal enough until you find out that Cecep is an orangutan and Anne is a human. When the two interacting characters are humans, the question of whether they were communicating and what was being communicated seems trivial and the answer is obvious. But when a nonhuman is involved, the standards of evidence for the interpretation rise. Cecep's behavior, and the behavior of other orangutans who pantomime what they want done to them, was the topic of a paper I wrote with Anne Russon, the Anne of the story above (Russon and Andrews 2011a). We argue that these orangutans are engaged in communicative acts, and that they use gesture to communicate. But others were not convinced. Some scientists suggest that the orangutan's actions were accidental, and were just interpreted as a request. Anne and I are convinced that Cecep's actions were not accidental and were a request, given the frequency we had observed him and the other young orangutans in his social group acting out the things that they wanted, and the frustration that arose when requests were not answered compared with the calm following the requests that were granted. It was also striking that this behavior was always directed at a human, and not another orangutan.

If Cecep was a human infant and Anne was his mother, there would be little concern about whether Cecep was really communicating. Since infants turn into language users, and language users are the paradigmatic communicators, less evidence is needed to demonstrate that an infant is communicating. But is the fact that a child will be a language user in the future genuinely relevant to the question of whether she is now communicating? We can't take that line of reasoning too far, because a six-month-old human fetus will also typically turn into a language user, and yet a pregnant woman who claims that she can communicate with her fetus would be looked upon with skepticism, even though there is an intimate relationship between the mother and the fetus, and they are constantly responding to each other's movements and biological processes. They are dynamically linked in a co-regulating relationship, but they are not doing anything we would typically understand as communicating. So mere potentiality for being a communicator doesn't a communicator make.

While the example with Cecep and Anne is a rather unusual case of communication between members of two species, communication of some sort appears to be common across many animal taxa. We see it in the social insects. Honeybees who come back from foraging will dance to indicate the location of a food source to other members of the hive (von Frisch 1967). Ant foragers will lay a pheromone trail from a food source back to the nest, which is followed by other ants (Aron et al. 1993). Swimmers also communicate. Golden shiner fish are able to arrive at consensus about which of two paths to take even though none of the individuals have a preference for the path (Miller et al. 2013). Male cuttlefish change their coloring when courting a female, but can deceive rival males by displaying female coloring only on the side of the body nearest the rival while continuing to present the courting color to the female (Brown et al. 2012).

Birds communicate as well. Chickens give different calls in the presence of food (Evans and Evans 1999). Ravens will gesture with their beaks and use eye contact to coordinate interactions with nonfood items such as twigs or moss (Pika and Bugnyar 2011). And mammals communicate too; for example, baboons have at least 14 different vocalizations verified by playback experiments, including alarm calls, reconciliation grunts, fear barks, contact barks, and threat grunts (Cheney and Seyfarth 2007). Prairie dogs (Kiriazis and Slobodchikoff 2006) and meerkats (Manser 2001) also have distinct alarm calls they use to warn group members about the appearance of various predators.

All these examples of communication share something; they involve two or more organisms coordinating their behaviors. But what else do they have in common? And how do they differ? Are they all instances of the same kind of communication? While linguistic communication is perhaps the variety of communication we are most familiar with, investigation can shed light on communication in nonlinguistic creatures. To untangle these questions we can look into what we really are interested in when we speak about communication. And we can examine what sorts of things animals can communicate about.

5.1 What is communication?

Humans obviously communicate using language, through spoken word as well as in writing, for example in books like this one. But humans also communicate in more subtle ways. We communicate a lot through body language, sometimes intentionally, with a smile or a touch, other times unintentionally. For example, our implicit racism can be communicated through body language, as indicated in a study of how white TV characters used more guarded body language when interacting with black characters than they did when interacting with white characters, even when the black and white characters shared the same high status (Weisbuch et al. 2009).

There are three importantly different kinds of theories of communication: biological theories, information processing theories, and intentional theories. As may already be obvious from the examples of purported communication presented so far, there are stronger and weaker constraints on what counts as communication. The biological approach to communication, which calls the behavior of ants and bees communicative, is the most minimal when it comes to cognitive requirements, whereas intentional accounts of communication can be very demanding. We will look at each account in turn.

5.1.1 Biological accounts

Biologists describe communication as a relationship between two organisms such that a change in the state of one organism causes a change in the state of the other organism. Maynard-Smith and Harper define communication as "any act or structure which alters the behaviors of other organisms, which evolved because of that effect, and which is effective because the receiver's response has also evolved" (Maynard-Smith and Harper 2003, 3). This account is a development of the view of communication held by biologist Richard Dawkins and zoologist John Krebs, which required two criteria: the behavior causes a change in the receiver and that change is beneficial to the sender (Dawkins and Krebs 1978). The courting cuttlefish is communicating to the female, because his change in coloring causes the female to approach, the courting color evolved in order to attract females, and it benefits the male to attract females. The cuttlefish is also communicating to the male who sees him present female coloring, because it causes the rival male to leave him alone, and that is an obvious benefit to a male seeking a mate.

This account of communication can also be used to describe human linguistic communication, in which one person's utterance of a sentence causes a change of belief in the communicative partner (assuming of course that language evolved for communicative purposes), because minimal criteria for communication are able to accommodate all candidate communicative interactions. But minimal criteria for communication also permit much simpler behavior to count as communicative. For example, bean plants who tell wasps to come and eat irritating bugs, and who can warn other bean plants of pests to come, are communicating. Why? Because a bean plant infested with aphids produces a chemical that attracts wasps to eat the aphids, and it will also send signals through fungus threads that connect the roots of neighboring plants, causing those other plants to produce the substance as a prophylactic (Babikova et al. 2013). Take another example: a fertilized egg will only be successfully implanted in a uterus if the uterus first sends the correct signals (Mohamed et al. 2005). Systems biology is rife with examples of cell signaling and communication.

Deceptive communication is also possible on this account. If the signaler derives some fitness benefit from signaling false information that causes another organism to engage in some behavior, then the signaler is deceptively communicating. Some plants are able to deceive in this way. For example, orchid species attract male wasps by looking like, and smelling like, female wasps. The males are attracted to the flower because of its appearance and its production of a chemical that smells like the mating pheromone of females, and the wasps try to mate with the flower. While the attempt at copulation fails for the wasp, it is extremely beneficial to the flower, because when the wasp flies off to try to mate with the next flower, he carries the flower's pollen on his head and deposits it on the new flower's stigma.

On this account of communication, Cecep and Anne were clearly communicating; the orangutan's behavior prompted the human's change in behavior (and vice versa). But that makes the answer to the communication question too simple. Though many animal cognition researchers use the biological sense of communication in their discussion of animal communication, this isn't the question we have before us about Anne and Cecep. The biological notion of communication is silent on intentionality—the ability of minds to think about something—and if we are interested in whether animals can communicate their thoughts— intentional communication—a different theory is required.

5.1.2 Information-based accounts

Computer scientists, linguists, mathematicians, and philosophers have offered an alternative, suggesting that communication is better understood as the exchange of information from one party to another. The mathematician Claude Shannon introduced the idea that a communication system involves a message sender that transmits a signal through some medium to a receiver that reconstructs the signal for the intended recipient of the message (Shannon and Weaver 1949). The message is seen as information that is encoded by the sender and decoded by the receiver.

Information processing accounts of communication raise the question of what counts as information. Not just any signal can be informative, since information signals are often accompanied by irrelevant noise. When someone speaks to you in a crowded coffee shop, the words and perhaps body language are part of the medium of the information being transferred, and the others chatting around the speaker are mere noise in the auditory signal. In order to address the question of what counts as information, Dretske suggests we understand information as a means of reducing uncertainty in the receiver, such that the probability of some state of affairs increases given the signal (Dretske 1981).

The information exchange model of communication is also one that is accepted by some animal cognition researchers (Wheeler et al. 2011). Like the biological model, the information model is non-cognitive, and so it permits researchers to talk about animal cognition without making any assumptions about the cognitive mechanism involved in the communicative act. For example, the honeybee dance can also be described in information exchange terms. The dancing bee encodes the location and quality of a potential new hive site and transmits it via a dance, which is decoded by the other bees who fly to the location and then return to the swarm to begin their own dances. The swarm uses the information gathered and communicated by the scout bees who return to the swarm and relay the information to other scouts. When all (or most) of the scouts dance for the same hive site, the scouts communicate to the bees in the rest of the swarm that it is time to take off and fly to the new site (Seeley and Visscher 2003).

Some information accounts combine the informational content with an action guiding aspect. For example, Millikan refers to the simplest animal representations as *pushmi-pullyu*, in order to convey the idea that they simultaneously give information about the situation and information about how to respond to the situation (Millikan 2006). These double-aspect representations lack the systematicity we find in natural language, and so are not couched in either external language or in some language of thought. Since the representations both describe what is the case and what should be done about it, Millikan suggests that they can serve as the mechanisms behind Gibsonian affordances, or perceptions that are inextricably tied up with actions; for example, a liana is perceived as something to swing from and a certain orientation of branches in a tree is seen as nestable. Millikan suggests that some animal signals, like the dances of bees, the chemical signaling of ants, and other fixed-action patterns, are best understood as mediated via pushmi-pullyu representations. Humans also commonly represent pushmi-pullyu relations. For example, it's a pushmi-pullyu representation of a particle that causes us to blink when any small object approaches our face; the blink both represents the object and is a response to it.

Pushmi-pullyu representations are intentional in the sense that they represent what they are about, even though they are not voluntary, or even necessarily something we need to be aware of. But they are limited to representing relations between objects or states of affairs and the perceiver. They don't allow for understanding objective properties or relations between two objects, and they cannot ground metacognition. For this reason, Millikan thinks that many human representations and signals, and probably many animals' representations and signals as well, will be more complex than pushmi-pullyu representations.

While Millikan doesn't include machines in her account, artifacts can also fit the double aspect of representing the world and telling another artifact what to do. Consider a time bomb; the clock represents the time, and tells the bomb to go off. The clock is communicating this information to the bomb, and the bomb responds appropriately given that information. Because informational accounts can include natural as well as artificial design, artifacts and artificial systems such as computer networks can communicate as well. Like the biological account of communication, this widening of the class of communicative interactions doesn't allow us to answer the question we are interested in, namely, were Cecep and Anne communicating in the way two humans do? To answer that question, we need to turn to intentional theories of communication.

5.1.3 Intentional accounts

If you want to know whether Cecep and Anne were *really* communicating, you might be thinking that there is something missing from the above accounts. Philosophical accounts of intentional communication have largely focused on human communication. What does it mean to say that two people are communicating? Can I intentionally communicate things I don't mean to communicate, like the TV characters who demonstrated their implicit racism? Am I communicating to you when you overhear my conversation with another person? We generally think not. The implicit racist's behaviors give us information about her, but such behavior is usually taken to be inflexible and automatic. Furthermore, the implicit racist doesn't know that she is expressing racist views, nor does she know that her audience is picking up on the message. This points us toward two basic elements we can associate with intentional communication: it needs to be flexible, and it requires expecting that another receives the message.

The discussion that follows is focused on various ways of cashing out the second criterion for intentional communication. There are three main approaches to intentional communication that involve different cognitive requirements: Gricean accounts that require having a theory of mind to communicate, weaker Gricean accounts such as intentional-semantics which require some understanding that other minds exist, and dynamical systems accounts, which are silent on cognitive mechanism, and instead stress co-regulation and behavior coordination between communicative partners.

Let us now look at how these accounts have been applied to nonhuman primates.

5.1.3.1 Gricean communication

An influential account of intentional communication comes from the work of the philosopher H.P. Grice, whose analysis of a speaker's meaning in terms of the speaker's communicative intentions is reflected in contemporary discussions of communication in children and other animals. Grice suggests that when we communicate with one another, we need to think about what others are thinking in order to understand what they mean; the words alone do not have meaning. In this way, Grice takes pragmatics to be an essential part of communication, because the context always needs to be considered to know what someone means. For Grice, a speaker means something by an utterance x if and only if the speaker utters x with the intention that: (1) it produces a response in the intended audience; (2) the audience recognizes the speaker's first intention; and (3) the audience's recognition of the speaker's first intention serves as a reason for the audience responding as it does (Grice 1957). When two agents interact in a meaningful way, they are communicating.

The Gricean account of communication is able to offer cognitive explanations of phenomena that appear to be communicative, however, it forces a high-level interpretation of what the communicative partners are up to. Dennett suggests we need a third-order belief (e.g. I *think* that she *thinks* that I *think*) to fulfill Grice's three conditions (Dennett 1987). If that is right, then only individuals with a sophisticated theory of mind, who are able to think about other's beliefs about beliefs, are able to communicate. This leaves out young infants and probably most animals. For example, in his article "Intentional Systems in Cognitive Ethology" Dennett addresses the question of what communicative animal calls might mean (Dennett 1983). To illustrate the issue, he discusses the vervet monkey alarm calls studied by Cheney, Seyfarth, and Marler. When a vervet monkey sees an eagle in the sky above his troop, then it is reasonable to predict that the monkey will utter the eagle alarm cry. Dennett offers the following possible interpretations of the monkey's alarm cry as:

First-order: The monkey *wants* to cause the other monkeys to run into the bushes.
Second-order: The monkey *wants* the other monkeys to *believe* that there is an eagle.

The first-order interpretation would make the monkey's vocalization non-meaningful and hence non-communicative on this view. But even the second-order interpretation, as richly mentalistic as it is, wouldn't suffice as a meaningful utterance. In order to make it meaningful on this account we would have to add that the monkey wanted the other monkeys to believe that he uttered the eagle alarm cry in order to give them a reason to run into the bushes.

So, in order to communicate, an animal would need third-order intentionality—the ability to think about the beliefs others have about one's own belief. The Gricean theory of communication, according to some interpretations, sets a very high standard. The interaction between Anne and Cecep wouldn't be classified as communication, because Cecep almost certainly lacks third-order intentionality. Individuals who lack a theory of mind—which some think includes white middle class Westerners younger than four (Wellman et al. 2001), Tainae from Papua New Guinea younger than 14 years (Vinden 1999), some people on the autistic spectrum, and perhaps all nonhuman animals—would not count as communicators. Babies may coo while looking in your eyes, they may call out "Mama" and "Dada", and they may point and yell out,"ba! ba!" every time they see a ball. But on the strong Gricean view, these babies mean nothing at all. And even once toddlers start stringing words together, they almost certainly lack the third-order intentionality the strong Gricean view requires for communication, so having a language isn't sufficient for communicating on his view. Such a counterintuitive consequence should lead us to question the strong Gricean account of communication.

5.1.3.2 Weaker versions of intentional communication

Rather than requiring that third-order intentionality be a necessary condition for communication, many who want to retain a kind of intention-based semantics but who are critical of the strong Gricean picture as too stringent to even account for human communication weaken the strong view requirements in various ways (Gómez 2007; Moore 2014; Sperber and Wilson 1986).

For Neo-Griceans, ostension is offered as a way of showing intention without requiring complex metacognition. Ostensive communication has two parts, a message and a signal that the message is intended. When we point at an apple, we direct attention to that apple. But the

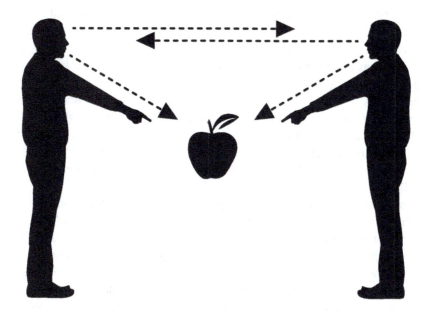

Figure 5.2 Eye contact with pointing is an example of an ostensive cue that signals intention.

point might not have been intended for anyone in particular, and it may have merely been some kind of truncated reaching for the apple. When we add an ostensive cue to the point, such as making eye contact with a recipient, we are able to show our intention that the recipient see the apple.

Eye contact is certainly used in many human cultures to signal intention; the eyes send many messages. Some of these messages can be aggressive. And what eye contact means might vary from species to species. For example, it is claimed that gorillas find eye contact aversive because it signals a threat, and people are advised to avoid eye contact with vicious dogs or bears for the same reason (see Argyle and Cook 1976; Goodenough et al. 1993). Young infants engage in eye contact with their mothers during an early stage of development that the psychologist Colwyn Trevarthen calls primary intersubjectivity (1979). Based on the coordinated behaviors of infants and mothers, Trevarthen thinks that humans are born into a world of intentionality and have much of the cognitive equipment of the social agent at birth. Infants can show that they are consciously regulating their interactions with a caregiver by using ostensive signals such as eye contact. By the time infants reach their ninth month, they are able to coordinate their body movements such as points with eye contact in a way that we naturally interpret as intentional communication.

Coordination is key to interpreting behavior as intentional communication. When behaviors and utterances are made appropriate to the social context, such as the give and take of conversation or the smiles in response to a smile, we read the interaction as meaningful and interpret our communicative partner as understanding our intentions. When human infants begin to coordinate their behavior in this way around nine months, they are moving from the dyadic phase of primary intersubjectivity, at which they are either engaged with an agent or with an object (but not both at the same time), to triadic interactions, the stage at which they share their object play with other people. Trevarthen calls this move to triadic interactions *secondary intersubjectivity*. He interprets this shift in behavior in terms of new motivations to act cooperatively. Human infants from 8 to 12 months engage in social play with others, with simple actions like offering a rattle to Mommy after trying and failing to manipulate it oneself, or inviting Mommy to pretend-bite a ball by pretend-biting the ball and handing it to her (Hubley 1983, as cited in Gómez 2010). Soon afterwards, infants begin engaging in more complex cooperative behaviors, such as digging a hole together in a sandbox, or pretending to serve tea. Around the point of the nine-month revolution, Trevarthen claims children have a rudimentary understanding of persons that allows them to participate in joint cooperative actions (Trevarthen and Hubley 1978).

While Trevarthen and many contemporary psychologists think that the cooperative interactions we see in human infants are uniquely human, the primatologist Juan-Carlos Gómez finds similar behavior among other great apes, including chimpanzees and gorillas. Using Trevarethan's criteria for secondary intersubjectivity, he analyzed the behavior of a captive infant gorilla named Muni, who was raised by humans at the Madrid Zoo in the early 1980s (Gómez 2010). By following Muni's behavior during the period of 6 to 36 months old, Gómez was able to systematically compare Muni's cooperative behavior with the typical cooperative behavior of human infants using the descriptive categories that Trevarthen and colleagues used in their studies. Gómez found two revolutionary periods in the development of Muni's cooperative behavior: at 18 months the gorilla started engaging in cooperative behaviors much more frequently, and at 30 months the complexity of the interactions also increased:

OBSERVATION 2: (10 months; 11-10-80). H shows M how to put pebbles through a hole in a big hollow plastic rectangular block. H then offers the block and the pebbles to Muni, who picks them up and laboriously tries to put the pebbles through the hole, first unsuccessfully with her hand, then successfully with her mouth [IMITATION]. MUNI then turns over the block and tries to retrieve the pebbles; H helps her by holding and moving the block together with her, which Muni accepts [ACCEPTS ASSISTANCE].

(Gómez 2010, 361)

OBSERVATION 5: (20 months; 5-8-81). While Muni watches, a human makes an object (the pointed half of a plastic egg) spin on the floor like a spinning top by giving it an initial rotating impulse with both hands. Muni watches the initial action and its result for a few seconds, then jumps upon the object catching it [FOLLOW MANIP]. H retrieves the egg and repeats the same action, which Muni again watches. She picks up the egg, watching it and handling it in a variety of ways [FOLLOW MANIP]; eventually she offers the egg to H, extending it towards H's chin but without touching it [OFFER], while making eye contact [EYE CONTACT]. H picks up the egg and makes it spin again. Muni catches it once more and offers it again to H as before [OFFER + EYE CONTACT]. The same is repeated twice more.

(Gómez 2010, 362)

OBSERVATION 20: (32 months; 4-8-82). Muni is hitting the floor with a fragment of red brick. H notices that the brick leaves marks on the floor, he takes the object from Muni [ACCEPTS ASSISTANCE], and shows her how to trace lines on the floor with the brick piece. H gives the brick back to Muni who takes it in her hand [TAKE]. However, she looks at him [EYE CONTACT], takes his hand [TOUCHES] and places it on the floor marks he had just made [TAKES HAND TO OBJECT], lets go of the hand and then places the brick just by H's hand [OFFERS], and watches both hand and brick waiting (no look at eyes). H repeats the tracing. H offers back the brick, and M takes it [TAKES OBJ]; Muni then moves it on the existing marks and manages to add a few herself [IMITATES].

(Gómez 2010, 364)

The eye contact as well as the more intricate interactions that emerge around 18 months lead to rather complex interactions between Muni and her human caregivers. Gómez takes this study as evidence that a gorilla follows the developmental trajectory of a human infant; it's only the ages at which the capacities are acquired that differ.

Gómez thinks that we can take these sorts of behaviors to be intentional and meaningful given his downgrading of the cognitive requirements associated with intentional communication. Whereas the original Gricean accounts require theory of mind, what Gómez requires is the ability to code a relation between an agent and some aspect of the world (Gómez 2009). The vervet monkeys are communicating because they not only respond appropriately to alarm calls by taking the correct evasive action, but they also scan the environment *looking for* the appropriate predator. Because the vervets look toward the ground when they hear the snake alarm, and look toward the sky when they hear the eagle alarm, Gómez suggests that the vervets are looking specifically for the predator that the signaler is worried about. Thus, rather than having to think about other's beliefs, a communicator uses her own representation of the world, or the world itself, as the content of what is being communicated. The communicative partner uses the signaler's behavior to understand what Gómez calls her *embodied intentions*, understood as the behavior that advertises the signaler's relationships to the target. Simple communicators can communicate only about the world, not about their representation of the world, or how the world might have been. Humans who mindread can, in addition to communicating about the world, also communicate about representations of the world, but Gómez thinks that this variety of communication isn't exhaustive of communication. If it were, we would have no good way of making sense of the behavior of human infants and other apes.

The psychologist Michael Tomasello also agrees that some ape signals are examples of intentional communication, and claims that intentional signals

are chosen and produced by individual organisms flexibly and strategically for particular social goals, adjusted in various ways for particular circumstances. These signals are *intentional* in the sense that the individual controls their use flexibly toward the goal of influencing others.

(Tomasello 2008, 14)

To make an intentional signal, Tomasello thinks one must be able to flexibly use the signal, be aware of the attentional state of the communicative partner, and be able to learn the signal. Similar definitions have been given by other primatologists, such as Katja Liebal and colleagues' definition of intentional communication according to which "one individual (a sender) does something in order that another does something (a receiver)" (Liebal et al. 2004). This requires that the sender's communicative actions be directed to a receiver through body orientation or eye gaze, and that the sender anticipate a response from the receiver (by waiting for a response, looking at the recipient, or persisting with or elaborating the signal).

Many psychologists conclude that great apes do intentionally communicate given these sorts of definitions. Tomasello claims that chimpanzees intentionally communicate only via gestures, because when gesturing but not when vocalizing apes monitor the gaze of communicative partners (Leavens and Hopkins 1998), and repair failed communication attempts by repeating a message or elaborating on it (Liebal et al. 2004; Leavens et al. 2005b). But other researchers argue that vocalizations also fulfill these criteria (Hopkins et al. 2007; see See 2014 for a review). Chimpanzees show sensitivity to a communicative partner when they modulate their vocalizations given the partner's location (Hostetter et al. 2001) and visual attention (Hostetter et al. 2007; Hopkins et al. 2007). Chimpanzees will also repeat or elaborate on a failed vocal message (Bodamar and Gardner 2002; Leavens et al. 2004).

5.1.3.3 Dynamical systems account of communication

A different approach to intentional communication comes from the philosopher Stuart Shanker and the anthropologist Barbara King. King and Shanker colorfully refer to communicative interactions as a dance, and the metaphor is meant to suggest all the subtle shifts in behavior one engages in while responding to the other, and the feedback loops that occur given these shifts (Shanker and King 2002; King and Shanker 2003). Like Trevarthen, King and Shanker are moved by the subtle and intense interactions between young infants and their caregivers. They take the interaction between communicating partners to be similar to the relationship between mother and infant in that it is one of co-regulation, a process of continual adjustment. In a successful communicative interaction, information is created between communicative partners, and mutual understanding is the result. One consequence of this view is that the larger context is essential to interpreting a signal; one gesture or sentence cannot be taken from the larger context and said to be independently meaningful. And because meaning is created by interactions across many sensory modalities, an exclusive focus on one modality will be misleading. Spoken human language can be perceived through auditory sensory modalities, but we also watch people's facial expressions and body language in order to actually understand what our communicative partner means. When humans lack cues, misunderstandings can result. This was common in the early days of email, when subtle meanings were lost. The invention of emoticons allowed us to replace the missing visual signals and improve electronic communication.

While the information transmission model is focused on sequential transmission and turn taking, the dynamical model focuses on coordination of simultaneous movements between the communicative partners (Shanker and King 2002). In their defense of the dynamical systems approach to studying ape communication, Shanker and King endorse the psychologist Alan Fogel's definition of communication as a "continuous unfolding of individual action that is susceptible to being continuously modified by the continuously changing actions of the partner" (Fogel 1993, 29).

King and Shanker offer the following examples of co-regulation among members of a captive bonobo family:

> Event 1. Female Elikya, two months of age, sits with her mother Matata. Her mother hands her over to her older sister Neema sitting nearby. From Elikya's facial pout, it is clear that she is distressed by this transfer. Three times in succession, she extends her arm and hand, palm up, back towards her mother. She is near enough to her mother to touch her, but she gestures instead. After the third gesture, her mother takes Elikya back. As Elikya relaxes against her mother, her sister pats her gently.

> Event 2. Elikya, eight months old, moves toward her sister Neema; she may lightly touch Neema's outstretched leg, but it is hard to be certain. Neema lowers her leg, then begins to stomp her feet on a platform as Elikya stands bipedally facing her. Elikya has a playface and raises her arms. Immediately Neema moves to Elikya and hugs her, covering her with her whole body, then quickly moves back and resumes her previous position.
>
> (King and Shanker 2003, 11).

King and Shanker think these two interactions show how the kind of gesture Elikya offers, along with her facial expression and body posture, helps to shape the behavior of her sister and mother. In a similar vein to Gómez's account of intentional communication, King and Shanker stress the embodied nature of communication. But King and Shanker are less interested in content than they are in understanding. Communication occurs when there is mutual understanding that "*emerges* as both partners converge on some shared feeling, thought, action, intention, and so forth" (2003, 608). When one communicates her desires, intentions, wishes or emotions, she is not communicating information, nor is she making accessible some hidden internal state or representation. Rather, as Gómez also suggests, communication is about things that are actually happening in the world.

The dynamic model is an embodied approach to communication that emphasizes the active nature of communication, in all its modalities. While eye contact, vocalizations, and gesture are part of the story, other elements are also important parts of communication. For example, humans as well as other great apes use touch to get attention, as well as to offer comfort and support. Neema patting Elikya after returning her to her mother has a communicative function. On the dynamic dance account of communication, chimpanzees who touch and hug another chimpanzee after he loses a fight (de Waal and van Roosmalen 1979) count as an example of communication.

Some researchers who work with other species also view communication in this way. Diana Reiss, a biologist who studies dolphin communication, describes how meanings are created when two different species come to use one another's signals. Rather than there being absolute meaning in a message that is encoded and then sent to a receiver who decodes it, meaning is created by our knowledge of one another's past behaviors and patterns, and we interpret signals based on our expectations, which come from this rich knowledge of the other.

Reiss describes her experiences communicating with a bottlenose dolphin during her PhD research. She was working with a newly captive dolphin named Circe, and was teaching her to eat dead fish and respond to basic husbandry commands. Part of the process of training dolphins often involves giving them a "time-out" when they don't do as the trainer desires. Reiss would give Circe a time-out when she broke a rule, such as leaving the training station before being dismissed. To give a time-out, Reiss would break social contact for a brief time by stepping back and silently waiting a few moments, Circe quickly learned to stay at the station until released.

Circe learned the time-out strategy so well that she began to use it herself whenever Reiss broke the rule by feeding Circe disgusting fish tails. As Reiss describes it:

> One day during a feeding I accidentally gave her an untrimmed tail. She immediately looked up at me, waved her head from side to side with wide-open eyes, and spat out the fish. Then she quickly left station, swam to the other side of the pool, and positioned herself vertically in the water. She stayed there against the opposite wall and just looked at me from across the pool. This vertical position was an unusual posture for her to maintain...I could hardly believe it. I felt that Circe was giving me a time-out!
>
> (Reiss 2011, 75)

Reiss decided to do an experiment to determine if the behavior would be repeated whenever the fish was not cut as Circe preferred, and, as she reported in her dissertation, Circe always gave Reiss a time out when fed fish tails (Reiss 1983). Though Reiss doesn't offer and test alternative hypotheses, and didn't do transfer tests to determine whether Circe would give her a time-out in other contexts, her report does serve as preliminary evidence that Circe was using a particular behavior that she learned from Reiss in order to communicate her displeasure.

While other models of communication set an upper limit for what communication can be, the dynamical approach to cognition places emphasis on the emergence of communicative ability. The dynamical approach is silent on the cognitive capacities that are required for communication, suggesting instead that we start with a behavioral account of communication, and use that to examine what is needed for the complex coordination and co-regulation of behavior that we see in some animals.

5.1.3.4 Studying intentional communication in other species

In all the intentional accounts of communication, the evidence that has been given in favor of animal communication has been limited to great apes, monkeys, and dolphins. Because—save for the dynamic dance—these accounts were introduced to explain human communication, they are most easily generalized to species that may communicate in ways similar to humans.

But the approach is more difficult to implement with species that do not share as many features with human beings.

Comparing the development of great ape infants to human infants is a methodology that works because the two species use shared sensory modalities, have a similar morphology, and live in similar social situations. For other species, such an approach is more difficult. Elephants use sound that travels miles; electric fish use pulses of electric charges through water to communicate. But difficulties arise even when it comes to the more familiar-seeming species like the great apes. Individuals may communicate by deliberate non-engagement, such as the orangutan's back turning "ignore" response to an approaching individual (Russon, personal communication).

Psychologists working with humans point to cues we can use to identify communication between human infants and adults, such as eye gaze and child-directed speech (Csibra and Gergeley 2009). But these cues are species-specific, and it wouldn't do to look for them in all species. In species with poor eyesight, or species that do not use vision as a primary sensory modality, eye contact may be less important than other cues, such as touch or synchronization of behavior. Dolphins, for example, do not rely on their eyesight to see underwater, but instead use echolocation. There are no visual cues that would let a dolphin know if another is echolocating, but there are aural cues; a dolphin's echolocation clicks can be heard. There is evidence that dolphins can eavesdrop on each others' echolocation clicks and click echoes in order to gain information about the dolphin and the environment (Gregg et al. 2007). Male dolphins synchronize their behaviors, swimming and surfacing in unison during social interactions, and especially in intense situations in which the males are chasing after and trying to herd a female (Connor et al. 2006). Dolphin mother and infant closely synchronize their movements for the first three months, which some scientists think helps the infant learn to actively synchronize and later to imitate behaviors, which in turn promotes social learning of actions such as sponge fishing and other cultural behaviors (Fellner et al. 2006). For dolphins, eye contact is likely not as important as auditory or tactile cues.

Study of intentional communication in various species will have to be sensitive to the modalities that are salient and under voluntary control for that species. This suggests that knowing the species well is essential to identifying which cues might signal intentional communication for that species.

5.2 Meaning in intentional communication

If animals are intentionally communicating, they must mean something by their communicative behaviors. Much research on the semantics of animal signals has focused on the question of whether animal signals are referential or whether they are emotive. That question matters, for if the signal is intentional it should be at least partially referential, or so it might seem. Emotive signals are automatic expressions of feelings about a situation, like a scream of fear or a sigh of pleasure. While these vocalizations are communicative, they need not be intentional. When the vervet monkey utters the eagle alarm cry after seeing an eagle, he might be referring to the eagle, or he might be merely expressing his eagle-fear.

5.2.1 Reference

The biologist Peter Marler suggested that the first step is to distinguish what he calls functionally referential from nonreferential utterances. A functionally referential utterance is one that has all the behavioral characteristics of a referential signal. This category is agnostic about the cognitive mechanisms underlying the behavior. Marler suggests that there are two criteria for a signal to be functionally referential: the production of the signal must be caused by the same kind of stimuli, and hearing or seeing the signal must cause the same effect as does hearing or seeing the object the signal refers to (Marler et al. 1992). For example, because vervet monkeys give the same signal to all perceptions of an eagle, and because vervets respond to the eagle alarm cry and the appearance of an eagle in the sky by hiding in a bush, the vervets' eagle alarm call counts as a functionally referential signal.

Many species will turn out to have referential calls if we apply Marler's critiera. For example, bantam chickens give different alarm calls in response to aerial predators such as hawks and ground predators such as foxes (Evans et al. 1993; Evans and Marler 1995). As well, they exhibit different behaviors in response to hawks and foxes, but will take the same evasive action at the sight of a hawk and the perception of the aerial predator alarm call. Dogs are more likely to avoid taking a bone when they hear a recording of a growl made by a dog guarding his food than when they hear a recording of a dog growling at a stranger (Faragó et al. 2010). Prairie dogs have alarm calls for hawks, humans, dogs and coyotes, and respond to the alarm calls the same way they respond to seeing members of those species (Kiriazis and Slobodchikoff 2006), and the alarm calls may be modified depending on the individual properties of the predator (Slobodchikoff et al. 2009). Meerkats have alarm calls that simultaneously indicate predator type and the degree of danger presented by the predator (Manser 2001).

Other animal calls thought to be functionally referential include food calls and social calls. When chimpanzees find food, their calls can indicate both that there is food available, and also how good a food source it is (Slocombe and Zuberbühler 2005, 2006). Chickens (Evans and Evans 2007), ravens (Bugnyar et al. 2001), and various other primate species (Hauser and Marler 1993; Kitzmann and Caine 2009) also have food calls that have been identified as functionally referential.

Contact calls are also taken as having referential properties, and in some cases they may function as names representing particular individuals. Contact calls are given to indicate the presence of individuals, and some species have specific calls for specific individuals. Across many species mothers can discriminate their offspring's contact calls from those of unrelated individuals. For example, bat mothers discriminate between the isolation calls of their own offspring and those of other young bats, and experienced mothers are better at making this discrimination than new mothers (Knörnschild et al. 2013). Dwarf mongooses identify individual adults by their contact calls; in a playback experiment mongooses who had acquired a desirable food item were more vigilant after hearing the contact call of higher ranking individuals than when they heard the calls of lower ranking individuals (Sharpe et al. 2013).

Baboons recognize alarm calls as well as reconciliation calls as coming from particular individuals (Cheney and Seyfarth 2007). Baboons can determine who is making a call, regardless of the type of call, and they respond differently depending on who is doing the calling. Cheney and Seyfarth write,

> Individual recognition occurs in so many contexts, with so many vocalizations, that it is hard to escape the impression that listeners have a mental representation, or concept, of Sylvia [a baboon] as an individual. If monkeys were human, we would call this a concept of a *person*.

> (2007, 262)

In a playback experiment, their research team presented recordings simulating a threat and fight between two females. When the fighting was consistent with the dominance ranks, observers were relatively uninterested. But when the recordings simulated a threat by a subordinate baboon to a dominant, the other baboons looked longer at the direction of the vocalizations. Cheney and Seyfarth take this as evidence that the baboons are aware of individual identity and family membership, as well as linear ranking between families.

Bottlenose dolphins also have a sophisticated system of individual identifiers based on the signature whistle. Bottlenose dolphins each create a unique signal that broadcasts their individual identity (by modifying calls heard around them early in life), and other dolphins learn to identify that signal with the individual (Janik et al. 2006). While females have a relatively stable signature whistle, males will modify their signature whistle to resemble the whistle of other males they have formed coalitions with (Watwood et al. 2004). Signature whistles are used to indicate one's approach to the group, which is useful given that dolphins often leave the group and return after some absence. Dolphins will also sometimes copy another's signature whistle, and this elicits a response in the named individual, who responds with his signature whistle (King and Janik 2013).

In addition to calls, some gestures may also have referential properties. In particular, pointing is taken to indicate reference to the object pointed at. As a deictic gesture—one that is only understood in a context—pointing occurs spontaneously in children and is interpreted as referential and triadic. The pointer indicates to the partner the existence of some referent in the environment. Because children begin pointing around nine months, and apes are not often observed pointing in natural contexts, many researchers assume that pointing is unique to human beings (Tomasello et al. 2007; Franco and Butterworth 1996; Povinelli et al. 2003; Moll and Tomasello 2007). However, great apes in captivity are often observed pointing to indicate objects for a human caregiver, and there are also a few observations of apes pointing for other apes (de Waal 1982; Pelé et al. 2009; Savage-Rumbaugh 1986). Formal studies confirm that chimpanzees point in the presence of a human observer, but not when alone (Leavens et al. 1996), and that they are produced with sensitivity to the attentional state of the recipient (Liebal et al. 2004). Leavens argues that pointing is a natural communicative behavior for chimpanzees who are enculturated—who live in non-institutionalized captive settings in which they enjoy daily interactions with human caregivers (Leavens, forthcoming). The studies of captive chimpanzees that find no evidence of pointing behavior use institutionalized chimpanzees as subjects, individuals who had no opportunity to learn the human communicative cue.

Leavens thinks that chimpanzees don't point in the wild, but that they easily adopt the human signal as part of the enculturation process.

However, some think that apes may also use pointing, or pointing-like gestures, in natural settings. For one, there are rare reports of pointing in wild bonobos (Veà and Sabater-Pi 1998) and chimpanzees (Hobaiter et al. 2013). Further, it may be that great apes, like humans in some cultures, use other gestures for pointing. For example, the Mohawks and Ojibway of North America point with their noses and chin, and lip-pointing, which is a deictic gesture that involves not only protruding the lips but also orientation of gaze and sometimes an eyebrow-raise, is common in Laos (Enfield 2001). In a similar sort of gesture, rehabilitant orangutans have been observed to show caregivers fruits by presenting them on their extended lower lip; the caregivers are allowed to examine the fruits, but if they fail to return them the orangutans become agitated (Andrews, unpublished data).

While one interpretation takes pointing to have the role of referring to the object pointed at, Tomasello thinks these gestures merely serve the function of getting others' attention (Tomasello 2008). Attention-getting gestures are intentional, because they are a reflection of the communicator's desire that the receiver engage in some action. But they aren't referential, given that the sender expects that if the recipient looks where the sender indicates, the recipient will do what is wanted—such as provide the object pointed at. For Tomasello only human pointing is genuinely referential, because it is cooperative, and can involve sharing information for the receiver's sake. Ape pointing, he thinks, is merely a request serving the sender's selfish motives.

5.2.2 Expressivism

Intentional signals can refer, but they can also express sensations, emotions, desires, and so forth. Darwin thought that animal signals are largely expressions of emotions, and that recipients use this information about the signaler's state (Darwin, 1973/2007). The cat with arched back who hisses at a dog is expressing her fear and anger toward the dog, and the dog with rump and tail up with head and paws on the ground is expressing her desire to play. These animal signals have long thought to be species specific and inflexible, thus leading to debates among ethologists about whether an animal's signal was referential or expressive. These two properties were taken to consist of an exclusive disjunction; a signal can either be expressive or referential, but not both. For example, the vervet eagle alarm cry couldn't mean "There is an eagle and I am *terrified* of it!"

Studies of animal communicative signals that look to correlate the intensity of the call with the degree of danger have found that there is an expressive element in alarm calls. Alarm calls across species are also observed in response to events or objects that don't correspond to the stimulus class; adults will give alarm calls to falling trees or non-predators (Arnold and Zuberbühler 2006), which suggests that there may be an emotive quality rather than merely a referential one. Many species give food calls in higher frequency when food is abundant (Hauser et al. 1993; Di Bitetti 2005), or of a high quality (including fowl (Marler et al. 1986), cottontop tamarins (Elowson et al. 1991), red-bellied tamarins (Caine et al. 1995) and spider monkeys

(Chapman and Lefebvre 1990)). These sorts of findings suggest to Rendall and Owren (2002) that animal signals are just expressions of the sender's emotion, which in turn causes an emotion in the receiver, who then behaves appropriately given that emotion.

However, rather than assuming a dichotomy between expressive signals and referential ones, some argue that animal signals can inform receivers about both motivational state and external objects or events (Marler et al. 1992; Manser et al. 2002). For example, suricates give different alarm calls to mammalian, avian, and reptilian predators, and they respond differently to the calls depending on the degree of urgency the call demonstrates (Manser et al. 2001). Playback experiments confirm that suricates respond differently to the three different alarm calls, and to different levels of urgency within each call class. For example, in response to a low urgency snake alarm recording, suricates will raise their tails, approach the loudspeaker, and sniff the area around it, but they will quickly resume their previous activity. However, if a high urgency alarm call is played, the suricates will continue the alarm response behavior for a significantly longer time.

Given this dual role for some alarm calls, some argue that animal alarm calls are best understood as neo-expressive avowals, which are self reports of one's current mental states that have both an action component and a semantic component (Bar-On 2013). Expressivism in the philosophy of language is the view that our utterances do not refer, but merely express. For example, expressivism in ethics is the idea that there is no truth-evaluable content to our moral claims, but instead they merely express our feelings about the topic. In this sense, when we say, "Murder is bad" what we really mean is "Yuck! Murder!" Neo-expressivism is a position in the philosophy of language developed by the philosopher Dorit Bar-On which combines the traditional expressive element with semantic content, such that an avowal is both an expression of a current mental state and a token with semantic properties (Bar-On 2004).

An application of this view to animal alarm calls suggests that they are best understood as expressing both motivational state and truth-evaluable propositional content (McAninch et al. 2009). To defend this claim, the authors argue that at least some animals meet the requirements for conceptual thought set out by York Gunther (2003). Gunther provides four principles of conceptualist thought and some of these principles are more easily applied to animal signals than others. The principle of reference determinacy, for example, appears to be easily fulfilled by creatures whose alarm cries are functionally referential. As well, the principle of force independence—the idea that different individuals can have different attitudes toward the same content, and hence can act differently toward it—also seems to be fulfilled by alarm calls. Because individuals respond differently to an alarm call depending on the context, there is a kind of force independence to the call; an eagle alarm call doesn't make you run into a bush if you are already hidden. Even in honeybee dances we see some degree of force independence, since scout bees who have found a candidate site for a new hive will often fail to bring all the other scout bees to the site; the bee's private experience with a different site is a relevant factor in her response to a scout's dance (Grüter et al. 2008). The idea that the same signal can mean something different based on the context of that signal gets at the heart of pragmatics. For example, when there are different responses to an infant and an adult giving the same signal, or a dominant and a submissive, there is evidence that the messages mean something different depending on whom they come from. Signaler identity affects the message in many species (Tibbetts and Dale 2007). Further, this suggests that there is flexibility in response to the message (Tomasello and Zuberbühler 2002). Thus, the force independence principle is met in many species.

The last two principles are a bit more difficult to apply to animal signals. Compositionality, or the idea that the organization of smaller parts determines the larger meaning, is a property that some think is unique to language. Nonetheless, repeating a message can change the meaning of the message, from honeybees who dance longer for better nest sites (Seeley and Buhrman 2001) to suricates, who indicate the level or urgency of an alarm call through a graded change in harmonics to a noisy structure (Manser 2001). Slobodchikoff claims that Gunnison's prairie dogs have alarm calls for different predators and features of predators, and that these modifiers indicate a communication system with correlates to nouns and adjectives (Slobodchikoff 2002). So McAninch and colleagues think there may be some animal correlates to this principle as well, though further research is required.

Finally, the cognitive significance principle may be met as well. This principle relates the meaning of a signal to a mental state about the content of the meaning. McAninch and colleagues suggest that vervet monkeys fulfill this requirement. A monkey may be seen by other monkeys as an unreliable signaler of one predator, but still reliable when it comes to other predators. When researchers reveal a monkey as unreliable about eagle alarm calls by playing back recordings of that individual's eagle alarm call in the absence of an eagle, conspecifics will begin to ignore his eagle alarm call. However, they will continue to respond to his alarm call for other predators (Cheney and Seyfarth 1990).

Animal signals, like human utterance, may at the same time express feelings and involve semantic content. There is no need to assume a dichotomy between these two elements. The empirical question that remains is to what extent do various species engage in avowals with semantic content.

5.2.3 Content vs. attention-getting signals

When the cat meows at the door, she wants outside. When she meows at her bowl in the morning she wants food. When she meows in front of her sitting human during a cold evening, she wants up on the lap. All these meows might sound the same, but they all mean something different. Or at least cat owners like to think so. Another possibility is that these signals have no content, but instead are attention-getting signals. They lead the cat's human to pay attention to her, and the human is capable of responding to fulfill the cat's current desire depending on the larger context. In this way the cat's meowing would be more like a baby crying than words in a human language.

Tomasello argues that it isn't just chimpanzee pointing that lacks referential content, but that none of the many great ape gestures refer. He draws a distinction between two kinds of gestures: attention-getting signals and intention-movement signals (Tomasello 2008). Attention-getting gestures are those that are intended to draw the recipient's attention to something with the expectation that the recipient will then act in a certain way. Intention-movement signals are truncated actions that provide information about the activity the signaler is about to perform, such as reaching toward an object he wants to obtain. He writes, because intention-movements are simply ritualizations (abbreviations) of initial steps in intentional actions, their "meaning" is built in; it is simply what the communicator intends the other to do in the interactions, which was already present in some preexisting act in the social interaction before the signal was ritualized.

(Tomasello 2008, 51–52)

In attention-getting signals, there is no referential content. Tomasello argues that what may look like pointing in ape behavior is instead an example of an attention-getting signal. When an ape points, the recipient looks at what is pointed at and, so long as the message is well received, gives the object to the signaler. Tomasello says that apes do not understand declarative points when they are presented to them, but take all points to be directives. Because of this, pointing and other attention-getting signals cannot be understood as having referential content, but they are better understood as requesting a certain behavior. Tomasello thinks that nothing apes do in their natural environments amounts to referential behavior, and that what distinguishes ape and human communication systems is this difference in reference.

Theories about what animal signals might mean are closely related to theories about the evolution of language. Accounts that see a smooth transition between animal signaling and human language in all its complexity are more inclined to interpret animals signals as having some properties of human language, such as reference, meaning, or truth-evaluability.

5.3 Evolution of language

Studies of the baboons of Botswana's Okavango Delta found that baboons have around 14 discrete vocalizations with different meanings. These vocalizations are learned, not reflexive; an individual appears to be able to choose whether to vocalize or remain silent. However, unlike human vocalizations, the baboons do not combine vocalizations to make new meanings. There is no syntax in the baboon communicative system. Because of this, it is difficult to determine exactly what the meaning of a baboon call is. For example, baboons make a wahoo sound when a lion approaches, and when individuals hear the call, they might look around to see a lion, or they might run into the trees. Because baboons will continue to give the call after others have seen the lion, as well as after they have run into the trees, it isn't just a call to action. But it also isn't just a reference to the lion. It seems to have both a motivational and a referential component. Despite the complexity of the baboon communication system, Cheney and Seyfarth don't call what the baboons have a language. In order to understand why they don't, we need to understand how psychologists and linguists use the term "language."

5.3.1 What is language?

The English word "language" derives from the Latin *lingua*, which literally translates as "tongue." And while we use the term to refer to systems of codes we use to program computers, few students have the opportunity to meet their language requirement by studying C++. Narrowly understood, "language" refers to the systems of communication demonstrated in humans, and the questions of whether animals have similar systems and how these systems evolved are based on premises about the properties shared by all natural human languages.

The linguist Noam Chomsky famously claimed that only humans have language. By this he meant that no animals have anything like a human language; while it is "obviously true" that animals have systems of communication (Chomsky 1980, 430), these systems of communication are different enough from human language to make the claim that animals do have language weaken the expressive power of our language. If we call animal communication systems "language" then we no longer have a word we need to draw important distinctions between types of communication systems.

Chomsky's theory of generative grammar is based on the idea that all human languages share a set of implicit rules that allows us to form sentences according to the hierarchical grammars of our natural languages (Chomsky 1965). While the grammars of natural languages differ, at a more abstract level they all share the same rules. Chomsky argues that human language can be described along six dimensions: structural principles, physical mechanisms, manner of use, ontogenetic development, phylogenetic development, and integration into cognitive systems. So far as we know (circa 1980), animal communication systems lack all of these features, says Chomsky. While in subsequent years we have learned about the physical mechanisms, manner of use, ontogenetic development, and integration of animal signaling (see e.g. Shettleworth 2010b, Chapter 14), Chomsky insists that structural principles are necessary for having a language. He thinks animal communication systems lack grammatical structure, lack a productive capacity (they don't allow a denumerably infinite number of distinct expressions), do not involve distinct elements, but are continuous, and do not exhibit recursion (the embedding of phrases inside other phrases to construct new phrases). Furthermore, the manner of use of animal communication systems and human languages is very different. Animals don't tell stories, they don't write poetry, don't request information for clarification, can't give monologues or engage in casual conversation about the weather. They can't talk about the past or discuss plans for the future. What they can do is indicate things like whether they are ready to mate, whether there is a predator around, or whether they will behave in a friendly or aggressive manner.

If the question "Do animals have language?" is understood to be the question of whether animal communication systems are *like* human language systems, then Chomsky concludes, it is clear that the differences are so great as to undermine the usefulness of the metaphor. Animals don't use language just as humans don't fly, even though humans can jump off tables and sail through the air for a second or two. More recently Chomsky argues that recursion might be the only structural feature that distinguishes human language from animal communication systems (Hauser et al. 2002). If we understand language to be recursion, which all human languages have in common, Chomsky concludes, no other species has language.

As linguistic anthropologists learn more about the diversity of human languages, and as animal cognition researchers learn more about how animals communicate, the claim that all humans and no animals engage in recursive signaling has been challenged. Research on European starlings demonstrates that we can train birds to discriminate a recursive grammar from among strings of starling sounds (Gentner et al. 2006). Research has shown similarities between human language and bird song along cognitive, neurological, genomic, and behavioral dimensions (Bolhuis et al. 2010). Because human children and baby birds both have to learn their communication systems through exposure to experts in those systems, and because both species go through a babbling phase, it may be that learning recursion is simply a part of learning a complex set of vocalizations. However, there is a difference between human children's easy acquisition of recursive forms, and their easy generalization from one to another, and the intensive training of the starlings that didn't permit as much generalization. There is also evidence that cotton-top tamarins may not be able to recognize embedded grammars (Fitch and Hauser 2004). This suggests that there may be some species that cannot recognize recursion, some species that can recognize recursion but cannot generalize to new patterns, and, on the other hand, humans, who can generalize recursion more widely. In addition, some challenge the claim that embedding of the sort found in the birds is necessary for recursion, though it is sufficient (Watumull et al. 2014). Another challenge comes from the linguist Daniel Everett, who claims that the language spoken by the Pirahã of Amazonian Brazil fails to demonstrate recursive properties (Everett 2005). Everett, one of the few to translate the language, also claims that there is a limit to how long sentences can be and so the language is finite. These claims, if true, would further undermine a clean distinction between animal systems and human systems of communication.

Further, brain areas associated with speech production in humans are also associated with bird song in zebra finches. Humans with a mutation of the FOXP2 gene have impaired speech production, and some claim this gene was key to the evolution of human speech and language (MacDermot et al. 2005). However, because the FOXP2 gene is expressed in the same part of the brain in finches, and because finches with damaged FOXP2 are also impaired in their song production (Haesler et al. 2007), it may be that this gene has a more general function.

Human and nonhuman communication systems might be continuous with one another, with animal systems having simpler aspects of many properties of human communication language. On the other hand, human language may be discontinuous with animal systems of communication, such that language is something entirely new under the sun.

5.3.2 Gestural origins of language evolution

When we think about language, we generally think about talking. The voices that surround us are the most salient aspects of our linguistic processes. So when wondering about how language evolved, a natural hypothesis is that it started from vocalizations, like grunts and clicks and song. While this is probably the dominant view of language evolution, and the reason why vocal imitation is emphasized in some accounts of language evolution (Fitch 2005), an alternative idea is that human language evolved from body movements, like gesture, miming, and dance. Because in many primates gestures appear to be under voluntary cortical control to a greater extent than are vocalizations, which appear to be controlled by the limbic system (Ploog 2004), there is an opportunity to recruit bodily movements for communicative purposes.

The psychologists Michael Corballis (1992, 2002) and Merlin Donald (1991) both promoted versions of this theory beginning in the early 1990s, though the idea has been around for hundreds of years. Early European traders who were able to communicate with foreign people through gesture helped promote the idea that languages of the hand may have preceded languages of the mouth (Corballis 2009). That experience continues today for travelers to foreign countries; my sister and I spent an afternoon in Saharan Morocco with a family with whom we shared but a word, though we were still able to offer a ride to the matriarch, accept an invitation into her home, and take tea with her family. Gesture-first advocates consider several properties of pantomime as critical stepping stones to language: it is productive (enables creation of novel messages), and because it can communicate meaning with propositional content it serves as an entryway to syntax, declaratives, and narrative (Arbib 2002; Arbib et al. 2008; Corballis 2002; Stokoe 2001).

Donald saw the beginnings of modern human language as stemming from what he calls "mimetic skill," which consists in the ability to control behavioral movements, rehearse them, and use them for communicative purposes (Donald 1991). Our ancestors were able to communicate by acting out what they wanted to say; by relying on pantomime they were able to communicate complex thoughts. Although Donald agrees that apes have a complex set of cognitive abilities, he thinks that their ability to store and use memories is quite limited, and so they "remain locked into an episodic lifestyle" (1993, 739). The ability for mimetic skill, which is the origin of language, he thinks is unique to humans. Tomasello also endorses a version of the gestural theory of language evolution, writing, "I personally do not see how anyone can doubt that ape gestures—in all of their flexibility and sensitivity to the attention of the other—and not ape vocalizations—in all of their inflexibility and ignoring of others—are the original font from which the richness and complexities of human communication and language have flowed" (Tomasello 2008, 55).

Corballis argues that contemporary human language not only has its source in gestures, but remains, in fact, a gestural system, where the gestures are those of our articulatory organs including the lips, tongue, and larynx (Corballis 2009). Contemporary support for the theory comes from the research of neuroscientist Michal Arbib, another prominent supporter of gesture first theories (Arbib 2005). Arbib and Corballis think the gestural system is based on the existence of the mirror system, which is a neural system found in humans and other primates that is active both when witnessing another engage in an action and when one engages in that action oneself (Rizzolatti and Craighero 2004). The mirror neuron system overlaps Broca's area in humans, which is a brain area associated with the production of speech, as well as with observing or imagining meaningful gestures. And in monkeys, the mirror neuron system is thought to involve a brain area homologous with Broca's area in humans (Rizzolatti and Arbib 1998).

Animal cognition researchers have continued pursuing this interest in gestural theories of language evolution by examining gestural communication in other species. There has been special interest in the great apes, whose gestures are individually variable in terms of their repertoires (Call and Tomasello 2007), flexibly used (Gentry et al. 2009), involve multi-modal communicative combinations (Leavens et al. 2010; Pollick and de Waal 2007; Tanner et al. 2006), are used in sequences (Genty and Byrne 2010; Tanner 2004), and are part of negotiation or co-regulation within communicative interactions, including elaborations of failed messages (Cartmill and Byrne 2007; Leavens et al. 2005b, 2010).

Perhaps most controversially, great apes have been reported to engage in pantomime, which involves more elaborate acting out of desired ends in an idiosyncratic way (Russon and Andrews 2011a, 2011b). Pantomime consists of a gesture or series of gestures in which meaning is acted out; in humans, it can be as simple as twirling a finger to indicate a vortex or as complex as a Balinese dance recounting the story of the Ramayana. Pantomime can be representational, symbolic, narrative in form, and fictional (McNeill 2000). There are a number of anecdotes about pantomime in captive great apes. For example Koko, a language-trained gorilla, mimed rolling a ball of clay between her hands to express "clay" (Tanner et al. 2006), Chantek, a language-trained orangutan, placed his thumb and index finger together and placed his lips on them, blowing, to indicate his desire for a balloon (Miles et al. 1996). The primatologist Christoph Boesch reports observing a wild chimpanzee acting out how best to crack a nut for her daughter (Boesch 1993). Wild chimpanzees also have been observed using a gesture called a "directed scratch" which involves an exaggerated scratching of a part of one's own body as a request to another chimpanzee to scratch that spot (Pika and Mitani 2006). And, as we saw in the interaction between Cecep and Anne, semi-free ranging orangutans have been known to act out what they want done to them (Russon and Andrews 2011a, 2011b). Another orangutan, Kikan, re-enacted a past event: a researcher, Agnes, had used a pencil to remove a sliver from the sole of Kikan's foot and then daubed latex from a fig leaf stem on the wound to protect it. A week later, Kikan pulled on Agnes' leg to get her attention, then picked a leaf and poked its stem at the sole of her (now healed) foot, just as Agnes had done while doctoring her. Anne and I think that Kikan's pantomime demonstrates narrative features, with the understanding that narrative is defined as "the representation of an event or a series of events" (Abbott 2002, 12). We also think it shows some of the components of episodic memory, or reconstructing one's own past experiences as situated in time (Suddendorf and Corballis 2007; Tulving 2005), because Kikan reconstructed key elements of a personally important experience.

While critics argue that pantomimes and other great ape iconic gestures exist only in the eye of the beholder (e.g. Guldberg 2010; Tomasello and Zuberbühler 2002), the aforementioned observations indicate the need for testing in experimental settings. Pointing, iconic gestures, and pantomime may be important keys to understanding great apes' gestures given great apes' remarkable motor flexibility and the opportunities we have for observing their production and comprehension.

Compelling studies of ape gesture focus on how an ape responds to a failed message. It may be that a gesture is just an accident, and has no meaning, if it isn't repeated or elaborated on when the purported communicative partner doesn't respond in the right way. But if the gesture is repeated or elaborated on, a good explanation for the behavior is that it is an instance of intentional communication.

Leavens and colleagues report that chimpanzees respond to failed messages by persisting, and elaborating their gestures (Leavens et al. 2005b, 2010). In one study, they looked at chimpanzees pointing behavior, which is usually understood as a request for the object pointed at (Leavens et al. 2005a). The researchers were a bit sneaky, and pretended not to understand the request in some conditions. When the researchers failed to give a whole banana to chimpanzees pointing at a banana, the chimpanzees either persisted by repeating the gesture, or elaborated on the gesture until they received the desired food.

Similarly, in another study, the psychologists Erica Cartmill and Richard Byrne (2007) found that captive orangutans continued to gesture until they received some requested food, but that they varied the types of gesture depending on the response of the caretaker. If the orangutans only received part of the food they were requesting, they would continue repeating the original gesture. However, if the caretaker engaged in an incorrect behavior, such as bringing the wrong food, the orangutans changed their gesture, or elaborated on the original one.

Apes elaborate, repeat signals, and substitute gestures when their message fails. The flexibility of the responses is comparable to that of human children, and such patterns of behavior, like the behavior of human children coming to learn human language, can be interpreted as intentional communication. If the apes were merely responding with frustration, we would expect them to respond to failures with species-typical frustration responses, but they do not. Instead, the apes act as though there is an appropriate way of responding to the request and the human fails to do so, and so they help get the message across by either giving the same signal with more vigor or changing the signal entirely.

Gestural communication has been observed in other species as well, including ravens who have been observed to use head and beak to indicate objects such as moss or twigs to their partner (Pika and Bugnyar 2011). Ravens show—pick up a non-food item by the beak and hold it for a few moments—or offer—pick up a non-food item by the beak and move the head up and down—items that have no obvious functional purpose for eating or nest building. Pika and Bugnyar think that the gestures serve to promote or test the bond between raven partners, given that ravens bond for life and rely on their partners to raise young, so that finding the right partner is a high-stakes activity.

Elephants have also been observed to use a number of gestures with one another; for example they orient their body to indicate where they want to go next (Poole and Granli 2011). And some elephants understand human pointing (Smet and Byrne 2013). While controlled studies of these species' gestural communication have not been done, observations of failed communications can help to illuminate the intentional nature of these other animal gestures.

Additional support for the gestural theory of language evolution comes from claims that chimpanzee vocalizations are involuntary (see Arbib et al. 2008, Hammerschmidt and Fischer 2008, and Seyfarth and Cheney 2010 for reviews), while gestures are supposed to be under voluntary control. Further, Tomasello claims that while chimpanzees are unable to learn vocalizations, they can learn new gestures (Tomasello 2008).

However, other researchers dispute these claims. Chimpanzee infants acquire the vocalizations that their mothers produce, whereas chimpanzees raised by humans in a nursery fail to acquire the same vocalizations (Taglialatela et al. 2012). In addition, wild chimpanzees living in adjacent communities have very different pant hoots, such that they are more different from one another than they are from far off communities, suggesting that the adjacent communities varied their calls to better distinguish in-group from out-group calls (Crockford et al. 2004).

Other species also learn to make sounds that serve as signals, such as the male zebra finch who normally will imitate his father's song, but who will develop a different song if exposed to another song model during the sensitive period for song learning (Eales 1985), or bottlenose dolphins who will modify their signature whistle to resemble the whistle of a coalition partner, and who will produce a partner's whistle to get the partner's attention (King et al. 2013). However, the common ancestor of humans and finches and the common ancestor of humans and dolphins is perhaps not where we need to look for information about the evolution of language.

Another possibility is that both gesture and vocalization were integral to the evolution of human language. The chimpanzee homologue to Broca's area is active when the chimpanzee intentionally gestures and intentionally vocalizes, but not during nonintentional vocalizations (Taglialatela et al. 2011). Taglialatela and colleagues suggest that this neurological evidence is evidence for a multi-modal theory of language evolution, one that involved our hominid ancestors both gesturing and making vocalizations in order to communicate.

5.3.3 Teaching animals language

In addition to observing how animals communicate with one another, we humans have been exceedingly curious about the possibility of teaching human language to other species. The cross fostering experiments in the first half of the twentieth century had humans bringing baby chimpanzees into their homes, treating them like human infants, and hoping that they would begin to speak (Kellogg and Kellogg 1933; Hayes 1951). Unlike parrots, however, chimpanzees don't have the vocal apparatus needed for making human sounds, and perhaps they also lack the cognitive mechanisms for vocal imitation (Fitch 2000) and so this research shifted to teaching chimpanzees and other apes American Sign Language and artificial symbolic communication systems. Early attempts appeared to be a success. The juvenile chimpanzee Washoe learned over 100 signs in American Sign Language, after laborious training by his researcher caregivers Beatrix and Allen Gardner. While they wanted Washoe to learn language like a human, his acquisition of symbols required shaping, molding, and modeling the appropriate gestures (Gardner and Gardner 1978). Around the same time, the psychologist David Premack introduced several chimpanzees, including Sarah, to a lexical communication system using plastic tokens for nouns, verbs, and logical connectives, in order to produce strings of symbols that obey syntactic rules (Premack 1971), and Francine Patterson introduced a modified form of American Sign Language (ASL) to Koko, a gorilla, who learned over 100 signs and combined multiple signs to make new ones (Patterson 1978). However, when the psychologist Herbert Terrace tried to replicate the findings of some of these studies, he failed. After acquiring an infant chimpanzee he named Nim Chimpsky, Terrace hired a series of caregivers to look after Nim and teach him ASL. Nim didn't acquire much in the way of signing, and those signs he did seem to learn appeared to Terrace to be imitations of signs just given by a caregiver. After reviewing videos of Washoe's signing, Terrace concluded that Washoe's performance was also best explained as imitation (Terrace et al. 1979).

Future ape language research controlled for alternative interpretations of results. Premack used transfer tests as evidence that the chimpanzee Sarah understands the symbols she was taught, showing that she could use symbols appropriately in a context different from the context in which she learned them (Premack 1971). Sue Savage-Rumbaugh was trying to teach Matata, a female bonobo, a lexical communication system when Matata's adopted son, Kanzi, spontaneously began using the lexicons (Savage-Rumbaugh 1986). Kanzi and other bonobos in Savage-Rumbaugh's care also came to comprehend spoken English, and in a formal study of comprehension of novel utterances Kanzi performed as well as a two-year-old human child (Savage-Rumbaugh et al. 1993).

The psychologist Tetsuro Matsuzawa taught the female chimpanzee Ai to use numerals, and he is currently studying the intergenerational transmission of this ability between Ai and her son Ayumu (Matsuzawa 2002).

Given what some apes are able to accomplish, some researchers have started to look at other species. The psychologist Lou Herman taught a gestural communication system to four bottlenose dolphins, who were able to comprehend nouns, verbs, modifiers, and (perhaps) some logical connectives (Herman 2010).

Irene Pepperberg taught spoken English to an African grey parrot, Alex, who was able to label objects by name, color, shape, and matter (Pepperberg 1999), and studies of other grey parrots' vocalizations suggest appropriate contextual use of words and phrases (Colbert-White et al. 2011) and semantic structure such as synonymy (Kaufmann et al. 2013). And studies of dogs' word learning suggest that border collies like Chaser and Rico understand that words refer to objects in the world (Kaminski et al. 2004; Pilley and Reid 2011).

Among the claims made about how other animals can come to use symbols for communicative purposes, we see evidence for semantics and syntax. Philosophical questions arise about what these studies tell us about the relationship between language and mind. Are there cognitive operations that an animal can do with a symbolic system and cannot do without it?

There is some suggestive evidence that having a symbol helps animals pass certain tasks. Chimpanzees in a reverse contingency task (in which what you pick goes to another, and you get what you don't pick) failed to maximize their own reward when they were presented with candies, but were able to maximize when they were given numerals rather than objects (Boysen et al. 1996, 1999). Capuchin monkeys are also reported to do better on this task when using tokens rather than food (Addessi and Rossi 2011). It seems that symbols may help animals control impulses. But what about other tasks? We use symbols to help us remember things or to do math problems, among other things. But these animals don't have the ability to use the symbols for themselves, for the most part. When a researcher provides them, the subjects can respond appropriately, and they are used to make requests for trips or treats. But if the full range of symbols is not available to the individual, they cannot come to rely on them or use them to develop novel solutions to other seemingly unrelated tasks. Dolphins and dogs who can comprehend symbols given to them by humans but have no means to produce symbolic communication are not going to be able to recruit such symbols for other purposes. Without the ability to use the system to communicate with other members of one's species, and without intergenerational transfer of the system to offspring in the group, it is unlikely that the system will develop. Consider the evolution of creoles from pidgins, as illustrated in the creation of a new sign language in Nicaragua in the late twentieth century. In a short period of time, a group of deaf children who were brought together created a language, by modifying elements of various home signs they brought with them to the school. As younger children joined the school, the system continued to change and increase in complexity, with grammatical structures like noun–verb agreement (Senghas and Coppola 2001). And while parrots should be able to autonomously use the symbols they acquire, Pepperberg reports that Alex didn't like the other parrots she brought into his community, and there are no reports that I can find of Alex talking with other parrots.

There are reports of great apes using their symbolic systems to communicate with one another. The ASL study that began with Washoe also included other apes, including Loulis, Washoe's adopted son, who learned signs from her (Fouts et al. 1982). Loulis reportedly used his signs to communicate about play with his young friend Dar. When the play got too rough Loulis would sign to Washoe to get comfort. He also appeared to blame Dar for starting a fight, by signing "good good me" to Washoe and then pointing and screaming at Dar (Fouts and Fouts 1993). Savage-Rumbaugh has conducted formal tests that indicate the chimpanzees Sherman and Austin can use lexigrams to communicate to one another; when one chimpanzee needed a tool that the other chimpanzee had access to, he could use the correct lexigram to request the appropriate tool, which would then be provided (Savage-Rumbaugh 1986). The real promise of the artificial animal language research program would be the development of communication systems by groups of individuals who, like the deaf Nicaraguan children, modify what they are given to create a new language. There is some evidence that groups of zebra finches who learned nonstandard songs will, over a few generations, develop a wild-type song in much the same way humans create creoles (Fehér et al. 2009), but unlike the symbol trained apes, humans know little about what zebra finch songs might mean to the birds. We have as of yet seen nothing like creolization in artificial animal language systems.

There are at least two ways in which having a symbolic language can be related to thought. The one we have already examined in preceding chapters is the claim that language is required for thought. The second, less controversial claim is that language and symbolic representational systems more generally, while not being a requirement for thought, do allow for a significant expansion of thought and cognitive processes because they permit a way of offloading cognitive work from the brain into the linguistic environment. With speech, language allows us to share tasks and solve problems through dynamic interaction, linking brains together. With written symbols, language allows us to make lists to help our memories, to prioritize and schedule our tasks, and to make inferences about complex relationships. Symbols allow us to better interact with others, to explain our actions and share our plans.

The use of animals' communication systems, both natural and artificial, appears at this point to lack one of the things that human language is used for, namely giving information to someone who doesn't already have it. In order to do that, one has to first understand what another does and doesn't know, and has to realize that the information would be useful to the other. We don't yet know whether other animals provide information in this way. We do know that many animal signals are subject to audience effects, such that a call will only be made when the appropriate audience is around. But the presence of an audience may be part of the stimulus that causes an animal to make a functionally referential call. For example, vervet monkeys may not give an alarm call when alone, but they will continue to produce alarm calls even after all the group members are safe (Cheney and Seyfarth 1996). Cheney and Seyfarth argue that because vervet monkeys lack a theory of mind, they fail in this basic aspect of communication and pragmatics.

5.4 Chapter summary

Like the question "Do animals have beliefs?," the question of whether animals communicate requires clarification in order to be answered properly. Biological, informational, and intentional views about the nature of communication will give different answers to the question in some cases, but they need not be in conflict with one another. And while intentional communication is of primary interest when it comes to looking at similarities and differences between humans and other animals, here again we see that our theories of intentional communication are still developing. Investigation into the cognitive requirements for intentional communication starts with our assumptions that human children communicate at an early age, and using the calibration method we can examine both our notion of intentional communication and the developing abilities of children to help us better understand in what sense different species might be engaged in intentional communication. But one thing seems clear: if communication, whether linguistic or nonlinguistic, is intentional, then it must involve some sort of social understanding. Intentional communication only occurs when one has an inkling that there is a communicative partner. In the next chapter we will turn to look at the research on social cognition, folk psychology, and theory of mind/mindreading in other species in order to determine what this understanding might look like.

Further reading

The anthology *Animal Communication Theory: Information and Influence*, edited by Ulrich Stegmann (2013), is a state of the art collection of papers by philosophers and scientists.

For two very different examples of theories of ape communication see *Origins of Human Communication* by Michael Tomasello (2008), and *The Dynamic Dance: Nonvocal Communication in African Great Apes* by Barbara King (2004).

There are lots of resources about teaching language to animals. The documentary film *Project Nim* is an emotional depiction of the attempts to teach American Sign Language to a chimpanzee. Nim's biography is also an excellent read: *Nim Chimpsky: The Chimp Who Would Be Human* by Elizabeth Hess (2008).

Sue Savage-Rumbaugh describes her work teaching a symbolic communication to Kanzi and other apes in her book *Kanzi: The Ape at the Brink of the Human Mind* (Savage-Rumbaugh and Lewin 1994). And Irene Pepperberg describes her work teaching English to Alex the parrot in *The Alex Studies: Cognitive and Communicative Abilities of Grey Parrots* (1999).

6 Knowing minds

Gelada baboons live in small groups led by a dominant male who has exclusive mating rights with all adult females. The subordinate males of the group aren't allowed any sex with females, and so they typically leave their natal group and try to take over a group of their own. Despite this, about a quarter of the babies born in a gelada group are not the dominant's offspring. Clearly, the baboons are up to something. Indeed, a controlled study of gelada mating behavior found that when baboons have unsanctioned sexual relations, they keep quiet, while when females mate with the dominant male, they vocalize loudly. Researchers think that cheaters take the dominant male's perspective into account, and position themselves out of his visual and acoustic perspectives (Le Roux et al. 2013).

What's going on here? Are the cheating baboons thinking about how best to fool the dominant, realizing that he will be angry if he sees them mating? Can they understand what he can see and hear? Do the baboons think about the mind of the other baboons?

If the cheaters were humans, it would be easy to find answers to these questions. We whisper about cheaters, and tell stories about their motivations and mistaken beliefs, anticipating the tragedy to come. This is what sells gossip magazines.

But imagine our world with no *US Weekly*, no *Star*, no celebrity section of the *Huffington Post*. Imagine spending no time thinking what others are doing and why they are doing it. While our lives probably wouldn't be affected for the worse if we were to stop gossiping about people we'll never have the chance to meet, our lack of interest in the minds around us would be devastating. Imagine what our world would be like if no one else cared about how we feel, what we think, our goals or our pains. We would have no group projects, because no one would be concerned with figuring out what our goals are, and so nobody would be cooperating. On the bright side, no one would fool us either, because they wouldn't be able to think about what they want us to think. But, in such a world, even if we were surrounded by people, we would remain utterly alone.

This imaginary world is so alien to a social species like ours, which thrives on having deep relationships with others. We manage our reputations by curating what we put out for public display, from the way we dress to our carefully crafted Facebook updates. When we talk to each other, we overwhelmingly discuss what people are doing and why they are doing it—as much as two-thirds of our conversational life is taken up with such gossip (Dunbar 1996). Children are like adults in this way, and little kids would rather talk about people and actions than about anything else (Hood et al. 1979).

Given our intense interest in others, a natural question is whether any other species shares our fascination. While the question seems simple enough, it very quickly becomes evident that it isn't so easy to answer. Since other animals don't use language, they don't gossip. And while social species are excellent at coordinating behavior—even sneaky sex—it isn't clear whether they are thinking about others' *minds* or others' *behavior*.

6.1 Mindreading (or theory of mind)

Whichever term you use (philosophers tend to prefer "mindreading" while psychologists use "theory of mind"), the topic is the same, namely the ability to view others as having a mind and mental states. We all assume that other humans read minds, and we have introspective evidence that we do it ourselves. Psychologists David Premack and Guy Woodruff were the first to ask whether chimpanzees do it too in their 1978 paper "Does the chimpanzee have a theory of mind?" They showed Sarah, a 14-year-old chimpanzee, short videos of a human beginning to engage in some typical chimpanzee or human goal-oriented behavior such as acquiring out-of-reach bananas or warming up a cold room with a heater. Sarah was then shown two photographs, one of which demonstrated the goal of the action, and she did a good job picking the correct photograph for her preferred trainer (interestingly, Sarah tended to choose photos depicting mishaps when shown pictures of a trainer she didn't like very much) (Premack and Woodruff 1978).

Premack and Woodruff claim that Sarah's performance shows that she understands that the actor has an *intention*. They suggest that the best interpretation of their findings is that Sarah does have a theory of mind, because "In looking at the video, [s]he imputes at least two states of mind to the human actor, namely, intention or purpose on the one hand, and knowledge or belief on the other" (Premack and Woodruff 1978, 518). To be fair, they say that additional research is necessary, but that nonetheless their study offers preliminary evidence that chimpanzees think about others' beliefs and desires or goals. They reason as follows: Belief alone, like purpose alone, may not be enough to make a correct prediction because cognitive states and motivational states are jointly necessary for behavior. A person might *want* to acquire the bananas, but without *knowing* where they are there's nothing she can do about it. Similarly, I may *want* to acquire a million dollars, but this desire alone isn't going to cause me to do anything in the absence of some belief about how to achieve that goal; if I *believe* that playing the lottery will help me gain a million dollars, and I desire to have a million dollars, I will play the lottery. Since Sarah is predicting what the human is going to do next, she must be thinking of both his belief and his goal/desire. The only other option, as they see it, would be that Sarah is reasoning about behavior. But that would require knowledge of a huge number of regularities unmediated by any unifying theory, and they think it is unlikely that that's what Sarah is doing. As they put it, "The ape could only be a mentalist. Unless we are badly mistaken, [s]he is not intelligent enough to be a behaviorist" (Premack and Woodruff 1978, 526).

This report was just the beginning of what has turned into a huge debate about mindreading in other species. Premack and Woodruff failed to convince many that Sarah has a theory of mind. In his commentary on the article, the anthropologist Ben Beck pointed out that chimpanzees and humans alike do not need a theory of mind to be good at predicting behavior. The philosopher Tyler Burge agreed, remarking that he can see a beetle stymied by an obstacle in its path and immediately understand its problem without attributing mental states to the beetle. While these insights were largely ignored, other commentaries played a central role in shaping future research. Daniel Dennett worried that Sarah's behavior could be explained via associative reasoning, and suggested an alternative experiment based on asking whether chimpanzees can think that others have *false* beliefs. He writes,

> Very young children watching a Punch and Judy show squeal in anticipatory delight as Punch prepares to throw the box over the cliff. Why? Because *they know Punch thinks Judy is still in the box.* They know better; they saw Judy escape while Punch's back was turned. We take the children's excitement as overwhelmingly good evidence that they understand the situation – they understand that Punch is acting on a mistaken belief (although they are not sophisticated enough to put it that way). Would chimpanzees exhibit similar excitement if presented with a similar bit of play acting (in a drama that spoke directly to their "interests")? I do not know, and think it would be worth finding out, for if they didn't react, the hypothesis that they impute beliefs and desires to others would be dealt a severe blow, even if all the P&W tests turn out positively, just because it can be made so obvious – obvious enough for four-year-old children – that Punch believes (falsely) that Judy is in the box.
>
> (Dennett 1978, 569)

Dennett's idea, which was shared by two other philosophers who wrote commentary on the study (Bennett 1978; Harman 1978), stemmed from a discussion in the philosophy of mind about the nature of belief and its role in mentality. There are two main ideas, only one of which was largely acknowledged by Premack and Woodruff. The first idea is that belief and desire together cause action, and thus there is a tight relationship between the two.

The second main idea is that beliefs are the sort of things that are true or false. If we didn't actually take belief to be the sort of thing that can be true or false, we wouldn't need to talk about beliefs at all. Instead, we could speak of knowledge, or even more distant from mentalism, we might say, "Such and such is the case, and T is familiar with such and such." As discussed in Chapter 4, when we use the term 'belief', we are often contrasting it with a contrary belief— "he believes that the shops are open Monday, because he doesn't know it is a holiday."

Gilbert Harman appears to be working from the insight that error is what gives belief its point when he offers a test to determine whether chimpanzees attribute beliefs:

Suppose that a subject chimpanzee sees a second chimpanzee watch a banana being placed into one of two opaque pots. The second chimpanzee is then distracted while the banana is removed from the first pot and placed in the second. If the subject chimpanzee expects the second chimpanzee to reach into the pot which originally contained the banana, that would seem to show that it has a conception of mere belief.

(Harman 1978, 576–578)

Harman's idea for testing mindreading was taken up by developmental psychologists who developed the false belief test for human children. The psychologists Hans Wimmer and Josef Perner (Wimmer and Perner 1983) showed children a puppet show in which Maxi puts away a piece of chocolate before leaving the room. While Maxi is out, his mother finds the chocolate and moves it to another location. Maxi returns to the scene, the show is stopped, and children are asked to predict where Maxi will go to look for his chocolate. If children predict that Maxi will look for the chocolate where he left it, then they demonstrate their ability to attribute false beliefs to others, or so it is thought. But the child that predicts that Maxi will look for the chocolate where it really is doesn't demonstrate an ability to attribute different beliefs to others, and so they might not yet have a concept of belief. In this original study, most children younger than four predict that Maxi will search for the chocolate where it is, and children older than four pass more often than not (Wimmer and Perner 1983). This test became known as the Sally-Ann task, after a version of the same story given to children on the autistic spectrum (Baron-Cohen 1995). After hundreds of tests, it seems pretty clear that typically developing children pass this test around four years of age (Wellman et al. 2001, but see Yazdi et al. 2006 for a critique of the metastudy).

While the false belief task became a popular research program in child development, the inability to tell such stories to chimpanzees made it difficult to use as a test for mindreading in other species. While there have been many studies purporting to show some understanding of intentionality, goals, desires, perceptions, and beliefs in chimpanzees, Premack and Woodruff's question remains a live one.

6.1.1 Is nonhuman mindreading empirically tractable?

Dozens of empirical studies of mindreading in great apes, monkeys, dogs, dolphins, and elephants have been performed already. It may seem that we just need to find the right test in order to determine whether another species thinks about mental states. However, there are some reasons to think that empirical research is the wrong way to proceed on this issue. As we saw in Chapter 4, José Bermúdez thinks that nonlinguistic animals cannot engage in logical thought because they cannot think about thought. If animals can't think about thought, then they certainly can't mindread. Bermúdez contends that mindreading isn't possible without language. This isn't an empirical claim; rather, it rests on the idea that in order to think about thought, thoughts need to be represented in some format that permits metacognition, and, he claims, only public language can do that.

The overall line of reasoning starts with what Bermúdez calls the argument from intentional ascent (or thinking about thoughts), which can be stated as follows:

1   For a thought to be the object of a second-order thought, it must be represented.
2   Representations are either symbolic (requiring the use of natural language) or pictorial.
3   In order for a thought to have an inferential role it must be composed of elements that play a role in other related thoughts.
4   Symbolic representations are composed of elements that play a role in other related thoughts.
5   Pictorial representations are not composed of elements that play a role in other related thoughts.
6   Therefore, for a thought to have an inferential role, it must be a symbolic representation, involving elements of a natural language.
7   Second-order thoughts require thoughts to have an inferential role.
8   Animals do not have language.
9   Therefore, animals do not have second-order thoughts.

The upshot of this argument is that thoughts can be the object of thoughts only if they take linguistic form. Bermúdez concludes that intentional ascent, or thinking about thoughts, requires semantic ascent, or thinking about words.

Premise (2) is key to this argument. Bermúdez considers two different mechanisms that would permit metacognition and logical thought, and then goes about showing how one of them cannot do the job. This argument is reminiscent of Davidson's claim that he can think of no other way than language to think about truth or falsity. Bermúdez goes one step further, proposing a possible alternative, and then arguing that it cannot succeed. That work is done in premise (5), which he defends by arguing that there is no structure to pictures, no joints at which to divide them, and so they cannot offer the structure needed for truth-evaluability and inferential roles.

However, other philosophers think that pictorial representations, such as maps or diagrams, offer a richer structure than Bermúdez gives them credit for, and they can account for some degree of rational inference (Braddon-Mitchell and Jackson 1996; Camp 2007; Lewis 1994; Rescorla 2009b). Imagistic map-like representations can take the place of mental sentences. They provide a great deal of information in virtue of their organization. The elements of maps are systematic and productive (e.g. if the map says "Minneapolis is north of Toronto" it also says "Toronto is south of Minneapolis"), and different maps can be made using the same elements to express new beliefs.

But can maps support logical inference? Camp (2007) thinks maps can express negation, disjunction, the conditional, and tense. She suggests that negation would be represented pictorially with colored icons that represent positive or negative information. Dynamic maps might represent disjunction and conditional via flashing lights, tense could be represented by italics. One could even represent some existential quantifiers, such as "There exists a school right here." However, she doesn't think maps can account for non-specific existentials such as "I know that the right guy is out there, I just need to find him!" or universal generalizations.

Camp concludes that although maps have fewer expressive limitations than one might suppose, they cannot account for the full expressive power of language.

In addition, one can worry about the claim in premise (2) that symbolic representations require natural language. Robert Lurz (2007) argues that premise (2) implies:

(T) Thinking about thoughts requires thinking about sentences in a public language.

In adopting this view, Bermúdez rejects language of thought, because all the required symbolic representations in the language of thought are at the subpersonal, or unconscious, level. Bermúdez is also deviating from views such as Davidson's, according to which thought requires language, because he thinks one can have thought, but not thoughts about thoughts, without language. Bermúdez is carving out a new conceptual space in the discussion of the relationship between thought and language.

However, there are reasons to be wary of Bermúdez's theory. Lurz argues that Bermúdez relies on two additional premises to defend claim (T). These are:

(L2) Necessarily, to think about thoughts, as in PA [propositional attitude] ascriptions, involves entertaining them consciously and considering how they relate to each other logically and evidentially.

(Lurz 2007, 276)

(L3) Necessarily, entertaining thoughts in the manner of second-order cognitive dynamics, as one does in having explicitly reasoned higher-order PAs, requires the representational vehicles of the thoughts to be (i) at the personal level and (ii) linguistic; and the only representational vehicles of thought that satisfy conditions (i) and (ii) are sentences in a natural language.

(Lurz 2007, 287–288)

Lurz argues that (L2) can't be true because we also unconsciously think thoughts about thoughts, and he cites empirical evidence showing that children are able to think about thoughts without considering their logical relations or the evidence we have for them. This evidence comes from showing that children who can pass false belief tasks, such as the Sally-Anne task, still have deficits when it comes to understanding implications of their beliefs and the evidence that led them to construct the belief that they did.

One way Bermúdez may respond to this critique is to challenge the idea that children who pass the false belief task are actually attributing beliefs to the characters in the story. As we will see later in this chapter, there are possible nonmentalistic heuristics that could be applied in order to pass this test. However, this move isn't really open to Bermúdez, since these children are able to *talk* about the beliefs of others. Since for Bermúdez speaking about belief is what it means to represent belief, he would have to accept that these children are able to think about thoughts.

Lurz also challenges (L3) by suggesting that Bermúdez's requirement that the vehicles of thought are at the personal or conscious level is unwarranted, because it assumes that if the vehicles were at the subpersonal level, the thoughts carried by that vehicle would also have to be at the subpersonal level. But there is no defense of the claim that for thoughts to be conscious the representational vehicle of the thought also has to be conscious. By asserting this, Bermúdez begs the question and denies a distinction many take to be essential, namely the distinction between first-order thought and metacognitive thought.

If Bermúdez is right, then the empirical research program dedicated to answering Premack and Woodruff's question is misguided, because the question is already answered a priori. If the animal doesn't talk about belief, the animal doesn't think about belief. But if Lurz is right, there is empirical work to be done.

6.1.2 The "logical problem"

If we move forward with the notion that Premack and Woodruff's question is one that can be answered empirically, the next question that arises is an epistemic one: what sort of evidence do we need to conclude that a nonhuman animal is a mindreader? Researchers inspired by the philosophical analysis of belief devised experiments that sought to determine whether chimpanzees can understand others' false mental states. Among all candidates, false perception has been of particular interest. But these studies have all been challenged by what the psychologists Daniel Povinelli and Jennifer Vonk refer to as involving "logical problems" (Povinelli and Vonk 2003, 160), which leads to what Susan Hurley and Matthew Nudds dubbed "the logical problem" (Hurley and Nudds 2006b). The problem arises when trying to decide between two kinds of hypotheses—mindreading and behavior reading. Povinelli and Vonk claim that because our mental state attributions are largely due to our observations of the person's behavior, whenever we are predicting behavior we might just as likely be relying on associations between behaviors as we are relying on associations between mental states and behavior.

Povinelli and Vonk introduce this puzzle as a critique of a study that purports to show that chimpanzees know what other chimpanzees can see. The psychologists Brian Hare, Josep Call, and Michael Tomasello investigated this question in the context of food competition between a dominant and subordinate chimpanzee. In one of the experimental conditions, they set up a room with a door at each end, and positioned a chimpanzee at each door. In all cases, one of the chimpanzees was dominant over the other. This is an important part of the experiment, because subordinate chimpanzees know that they are not allowed to take food from a dominant chimpanzee; they risk getting beaten up. The experimenters set up the room so that there were two cloth bags in the middle of the room, and they placed a piece of banana or apple on the subordinate's side of the bag. The subordinate was allowed to watch the room set up in all conditions, but the dominant was only allowed to watch the placement of the food in the informed condition, otherwise the food was hidden while the dominant chimpanzee was behind

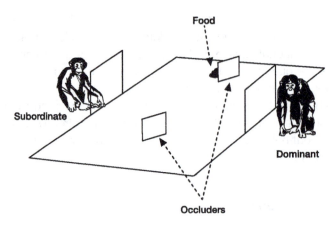

Figure 6.1 Chimpanzee food competition set up. The subordinate only seeks the food the dominant cannot see. (Source: Hare et al. 2001)

a door. The subordinate chimpanzee was very good at avoiding the food the dominant saw being hidden, and seeking out the food that the dominant didn't see being hidden. The researchers concluded from these findings that chimpanzees understand the mental state of seeing (Hare et al. 2001).

However, Povinelli and Vonk have a different interpretation of what's going on in this study. Chimpanzees have lots of opportunities to watch other chimpanzees move toward food, and so they had ample opportunity to notice that some particular behavior or bodily posture, such as turning one's head toward food, usually results in the dominant animal moving toward the food item. Given past experience, the subordinate need only notice the dominant's bodily orientation in order to predict that the dominate who turned his head toward the food will now move toward the food. Povinelli and Vonk write,

> Techniques that pivot upon behavioral invariants (looking, gazing, threatening, peering out the corner of the eye, accidentally spilling juice versus intentionally pouring it out), will always presuppose that the chimpanzee (or other agent) has access to the invariant, thus crippling any attempt to establish whether a mentalistic coding is also used.
>
> (Povinelli and Vonk 2003, 159)

They conclude that no experiment that relies on behavioral invariants can decide between a mindreading and a behavior reading explanation.

Povinelli and Vonk argue that in order to avoid the possibility that the chimpanzees predict based on behavioral invariants rather than taking the extra step of inferring mental state from behavior, mindreading tests need to be devised so that the task can't be solved by reference to past experience with others' behavior. The task should be set in an unfamiliar context that requires the chimpanzee to draw inferences in order to predict a new behavior, one that he hasn't any behavioral abstractions for. They think that a version of the experiment proposed by Heyes (1998) would suffice:

Subjects would first be exposed to the subjective experience of wearing two buckets containing visors which look identical from the outside, but one of which is see-through, the other of which is opaque. The buckets would be of different colors and/or shapes in order to provide the arbitrary cue to their different experiential qualities. Then, at test, subjects are given the opportunity to use their begging gesture to request food from one of two experimenters, one wearing the <seeing> bucket and the other wearing the <not seeing> bucket ... By definition, S_b has no information that would lead the subjects to generate this response. In contrast, a system that first codes the first person mental experience, and then attributes an analog of this experience to the other agent (in other words, S_{b+ms}) could have relevant information upon which to base a response.

(Povinelli and Vonk 2004, 14)

This experiment seems promising, because the chimpanzee subjects would not have the prior experience of seeing humans wearing buckets. But would the success of this study really avoid the logical problem? I think not. The chimpanzee who successfully begs from the experimenter wearing the <seeing> bucket could have, *from his own experience*, made the connection between wearing the see-through bucket and being able to do things—like walking around without bumping into things, or acquiring food items in the enclosure (Andrews 2005). Rather than generalizing from one's own *mental* experience, the chimpanzee could be generalizing from his own *physical* experience. One can solve this task by making the behavioral connection between wearing the opaque bucket and *not being able to do things*, and from that decide to beg from the person who can do things.

While the logical problem wasn't presented as a logical barrier to doing empirical research on chimpanzee theory of mind, the worry arises that no experiment can in principle avoid these alternative interpretations. However, Povinelli and Vonk think that the problem is surmountable, as does Lurz. He argues that we can overcome the logical problem by designing an experiment where the chimpanzee's behavior isn't subject to a *complementary* behavior reading hypothesis—a hypothesis that takes the same features of the environment that are used to ascribe mental states to be, by themselves, sufficient to anticipate behavior (Lurz 2011).

Lurz thinks that we can gain new insight about how to devise such an experiment by considering the adaptive function of mindreading. He suggests that the reason why we mindread is that our ancestors found it useful to predict the behavior of conspecifics who were looking at ambiguous stimuli, such as camouflaged predators or prey. The function of mindreading is to predict others' behavior in opaque environmental contexts, such as in the face of visual illusions. Because the natural world is rife with camouflage, Lurz thinks that recognizing something as camouflage, such as seeing that what looks like a leaf is in fact a bug, was the first step in perceptual mindreading. The next step would be to recognize that another individual didn't see the "leaf" as a bug, but that he saw the "leaf" as a leaf. In order to do that, one has to be able to introspect one's own perceptual state and then compare it with the perceptual state of the other individual. Lurz doesn't elaborate on the specific benefits that would accrue to an individual with this ability, but he does use this idea to design a series of experiments that examine whether an animal can predict what another will do based on the recognition that the other is experiencing a perceptual illusion.

In one case, Lurz suggests a modification of the chimpanzee food competition study in which researchers train a subordinate and a dominant chimpanzee that orange bananas are not real bananas. The chimpanzees already love yellow bananas. After training, the subordinate is exposed to translucent red barriers that make real yellow bananas look like fake orange ones. Once the subordinate understands how the barriers work, a naive dominant is invited in for the test. The room is baited with two yellow bananas on the subordinate chimpanzee's side of two barriers. Because one barrier is transparent and the other is translucent red, the subordinate who can perceptually mindread will seek out the banana behind the red barrier, because the dominant will think it is a fake orange banana, and will go for the yellow treat behind the transparent barrier.

Lurz criticizes the original food competition task, which can be explained in terms of the complementary behavior reading hypothesis by appealing to direct line of gaze (a facial/bodily orientation of the chimpanzee toward the object): the dominant has always eaten food to which he has a direct line of gaze; in the study, the dominant has direct line of gaze to the food in the open, but not to the food behind the barrier, so the dominant will move toward the food in the open. Because in his task the subordinate chimpanzee has never observed anyone interact with a red barrier, Lurz claims there is no complementary behavior reading hypothesis about direct line of gaze through translucent red barriers. However, such an interpretation is available (Andrews 2012b). Because the subordinate might see the transparent barriers as offering a direct line of gaze and the red translucent barriers as strange blockers or modifiers of direct line of gaze, the subordinate could predict that the dominant would move toward the banana to which the dominant has a direct line of gaze, rather than toward the banana to which the dominant's gaze is obstructed by an odd barrier. This doesn't require that the subordinate think anything about how the bananas *appear* to the dominant chimpanzee.

More recently, Lurz and the psychologist Carla Krachun proposed a different test of chimpanzee mindreading based on Lurz's evolutionary account (Lurz and Krachun 2011). Krachun has found that chimpanzees are able to learn about the affordances of minimizing and magnifying glasses to choose the largest grape, even when it is under a minimizing lens and looks small (Krachun et al. 2009). They propose using a violation of expectation task, in which a chimpanzee is watching a human competitor choose a grape that the chimpanzee alone saw placed in a minimizing or maximizing box. The chimpanzee expects that the human will try to get the largest grape, and so should be surprised if, for example, the human reaches for the grape that looks smaller but is actually bigger. While Lurz and Krachun think there is no complementary behavior reading hypothesis available to interpret success on this task, the training trials would teach the chimpanzee that the human reaches for objects with a relative size difference. The chimpanzee can use this experience with the human's past behavior to expect that the human will continue reaching for the large-looking grape, even though the chimpanzee himself would prefer the other grape (the chimpanzee could do this because he would have a past experience of the actual size that he could use to set his own goal, but he need not know *why* he was able to solve the task). So the logical problem appears to remain unsolved.

6.1.3 Do we need to solve the logical problem?

The challenge to come up with an experiment that avoids the logical problem may be a red herring. While for any one experiment we may be able to come up with an alternative behavior reading explanation, science doesn't usually proceed by relying on a single groundbreaking experiment to prove a theory true. Instead, a research program arises, involving many different researchers, studies, and approaches, and which aims to investigate the phenomenon from a variety of angles. How science progresses has been a matter of some debate among philosophers of science—from Karl Popper's view that science proceeds by attempting to falsify theories and rejecting those theories whose predictions are not supported by experimental results, to Thomas Kuhn's view that scientific change only happens after too many problems arise with a theory which in turn leads to a paradigm shift, to Imre Lakatos' view that science progresses through the construction of auxiliary hypotheses to explain false predictions, which in turn permit new and more precise predictions. On all these views, scientific progress isn't a deductive practice; the evidence for a hypothesis cannot *guarantee* the truth of the hypothesis. Rather, the evidence offers support.

In order to gain support for a hypothesis, we may seek to confirm it. Confirmation, however, isn't as straightforward as it might seem. There exist various accounts of what it is to confirm a hypothesis. For example, according to the hypothetico-deductive model, we can confirm a hypothesis when it, plus any necessary auxiliary hypotheses, entails the observable evidence. Experimentalists use this method when they form predictions from their hypotheses, and test whether their predictions come true. A successful prediction then offers some evidence for the theory that, along with auxiliary hypotheses, entails it. However, on this view, a false prediction isn't able to disconfirm a theory. As Lakatos points out, what often happens in science is that either the theories are modified to take into account the new predictions or different auxiliary hypotheses are constructed. For example, when Newton's theory of celestial mechanics made a false prediction about the orbit of Uranus, scientists didn't reject Newton's theory. Instead, they questioned some of the auxiliary hypotheses, including the hypothesis that the solar system had only seven planets. This move led astronomers to discover the planet Neptune. When we turn to hypotheses dealing with entities that are not directly observable, like particles, waves, or beliefs, any empirical finding is going to be consistent with multiple hypotheses, because hypotheses dealing with unobservables are even more deeply entrenched in a set of auxiliary hypotheses that led to the postulation of the entity in the first place. So we shouldn't be surprised by the fact that when examining chimpanzee theory of mind using the hypothetico-deductive method, researchers are faced with competing hypotheses. The philosopher W.V.O. Quine suggests that when we deal with competing hypotheses we should reject the hypothesis that is less entrenched in our web of belief. If the hypothesis has lots of other hypotheses resting on it—such as our hypothesis that there exists an external world—then we shouldn't reject it if we can instead reject a hypothesis that plays a less crucial role in the system.

Another account of confirmation comes from probability theory. Bayesian approaches to confirmation share the idea that evidence increases the probability that a hypothesis is true. In an attempt to examine claims about the chimpanzee's mental capacities more generally, Sober examines the evidence for mental continuity between humans and chimpanzees from a Bayesian confirmation approach (Sober 2012). The hypothesis he investigates is: "if human beings and a closely related species (e.g. chimpanzees) both exhibit behavior B, and if human beings produce B by occupying mental state M, then this is *evidence* that M is also the proximate mechanism that chimpanzees deploy in producing B" (2012, 230). That is, given that both chimpanzees and humans engage in the same behavior, we can examine which probability is greater: that chimpanzees have the mental cause of that behavior given that humans have that mental cause, or that chimpanzees have that mental cause alone. From the fact that humans and other apes share a common ancestor, we can examine whether the two effects trace back to a common cause. Unfortunately, Sober concludes, we don't yet have enough evidence to draw a good conclusion about the truth of the hypothesis. What do we need? More evidence, which means more empirical study, of both behavior and biology.

Whatever your account of confirmation is, when doing science you will always have competing hypotheses, but scientists need not worry that there are alternative hypotheses explaining a phenomenon. Instead, they need only to defend the claim that their chosen hypothesis best accounts for the *overall* body of data. As Heyes reminds us, inference to the best explanation arguments rely on the existence of alternative hypotheses. But they also rely on having plenty of data. When we are deciding between competing hypotheses, we appeal to the body of data at hand, and can use Quine's test to decide which one to accept for now. The fact that each piece of evidence has its own, different alternative interpretation need not be of much significance. So while we need not worry about solving the logical problem, we do need to have the right kind of data in order to draw conclusions between competing hypotheses. Given that at this point there is quite a bit of experimental data on chimpanzee social cognition, we can now turn to the question of whether we have the right sort of data to answer Premack and Woodruff's question.

6.1.4 Benefits of mindreading

One way to examine mindreading in other species is to examine what benefits might accrue to individuals who mindread, and then look for evidence that animals enjoy those benefits. As has already been mentioned, one benefit of mindreading might be improved ability to predict behavior. Another benefit of mindreading might be the ability to explain behavior.

The benefits of mindreading are often discussed in the context of the Social Intelligence Hypothesis, according to which the reason why humans and other primates are so smart is because they are so social. Complex cognitive capacities arose due to the pressures associated with living in large social groups, not due to other, more ecological pressures such as foraging or avoiding predators. The Social Intelligence Hypothesis predicts that intelligence will be a function of social group size for all animal species (except for the eusocial insects).

The idea that mindreading facilitates prediction took hold in the Machiavellian version of the Social Intelligence Hypothesis, which suggests that the reason why social life led to such a problem for our ancestors is that they lived in a cutthroat environment, and access to food and mates was always a struggle (Whiten and Byrne 1988). Learning how to outwit one's competitors through deception was a valuable trick, and offered selective advantage to those who learned it. True deception, of course, involves making someone believe something that isn't true, and it is useful to deceive others in order to manipulate them to act in a certain way. As individuals gain a more sophisticated theory of social action and greater predictive success, they up the stakes for other members of their community, thus creating an evolutionary arms race. Since attributing propositional attitudes is needed for making the most accurate predictions of behavior, the arms race led to the development of mental state concepts such as belief as well as a theory of how beliefs and desires cause behavior. It takes sophisticated cognition to develop these abilities, because it requires the postulation of theoretical entities such as belief and desire, and it requires the development of some mechanism for using these theoretical entities to make predictions of behavior. And this was the thinking that led to the idea that belief attribution evolved to make better predictions of behavior in a competitive social environment.

If mindreading evolved to predict another's behavior better, then it makes sense to look for mindreading in the predictive behaviors of other animals, particularly in situations where animals benefit from deceiving another. However, it may be that mindreading isn't necessary for engaging in deceptive behavior. One could develop the skill of deceiving and manipulating others without mindreading, but rather by being a good behavior-reader. For example,

> Our ancestors could have engaged in the very behaviors that have been touted as evolutionarily advantageous, such as hiding food or having forbidden sex, without attributing mental states to one another. For example, an ancestor may have come to notice that every time he found food, he made a certain sound, and when he made that sound, everyone else came and took away some of the food. He may have wondered what made everyone come running when he found food, and perhaps he experimented with different aspects of his food-finding behavior. One variable he tested was the food-discovery cry. Once he noticed that people came when he uttered the cry, he learned not to utter the cry when he wanted to keep the food for himself. We describe this behavior as deceptive, and coming up with this trick would surely have been an advantage for our ancestor, as it represents a cognitive step toward scientific reasoning and would offer him a benefit when living in a large social group. However, it does not require the attribution, or even the concepts, of belief or desire.
>
> (Andrews 2012a, 109)

While the Machiavellian version of the Social Intelligence Hypothesis offers one reason to think that mindreading abilities are best found in competitive predictive situations, cooperative versions of the hypothesis suggest looking in other places. Our hominid ancestors didn't only compete with one another, but they innovated tools and shared their knowledge with others; they lived in communities, built shelters, and engaged in joint activities such as child rearing, foraging, and hunting. These early cooperative behaviors led to the development of different social traditions and cultures—differences in language, in norms, in dress, in food, and in art. The creation of culture, and of social groups within a culture, also relies on complex cognition and may hugely benefit from mindreading abilities. Being able to explain the behaviors of group members in terms of their reasons for action could offer a significant advantage to cooperative societies, for it permits the spread of new behaviors that may be beneficial.

To take a simple, but probably apocryphal example, consider the innovation of cooking meat (Andrews 2012a). Learning to put meat in fire before eating it offered great nutritional benefits to hominids. However, imagine the innovation of cooking: one individual takes the meat from a difficult hunt and sticks it in the fire. Fire, known to be destructive, might seem like a bad place to put your valuables. But if the individual's community members were able to consider reasons for his behavior, they wouldn't cast him out for damaging their food supplies; rather, they would give him an opportunity to explain. Knowing that people act from mental states allows us to understand that there may be opaque reasons to engage in the behavior, no matter how strange the behavior might seem.

Mindreading for explanation seeking makes sense of the host of cooperative social behaviors we see in humans and some other species. Social animals don't just compete and have sneaky sex, but they also engage in collaborative activities. For example, social learning, or coming to perform actions that you see demonstrated by others, and tolerating naive individuals' attention to your skilled performances, is one of those activities. Many species demonstrate social learning abilities, from rats, guppies, and cowbirds, to monkeys, dolphins, and elephants. While there are probably various mechanisms involved in social learning, they all require some sort of recognition that a particular behavior is valuable and worthy of performing. And because social learning leads an individual to copy group members, different behaviors can arise in different groups in the same species, even when the groups share a similar environment. This leads to what researchers describe as cultural traditions, understood as population-specific differences in behavior that are not ascribable to purely ecological differences in communities, socially learned, and which persevere for some time. The Japanese primatologist Kinji Imanishi is the first one who suggested that other animals also have culture, based on the observation that the Japanese macaques on Koshima Island wash sweet potatoes in the water before eating them (Imanishi 1957). This unusual behavior led to further investigation of differences between macaque communities across Japan, and Imanishi and his colleagues found differences in social behavior as well as food processing among these communities. While careful to distinguish human cultural achievement such as religion and music from the culture we see in other species, Imanishi, who was later joined by Western anthropologists and psychologists, was convinced that the behavior we see in macaques (as well as various species including all the great apes, dolphins and whales, monkeys, and several bird species) is evolutionarily continuous with the more rarified aspects of human culture.

These considerations suggest that we can learn about how animals understand other minds by doing research that goes beyond the standard false belief task, and by examining naturalistic behaviors, including explanation-seeking and social learning, and using those observations to devise experiments that go beyond the framework of behavior prediction. Animals may mindread to learn, to satisfy their curiosity, and to understand how to help others, in addition to using it to cheat and deceive. Mindreading might help explain why adult chimpanzees at the Lincoln Park Zoo don't put on their usual dominance displays toward Knuckles, a juvenile male who has cerebral palsy. Rather than screaming at him when he approaches, the dominant male tolerates Knuckles, and even grooms him. Frans de Waal reports that physically disabled chimpanzees have lived to adulthood in the wild, as evidenced by the discovery of skeletons. He suggests that these individuals could only have lived that long if they had been fed by group members who were able to understand their needs and abilities (2009). Mindreading could have assisted there too.

By looking at these other examples of where and how mindreading could be beneficial for social animals, we are confronted with a more basic question about animal social understanding than that which Premack and Woodruff were addressing, namely, do animals think that other animals are agents, and if so, how do they think about their minds. In order to think about someone's beliefs, we first need to realize that they are the right sort of thing to ascribe beliefs to. Which other species can identify agents, and how do they do it? When we look at animal social cognition and folk psychology through a wider lens, we can ask questions about other creatures' understanding of various aspects of the mind.

6.2 Understanding intentional agency

David Hume could sit in front of his fire alone at home and question causality, but as soon as he moved he accepted causal powers. The same goes for other mind skeptics—as soon as the skeptic is in a social environment, she can't help but act as if there are minds—or intentional agents. We see other people as self-propelled, as goal-oriented, and as able to flexibly change their goals and their paths toward their goals given changes in their environment. For most humans, it is easy to sort agents from non-agents. Here we differ from the ants who will carry their folic-acid-painted nestmate to the graveyard alive and kicking. The ants have one cue for death, and don't take the behavior of other ants as evidence for life or intentionality. A human, on the other hand, would probably open a coffin if she heard someone knocking.

Not all humans share the ability to easily distinguish agents from non-agents. Some children with autism show impairments in this regard. The psychologist Leo Kanner, who first identified autism as a disorder, described one child he worked with in the following manner: "on a crowded beach he would walk straight toward his goal irrespective of whether this involved walking over newspapers, hands, feet or torsos, much to the discomfort of their owners ... It was as if he did not distinguish people from things or at least did not concern himself about the distinction" (quoted in Baron-Cohen 1995, 61). Some people on the autistic spectrum recognize their struggles with identifying intentionality; one youth says, "I really didn't know there were people until I was seven years old ... I then suddenly realized there were people. But not like you do. I still have to remind myself that there are people" (Hobson 1993, 3).

This agent-blindness is rare among humans. We generally take others as having minds, intentional actions, personality traits, emotions, and moods, and we do it from an early age—maybe as early as two months (Trevarthen 1977, 1979). By twelve months human infants are pretty good at identifying agency, in people, animals, as well as in inanimate objects of the right sort. For example, the psychologists György Gergely and Gergely Csibra showed infants a video of a small circle first pulse, then move toward and jump over a wall, and then continue to a big circle and pulse again. The video was shown until the infant lost interest in it (Gergely and Csibra 2003).

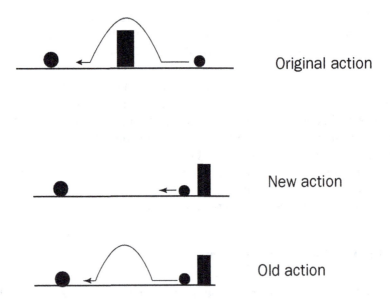

Figure 6.2 Stimuli shown to infants in the teleology study. (Source: Gergely and Csibra 2003)

Then the child was shown a new video, either a New Action video or Old Action video. In both videos, the two circles remain, but the wall has been removed. Infants who watch the Old Action video, in which the small ball continues to hop even though the wall is gone, show renewed interest. Infants who watch the New Action video, in which the small ball now moves in a straight line to the large ball, are still bored. It seems that the infants think that the little ball wants to get to the big ball, and so they predict that the little ball will take the most direct path to the big ball—an attribution of intentionality to the little ball.

If we take these sorts of behavior as evidence that infants understand intentionality, then we must agree there is evidence that great apes also understand other apes as intentional agents. As we saw in the last chapter, chimpanzees engage in primary intersubjectivity behaviors with human and chimpanzee caregivers. In addition, infant chimpanzees pass the Gergely and Csibra test (Uller 2004).

Other studies purport to show that chimpanzees understand intentionality. Some of these come from the studies on elaboration after a failed message that we saw in the previous chapter, but other research comes from studies in which humans fail to meet a chimpanzee's expectation. For example, chimpanzees are more likely to protest when a person is unwilling to give them food compared with a person who is unable to give them food (Call et al. 2004). And when a human caregiver needs help retrieving a dropped or out of reach object, chimpanzees will help out by retrieving the object for the caregiver (Warneken and Tomasello 2006).

The logic of the arguments here is based on analogy: human infants who pass tests P and Q demonstrate that they see others as agents, so chimpanzees who pass chimpanzee versions of tests P and Q likewise demonstrate that they see others as agents. But as we discussed in Chapter 2 in the context of large studies comparing a number of different species on the same task, it isn't clear that we can give chimpanzees the same task we can give to human children, because it might not strike the subjects as the same task. We can't test animals on their sensitivity to human signals if those animals are not at all interested in humans, or are frightened of humans, or cannot even interact with humans at all. The species that have been tested along these sorts of lines are those who do enjoy some social relationships with humans, and those who have a rich social structure. But not all species will be able to take the same test off the shelf in order to demonstrate understanding of intentionality.

Take for example the ability to follow points. In the last chapter we discussed chimpanzee pointing, which some chimpanzees who live with humans come to do, as well as perhaps some wild chimpanzees. Comprehending points, something one-year-old human infants can do, also suggests understanding of intentionality, because it is a response to directing one's attention to something of interest. In object choice tasks, where a human informant points to indicate where food is hidden, many chimpanzees have problems using the cues to correctly locate food (Call and Tomasello 1994; Kirchhofer et al. 2012). Leavens notes, however, that the chimpanzees who fail these tasks are the ones who have not lived with humans. The fact that domestic dogs (Kirchhofer et al. 2012; Hare and Tomasello 1999; Miklósi and Soproni 2006), human habituated wolves (Udell et al. 2008), and captive bottlenose dolphins (Herman et al. 1999; Tschudin et al. 2001) do respond appropriately to human pointing gestures supports the claim that understanding points comes from living with humans who point.

To conclude from these studies that chimpanzees don't understand intentionality because they fail the object choice task is to draw too hasty a conclusion. The problem arises when we focus on a single behavior, and ignore evidence from other domains. Just as a chimpanzee's failure to follow points doesn't undermine his sensitivity to agency, dolphins' and dogs' success in so doing doesn't alone show that they are sensitive to agency. To defend claims such as those we would need to look at the whole body of evidence on dog or dolphin behavior. (If you are interested in these species, look at Hare and Woods 2013 for a review of the social cognition research on dogs and Pack and Herman 2006 for one on dolphins.)

If we have evidence that an animal understands agency, we already have preliminary evidence that the individual understands goals. Since an agent is someone who acts, the evidence for agency is *goal-directed behavior*. Therefore, if we show that members of a species can attribute goals, we establish that they understand agency. Explicit tests of goal attribution have been done with several species including chimpanzees. In fact, the original test for theory of mind in chimpanzees was actually a test to see if a chimpanzee could identify a human's goal.

6.3 Understanding others' emotions

When we understand that another person is in an emotional state, we know how they feel, but not necessarily what they think. And emotions are not always about something. When I am afraid of a bear, my fear is about the bear, but when I wake up sad, my sadness isn't about anything in particular. Emotions are affective states that may or may not be intentional.

Emotions have a physiological grounding and are associated with specific bodily movements. The psychologist Paul Ekman discovered the subtle muscle movements associated with different emotions, and he argues that these are innate to humans, found cross culturally and occur without training (Ekman 1992). There is some evidence that the facial expressions associated with an emotional state cause the emotion as well as express the emotion. For example, if you take a pencil and hold it between your teeth, you make a grimace that recruits the same muscles as a smile does. And when you hold a pencil between your lips, you recruit the same muscles you do when you frown. Psychologists have tested people in these two conditions, and they find that people forced to smile give more positive responses than do people with the pencil between their lips; for example, they report more intense humor responses to a set of cartoons (Strack et al. 1988; see Adelmann and Zajonc 1989 for a review of the literature).

Given this connection between expressing the emotion and feeling an emotion, some philosophers and psychologists have claimed that our ability to recognize emotions in others is associated with our feeling the same emotion when we see their body movements. Some philosophers who think we understand other minds by simulating what it is like to be that person in that situation suggest that seeing others in a particular emotional state causes us to come into that state as well. For example, Alvin Goldman suggests that we understand others' emotions by subtly imitating their facial expressions, and then experience the emotion ourselves, realizing that emotion is shared with the observed other (Goldman 2006; Goldman and Sripada 2005). Evidence for this claim comes from studies of face-based emotion recognition; people with certain neurological deficits are impaired in both feeling an emotion and attributing the emotion to others. This mirroring of emotional states is part of a larger mirroring system found in humans and other animals, which activates the same neural pathways whether one is observing another engage in an action or engaging in that action oneself (Gallese et al. 1996; Rizzolatti, Foggasi, and Gallese 2001.) Because those who have impairments in the areas of the brain that experience fear cannot use those parts of the brain to mirror others' experience of fear, they cannot recognize fear in others.

That other species share the biology, chemistry, and behavior associated with human emotional states is evidence that those animals also experience emotions. As discussed in Chapter 3, rats appear to laugh and fish seem to fear. Since Darwin's book *The Expression of the Emotions in Man and Animals* (1873/2007), scientists have investigated emotions in different species. Stress associated with the release of cortisol, bonding and pleasurable love feelings associated with oxytocin, and brain activity associated with fear or anger have all been found in other species.

One topic of interest these days is the investigation of mental illness in other species. This is of particular interest for those working with captive animals who are often subjected to stressful living situations without the kind of social structures and physical environments that allow them to thrive in a natural environment. The physician Hope Ferdowsian and the psychologist Gay Bradshaw have shown that captive animals such as chimpanzees used for medical research often suffer from a range of psychological disorders we see in humans such as post traumatic stress disorder (Ferdowsian et al. 2011; Bradshaw et al. 2008), and psychologists studying human mental disorders take animal models to be useful research tools (see Haug and Whalen 1999). William McGrew has documented the different self-destructive behaviors he finds in some captive chimpanzees, such as pulling out hair and self-mutilation, which are not seen among wild chimpanzees. Dogs working for the American military in war zones track enemy fighters and sniff out bombs, and these experiences often cause the dog soldiers to experience symptoms of post traumatic stress disorder. According to a 2011 *New York Times* article, these dogs have been successfully treated by military veterinarians using drugs and desensitization treatments that work on humans (Dao 2011). Even honeybees show behavioral traits that we associate with depression and stress; when a beehive is shaken, simulating an attack, the bees are less willing to explore new tastes, and they show changes to their neurochemistry that are associated with depression in humans (Bateson et al. 2011).

Researchers also investigate emotions in animals associated with the death of companions—what we call grief in humans. Different species handle death in different ways; to take a few examples, chimpanzee mothers have been known to carry their dead infants for days, even after they start rotting, elephants visit the bones of their dead group members year after year, and crows and ravens gather around a dead conspecific, rarely touching the body but sometimes laying grass or twigs next to the corpse. There are many reports of animal responses to death made by psychologists, biologists, and anthropologists; see, for example, Marzluff and Angell 2012; King 2013; and Bekoff 2013. While I was in Borneo working with rehabilitant orangutans, I spoke to a woman named Wiwik—an orangutan babysitter—about an infant orangutan they had taken in who was quite lethargic and ill, but who came to bond with her and started doing much better. Soon Wiwik had to go off to school, leaving the baby orangutan behind. The infant started going downhill, and the other babysitters thought that she missed Wiwik, so they gave the infant a photograph of her. I was told that the baby held on to that photograph for dear life, carrying it with her, but she continued to decline and soon died. Stories like this are rife in the animal literature, and are currently the subject of much scientific interest (as well as a fair amount of skepticism).

Granting animal consciousness, the analogical reasoning used in these sorts of studies showing similarity in physiology and behavior to humans in various emotional states provides evidence that particular species experience particular emotions. Claims regarding the existence of specific emotions experienced by animals can be controversial, especially when it comes to complex emotions such as grief. However, in light of all the evidence, the claim that animals experience emotions of *some* sort seems indisputable.

Experiencing emotions can be adaptive; fearing a predator will keep you alive longer than stupid bravery. We can read others' emotions, and form expectations of others' future behavior based on their emotions. But do other animals track the emotional states of their friends and foes as well? And how could we tell? Studies can investigate whether seeing a highly charged emotional state in another affects one's behavior, neural states, or cognitive capacities in the same ways that humans are affected in such situations. And there is some evidence that animals are sensitive to others' emotional states from research on empathy.

Cognitive studies of emotion recognition are largely limited to the great apes. Researchers have found that chimpanzees are better able to remember photographs of aggressive chimpanzees than photographs of relaxed chimpanzees from a set of photographs (Kano et al. 2008). Lisa Parr, a psychologist who studies emotion in chimpanzees, found that primate facial muscles are very similar across species, and that chimpanzees' facial muscles are almost identical to those of humans. From this she infers that we can make direct comparisons between chimpanzee and human facial expressions in terms of the emotions they indicate. Using this information, and following Ekman's research, Parr has developed a catalog of chimpanzee facial expressions and the emotions they express.

Parr reported that chimpanzees can identify computer generated chimpanzee emotional facial expressions with photographs of chimpanzees displaying the same emotion (Parr 2003; Parr et al. 2007). This suggests to her that chimpanzees recognize basic emotions, such as friendliness, aggression, fear, pouting—wanting something that you're not getting—and that other chimpanzees respond appropriately to others based on the emotions they are expressing. Given the conservation in musculature between humans and chimpanzees, the fact that chimpanzees display facial expressions in emotional settings, and that other chimpanzees respond appropriately given those displays, we have some behavioral evidence that chimpanzees track others' emotions.

Of course, as we saw in the last chapter many species display signals associated with their emotional state that indicate how they might respond to others' behavior. A dog's play bow lets another dog know that he isn't being threatened, a cat's arched back and erect fur indicates fear and signals that an attack may be coming. It is adaptive for conspecifics to respond appropriately to the signals of others, so we shouldn't be surprised that other species can track the emotions of others. To figure out whether these animals understand emotion, we would want to examine their emotion tracking behavior in conjunction with their physiological responses. Given the simulation model of human emotion, we would predict that if an animal responds appropriately to an expression of emotion in another animal, its neural pathways associated with that emotion will also be activated. With such a correspondence of behavioral and physiological evidence, we could reasonably conclude that the individual understands the other's emotion. Brain scanning in other species offers some methodological challenges, but researchers are overcoming them, training dogs to stand still in specialized harnesses while being scanned in a fMRI machine (Berns et al. 2012; Berns 2013), scanning monkeys, rats, and mice to better understand PTSD, stress, and autism in those species (see Marzluff and Angell 2012).

Researchers are already using these brain imaging techniques to study animal emotions; John Marzluff and colleagues used PET scanning to determine what parts of the brain are active when a wild crow sees a dangerous person compared to a caring person, and they found that in such situations crows use parts of their brains homologous to the relevant parts of human brains. Marzluff and colleagues take this as evidence that birds feel fear in a way similar to the way humans experience fear (Marzluff et al. 2012).

Testing other species' understanding of emotion in others is the next step in the current interest in animal emotions. It is a ripe area of research.

6.4 Understanding perceptions and attributing personality traits

While behavior rules may help an individual track others' perceptual states, by, for example, telling an animal to look in the direction that another animal's head is turned in order to see something interesting, mindreading perceptual states goes beyond this. If animals think about what others see or hear, they are attributing some sort of perceptual state. If animals can also think about another's false perception, then they have also acquired the ability to think about the correctness conditions of perception, which puts them one step closer to being able to think about belief. Just as truth is what gives belief its point, accuracy is what gives perception its point. Perspective, by its very nature, is contrastive, and implies the existence of multiple different ways of seeing the world. When I wonder about someone's perspective on a landscape or an abstract problem, I am wondering how it appears to the other, and whether it appears differently than it does to me. When I say that Frank perceives the red fruit, I mean that there is red fruit, and that Frank understands that there is red fruit.

Compare this with the cognitive requirements needed for attributing emotions. While we see normative constraints on the kind of emotions people should have in particular circumstances— you should be happy that your sister won the prize, you should be sad that your cat died—in no sense can someone have a false or illusory emotion the way they can have a false belief or an illusory perception. You might be wrong about what's causing the emotion, you might apply labels to your emotions in non-standard ways, but what you are feeling is what you are feeling, and many think that we have private and privileged access to our own emotions. If that's the case, then there are no correctness conditions for emotions in the same way there are for belief.

While beliefs take propositions as their content, perception takes as its objects the world, as well as states of affairs (and perhaps mental states too, as direct perception accounts of mindreading suggest). While we can perceive an object, we cannot believe an object. Belief differs from perception because we believe things that can be expressed in sentences—I can see a ball, and I can see that there is a ball, but when it comes to belief, I can only believe that there is a ball. Seeing, unlike belief, is factive: if you see that X is the case, then X is the case. This doesn't hold for belief; if you believe that X is the case, it doesn't follow that X is the case.

In developing the idea that perceptual mindreading is a less complex type of mindreading than belief mindreading, Bermúdez suggests that perceptual mindreading takes the form of representing: (i) a particular individual; (ii) perceiving; (iii) a particular state of affairs. On this view, we can only perceive states of affairs, not mental states or propositions (Bermúdez 2011). While the perceptual mindreader has to represent an individual perceiving a state of affairs, she doesn't represent the individual perceiving anything representational. And because a perceptual mindreader typically already perceives what she can think someone else perceives, to make the move from perceiving to mindreading perceptions is simply to add to her representation of the state of affairs a relation between the perceiver and the state of affairs. The perceptual mindreader can reason like this: I see the ripe fruit, and Putri is facing the ripe fruit, so Putri sees the ripe fruit too. But the perceptual mindreader isn't able to take into account that Putri might not see that the fruit is ripe, for example. She doesn't understand that things can appear differently to different individuals. On Bermúdez's account, perceptual mindreading does not have correctness conditions, and does not involve metarepresentation. (One might question Bermúdez's choice of calling this kind of understanding mindreading!)

However, there are other ways of understanding perceptual mindreading such that it has some, but not all, of the logical properties of belief mindreading. Robert Lurz introduces a distinction between two kinds of perceptual mindreading—attributions of seeing, and attributions of seeing-as (Lurz 2011). An attribution of a simple seeing may go very much like Bermúdez describes, but an attribution of a seeing-as state is more complex. Seeing-as is taken to be an intentional state, and attributing a seeing-as, such as in the case of an illusory perception, requires that one attributes to another the perception of an object/event *as* F when the attributor himself does not believe that the object/event *is* F. The seeing-as mindreader can attribute to Putri that she sees the fruit as unripe, even though it is ripe, for example.

Though they involve a more complex state than simple seeing, seeing-as attributions differ from belief attributions in that the former are not revisable in light of additional information the way that belief attributions are. Lurz suggests that even the most sophisticated perceptual mindreader would be unable to predict that an animal who saw what appeared to be a bent stick in a glass of water would treat the stick as whole given that he observed the stick being lowered into the water. In order to calibrate attributions in this way, belief attribution is needed. The reasoning is that only with belief attributions can one make the logical inferences needed to update attributions.

However, we may be able to do quite a bit of reasoning about others without attributing beliefs to them. A new attempt to find some middle ground between belief mindreading and behavior reading has been developed by the psychologist Ian Apperly and the philosopher Stephen Butterfill. They introduce the notion of minimal mindreading, which has some of the properties of belief attribution, such as correctness conditions and goal directed causal powers, and two relations: encountering and registration. The encountering relationship holds between an individual and an object in a location within the individual's field (Apperly and Butterfill 2009; Butterfill and Apperly 2013). When we attribute encountering an object to another, we are not appealing to any other psychological states; the attribution is a proxy for "perceiving." Registration, on the other hand, serves as a proxy for belief. A registration is an encountering relationship that remains even once the object is no longer in the agent's field. "One stands in the registering relation to an object and location if one encountered it at that location and if one has not since encountered it somewhere else" (Apperly and Butterfill 2009, 962). While there are no truth conditions for registration attributions, there are correctness conditions. Registration attribution allows one to respond to changing perceptual information in ways that track the behavior of the target. But what it doesn't allow one to do is to robustly track all kinds of false belief and false perception. Rather, there may be signature limits such that someone with a minimal theory of mind cannot understand modes of presentation or pass level-2 mindreading tasks, but can track behavior in a Sally-Anne style task. For example, they suggest that a minimal mindreader, but not a full-blown mindreader, would make the following invalid inference:

1   Mitch believes that Charly is in Baltimore.
2   Charly is Samantha.
3   Therefore, Mitch believes that Samantha is in Baltimore.

The minimal mindreader makes this inference because she uses a registration relation to reason:

1   Mitch registers <Charly, Baltimore>.
2   Charly is Samantha.
3   Therefore, Mitch registers <Samantha, Baltimore> (Butterfill and Apperly 2013, 622).

Chimpanzees can pass the food competition task described earlier using the encountering relation, by realizing that the dominant chimpanzee doesn't encounter the food, and because of that he will not approach it. While most chimpanzees pass this task, they tend to fail in the misinformed condition, where the subordinate watches as the dominant sees food being hidden, then sees the dominant's view blocked while the food is moved to a new location. When released into the enclosure, the subordinates avoid the location of the food, even though the dominant doesn't know its current location. Here the dominant encounters the food, but doesn't correctly register it.

Whether or not human children or nonhuman animals are in registration relations to others or attribute beliefs to others (or neither!) is a matter for ongoing empirical research and theoretical debate. But, it is important to be skeptical of any claim that some tasks can only be solved by attributing beliefs to others. Our ability to think of alternative explanations for behaviors is limited to a greater extent by our own lack of imagination than by physical or psychological constraints on the subjects. Belief is easy for us to think of, but the human interest in others' beliefs may act as a blinders that hide the true cognitive mechanisms behind our actions, and the actions of other animals.

6.4.1 Research on perceptual mindreading in animals

While the studies on belief and perception attribution stem from the tests Premack and Woodruff did with the chimpanzee Sarah back in the 1970s, it continues today. As was discussed earlier, research into the question of whether chimpanzees understand what others can see has been one area of interest. There has long been ethological evidence that chimpanzees as well as other primates routinely track others' perceptual states (Plooij 1978; Byrne and Whiten 1988; Whiten and Byrne 1997). Experimental work confirms that great apes will follow human gaze around barriers and past distractors, and will use such cues to find food in hiding places (Itakura et al. 1999; Bräuer et al. 2005). As early as 13 months chimpanzee infants are already tracking eye direction in a human experimenter (Okamoto et al. 2002). Chimpanzees also seem to know about the affordances associated with seeing. They will seek out food that a dominant chimpanzee cannot see, but will avoid food that the dominant can see (Hare et al. 2001).

However, great apes have trouble in nonverbal versions of the false belief task. In one set of studies, chimpanzees and orangutans were trained that there was food hidden in one of two identical containers, and that a human would mark the location of the food with a wooden block. Though the apes were good at retrieving food from the correct location in this case, they were bad at using the cue to retrieve food when they had reason to think the human had a false belief—when the containers were switched when the communicator was out of the room (Call and Tomasello 1999).

Chimpanzees were not even able to take humans' informational state into account in a competitive version of this task, though they did look toward the actual location of the food when their competitor was attempting to open the wrong container (Krachun et al. 2009).

In addition to great apes, researchers have investigated perceptual mindreading in corvids (Emery and Clayton 2001; Dally et al. 2006; Clayton et al. 2007), monkeys (Flombaum and Santos 2005; Santos et al. 2006), dogs (Hare et al. 1998; Hare and Tomasello 1999; Miklósi et al. 2004; Bräuer et al. 2006), and wolves (Udell et al. 2008). Scrub jays seem to be sensitive to what others can see. Because scrub jays store food to eat later, and their food caches are subject to plundering by other scrub jays, scrub jays have developed a strategy of rehiding food if their original caching behavior is observed by another. It looks like the bird is pretending to hide its food, knowing a competitor is watching, and then when no one is around, hides it again, for real this time. But not all scrub jays appear to do this; in an experimental test, only those scrub jays with previous experience *stealing* food would recache their food store (Clayton et al. 2007). Clayton and colleagues suggest that the scrub jays may be simulating, or thinking about what they would do if they were the observing bird, and so they hide their food again when being observed.

Rhesus macaques also show evidence of some sort of perceptual mindreading. Free-ranging monkeys on the island of Cayo Santiago were faced with human competitors in a foraging task. In one study, two experimenters approached a lone monkey, but in such a way that only one of the humans could see the monkey. Both humans had a grape, and the monkeys would tend to steal the grape from the human who couldn't see them (Flombaum and Santos 2005). The monkeys were also good at passing auditory versions of the task, preferring to steal a grape from a quiet box than from a noisy box when a human wasn't watching them. However, when a human was obviously looking at the monkey, he would take the grape and run, without worrying about whether he'd make a noise (Santos et al. 2006).

Canids have also been subject to a number of perceptual mindreading tasks. Scientists have confirmed what dog lovers have long known, that dogs use human gaze to locate objects, and they often make eye contact before initiating play (Hare et al. 1998; Hare and Tomasello 1999; Miklósi et al. 2004; Bräuer et al. 2006). Wolves who have been raised with humans also show a sophisticated ability to follow human social cues (Udell et al. 2008), as do coyotes (Udell et al. 2012). The tests of perceptual mindreading in canids typically take the form of preferential begging tasks—and many individual canids prefer to seek food from a human who can see the subject rather than a human who cannot see him, though there are wide individual differences within species (see Gácsi et al. 2004; Udell et al. 2011). One worries that these tests show that canids can learn to use behavioral cues to determine how best to get food from a human. However, other studies that find that dogs misbehave only when a human cannot see them offer some converging evidence that canids can generalize from their experiences with humans across situations, which serves as evidence of perceptual mindreading.

In one such deceptive situation, dogs were given a command to do something, such as lying down, or to refrain from doing something, such as eating food. Researchers found that the dogs obeyed the commands better when the human looked at the dog than when the human was distracted or looking away (Gácsi et al. 2004). And like the rhesus macaques, dogs preferred to take food from a silent container than a noisy one when humans were not looking (Kundey et al. 2010). And when dogs are explicitly commanded to leave the food alone, they also prefer to make a silent approach to steal the food, even when they cannot see the human (Bräuer et al. 2013).

In cooperative situations, too, dogs engage in behaviors that show sensitivity to human perspective. When a human asked a dog to fetch a toy, and the human could only see one toy and the dog could see two, the dogs were more likely to fetch the toy that the human could see (Kaminski et al. 2009).

6.4.2 Research on personality understanding in animals

Researchers in animal personality have used the same factoring analysis used in human psychology in order to identify individual differences in a variety of species, from great tits (Amy et al. 2010) and octopuses (Mather and Anderson 1993) to dogs (Gosling and John 1998) and orangutans (Weiss et al. 2006; see Freeman and Gosling 2010 for a review of personality research in primates). As in human personality research, the nonhuman animal personality research uses instruments such as the Five-Factor Personality Inventory (FFPI) to rank subjects on properties such as extraversion, agreeableness, and neuroticism.

While one goal of the personality research is to determine whether there are personality differences in other species, researchers can also look at whether conspecifics seem to understand personality differences among individuals. The psychologist Francys Subiaul began this work by asking whether chimpanzees can learn some of the traits of unfamiliar humans by watching them interacting with another chimpanzee, and it turns out they can (Subiaul et al. 2008). Further work shows that orangutans can also formulate reputation judgments by observing a human interacting either nicely or meanly with another orangutan (Herrmann et al. 2013).

6.5 Chapter summary

Justification for the existence of some psychological property in animals should come from a convergence of good empirical evidence and careful conceptual analysis, and this is also true for cognitive capacities such as mindreading. As research continues on the question of whether other animals consider the beliefs, perceptions, emotions, or personality traits of others we can develop a body of data that can be used to make inference to the best explanation arguments for the existence, or nonexistence, of these abilities. As part of our investigation into the nature of nonhuman social cognitive abilities and the distribution of abilities across species, we should also look at the development of the various associated skills in human children.

The mindreading capacity that has been of so much interest is a particularly difficult capacity to measure because, to begin with, it isn't clear under what circumstances humans use it. Rather than a piece of folk psychology, the notion of "theory of mind" is a scientific construct, and covers a range of capacities associated with perspective taking, teleological reasoning, and emotion attribution. There is reason to widen it further to include the various different ways humans understand other humans, and so the bourgeoning research program in animal reputation and personality can also be seen as part of the theory of mind matrix.

In addition to studying different aspects of social cognition, different kinds of studies can be done, and different sorts of individuals can be studied. For example, rather than considering only predictive tasks, researchers can also look at devising explanatory tasks, and rather than focusing just on competitive tasks, individuals can be given competitive and cooperative versions of similar tasks in order to investigate the different situations in which social cognition might be present.

In great ape research, subjects consist almost entirely of animals born into zoos or research labs, with some work done on sanctuary animals. Finding ways to test for mindreading abilities in wild ape populations is a challenge that is worth taking on. As in the canid research, where pound dogs are tested alongside pets, and wolves habituated to humans are compared to wild wolves, the population differences and similarities between captive and wild apes, and apes in different social situations, can be investigated.

Further reading

For background on the different theories of mindreading, Ian Ravenscroft has a *Stanford Encyclopedia of Philosophy* entry called "Folk psychology as a theory" and Robert Gordon has an entry called "Folk psychology as mental simulation" (http://plato.stanford.edu/). Two recent books have investigated the philosophical questions associated with animal mindreading—my own *Do Apes Read Minds? Toward a New Folk Psychology* (2012) and Robert Lurz's *Mindreading Animals* (2011).

One of the first texts about perceptual mindreading in apes comes from the skeptic Daniel Povinelli and his colleagues in *Monographs of the Society for Research in Child Development* called "What young chimpanzees know about seeing" (1996). For a good anthology of articles on social cognition in animals, Nathan Emery and colleagues edited *Social Intelligence: From Brain to Culture* (2008).

Brian Hare, the psychologist who ran the food competition task with chimpanzees, studies dogs as well as primates. He and his partner Vanessa Woods wrote a very readable overview of what we know about dog, wolf, and fox sociality, *The Genius of Dogs: How Dogs are Smarter Than You Think* (2013). They defend Hare's theory that dog social cognition is superior to chimpanzee social cognition due to the co-evolution of humans and dogs.

7 Moral minds

In December 2013, lawsuits were filed on behalf of four captive chimpanzees in New York State: Tommy, a 26-year-old chimpanzee living in a cage in a dark shed, Hercules and Leo, two young male chimpanzees used in a locomotion research experiment at Stony Brook University, and Kiko, a 26-year-old chimpanzee living in Niagara Falls, NY, who is a former entertainment actor. The lawsuits demanded that the courts grant the chimpanzees the right to bodily liberty via a writ of *habeas corpus*. The attorney for the case, Steven Wise, said:

> Not long ago, people generally agreed that human slaves could not be legal persons, but were simply the property of their owners ... We will assert, based on clear scientific evidence, that it's time to take the next step and recognize that these nonhuman animals cannot continue to be exploited as the property of their human 'owners' ... When we go to court on behalf of the first chimpanzee plaintiffs, we'll be asking judges to recognize, for the first time, that these cognitively complex, autonomous beings have the basic legal right to not be imprisoned.
>
> (Nonhuman Rights Project 2013)

Wise thinks that because scientific evidence shows that great apes, cetaceans, and elephants are self-aware and autonomous, they should have basic rights as legal persons.

7.1 Moral status

Wise's legal argument suggests that the chimpanzees have the kind of cognitive properties that lead us to respect humans as persons. The idea that chimpanzees or dolphins are persons led to a backlash from people outraged that animals are being compared to humans who had been enslaved. Only humans can be persons—that's just what a person is, so goes the objection.

But when watching nature shows, calm voices and compelling music encourage us to think of animals as persons. The television series *Meerkat Manor*, which followed the Wisker family, portrayed the meerkats' behavior in soap opera format, replete with storylines of infidelity and family drama. In a *Time Magazine* article, James Poniewozik wrote,

> Like the meerkats, *Manor* is an odd beast. The crew is forbidden to intervene, and the producers don't sugarcoat the animals' less cuddly habits (infidelity, abandonment of young, occasional cannibalism). But the meerkats are named and given human traits ('courageous,' 'caring,' 'bully[ing]'), and their antics and tragedies take place over a sound track. *Manor* is both brutal and melodramatic and thus more devastating than most documentary or scripted drama.
>
> (Poniewozik 2007)

The producers of *Meerkat Manor* treated the little mongooses like people, and that seems to explain why the show was so successful (Poniewozik 2007).

While availability heuristics lead us to think that persons must be humans, because we think first of individual humans when asked for examples of persons, we can calibrate our understanding of "person" by considering other ways in which we use the term. Anyone reading science fiction literature can quickly realize that the category of human isn't the same as the category of persons. Aliens such as Luke Skywalker, Dr. Spock, mutants such as Iceman, Angel, and Beast, and others who aren't human are clearly treated as persons. They, like human characters, have feelings, work toward achieving goals, enjoy good and bad relationships, make plans and think about what to do next—they are much like us even if they lack some of our characteristics. But once we've drawn the distinction between person and biological human beings, how do we decide what else might count as a person?

The personhood question is a core issue that arises at the intersection of animal cognition research and ethics. Related to it are questions about whether animals are moral patients and about whether they are moral agents. A moral patient is someone who is granted some kind of moral consideration, whereas a moral agent is someone who can be held morally responsible for her actions. A human infant is a moral patient, most people think, but not a moral agent. Why not? Because being held responsible for one's actions requires certain cognitive capacities, which she doesn't yet have.

Moral agents are individuals who act in the moral sphere in such a way that they can be held morally responsible for their actions. What this way of acting amounts to is a matter of debate, but potentially necessary conditions include the ability to make self-reflective choices about one's actions, the ability to feel empathy for others, and the ability to realize the consequences of one's actions and to be able to choose from among those consequences.

There is also an attempt to find a middle ground between being a moral patient and having full-blown moral responsibility. The philosopher Mark Rowlands suggests we can think of a moral subject as someone who is *sometimes* motivated to act by moral reasons, even if that individual can't consider those moral reasons, or act to change them (and so isn't responsible for her actions). And Gary Varner, who takes personhood to require moral agency, argues that some animals, such as corvids, elephants, dolphins, and apes, are near-persons, and have a special moral significance for that reason. We will review the arguments for animals as moral patients, as moral subjects, and as moral agents, and consider what aspects of mind an animal would need in order to be included in each of these categories.

7.1.1 Utilitarian accounts of moral status

While the phrase that might come to mind when you think about animals as moral patients is "animal rights," Peter Singer, the moral philosopher who is known for his concern for animal welfare, does not frame the problem in this manner. Rather than thinking about moral rights, Singer focuses on the ability to feel pain (Singer 1990). As we saw in Chapter 3, scientists studying pain in animals are committed to the idea that the experience of pain is quite widespread, and is present at least in fish, birds, and mammals. The fact that animals experience pain, combined with an acceptance of utilitarianism, the moral theory according to which we ought to maximize overall utility—often operationalized as absence of pain and presence of pleasure—lead utilitarians to count animals who can feel pain or pleasure as moral patients.

For Singer, what makes an individual a moral patient isn't her intelligence, abilities, or skills; for any of these properties, we can identify a human who lacks the property, but who we still think has moral standing. A human in a vegetative state, or an infant, or a baby with spina bifida may not be as intelligent or as skillful as a chimpanzee, an elephant, or a scrub jay. So, these properties can't be relevant for the question of which individuals to include in the sphere of moral patients. What is relevant? Suffering—anything that can suffer has moral standing.

Once you've accepted that a property—say suffering—is what establishes moral standing, it is unjustified discrimination to hold that an animal cannot have moral standing by virtue of not being human. Speciesism, or discriminating against individuals based on their species membership rather than considering them for their individual characteristics, is a moral flaw. The speciesist thinks that the interests of her own species overrides the greater interests of members of other species. For example, a speciesist might try to justify her catch-and-release fishing by saying that she really enjoys it, and thinks that the pain of a fish doesn't matter morally. Vegetarians and vegans who take a utilitarian perspective will argue that eating animals and their products doesn't, in fact, maximize happiness, due to the pain inflicted by raising, killing, and using animals in agriculture.

Some philosophers have raised worries about the reliance on a classical utilitarian approach to animal moral standing because on this view no individual has rights; individual interests can be overridden by the greater good. Varner argues that R.M. Hare's two-level account of utilitarianism can avoid this criticism, and indeed can serve as a defense for the claim that animals are morally significant. One level follows internalized intuitive-level rules that are culturally variable and can be revised, and the other requires critical thinking, which permits deviations from the intuitive rules in particular circumstances. The existence of intuitive-level rules makes sense of our deontological intuitions, and it explains why violating such rules when acting from the position of a critical thinker can cause guilt or anguish in the actor. For most humans alive today, there doesn't seem to be any intuitive-level rule against eating animals or their products, but there might be some vague rules about not needlessly torturing them. Though Varner doesn't go so far as to advocate veganism or vegetarianism, he argues that, given that all vertebrates are capable of suffering, we should modify our intuitive-level rules in order to limit meat consumption and end factory farming for meat and animal products such as milk and eggs.

7.1.2 Rights-based accounts of moral status

The notion of human right suggests that certain rights are given to all humans regardless of their race or gender or ethnicity, but also regardless of their cognitive abilities, personality traits, or physical capacities. The philosopher Tom Regan defends a rights-based view of animal moral standing by starting with the assumption that all humans have rights (Regan 2004). He investigates what sorts of properties might justify granting all humans such rights. It can't be rational agency, because we grant human rights to humans who lack full-blown rational agency (in children, in those with dementia, and in those with cognitive deficits). If the justification were simply the biological property of having human DNA, then the position would be a blatant example of speciesism, which is itself as unjustifiable as racism or sexism. Rather, Regan thinks that what gives all human rights is that they are experiencing subjects of a life. His argument can be understood as follows:

1   Typical humans have the right not to be treated as a mere resource for others.
2   If typical humans have that right, then any individual that is the experiencing subject of a life has a right not to be treated as a mere resource for others.
3   Many nonhuman animals are the experiencing subjects of a life.
4   Therefore, many nonhuman animals have the right not to be treated as a mere resource for others.

Premise (1) is justified by arguments in favor of rights-based views. Premise (2) is justified too; being an experiencing subject of a life is arguably the only thing all conscious humans have in common, and so it seems to be the ground for the existence of rights. Premise (3) is defended by arguments in favor of animal consciousness and animal thought, which we reviewed in Chapter 3 and Chapter 4. To challenge the conclusion that many nonhuman animals should not be used for food, clothing, entertainment, etc., one would have to challenge one of the premises.

The philosopher R.G. Frey (1980) takes both the second and the third premise to be false: the third because animals lack beliefs and desires, which are needed to be the experiencing subject of a life, and the second because there are degrees of value, and humans can have more value than other animals because human lives are richer—we have love, marriage, children to educate, jobs, hobbies, sporting events, cultural pursuits, intellectual development, and so forth. And, importantly, we have freedom to choose our own path. But if Frey's view holds, then some humans, namely those with less rich lives, would turn out to be less valuable. This seems to be a problematic consequence of the view.

Other arguments for animal moral standing come from their ability to flourish. Animals might not suffer when they are not flourishing, just as humans might not suffer just in virtue of missing something that would contribute to their flourishing. Martha Nussbaum suggests that because other animals can flourish too, they have certain entitlements (Nussbaum 2004, 2006). Animals should not be killed, because they are entitled to bodily health and bodily integrity. Captive animals should be given the opportunities to flourish in ways that make sense for their species, to move about and play, to make choices, and to live in communities that fulfill their emotional needs.

7.1.3 Social accounts of moral status

Another way to think about our responsibility to animals depends not on what sort of psychological properties they have, but rather on what sort of relationships humans have formed with them. Many animal species are social, and they have relationships with conspecifics. But we humans also have relationships with the animals around us. Whether they are the cats, dogs, and rats who live with us in harmony, the ants, raccoons, and rats who invade our home, the domesticated farm animals we raise for food, or the wild animals whose habitats we actively protect or cut down, we have relationships with those around us.

Taking as their starting position political theory and the nature of citizenship, Sue Donaldson and Will Kymlicka argue that given our relationships with them, we need to include nonhuman animals in our political environment (2011). Just as disabled humans who cannot speak for themselves are still citizens whose rights and responsibilities can be fulfilled through those they have relationships with, humans with similar relationships with animals can act as their stewards. Domesticated animals, which we created by capturing wild animals and breeding them for hundreds or thousands of years, should be given citizenship status and a right to share the benefits of citizenship. Wild animals should be granted sovereignty over their habitats and bodies. And the non-domesticated animals that live in our cities and among our homes should be granted denizen status, which gives them the right to live among us without risking extermination. While on this view animals' psychological features must be taken into account in order to determine how to treat them as a citizen, a sovereign, or as a denizen, it is their relationship to us, not their psychological makeup, which grants them the rights under these categories. Of course these rights won't include things like voting rights—they will be rights appropriate to the needs of the individuals who have them.

Others who emphasize the importance of our relationships with animals over their individual psychological properties worry that the rights approach undermines the value of animals. In response to the lawsuits aimed at gaining personhood rights for chimpanzees, Lori Gruen argues that the rights approach undermines the relationships we have with other species. Having a right allows us to make a claim against another, and encourages a competitive and combative relationship between rights bearers. "We end up focused on what we can extract from each other or how we can protect what we have, rather than focusing on how we might work together to improve each other's lives" (Gruen 2014).

The rights approach also encourages us to see similarities and undervalue differences which can be just as valuable, according to Gruen. When we are anthropocentric, just as when we are Western centric, we end up valuing those like us more than those who are different, for no good reason. By arguing that we ought to protect animals because they share with us the qualities that we have that we take to make us morally considerable, Gruen thinks we thereby "assimilate them into our human-oriented framework; we grant them consideration in virtue of what we believe they share with us, rather than what makes their lives meaningful and valuable by their own lights" (Gruen 2014).

While these conceptions of what makes an animal worthy of moral consideration differ, they (mostly) all share some understanding that it is something about animals' minds that make them worthy of our concern. Animals who can feel pain, who can experience their lives, who can flourish, or who can enter into relationships share one thing—they are conscious. Hence, one way of deciding whether an entity has moral status is to determine whether it is conscious.

7.2 Moral subjects and near-persons

Many animal species are social. They live in groups and are presumably equipped with special cognitive mechanisms for dealing with the demands that arise from social living. While arguments for animals as moral patients may be familiar, little attention has been given to the idea that animals might *have* morality until recently. Can animals be autonomous agents, can they have social norms, moral emotions? Do they possess concepts of right and wrong?

Some animals are not only conscious, but, as reviewed in Chapter 6, also have social cognitive capacities that permit them to be sensitive to the suffering and well-being of others. Humans can suffer in more cognitive ways, when they use their cognitive capacities for mental time travel to anticipate their futures or by thinking counterfactually about how things might have been, and this may be true of some other species as well. Once one is able to consider others' feelings, and think about the future and counterfactual situations, they are demonstrating qualities that are associated with moral agency—being responsible for action. While no other species my have those capacities, some philosophers have suggested other moral categories that animals might fit into.

As was mentioned briefly above, Varner identifies a morally relevant intermediate position between persons and non-persons, which he calls *near-persons*. While all vertebrates are conscious and hence worthy of moral concern, none are persons (full-blown moral agents) because persons have a narrative sense of self, and no animals tell stories about themselves, or set long-term goals to work toward. Following the philosopher Marya Schechtman, Varner accepts that a person is necessarily rational, self-conscious, autonomous in the sense of having second-order desires, and hence is a moral agent. In addition, a person must have the following four concepts from which to construct a self-narrative: self, birth, death, and personality. Varner argues that in order to have the ability to self-narrate, one needs language, and we currently have no evidence of animal language. (While Varner thinks that cetaceans might have language, given the complexity of their vocalizations, he also thinks apes cannot have language, given their lack of vocalizations—and in so doing ignores the possibility of gestural language discussed in Chapter 5.) Varner admits that children may not acquire the cognitive abilities associated with narrative selves until adolescence, but this isn't a concern, because children will become persons, and so we have reasons for treating them as "persons in training."

While no animal is a person, some species are near-persons, thereby occupying a middle ground between merely sentient beings and persons. Chimpanzees, dolphins, elephants and scrub jays are near-persons; rats, monkeys and parrots might be near-persons, too.

Near-persons don't construct self-narratives, but they can engage in past and future thinking—Tulving's mental time travel. This ability is significant because it allows an individual to consciously re-experience events and to make and accomplish future plans, which in turn gives her more opportunity for happiness (re-experiencing pleasurable experiences and fulfilling plans) and unhappiness (dreading unpleasant experiences and failing to achieve goals). In addition, a near-person has a present sense of self insofar as he has a theory of mind. Varner's review of the mindreading literature leads him to conclude that monkeys, apes, elephants, dolphins, and scrub jays have the ability to attribute perceptual states to others.

As we saw in Chapter 6, however, there are alternative explanations to the mindreading explanation in these other species. For example, while Emery and Clayton think that scrub jays may engage in a kind of experience projection—a simulation version of mindreading—Varner is more optimistic, writing, "it is unclear how else to explain this striking result than by saying that the jays were using ToM" (Varner 2012, 214). However, the scrub jays who moved their food could have learned about behavior by making an association between the presence of a competitor and the loss of food. For example, the scrub jays might have remembered their past pilfering, they might have formed the association, and then they might have simply flipped the roles of self and other.

An individual's status as a near-person doesn't preclude her being used, though it does grant additional moral standing on Varner's account. Varner thinks that near-persons can be used in some biomedical research, and that wildlife policy should treat near-persons as replaceable, because of what he takes to be bad consequences of recognizing a right to life for such creatures.

An alternative way of finding a middle ground for animals in the moral sphere comes from Mark Rowlands (2012), who takes a hybrid virtue/sentimentalist approach, and argues that animals can be the subjects of moral emotions. The content of moral emotions provides moral reasons for an animal's actions. Rowlands take these emotions to provide reasons, rather than merely causing behavior. For example, if I am angry then the thought that "He deliberately hurt me" can provide a reason to retaliate—the anger isn't just the experience of anger sensations. As Rowlands puts it, animals can be *sensitive* to some morally salient features of their environments, and the mechanism underlying the sensitivity is a reliable mechanism that produces the appropriate emotion in the appropriate circumstance (most of the time). This makes animals moral subjects who are able to act for moral reasons, but not moral agents who are responsible for their actions. As an example of a moral subject, Rowlands describes his dog Hugo and Hugo's interaction with Rowlands' son. Hugo is a German Shepherd who is trained in protection, and as part of his training he will bite a kevlar sleeve that Rowlands puts on his arm. But when his five-year old-son puts on the bite sleeve, Hugo will only gently chew on it. This different treatment of different individuals in the same circumstance, coupled with Hugo's strong desire to bite the sleeve at any opportunity, leads Rowlands to conclude that Hugo is a moral subject. Hugo

> exhibits concern for my son, and as a result inhibits his desires when doing so is necessary. This is enough for him to qualify as a moral subject: one motivated to act by moral reasons. The concern he exhibits is bequeathed him both by natural history and by form of life. And the latter comes by way of the deed.
>
> (Rowlands 2012, 213)

For one's emotions to count as reasons rather than just causes, the emotions must have some normative force—they must be things that the agent endorses in some sense. A natural way to spell out this requirement may be in metacognitive terms, by claiming that one needs to scrutinize one's emotions and recognize that they are appropriate. However, Rowlands argues that this merely pushes the question up a level, because the question of normative force simply reappears at the level of critical scrutiny.

Following the work of philosopher Julia Driver, Rowlands develops an account of moral reason that is both consequentialist and externalist. A motivational state is moral if it has the actual consequence of achieving good consequences, and it is externalist in the sense that the moral quality of one's actions are determined at least partially by features external to the individual's agency. Rowlands defines moral subject as follows: "X is a *moral subject* if X possesses (1) a sensitivity to the good- or bad-making features of situations, where (2) this sensitivity can be normatively assessed, and (3) is grounded in the operations of a reliable mechanism (a 'moral module')" (Rowlands 2012, 230).

The gist of the position is that moral subjects are those individuals that feel emotions such as happiness or sadness because the situation is good or bad. Such an individual feels happiness in the face of others' happiness, and sadness in the face of their suffering. And when she feels sad, it is sadness about the suffering of others, such that the content of the subject's belief is what the emotion is intentionally directed at. And while her response is reliable, she can get it wrong. This is what gives the emotion normative force—e.g. the dog was happy about biting the little boy, but he should have been sad, so we need to do more to train the dog to respond appropriately to others. According to Rowlands, a moral agent has more— she understands that she tracks moral features of the world, she can evaluate her actions and their consequences—but since the moral subject already has normativity, he is already within the domain of the moral, and his behaviors can be good or bad.

This view requires a number of cognitive capacities in order to fulfill the sufficient requirements for being a moral subject. Perhaps we should say that the moral subject has beliefs about moral circumstances as well as emotions about those beliefs that leads her to act accordingly. On this interpretation, a moral subject minimally has beliefs and emotions. If animals cannot have beliefs or emotions, then they cannot fulfill the criteria for being a moral subject. The arguments for and against animal belief were discussed in Chapter 4, and in Chapter 3 we saw strong evidence for emotion in animals. Insofar as the arguments for animal belief and emotion are compelling, the question becomes whether some species have the right kinds of beliefs, emotions, and corresponding behaviors in order to count as moral subjects, and whether we should accept the existence of this sort of moral status.

7.3 Moral agency

While moral agency requires more in the way of cognitive capacities than moral subjects or near-personhood, there are arguments that some species, such as the great apes, should be considered moral agents or granted a moral status along these lines.

For example, Frans de Waal argues that morality and empathy are deeply entrenched in humans, and that we can find the evolutionary precursor to our full-fledged morality in other species (de Waal 2006). In opposition to those endorsing social contract views according to which ethical codes have developed in order to protect us from mean, nasty, selfish humans, de Waal claims that moral emotions, such as empathy and reciprocal behaviors, are evolutionarily old and so moral behavior is internally motivated rather than externally impressed upon us in order to control our nasty impulses. His argument can be stated as follows:

1   Humans act according to ideals of morality.
2   Nonhuman animals act according to ideals of morality.
3   There is an evolutionary explanation for why morality is beneficial to individuals (in terms of kin selection and reciprocal altruism).
4   If human and nonhuman animals act according to some ideal, and there is an evolutionary explanation for that ideal, then (given considerations of parsimony) we should expect that the ideal is real, natural, and continuous across species.
5   Therefore, morality is real, natural, and continuous across species.

Moral creatures require moral emotions such as empathy, which involves understanding another's emotional state (for example, by imagining what it is like to be someone else). De Waal provides a number of anecdotes that great apes have empathy. In one of the most evocative examples, de Waal describes the behavior of a bonobo in an English zoo:

> One day Kuni captured a starling. Out of fear that she might molest the stunned bird, which appeared undamaged, the keeper urged the ape to let it go ... Kuni picked up the starling with one hand and climbed to the highest point of the highest tree where she wrapped her legs around the trunk so that she had both hands free to hold the bird. She then carefully unfolded its wings and spread them wide open, one wing in each hand, before throwing the bird as hard as she could towards the barrier of the enclosure. Unfortunately, it fell short and landed onto the bank of the moat where Kuni guarded it for a long time against a curious juvenile.
>
> (de Waal 2007, 55)

These days, examples like this abound in YouTube videos shared by bored office workers and animal lovers. As further evidence of empathy, de Waal cites examples of targeted helping in apes who are able to respond to another individual's needs and help her fulfill them. He often tells the story of Binti Jua, a gorilla at the Brookfield Zoo who rescued a human child who fell into the moat surrounding the enclosure. Binti Jua approached the child, picked her up, and carried her over to a zookeeper. Other examples of empathy in animals come from consolation behavior, in which an uninvolved bystander gives physical reassurance in the form of physical contact to an individual who just lost a fight.

De Waal thinks another feature of morality is reciprocity, understood as a capacity to engage in exchanges that are mutually beneficial. We treat people well who treat us well. Humans follow norms of exchange when it comes to goods, work, or dinner invitations. For chimpanzees, exchanging food for grooming may be one example of a reciprocal behavior. This approach to the evolutionary continuity of morality across species is supported by biological theories of reciprocity. If it isn't advantageous for an individual or a species to act morally, then it seems that from a Darwinian perspective, it wouldn't make biological sense to act morally. However, there are evolutionary explanations for why morality is beneficial to individuals in terms of kin selection and reciprocal altruism (which are discussed in detail in Chapter 2 of Justin Garson's *The Biological Mind* (Garson 2014)). Kin selection is thought to be a mechanism that promotes the survival of close relatives even at the expense of the individual. It is beneficial to you to help you family members survive because by helping your family members you are also helping your own genes. Reciprocal altruism is the theory that explains altruism as beneficial to the self because when one individual helps another individual, the helper is later rewarded by the individual he earlier helped, so that the helper is making an investment in his future survival.

Given that he finds empathy and reciprocity in animal species, de Waal concludes that morality is real, natural, and continuous across species. What he calls the *veneer theory*, according to which morality is a cultural innovation that barely hides the intrinsically selfish nature of individuals, cannot be correct. Instead, he supports what he calls *evolutionary ethics*, the idea that morality is based on the natural emotional responses we have to others, including empathy, and the need for social species to cooperate. De Waal's Darwinian ethics proposes the existence of a Perception–Action mechanism that promotes emotional contagion. On his view, the development of mindreading abilities allows for cognitive empathy, and one needs to be able to fully adopt another's perspective in order to attribute mental states. And while human moral behavior is more elaborate than animal moral behavior, human behaviors and motivations aren't unique, but are continuous with the moral sentiments and behaviors of animals. What humans have that animals don't is the ability to make morality universal, to create moral rules and apply them indiscriminately to others. Since animals lack moral systems, explicit moral rules, and moral education, they are not full-fledged moral agents who can be held responsible for their actions. But they are on the continuum, and the difference is only a matter of degree.

Taking a different approach, Marc Bekoff and Jessica Pierce argue that morality is to be understood as relative to species, and animals are moral agents in light of various notions of morality (Bekoff and Pierce 2009). Unlike de Waal, they argue that other species have distinct forms of morality that are not a precursor to human morality. Because they take *morality* to mean "a suite of other-regarding behaviors that cultivate and regulate complex interactions within social groups" (Bekoff and Pierce 2009, 82), they take the complexity of animal behavior, social organization, and cognitive flexibility to demonstrate that other species have morality in this sense. They identify three clusters of moral behavior: cooperation, empathy, and justice, and they argue that many species engage in behaviors that fall into one or more of these categories. Central to the view is that different species have different norms, and that this makes animal morality species-relative. Despite the differences found between species, similarities include the capacities for empathy, altruism, cooperation, and a sense of fairness.

Vampire bats, for example, cooperate by sharing blood. Dogs and wolves punish others who violate social norms by giving false signals. And de Waal has provided us with examples of empathy in great apes. Their idea is that since we can see behaviors that fall into these categories, we have evidence of morality in these species, and by observing these behaviors in other animals we can learn more about their own systems of morality.

Unlike de Waal's focus on the mechanisms of morality, Bekoff and Pierce are only concerned with the behaviors, and behavioral regularities, which they identify functionally in terms of the benefits offered to the group. By focusing on behaviors rather than the mechanisms that lead to the behaviors, one might worry that Bekoff and Pierce are watering down the notion of morality, and that they miss the point of what we take to be moral agency.

As usually understood, a moral agent is someone who can be held responsible for her behavior, whose behavior can appropriately be judged morally acceptable or not. The behavior is not enough; there are some additional cognitive requirements usually associated with moral agency. The behavior has to be caused in the right kind of way. Imagine a robot programmed according to the science fiction author Isaac Asimov's three laws of robotics:

1   A robot may not injure a human being or, through inaction, allow a human being to come to harm.
2   A robot must obey the orders given to it by human beings, except where such orders would conflict with the First Law.
3   A robot must protect its own existence as long as such protection does not conflict with the First or Second Law.

Such a robot may exhibit seemingly moral behavior quite consistently, but we might hesitate to call it a moral agent. The robot need not know why it shouldn't injure a human, it need not feel any emotions or moral outrage when it sees a human being injured, and it need not feel empathy when seeing a living being in pain in order to exhibit moral behavior. If the robot is programmed to deterministically follow the rules stated above, it cannot make a choice to follow them or not; it can only determine how best to implement them. Is this sufficient for being a moral agent?

To help consider that question we can look at a general definition of moral agency in The Routledge Encyclopedia of Philosophy:

> Moral agents are those agents expected to meet the demands of morality. Not all agents are moral agents. Young children and animals, being capable of performing actions, may be agents in the way that stones, plants and cars are not. But though they are agents they

are not automatically considered moral agents. For a moral agent must also be capable of conforming to at least some of the demands of morality.

(Haksar 1998)

This definition, in a similar vein to Bekoff and Pierce's approach and Asimov's laws, is consistent with looking only at behavior. But depending on what it means to meet a demand of morality, considering behavior alone may not be sufficient. And the demands of morality will differ according to one's theory of morality.

For the Humean, emotions allow us to discriminate between good and bad actions, and without those emotional responses nothing would be morally good or bad. There is no morality for someone who lacks emotions or empathic understanding. For a Kantian, who thinks that a moral agent must be able to consider her reasons for acting and act on principles that she understands and endorses, someone who lacked metacognitive abilities would fail to be a moral agent. For a Utilitarian who thinks that a moral agent should know how to maximize overall happiness, the ability to make predictions about people's emotions is essential. Virtue ethics views would require having the appropriate personality traits, and particularist views would require knowing how to recognize moral similarities between situations and being able to act accordingly. Different moral theories make different demands on a moral agent.

However, all these theories go beyond the idea of taking only behavior into consideration, which suggests that Bekoff and Pierce's view doesn't reflect the mainstream ethical approaches to moral agency. Indeed, it seems they want to move away from mainstream philosophical approaches, given that they reject the moral agent/moral patient distinction as unhelpful and misleading. To be precise, they don't think that animals are moral agents (because they reject the category); rather, they think that many nonhuman species "have morality." What does this mean? Bekoff and Pierce's claim rests on the autonomous existence of norms in animal societies. They define a norm as "an expected standard of behavior within a group [that is] enforced by the group" (13). They suggest that the social complexity of a social group correlates with norms of behavior, presumably because the more complex, the more rules there are to follow.

Social insects are clear examples of complex social animals where there are standards of behavior that are enforced by the group. Consider the phenomenon of worker policing in ants, bees, and wasps, whereby worker females eat the eggs that have been laid by other workers in order to protect the queen's heirs and descendants. Here we have an example of a norm in a group—that only the queen should successfully reproduce—that is enforced by the group. This seems like it fits Bekoff and Pierce's definition of a norm, and so ants, bees, and wasps will be examples of animals that "have morality."

How do the insects accomplish these behaviors? Scientists suggest that the eggs that workers lay lack a hydrocarbon marker that the queen's egg has, and so the worker policing is accomplished by automatically destroying any egg that lacks the marker. Like Asimov's robot, little consideration needs to go into the behavior—one identifies the situation and responds appropriately to it. This may be too little cognitive engagement to satisfy most people's intuitions about what it means to be a moral agent, and hence little motivation to try to calibrate our concept of moral agency to limit its cognitive requirements. Like with the term "language", applying the term "morality" too broadly will damage the expressive power of the language, because we will no longer have a term that will be able to draw distinctions between "moral" ants and moral humans. In morality, too, we should examine both the similarities and the differences between species.

7.4 Psychological properties and morality

If performing particular behaviors seems insufficient for morality, it may be because there is little cognitive flexibility built into the behaviors that satisfy the moral requirement implicit in Bekoff and Pierce's notion of morality. To return to the approach of Tom Reagan, we might ask what cognitive capacities do we think humans need in order to "have morality" in some sense, and once we establish that, we can ask whether other animals have those cognitive capacities. There are at least four kinds of psychological properties that animals might need as a cognitive requirement for entering into the sphere of morality beyond being morally considerable. Corresponding to major ethical theories, we have the following candidates: consciousness and metacognition (Kantianism), empathy or other-regarding emotions (sentimentalism and utilitarianism), personality traits and ability to improve them (virtue ethics), and social relations (feminist ethics).

The psychological requirement for morality that has been discussed the most in the context of animal morality has been metacognition, which Kantians think is required for an individual to have autonomy. The conscious metacognitive requirement is needed according to ethical views in which an agent needs to be an autonomous being that considers her own reasons for action. To act from reasons is different than acting according to reasons, says Kant, and a moral being does the right thing for the right reason. Therefore, she has to know her reason for acting, and she has to be able to evaluate her reasons. The philosopher Christine Korsgaard uses this approach to argue against animal morality. Because animals can't mindread, they cannot decide whether or not some behavior is justified and act from that judgment. Instead, she suspects animals just act from their desires. She writes:

> What it [normative self-government] requires is a certain form of self-consciousness: namely, consciousness of the grounds on which you propose to act *as grounds*. What I mean is this: a nonhuman agent may be conscious of it as *fearful* or *desirable*, and so as something to be avoided or to be sought. This is the ground of his action. But a rational animal is, in addition, conscious *that* she fears or desires the object, and *that* she is inclined to act in a certain way as a result. That's what I mean by being conscious of the ground *as a ground*. She does not just think about the object that she fears or even about its fearfulness but about her fears and desires themselves.
>
> (Korsgaard 2006, 113)

Here is one way of putting Korsgaard's argument against animal moral agency:

1   In order to be a moral agent, one needs to be autonomous.
2   An autonomous agent is able to act for reasons.

3   Acting for reasons requires the ability to recognize *that* one has reasons for actions.
4   Reasons for actions are sets of beliefs and desires that motivate behavior.
5   Mindreading is required to recognize one's beliefs and desires.
6   Therefore, it follows that acting for reasons requires mindreading.
7   Therefore, moral agents must mindread.
8   No nonhuman animal mindreads.
9   Thus, no nonhuman animal is a moral agent.

Returning to Regan and Singer's strategy of identifying animal morality in terms of our intuitions about human morality, we might worry that the conscious metacognitive requirement for morality is too stringent a criterion. For one, on this view, a child isn't moral until she acquires metacognition. As we saw in Chapter 6, the age at which children acquire metacognition is an ongoing research issue, with some arguing it occurs before the first year of life, and many others thinking it occurs around four years-old, or later, in some cultures. But even if children are beginning to understand the nature of belief at four, there is evidence that it isn't until mid-childhood that children are able to understand the logical properties of belief, such as its opacity (Apperly and Robinson 2001, 2002, 2003) and that before adolescence humans may be impaired in their ability to evaluate the reasons they may know they have (Pillow 1999; Morris 2000; Moshman 2004). Evaluating one's reasons for action is the hallmark of agency on Korsgaard's view. This would suggest that human adolescents are not autonomous agents; therefore, they are not moral agents. While we do not hold adolescents fully legally responsible for their actions, most cultures do treat young humans as moral agents, at least as part of children's moral education. While we may not know exactly when the infant becomes a child who is morally responsible, the suggestion that the child is outside the realm of moral agency until a teenager is counterintuitive to many. For example, if a nine-year-old child burns a cat, we might want to condemn this behavior as immoral, and hold him responsible for his actions. However, on Korsgaard's view, the child cannot be held morally responsible, because he isn't yet able to evaluate his reasons for actions, even though we know that such children likely grow up to be anti-social toward humans. If we want to call the child immoral, we need a way of understanding moral agency that doesn't require sophisticated conscious metacognitive abilities.

As well, the idea that normal adolescent humans are not autonomous agents is inconsistent with research in moral psychology, because psychologists start with the assumption that young children are in the sphere of the moral. The psychologist Lawrence Kohlberg, who examined the moral development of ten year-old boys, claims to have found moral reasoning of some sort at this age (Kohlberg 1981). And Elliot Turiel and colleagues examined whether toddlers have a distinction between moral and conventional rules (Nucci and Turiel 1978).

That we recognize children as not *fully* responsible for their actions is reflected in their legal status. Children are still developing their cognitive capacities, are still learning how to evaluate reasons and control their impulses and emotions, so they are limited in what they can do. Given the "ought implies can" principle, children cannot be fully responsible for all the things that humans are generally responsible for. But for those things that they can control, they are responsible.

The requirement that moral agents have conscious metacognition of the reasons for their moral actions and are able to analyze their reasons also runs into problems when we consider adult human cognition. Research on adult moral reasoning suggests that adults do not generally consider their reasons when making moral judgments (Haidt 2001; Cushman et al. 2006). Haidt's research suggests that humans are moved by emotional considerations, and that their ability to construct moral rules is more of a post hoc confabulation than evidence that they consider and follow rules of action.

As an example of a human acting morally but not consciously understanding the moral norm he is following, consider this passage from Huckleberry Finn:

> They went off and I got aboard the raft, feeling bad and low, because I knowed very well I had done wrong, and I see it wasn't no use for me to try to learn to do right; a body that don't get STARTED right when he's little ain't got no show—when the pinch comes there ain't nothing to back him up and keep him to his work, and so he gets beat. Then I thought a minute, and says to myself, hold on; s'pose you'd a done right and give Jim up, would you felt better than what you do now? No, says I, I'd feel bad—I'd feel just the same way I do now. Well, then, says I, what's the use you learning to do right when it's troublesome to do right and ain't no trouble to do wrong, and the wages is just the same? I was stuck. I couldn't answer that. So I reckoned I wouldn't bother no more about it, but after this always do whichever come handiest at the time.
>
> (Twain 1992, 237)

Huck implicitly tracks the moral norms that slavery is wrong, even though he also knows that the legal principles of his society were in conflict with his intuitions, and so he lies that he didn't see Jim, the runaway slave he's sharing a raft with. Just as Huck Finn can track norms that he isn't explicitly aware of, other animals may also be able to follow norms without metacognitive awareness.

However, even if it is true that humans don't always consider their reasons for action when acting morally, it is still true that most adult humans can consider their reasons for acting. Nonetheless, if to qualify as autonomous the reasons for the act must be considered, it would follow that most of our actions could not be understood as autonomous. Rather than concluding that most moral-seeming human action is amoral, we may lower the cognitive requirements for autonomy. If children are already within the realm of the moral, even if they lack full-fledged morality, we could examine the other psychological requirements to see to what extent they are found in young children.

De Waal's account emphasizes the role of theory of mind and empathy in morality. Recall his idea that understanding other minds leads to the development of morality across evolutionary time. The idea seems to go like this: in order to know how another feels, what they will do next, and how to comfort someone, one needs to understand mental states. De Waal thinks that apes are able to take others' perspectives, and have a theory of mind in this sense. He suspects this ability evolved in order to help animals coordinate their behavior in cooperative societies. He writes, "At the core of perspective-taking is emotional linkage between individuals—widespread in social mammals—upon which evolution (or development) builds ever more complex manifestations, including appraisal of another's knowledge and intentions" (de Waal 2006, 72).

While de Waal speaks of this ability as one in line with mindreading capacities, there are a couple of reasons to see these as separate. At least, as understood in terms of belief reasoning, I think there are good reasons for distinguishing the development of morality from the development of mindreading. For one, as I have argued, if mindreading is involved significantly more in explaining anomalous behavior than it is in predicting behavior, then we shouldn't take mindreading to play an important role in the anticipation of future actions. While one might think that to be a moral agent, one has to predict behavior, it is not clear that one needs to mindread to predict behavior. I argue that mindreading doesn't facilitate behavior prediction in the expected ways (Andrews 2012a). Since we can predict behavior without thinking about others' mental states, it is in explaining behavior that mindreading offers an advantage. Once we have an explanation for someone's unusual behavior, we can generate predictions about future behavior, or at least limit the domain of expected behaviors. And we can understand the behavior, and the person, better. This offers certain advantages, such as accepting innovative behaviors into one's community, which leads to the development of cumulative culture. Given that innovation might involve anomalous behavior, the desire to explain anomalous behavior together with a mechanism for producing reason explanations offer an evolutionary advantage.

On this story, it is odd behavior that we seek to explain; there is no need to explain normal behavior. And, importantly, to realize that a behavior is in need of explaining is to realize that it is not normal. This in turn requires understanding what is normal, what individuals should be doing, or how we do things around here. It requires sensitivity to normativity. This normativity is more than just a statistical regularity, reflecting how we happen to do things around here. For example, in the West using your left hand to eat isn't a violation of a social norm, just a statistically unusual behavior. However, in India there is a social norm against eating with the left hand, and it is in India, not in North America or Europe, where eating with the left hand will lead one to question why the person is using that hand. The violations of statistical norms that are the typical subject of explanatory interest are the ones that indicate the existence of social norms. The upshot is that a society in which mindreading might develop is a society that already has social norms, so rather than thinking that mindreading leads to morality, I suggest that a proto morality facilitates mindreading beliefs.

Another reason to reject a view that requires mindreading comes from views that emphasize that morality is about relationships. Having been developed by feminist philosophers and psychologists, such views suggest that there are important aspects of morality having to do with community that are ignored when looking abstractly at the individual and his cognitive capacities. For example, the psychologist Jonathan Haidt defends the view that there are at least five foundational dimensions of morality: care/harm; fairness/cheating; loyalty/betrayal; authority/subversion; sanctity/degradation (Haidt and Joseph 2008). These dimensions reflect community concerns about proper behavior, respect for authority figures, and loyalty to one's ingroup over outgroup members. And the philosopher Lori Gruen argues that the kind of empathy that is foundational to morality is what she calls "entangled empathy" (Gruen 2013), which emphasizes the interconnectedness of individuals and their situations in such a way that allows us to understand and know how to respond to others according to their own situation. Entangled empathy involves an appropriate response to another individual's lived experience.

Gruen points out that individuals in many species have rich social relationships. They sacrifice their own safety to protect others, they grieve dead relatives and friends, they support disabled individuals, and they stay with sick or injured ones (Gruen 2013; Andrews and Gruen 2014). Gruen's approach dovetails with research in moral psychology, and suggests that we find many of Haidt's dimensions of morality in other species. To deny any moral qualities to other animals is to focus on the most rarified example of human morality, such as what we find in a philosophical ethics class, and ignore the moral behavior that runs like a thread through our daily activities. The philosopher Adam Morton asks us to think of ethics not just as dealing with questions about life and death, but also in terms of the small ways in which we can help and harm others around us in our daily behaviors, like walking down a crowded sidewalk, or giving a seat to a young child on the subway (Morton 2003). When we share someone's joy at her success, or when we shout out to a person who dropped her wallet on the street, we are acting morally, from our emotions and from developing practices that support a functioning community. If we ignore these sorts of moral actions, we are overintellectualizing human morality here too; remember Morgan's Challenge: "To interpret animal behavior one must learn also to see one's own mentality at levels of development much lower than one's top-level of reflective self-consciousness" (Morgan 1930, 250).

Finally, there is an approach to ethics stemming from Aristotelian virtue ethics, according to which moral behavior is the result of being a moral person, of having the correct personality traits and acting to improve one's traits. This approach requires two elements, having personality traits and the ability to self-create by purposefully changing oneself. As we saw in Chapter 6, psychologists have found personality dimensions in many different species, from apes to octopuses. However, comparatively little attention has been given to the question of whether other animals act to change themselves by practicing novel behaviors and developing new traits. We do know that many species engage in social learning, closely observing others' behaviors in order to learn them (Whiten 2000; Tomasello et al. 1987; Call and Tomasello 1994). For example, orangutans will stick their heads a few inches away from the behavior that they are observing, and then attempt the behavior themselves (Call and Tomasello 1994). Some scientists think that great apes practice behaviors in order to develop competences (Anne Russon, pers. communication). Future personality research could examine whether individuals understand their own personality traits, and whether they act to modify them.

7.5 Moral differences

While one strategy in investigating animal morality is to look for similarities between animals and humans, differences can also be instructive. If there are dimensions of morality, as Haidt suggests, then species may differ in their behaviors, cognitive capacities, and sentiments yet still be within the domain of the moral.

While measuring animal morality against human morality is de Waal's strategy, Bekoff and Pierce's approach encourages us to step aside from a human centered perspective in order to see how morality might function in different species. Their approach dovetails with cross cultural approaches to studying human moral behavior, where we see both similarities and differences between cultures. Some of these differences might be rather superficial (like how to eat at a table, or how to show respect for others), but be based on the same foundation. One worry about using human morality as the baseline for determining whether other animals have morality is that we may be blinded by superficial differences.

Consider an ongoing debate about whether chimpanzees have a sense of fairness, based on an experiment designed to investigate rationality in humans. In the ultimatum game, which was designed by the economist Werner Güth and his colleagues, two individuals are randomly assigned the roles of proposer and responder. The proposer is offered a sum of money and can decide to offer some portion of it to the responder. If the responder accepts the offer, both parties keep the money. However, if the responder does not accept the offer, then neither player gets anything (Güth et al. 1982). While a rational maximizer should accept any offer given, Güth and colleagues found that people tended to reject offers if they were too low. This finding is often interpreted as evidence that humans value the norm of fairness in the distribution of resources over their own personal gain. It seems that humans will make personal sacrifices to punish those who don't follow social norms about fair distributions of resources.

In a chimpanzee version of this test, the psychologist Keith Jensen and colleagues gave a version of the ultimatum game to a group of 11 chimpanzees in a controlled laboratory setting (Jensen et al. 2007). Unlike the humans, the chimpanzees acted as rational maximizers, accepting any offer given, no matter how small. The authors of this study conclude that chimpanzees are not concerned with fairness: "These results support the hypothesis that other-regarding preferences and aversion to inequitable outcomes, which play key roles in human social organization, distinguish us from our closest living relatives" (Jensen 2007, 107).

However, showing that chimpanzees don't object when food isn't distributed in a way we think is fair doesn't demonstrate that chimpanzees lack other-regarding preferences. For one, consider that the cross-cultural data on the ultimatum game shows a great diversity of responses. For example in non-industrialized human communities that lack a market economy, people will accept much smaller offers than in the West, and in larger communities we see greater rates of punishment. Given such findings, the anthropolgist Joseph Henrich and colleagues suggest that the norms associated with what we consider fair division of goods coevolved with market economies and sedentary populations (Henrich et al. 2010). And anthropologists are sensitive to how different cultures might approach what appears to be the same game. In commenting on Henrich's article, Baumard and Sperber suggest the possibility that:

> behavioural differences observed in economic games are not due to deep psychological differences per se, but rather due to different interpretations of the situation ... For example, Henrich et al.'s (2005) study in 15 small-scale societies reveals a striking difference between the Lamalera, who make very generous offers in the ultimatum game, and the Tsimane and the Machigenga, who make very low offers in the very same game. But the game is likely to be construed very differently within these societies. The Lamalera, being collective hunters, may indeed see the money as jointly owned by the proposer and the recipient. By contrast, the Tsimane and the Machigenga, who are solitary horticulturalists, may see the money as their own property and therefore feel entitled to keep it. In the same way, Westerners may appear as outliers not because they have a different moral psychology, but rather because, living in very large, democratic and capitalist societies, they make

different assumptions in economic games (e.g., that, not knowing the other participant – a situation of anonymity that is common in large-scale urban societies – they have no particular duty to share the stake with her).

(Baumard and Sperber 2010, 85)

Just as different cultures honor relatives in different ways—in North America people will sometimes put their visiting family members in a hotel, while in other cultures not sharing your home with your parents would be a huge insult—different cultures display their other-regarding sentiments in different ways. And just as different cultures display their other-regarding sentiments in different ways, different species can as well. To claim that the chimpanzees do not have a sense of fairness because they fail a test based on cultural human norms is based on an anthropomorphic, and perhaps a Western centric, assumption about what fairness looks like. In order to examine the question of whether chimpanzees have other-regarding tendencies that we might consider a sense of fairness, we need to look at species-specific behavior. For chimpanzees, there appears to be no norm about sharing food resources; it is not part of their natural interactions. While chimpanzees do share food in some circumstances, such as the meat that is acquired through cooperative hunting, the ultimatum game does not reflect a norm about sharing jointly earned resources. If this research had been based on an understanding of wild chimpanzee behaviors, researchers would never have asked whether chimpanzees have a concept of fairness by examining whether they accept inequitable distributions of food items. It is like testing humans on their sense of fairness by asking them to share their toothbrush with a classmate. If you won't share your toothbrush, you must not have any other-regarding preferences! And, interestingly, in a more recent study looking at chimpanzee performance on the ultimatum game, researchers found that, when two individuals would play the game together many times, the proposing chimpanzee will respond to verbal protests at selfish offers by making a fair offer (Proctor et al. 2013). That is, when a food sharing situation is forced upon individuals who don't have a food sharing norm, they can quickly develop one after some experience with the situation.

Ethological studies of chimpanzees suggest that chimpanzees do have other-regarding preferences, and something like a sense of fairness. In one case Frans de Waal writes, "I once saw an adolescent female interrupt a quarrel between two youngsters over a leafy branch. She took the branch away from them, broke it in two, then handed each one a part" (de Waal 2009, 190).

In their normal habitat, chimpanzees live in fission-fusion societies, which means there are small subgroups of chimpanzees who come together to form a larger community on a regular basis. Lori Gruen and I argue that in such large groups, and especially with a species as volatile as chimpanzees, having social norms would best facilitate the ability to share resources, exchange information, and to manage social interactions, and the complex behaviors we see among chimpanzees are best explained in terms of their having social norms (Andrews and Gruen 2014).

For example, in a region of Guinea called Bossou, human development encroaches on chimpanzee territory, and chimpanzees sometimes have to cross busy roads. The primatologist Kimberly Hockings and colleagues examined how chimpanzees manage the dangerous crossing, and found that adult males flank a line of chimpanzees, protecting adult females and young in the middle. The position of the dominant and bolder individuals depends on how risky the road crossing is—some roads are busier than others—and how many males are in the group. Hockings interprets this as cooperative action aimed at maximizing group protection—a case of risk taking for the sake of others. Similar risk taking is found in chimpanzee border patrolling, whereby chimpanzees seek to guard their territory from neighboring communities of chimpanzees. The anthropologist John Mitani found that chimpanzees in Ngogo, in Kibale National Park in Uganda, will raid one another's territories, killing males from another community in order to gain territory (Mitani and Watts 2001). Chimpanzees work together to protect their community from such threats as well as to attack and gain territory.

Another possible norm concerns the proper treatment of infants. Adult males show great tolerance with infant behavior, and will allow little ones to climb over them, and even steal food and tools—behaviors juveniles or adults would never get away with. Infanticide is extremely rare among chimpanzees, but it does happen. When threats of infanticide occur, adult female group members have been observed to respond with "massive reactions," including screaming, barking, and risky attempts to intervene (as discussed in von Rohr et al. 2011, 2012).

Looking at chimpanzee other-regarding preferences from the perspective of their natural behaviors as well as at the norms that develop for the unique situations of a group or species will help us better understand how other-regarding preferences might manifest themselves differently in different populations—of humans, and of species.

7.6 Chapter summary

Where different animals fit into the moral sphere may depend on their psychological properties, such as their ability to feel pleasure and pain, to develop positive personality traits, to respond emotionally to moral stimuli, or to think about their reasons for action. Or it may depend on the relationships they enter into with others. Objections to animals fitting somewhere in the moral sphere are typically based on their lack of some cognitive requirement—they aren't smart enough to have morality, or they only have simple emotions but lack the moral emotions, they can't empathize, aren't rational, and so forth. The issue then becomes the sort of capacity required to make the moral-looking behavior into truly moral behavior.

As we learn more about animals, their lives free from human encroachment, their cognitive capacities, their emotions and their needs, the calibration method will be useful in order to help decide the place of animals in the moral sphere. The outcomes of such decisions depends greatly on the work of philosophers and psychologists who study moral psychology and the nature of normativity, as well as on the more general research into the cognitive capacities of other animals.

Further reading

Lori Gruen's textbook *Ethics and Animals: An Introduction* (2011) is a great place to start if you are interested in animal ethics and related issues about animal minds. Classic arguments for animal moral considerability can be found in Peter Singer's *Animal Liberation* (1990), David DeGrazia's *Taking Animals Seriously: Mental Life and Moral Status* (1996), and Rosalind Hursthouse's *Ethics, Humans and Other Animals* (2000).

Jonathan Safran Foer's *Eating Animals* (2009) is a critique of our current treatment of farm animals that makes for some important, albeit very difficult, reading.

Arguments in favor of some kind of moral understanding in animals are presented in each of the following four books: Marc Bekoff and Jessica Pierce's *Wild Justice: The Moral Lives of Animals* (2009); Frans de Waal's *Primates and Philosophers: How Morality Evolved* (which includes commentary by a number of philosophers) (2006); Mark Rowlands' *Can Animals Be Moral?* (2012); and Gary Varner's *Personhood, Ethics, and Animal Cognition: Situating Animals in Hare's Two Level Utilitarianism* (2012).

Glossary

Access consciousness: A type of consciousness that characterizes mental states which are available to the individual, and does not require a qualitatively distinct aspect. The distinction between access consciousness and phenomenal consciousness was introduced by Ned Block.

Affordances: Perceptions that are inextricably tied to actions.

Analogy: An analogy is a relationship of similarity between entities. There are two factors relevant to the strength of an analogy—(a) the number of properties that are thought to be similar and (b) the level of similarity between those properties. The higher the number of similar properties and the higher the level of similarity between them, the stronger the analogy is.

Anthropectomy: (Gk. anthropos—human; ektomia—to cut out). The denial of human properties to non-human animals, usually with the suggestion that the denial isn't justified.

Anthropomorphism: The attribution of a human psychological, social, or normative property to a non-human animal, usually with the suggestion that the attribution isn't justified.

Associative learning: A type of learning that involves associating two events, which is involved in classical and instrumental conditioning. Associative learning is sometimes given as an example of a low-level cognitive process.

Belief: The propositional attitude that one has whenever one takes something to be true.

Cartesian dualism: The doctrine, articulated by René Descartes, that there are two kinds of substance—mental, non-material substance and physical substance.

Classical conditioning: A type of learning that takes place when an unconditioned stimulus is paired with a conditioned stimulus. It is also referred to as Pavlovian conditioning and is a form of associative learning.

Concept: A constituent of thought, usually taken to be necessary for a number of psychological processes such as categorization, logical reasoning, memory, and learning.

Content: Intentional mental states have content; they are about things. The thing that an intentional mental state is about is referred to as the content of that mental state. While content is usually taken to be propositional, in recent years non-propositional notions of content have been articulated.

De re/de dicto: A distinction between two ways of interpreting sentences in opaque contexts, such as propositional attitude attributions. "De re" roughly means "concerning the thing" while "de dicto" roughly means "concerning the sentence." Here is an example of the use of the distinction: Superman—the superhero who can fly unaided through the air—and Clark Kent—the mild-mannered reporter—are the same person, but Lois Lane does not know this fact; she thinks they are two different men. Does Lois Lane believe that Clark Kent can fly? No, in the *de dicto* sense, because she would not agree that this sentence is true: "Clark Kent can fly." This is what it means to say that propositional attitudes are opaque; substituting equivalent terms in a propositional attitude attribution can change the truth value of the attribution. But in the *de re* sense, she does believe that Clark Kent can fly because she believes *of the person* who is Clark Kent (i.e. Superman) that he can fly.

Dispositionalism: Dispositionalist accounts explain phenomena in terms of dispositions— ready tendencies of objects to do certain things. The dispositionalist view of belief takes belief to be a disposition of an individual to act or feel in certain ways.

Epiphenomenalism: The view of the relationship between the mental and the physical according to which physical things can cause other physical things, and they can cause mental things, but mental things can't cause anything.

Episodic memory: Memory for specific episodes belonging to one's past. It is usually contrasted with semantic memory, understood as memory of concepts or propositions.

Ethology: A branch of biology that investigates the natural behaviors of animals.

Evolutionary parsimony: A principle that suggests that evolutionary explanations that postulate fewer entities or processes are superior to those that postulate more entities or processes.

Explanandum: A phenomenon that requires an explanation. The explanation is called *explanans*.

Fixed action pattern: A sequence of behaviors that cannot be altered and that is carried through to completion once initiated by a stimulus. One classical example is the egg retrieval response of the greylag goose.

Functionalism: The view of the mind according to which the nature of mental states is to be explained in terms of their causal roles, and in particular an input–output relationship that holds in virtue of the mental state.

Intentionality: The "aboutness" of some mental states—the aspect of some mental states that allows them to be described as being directed towards an object. Intentionality is taken to be an essential feature of the mental domain, and is distinguished from consciousness.

Interpretationism: The view according to which mental states are only had by an individual insofar as the individual is interpretable as having those mental states. Interpretationism has been defended by Donald Davidson and Daniel Dennett.

Intersubjective: The property of being shared by at least two minds.

Kin selection: An explanation for altruistic behavior in terms of an organism's having a gene that successfully reproduces because it causes the organism to help close relatives.

Mental representation: A psychological object thought to have intentional properties such as content, success conditions, or reference, and which is essential for thought on mainstream views in philosophy and psychology. A mental representation relates to what it is about the way a map of Toronto relates to the city of Toronto.

Mental time travel: The ability to project oneself mentally either backward or forward in time, which allows one to remember past events or envision future events.

Metacognition: The ability to represent mental states. Typically, metacognition is understood as the ability to have thoughts about mental states, while mindreading is understood as the specific ability to have thoughts about others' mental states.

Metaphysics of mind: The philosophical project that investigates the nature and essential features of the mental.

Mindreading (Theory of mind): The practice of attributing mental states to oneself and others.

Moral agency: The ability to act morally. Moral agency entails responsibility for one's actions.

Moral particularism: An approach to ethics that eschews moral principles and focuses on judgments about particular cases.

Multiple realizability: In the philosophy of mind, the idea that different physical states and events can play the right kinds of roles to count as the same mental state or event. For example, if the neuronal configuration in human Poppy's brain plays the right kind of causal role, then it is right to say that Poppy believes that water is wet. If a very different neuronal configuration in dolphin Frank's brain plays the right kind of causal role, then it is right to say that Frank believes that water is wet. In other words, Poppy's belief that water is wet and Frank's belief that water is wet are realized by different physical structures. It is often thought that functionalism's ability to accommodate multiple realizability is an advantage of functionalism.

Ontogeny: The development of an organism over the lifespan.

Opacity: See de re/de dicto.

Operant conditioning: A type of learning through which a behavior that is followed by a reinforcer becomes more frequent, while behavior that is followed by a punishment becomes less frequent. It is also referred to as instrumental learning, and is a form of associative learning.

Operationalize: A term used in scientific research to refer to the process through which a phenomenon receives a definition that renders it measurable.

Panpsychism: The view according to which the fundamental building blocks of reality are minded.

Peak-end rule: The theory that describes the way in which human beings evaluate past experience, namely by its most intense point and its end, as opposed to its average intensity.

Phenomenal consciousness: The property of mental states that have a "what it is like" character, or a distinctively qualitative dimension that is accessible only to the subject.

Phylogeny: The evolutionary history of an organism or taxa.

Physicalism: The view that everything that exists, including the mind and the mental is physical.

Proposition: That which is expressed by a declarative sentence, and which is typically viewed as the object of belief. The same proposition may be expressed by different sentences. For example, "It is raining" and "Il pleut" express the same proposition.

Qualia: The distinctive subjective character of conscious mental states. Examples might include the hurty-ness of pain (for you), the redness of the color red (for you), or the extreme irritation you might feel when someone runs her fingernails across a chalkboard.

Reciprocal altruism: A type of behavior in which one individual helps another individual with the expectation that the helped individual will provide a reward later on. If this expectation is warranted, then the helping behavior will not result in a loss of fitness for the helper.

Sentimentalism: The meta-ethical view according to which morality is grounded in emotions.

Social intelligence hypothesis: The hypothesis according to which the challenges of social interaction drives the development of sophisticated cognitive capacities. This view was developed by Alison Jolly and Nicholas Humphrey.

Solipsism: The doctrine that all that exists is one's own mind and its contents.

Systematicity: The property of thought that entails that the ability to entertain one thought is essentially linked with the ability to entertain other thoughts.

Theoretical entity: The entity designated by a theoretical term within a theory, and which is essentially unobservable.

Utilitarianism: The view according to which actions are morally right insofar as they maximize utility—pleasure, happiness, general well-being, or some other kind of goodness.

Veneer theory: The view according to which morality is a cultural innovation that barely hides the instrinsically selfish nature of individuals.

Virtue ethics: An ethical theory that insists on the essential role played by the cultivation of character traits and character in moral behavior.

Bibliography

Abbott, H. Porter. *The Cambridge Introduction to Narrative*. New York: Cambridge University Press, 2002.

Achenbach, Thomas M., and Craig S. Edelbrock. *Manual for the Child Behavior Checklist and Revised Child Behavior Profile*. Burlington, VT: T.M. Achenbach, 1983.

Adams, Christopher D., and Anthony Dickinson. "Instrumental Responding Following Reinforcer Devaluation." *The Quarterly Journal of Experimental Psychology Section B* 33, 2 (1981): 109–121.

Addessi, Elsa, and Sabrina Rossi. "Tokens Improve Capuchin Performance in the Reverse–reward Contingency Task." *Proceedings of the Royal Society B: Biological Sciences* 278, 1707 (2011): 849–854.

Adelmann, Pamela K., and Robert B. Zajonc. "Facial Efference and the Experience of Emotion." *Annual Review of Psychology* 40, 1 (1989): 249–280.

Aglioti, Salvatore, Joseph F.X. DeSouza, and Melvyn A. Goodale. "Size-Contrast Illusions Deceive the Eye but Not the Hand." *Current Biology* 5, 6 (1995): 679–685.

Allen, Colin. "Animal Concepts Revisited: The Use of Self-Monitoring as an Empirical Approach." *Erkenntnis* 51 (1999): 537–544.

—— "Transitive Inference in Animals: Reasoning or Conditioned Associations?" In *Rational Animals?* edited by Susan Hurley and Matthew Nudds, 175–185. Oxford: Oxford University Press, 2006.

—— "The Geometry of Partial Understanding." *American Philosophical Quarterly* 50, 3 (2013): 249–262.

Allen, Colin, and Marc Bekoff. *Species of Mind: The Philosophy and Biology of Cognitive Ethology*. Cambridge, Mass.: MIT Press, 1997.

Allen, Colin, and Marc D. Hauser. "Concept Attribution in Nonhuman Animals: Theoretical and Methodological Problems in Ascribing Complex Mental Processes." *Philosophy of Science* (1991): 221–240.

Allen-Hermanson, Sean. "Insects and the Problem of Simple Minds: Are Bees Natural Zombies?" *Journal of Philosophy* 105 (2008): 389–415.

Amy, Mathieu, Philipp Sprau, Piet de Goede, and Marc Naguib. "Effects of Personality on Territory Defence in Communication Networks: A Playback Experiment with Radio-Tagged Great Tits." *Proceedings of the Royal Society B: Biological Sciences* 277, 1700 (2010): 3685–3692.

Anderson, James R., and Gordon G. Gallup. "Which Primates Recognize Themselves in Mirrors?" *PLoS Biol* 9, 3 (2011).

Andics, A., M. Gácsi, T. Faragó, A. Kis, and Á. Miklósi. "Voice-Sensitive Regions in the Dog and Human Brain Are Revealed by Comparative fMRI." *Current Biology*, 24, 5 (2014): 574–578.

Andrews, Kristin. "Interpreting Autism: A Critique of Davidson on Thought and Language." *Philosophical Psychology* 15 (2002): 317–332.

—— "Chimpanzee Theory of Mind: Looking in All the Wrong Places?" *Mind & Language* 20, 5 (2005): 521–536.

—— "Politics or Metaphysics? On Attributing Psychological Properties to Animals." *Biology & Philosophy* 24, 1 (2009): 51–63.

—— "Beyond Anthropomorphism." In *The Oxford Handbook of Animal Ethics*, edited by Tom L. Beauchamp and R.G. Frey, 469–493. Oxford: Oxford University Press, 2011.

—— *Do Apes Read Minds? Toward a New Folk Psychology*. Cambridge, Mass: MIT Press, 2012a.

—— "Robert W. Lurz, Mindreading Animals: The Debate over What Animals Know about Other Minds." *Notre Dame Philosophical Reviews* (2012b). http://ndpr.nd.edu/news/29824-mindreading-animals-the-debate-over-what-animals-know-about-other-minds/. Accessed July 25, 2014.

—— "Great Ape Mindreading: What's at Stake?" In *The Politics of Species: Reshaping Our Relationships with Other Animals*, edited by Raymond Corbey, and Annette Lanjouw, 115–125. Cambridge: Cambridge University Press, 2013.

Andrews, Kristin, and Lori Gruen. "Empathy in Other Apes." In *Empathy and Morality*, edited by Heidi L. Maibom, 193–209. Oxford: Oxford University Press, 2014.

Andrews, Kristin, and Brian Huss. Anthropomorphism, anthropectomy, and the null hypothesis. *Biology & Philosophy*, 1–19 (2014).

Andrews, Kristin, and Ljiljana Radenovic. "Speaking without Interpreting: A Reply to Bouma on Autism and Davidsonian Interpretation." *Philosophical Psychology* 19 (2006): 663–678.

Apperly, Ian A., and Stephen A. Butterfill. "Do Humans Have Two Systems to Track Beliefs and Belief-like States?" *Psychological Review* 116, 4 (2009): 953–970.

Apperly, I.A., and E.J. Robinson. "Children's Difficulties Handling Dual Identity." *Journal of Experimental Child Psychology* 78, 4 (2001): 374–397.

—— "Five-Year-Olds' Handling of Reference and Description in the Domains of Language and Mental Representation." *Journal of Experimental Child Psychology* 83, 1 (2002): 53–75.

—— "When Can Children Handle Referential Opacity? Evidence for Systematic Variation in 5- and 6-Year-Old Children's Reasoning about Beliefs and Belief Reports." *Journal of Experimental Child Psychology* 85, 4 (2003): 297–311.

Arbib, Michael A. "The Mirror System, Imitation, and the Evolution of Language." In *Imitation in Animals and Artifacts*, edited by Chrystopher L. Nehaniv and Kerstin Dautenhahn, 229–280. Cambridge, Mass.: MIT Press, 2002.

—— "From Monkey-like Action Recognition to Human Language: An Evolutionary Framework for Neurolinguistics." *Behavioral and Brain Sciences* 28, 02 (2005): 105–124.

Arbib, Michael A., Katja Liebal, and Simone Pika. "Primate Vocalization, Gesture, and the Evolution of Human Language." *Current Anthropology* 49, 6 (2008): 1053–1076.

Argyle, Michael, and Mark Cook. *Gaze and Mutual Gaze*. New York: Cambridge University Press, 1976.

Aristotle. *The Complete Works of Aristotle. Volume One.* Edited by Jonathan Barnes. Princeton: Princeton University Press, 1984.

Arnold, Kate, and Klaus Zuberbühler. "Language Evolution: Semantic Combinations in Primate Calls." *Nature* 441, 7091 (2006): 303.

Aron, Serge, R. Beckers, Jean-Louis Deneubourg, and J.M. Pasteels. "Memory and Chemical Communication in the Orientation of Two Mass-Recruiting Ant Species." *Insectes Sociaux* 40, 4 (1993): 369–380.

Aronson, Lester Ralph. "Orientation and Jumping Behavior in the Gobiid Fish Bathygobius Soporator. American Museum Novitates; No. 1486" (1951). http://digitallibrary.amnh.org/dspace/handle/2246/3993. Accessed July 25, 2014.

—— "Further Studies on Orientation and Jumping Behavior in the Gobiid Fish, Bathygobius Soporator." *Annals of the New York Academy of Sciences* 188, 1 (1971): 378–392.

Arrington, Robert L., and Hans-Johann Glock. *Wittgenstein and Quine*. New York: Routledge, 1996.

Audi, Robert. "Dispositional Beliefs and Dispositions to Believe." *Noûs* 28, 4 (1994): 419–434.

Babikova, Zdenka, Lucy Gilbert, Toby J.A. Bruce, Michael Birkett, John C. Caulfield, Christine Woodcock, John A. Pickett, and David Johnson. "Underground Signals Carried through Common Mycelial Networks Warn Neighbouring Plants of Aphid Attack." Edited by Nicole van Dam. *Ecology Letters* 16, 7 (2013): 835–843.

Baillargeon, Renee, Rose M. Scott, and Zijing He. "False-Belief Understanding in Infants." *Trends in Cognitive Sciences* 14, 3 (2010): 110–118.

Balter, Michael. "Stone-Throwing Chimp Is Back – And This Time It's Personal." *Science Now*, May 9, 2012. http://news.sciencemag.org/2012/05/stone-throwing-chimp-back-and-time-its-personal. Accessed July 25, 2014.

Bar-On, Dorit. "The Origin of Meaning: Must We 'Go Gricean'?" *Mind and Language* 28, 3 (2013): 342–375. *Speaking My Mind: Expression and Self-Knowledge*. New York: Oxford University Press, 2004.

Bard, Kim A., Brenda K. Todd, Chris Bernier, Jennifer Love, and David A. Leavens. "Self-Awareness in Human and Chimpanzee Infants: What Is Measured and What Is Meant by the Mark and Mirror Test?" *Infancy* 9, 2 (2006): 191–219.

Bargh, John A., Mark Chen, and Lara Burrows. "Automaticity of Social Behavior: Direct Effects of Trait Construct and Stereotype Activation on Action." *Journal of Personality and Social Psychology* 71, 2 (1996): 230–244.

Barkow, Jerome H., Leda Cosmides, and John Tooby. *The Adapted Mind: Evolutionary Psychology and the Generation of Culture*. New York: Oxford University Press, 1995.

Baron-Cohen, Simon. *Mindblindness: An Essay on Autism and Theory of Mind*. Cambridge, Mass.: MIT Press, 1995.

Barrett, Louise. *Beyond the Brain: How Body and Environment Shape Animal and Human Minds*. Princeton: Princeton University Press, 2011.

Barrett, Louise, Peter Henzi, and Drew Rendall. "Social Brains, Simple Minds: Does Social Complexity Really Require Cognitive Complexity?" *Philosophical Transactions of the Royal Society B: Biological Sciences* 362, 1480 (2007): 561–575.

Barth, Hilary, Nancy Kanwisher, and Elizabeth Spelke. "The Construction of Large Number Representations in Adults." *Cognition* 86, 3 (2003): 201–221.

Bateson, Melissa, Suzanne Desire, Sarah E. Gartside, and Geraldine A. Wright. "Agitated Honeybees Exhibit Pessimistic Cognitive Biases." *Current Biology* 21, 12 (2011): 1070–1073.

Baumard, Nicolas, and Dan Sperber. "Weird People, Yes, but Also Weird Experiments." *Behavioral and Brain Sciences* 33, 2–3 (2010): 84–85.

Beck, Jacob. "The Generality Constraint and the Structure of Thought." *Mind* 121, 483 (2012): 563–600.

—— "Why We Can't Say What Animals Think." *Philosophical Psychology* 26, 4 (2013): 520–546.

Behne, Tanya, Malinda Carpenter, and Michael Tomasello. "One-Year-Olds Comprehend the Communicative Intentions behind Gestures in a Hiding Game." *Developmental Science* 8, 6 (2005): 492–499.

Bekoff, Marc. *Why Dogs Hump and Bees Get Depressed: The Fascinating Science of Animal Intelligence, Emotions, Friendship, and Conservation*. Novato, California: New World Library, 2013.

Bekoff, Marc, and Dale Jamieson (eds). *Interpretation and Explanation in the Study of Animal Behavior: Vol. 1, Interpretation, Intentionality, and Communication*. Boulder: Westview Press, 1990.

Bekoff, Marc, and Jessica Pierce. *Wild Justice: The Moral Lives of Animals*. Chicago: University of Chicago Press, 2009.

Bekoff, Marc, Colin Allen, and Gordon M. Burghardt. *The Cognitive Animal: Empirical and Theoretical Perspectives on Animal Cognition*. Cambridge, Mass.: MIT Press, 2002.

Bennett, Edward L., David Krech, and Mark R. Rosenzweig. "Reliability and Regional Specificity of Cerebral Effects of Environmental Complexity and Training." *Journal of Comparative and Physiological Psychology* 57, 3 (1964): 440–441.

Bennett, Jonathan. "Some Remarks about Concepts." *Behavioral and Brain Sciences* 1 (1978): 557–560.

Beran, Michael J., Bonnie M. Perdue, Jessica L. Bramlett, Charles R. Menzel, and Theodore A. Evans. "Prospective Memory in a Language-Trained Chimpanzee (Pan Troglodytes)." *Learning and Motivation* 43, 4 (2012): 192–199.

Beran, Michael J., J. David Smith, Joshua S. Redford, and David A. Washburn. "Rhesus Macaques (Macaca Mulatta) Monitor Uncertainty during Numerosity Judgments." *Journal of Experimental Psychology: Animal Behavior Processes* 32, 2 (2006): 111–119.

Bermúdez, José Luis. *Thinking without Words*. Oxford University Press, 2003.

—— "The Force-Field Puzzle and Mindreading in Non-Human Primates." *Review of Philosophy and Psychology* 2, 3 (2011): 397–410.

Berns, Gregory. *How Dogs Love Us: A Neuroscientist and His Adopted Dog Decode the Canine Brain*. New York: New Harvest, 2013.

Berns, Gregory S., Andrew M. Brooks, and Mark Spivak. "Functional MRI in Awake Unrestrained Dogs." Edited by Stephan C.F. Neuhauss. *PLoS ONE* 7, 5 (2012): e38027.

Biro, Dora, and Tetsuro Matsuzawa. "Use of Numerical Symbols by the Chimpanzee (Pan Troglodytes): Cardinals, Ordinals, and the Introduction of Zero." *Animal Cognition* 4, 3–4 (2001): 193–199.

Block, Ned. "On a Confusion about a Function of Consciousness." In *The Nature of Consciousness: Philosophical Debates*, edited by Ned Block, Owen Flanagan, and Güven Güzeldere. Cambridge, MA: MIT Press, 1998.

Bloom, Paul. "Can a Dog Learn a Word?" *Science* 304, 5677 (2004): 1605–1606.

Bodamar, Mark D., and R. Allen Gardner. "How Cross-Fostered Chimpanzees (Pan Troglodytes) Initiate and Maintain Conversations." *Journal of Comparative Psychology* 116, 1 (2002): 12–26.

Boesch, Christophe. "Aspects of Transmission of Tool-Use in Wild Chimpanzees." In *Tools, Language and Cognition in Human Evolution*, edited by K.R. Gibson, 171–183. New York: Cambridge University Press, 1993.

—— "Cooperative Hunting in Wild Chimpanzees." *Animal Behaviour* 48, 3 (1994): 653–667.

—— "Cooperative Hunting Roles among Taï Chimpanzees." *Human Nature* 13, 1 (2002): 27–46.

Boesch, Christophe, and Hedwige Boesch. "Mental Map in Wild Chimpanzees: An Analysis of Hammer Transports for Nut Cracking." *Primates* 25, 2 (1984): 160–170.

Bolhuis, Johan J., Kazuo Okanoya, and Constance Scharff. "Twitter Evolution: Converging Mechanisms in Birdsong and Human Speech." *Nature Reviews Neuroscience* 11, 11 (2010): 747–759.

Borgia, Gerald. "Bower Quality, Number of Decorations and Mating Success of Male Satin Bowerbirds (Ptilonorhynchus Violaceus): An Experimental Analysis." *Animal Behaviour* 33, 1 (1985): 266–271.

Bower, Bruce. "The Hot and Cold of Priming: Psychologists Are Divided on Whether Unnoticed Cues Can Influence Behavior." *Science News* 181, 10 (2012): 26–29.

Boysen, Sarah T., Gary G. Berntson, Michelle B. Hannan, and John T. Cacioppo. "Quantity-Based Interference and Symbolic Representations in Chimpanzees (Pan Troglodytes)." *Journal of Experimental Psychology: Animal Behavior Processes* 22, 1 (1996): 76–86.

Boysen, Sarah T., Kimberly L. Mukobi, and Gary G. Berntson. "Overcoming Response Bias Using Symbolic Representations of Number by Chimpanzees (Pan Troglodytes)." *Animal Learning & Behavior* 27, 2 (1999): 229–235.

Braddon-Mitchell, David, and Frank Jackson. *The Philosophy of Mind and Cognition*. Oxford: Blackwell Publishers, 1996.

Bradshaw, G.A., Theodora Capaldo, Lorin Lindner, and Gloria Grow. "Building an Inner Sanctuary: Complex PTSD in Chimpanzees." *Journal of Trauma & Dissociation: The Official Journal of the International Society for the Study of Dissociation (ISSD)* 9, 1 (2008): 9–34.

Braithwaite, Victoria. *Do Fish Feel Pain?* Oxford: Oxford University Press, 2010.

Bräuer, Juliane, Josep Call, and Michael Tomasello. "All Great Ape Species Follow Gaze to Distant Locations and around Barriers." *Journal of Comparative Psychology* 119, 2 (2005): 145–154.

Bräuer, Juliane, Juliane Kaminski, Julia Riedel, Josep Call, and Michael Tomasello. "Making Inferences about the Location of Hidden Food: Social Dog, Causal Ape." *Journal of Comparative Psychology* 120, 1 (2006): 38–47.

Bräuer, Juliane, Magdalena Keckeisen, Andrea Pitsch, Juliane Kaminski, Josep Call, and Michael Tomasello. "Domestic Dogs Conceal Auditory but Not Visual Information from Others." *Animal Cognition* 16, 3 (2013): 1–9.

Brook, Andrew, and Kathleen Akins. *Cognition and the Brain: The Philosophy and Neuroscience Movement*. New York: Cambridge University Press, 2005.

Brooks, Rodney A. "Intelligence without Representation." *Artificial Intelligence* 47, 1–3 (1991): 139–159.

Brown, Culum, Martin P. Garwood, and Jane E. Williamson. "It Pays to Cheat: Tactical Deception in a Cephalopod Social Signalling System." *Biology Letters* 8, 5 (2012): 729–732.

Bshary, Redouan, Andrea Hohner, Karim Ait-el-Djoudi, and Hans Fricke. "Interspecific Communicative and Coordinated Hunting between Groupers and Giant Moray Eels in the Red Sea." *PLoS Biology* 4, 12 (2006).

Buckner, Cameron. "Morgan's Canon, Meet Hume's Dictum: Avoiding Anthropofabulation in Cross-Species Comparisons." *Biology & Philosophy* 28, 5 (2013): 853–871.

Bugnyar, Thomas, Maartje Kijne, and Kurt Kotrschal. "Food Calling in Ravens: Are Yells Referential Signals?" *Animal Behaviour* 61, 5 (2001): 949–958.

Burghardt, Gordon M. *The Genesis of Animal Play: Testing the Limits*. Cambridge, Mass.: MIT Press, 2005.

Burkhardt, Richard W. *Patterns of Behavior: Konrad Lorenz, Niko Tinbergen, and the Founding of Ethology*. Chicago: University of Chicago Press, 2005.

Buttelmann, David, Malinda Carpenter, and Michael Tomasello. "Eighteen-Month-Old Infants Show False Belief Understanding in an Active Helping Paradigm." *Cognition* 112, 2 (2009): 337–342.

Butterfill, Stephen A., and Ian A. Apperly. "How to Construct a Minimal Theory of Mind." *Mind & Language* 28, 5 (2013): 606–637.

Byrne, Richard W. "What's the Use of Anecdotes? Distinguishing Psychological Mechanisms in Primate Tactical Deception." In *Anthropomorphism, Anecdotes, and Animals*, edited by Robert W. Mitchell, Nicholas S. Thompson, and H. Lyn Miles, 134–150. Albany: State University of New York Press, 1997.

Byrne, Richard W., and Anne E. Russon. "Learning by Imitation: A Hierarchical Approach." *Behavioral and Brain Sciences* 21, 5 (1998): 667–684.

Byrne, Richard W., and Andrew Whiten (eds). *Machiavellian Intelligence: Social Expertise and the Evolution of Intellect in Monkeys, Apes, and Humans*. Oxford: Oxford University Press, 1988.

Caine, Nancy G., Rebecca L. Addington, and Tammy L. Windfelder. "Factors Affecting the Rates of Food Calls given by Red-Bellied Tamarins." *Animal Behaviour* 50, 1 (1995): 53–60.

Call, Josep. "Inferences about the Location of Food in the Great Apes (Pan Paniscus, Pan Troglodytes, Gorilla Gorilla, and Pongo Pygmaeus)." *Journal of Comparative Psychology* 118, 2 (2004): 232–241.

—— "Inferences by Exclusion in the Great Apes: The Effect of Age and Species." *Animal Cognition* 9, 4 (2006): 393–403.

Call, Josep, and Michael Tomasello. "The Social Learning of Tool Use by Orangutans (Pongo Pygmaeus)." *Human Evolution* 9, 4 (1994): 297–313.

—— "A Nonverbal False Belief Task: The Performance of Children and Great Apes." *Child Development* 70, 2 (1999): 381–395.

—— (eds). *The Gestural Communication of Apes and Monkeys.* New York, NY: Taylor & Francis Group/ Lawrence Erlbaum Associates, 2007.

Call, Josep, Brian Hare, Malinda Carpenter, and Michael Tomasello. "'Unwilling' versus 'Unable': Chimpanzees' Understanding of Human Intentional Action." *Developmental Science* 7 (2004): 488–498.

Camaioni, Luigia. "Continuity versus Discontinuity in the Development of Pre-Linguistic and Linguistic Communication." *Sistemi Intelligenti* 5, 2 (1993): 189–197.

Camp, Elisabeth. "Thinking with Maps." *Philosophical Perspectives* 21, 1 (2007): 145–182.

—— "A Language of Baboon Thought?" In *Philosophy of Animal Minds*, edited by Robert Lurz. New York: Cambridge University Press, 2009.

Capitan, W.H., and D.D. Merrill. *Art, Mind, and Religion.* Pittsburgh, PA: University of Pittsburgh Press, 1967.

Carey, Susan. *The Origin of Concepts.* New York, Oxford: Oxford University Press, 2009.

Carpenter, Malinda, Nameera Akhtar, and Michael Tomasello. "Fourteen- through 18-Month-Old Infants Differentially Imitate Intentional and Accidental Actions." *Infant Behavior and Development* 21, 2 (1998): 315–330.

Carruthers, Peter. "Brute Experience." *The Journal of Philosophy* 86, 5 (1989): 258–269.

—— "Suffering without Subjectivity." *Philosophical Studies* 121 (2004): 99–125.

—— "Meta-Cognition in Animals: A Skeptical Look." *Mind & Language* 23, 1 (2008): 58–89.

—— "How We Know Our Own Minds: The Relationship between Mindreading and Metacognition." *Behavioral and Brain Sciences* 32 (2009): 121–182.

—— "Introspection: Divided and Partly Eliminated." *Philosophy and Phenomenological Research* 80, 1 (2010): 76–111.

—— *The Opacity of Mind: An Integrative Theory of Self-Knowledge.* Oxford: Oxford University Press, 2011.

—— "Animal Minds Are Real, (distinctively) Human Minds Are Not." *American Philosophical Quarterly* 50 (2013): 233–247.

Carruthers, Peter, and J. Brendan Ritchie. "The Emergence of Metacognition: Affect and Uncertainty in Animals." *Foundations of Metacognition* (2012): 76–93.

Cartmill, Erica A., and Richard W. Byrne. "Orangutans Modify Their Gestural Signaling According to Their Audience's Comprehension." *Current Biology* 17, 15 (2007): 1345–1348.

Cavalieri, Paola, and Peter Singer. *The Great Ape Project: Equality beyond Humanity.* New York: St. Martin's Press, 1993.

Chalmers, David J. "Facing Up to the Problem of Consciousness." In *Toward a Science of Consciousness*, edited by Stuart R. Hameroff, Alfred W. Kaszniak, and Alwyn C. Scott, 1: 5–28. Cambridge, MA: MIT Press, 1996.

Chapman, Colin A., and Louis Lefebvre. "Manipulating Foraging Group Size: Spider Monkey Food Calls at Fruiting Trees." *Animal Behaviour* 39, 5 (1990): 891–896.

Chater, Nick, and Cecilia Heyes. "Animal Concepts: Content and Discontent." *Mind and Language* 9 (1994): 209–246.

Cheney, Dorothy L., and Robert M. Seyfarth. "Attending to Behaviour versus Attending to Knowledge: Examining Monkeys' Attribution of Mental States." *Animal Behaviour* 40, 4 (1990): 742–753.

—— *How Monkeys See the World: Inside the Mind of Another Species.* Chicago: University of Chicago Press, 1996.

—— "Constraints and Preadaptations in the Earliest Stages of Language Evolution." *The Linguistic Review* 22, 2–4 (2005): 135–159.

—— *Baboon Metaphysics: The Evolution of a Social Mind.* Chicago: University of Chicago Press, 2007.

Chomsky, Noam. *Aspects of the Theory of Syntax.* Cambridge, MA: MIT Press, 1965.

—— "Human Language and Other Semiotic Systems." In *Speaking of Apes: A Critical Anthology of Two-Way Communication with Man*, edited by Thomas A. Sebeok and Jean Umiker-Sebeok, 429–440. New York: Plenum Press, 1980.

Churchland, Paul M. "Eliminative Materialism and the Propositional Attitudes." *The Journal of Philosophy* 78 (1981): 67–90.

Clark, Andy, and David Chalmers. "The Extended Mind." *Analysis* 58, 1 (1998): 7–19.

Clark, Andy, and Josefa Toribio. "Doing without Representing?" *Synthese* 101, 3 (1994): 401–431.

Clayton, Nicola S., and Anthony Dickinson. "Episodic-like Memory during Cache Recovery by Scrub Jays." *Nature* 395, 6699 (1998): 272–274.

Clayton, Nicola S., Joanna M. Dally, and Nathan J. Emery. "Social Cognition by Food-Caching Corvids. The Western Scrub-Jay as a Natural Psychologist." *Philosophical Transactions of the Royal Society B: Biological Sciences* 362, 1480 (2007): 507–522.

Clifford, William. "Body and Mind." In *Lectures and Essays.* Vol. 2. London: Macmillian, 1874.

Colbert-White, Erin N., Michael A. Covington, and Dorothy M. Fragaszy. "Social Context Influences the Vocalizations of a Home-Raised African Grey Parrot (Psittacus Erithacus Erithacus)." *Journal of Comparative Psychology* 125, 2 (2011): 175–184.

Connor, Richard C., Rachel Smolker, and Lars Bejder. "Synchrony, Social Behaviour and Alliance Affiliation in Indian Ocean Bottlenose Dolphins, Tursiops Aduncus." *Animal Behaviour* 72, 6 (2006): 1371–1378.

Corballis, Michael C. "On the Evolution of Language and Generativity." *Cognition* 44, 3 (1992): 197–226.

—— *From Hand to Mouth: The Origins of Language.* Princeton: Princeton University Press, 2002.

—— "Language as Gesture." *Human Movement Science* 28, 5 (2009): 556–565.

Corbey, Raymond, and Annette Lanjouw (eds). *The Politics of Species: Reshaping Our Relationships with Other Animals.* Cambridge: Cambridge University Press, 2013.

Cosmides, Leda, and John Tooby. "Cognitive Adaptations for Social Exchange." In *The Adapted Mind: Evolutionary Psychology and the Generation of Culture*, edited by J. Barkow, L. Cosmides, and J. Tooby, 163–228. New York: Oxford University Press, 1992.

Crick, Francis, and Christof Koch. "Are We Aware of Neural Activity in Primary Visual Cortex?" *Nature* 375, 6527 (1995): 121–123.

Crockford, Catherine, Ilka Herbinger, Linda Vigilant, and Christophe Boesch. "Wild Chimpanzees Produce Group-Specific Calls: A Case for Vocal Learning?" *Ethology* 110, 3 (2004): 221–243.

Crystal, Jonathon D. and Allison L. Foote. "Metacognition in Animals." *Comparative Cognition and Behavior Reviews* 4 (2009): 1–16.

Csibra, Gergely. "Recognizing Communicative Intentions in Infancy." *Mind & Language* 25, 2 (2010): 141–168.

Csibra, Gergely, and György Gergely. "Natural Pedagogy." *Trends in Cognitive Sciences* 13, 4 (2009): 148–153.

Cushman, Fiery, Liane Young, and Marc Hauser. "The Role of Conscious Reasoning and Intuition in Moral Judgment Testing Three Principles of Harm." *Psychological Science* 17, 12 (2006): 1082–1089.

Dally, Joanna M., Nicola S. Clayton, and Nathan J. Emery. "The Behaviour and Evolution of Cache Protection and Pilferage." *Animal Behaviour* 72, 1 (2006): 13–23.

Dao, James. "More Military Dogs Show Signs of Combat Stress." *The New York Times*, December 1, 2011, sec. U.S. http://www.nytimes.com/2011/12/02/us/more-military-dogs-show-signs-of-combat-stress.html. Accessed July 25, 2014.

Darwin, Charles. *Descent of Man, and Selection in Relation to Sex*. New York: D. Appleton and Company, 1880.

—— *The Expression of the Emotions in Man and Animals*. Mineola, NY: Dover Publications, 2007.

Daston, Lorraine, and Gregg Mitman (eds). *Thinking with Animals: New Perspectives on Anthropomorphism*. New York: Columbia University Press, 2005.

Davidson, Donald. "On the Very Idea of a Conceptual Scheme." *Proceedings and Addresses of the American Philosophical Association* 47 (1973): 5–20.

—— "Thought and Talk." In *Mind and Language*, edited by S Guttenplan, 7–24. Oxford: Oxford University Press, 1975.

—— "Rational Animals." *Dialectica* 36 (1982): 317–327.

—— *Inquiries into Truth and Interpretation*. Oxford: Oxford University Press, 1984.

—— "Three Varieties of Knowledge." *Royal Institute of Philosophy Supplements* 30 (1991): 153–166.

Davidson, Donald. *Subjective, Intersubjective, Objective*. Oxford, New York: Clarendon Press, Oxford University Press, 2001.

Dawkins, Richard, and John R. Krebs. "Animal Signals: Information or Manipulation." *Behavioural Ecology: An Evolutionary Approach* 2 (1978): 282–309.

De Lillo, C., D. Floreano, and F. Antinucci. "Transitive Choices by a Simple, Fully Connected, Backpropagation Neural Network: Implications for the Comparative Study of Transitive Inference." *Animal Cognition* 4, 1 (2001): 61–68.

De Waal, Frans B.M. *Chimpanzee Politics: Power and Sex among Apes*. New York: Harper & Row, 1982.

—— "Complementary Methods and Convergent Evidence in the Study of Primate Social Cognition." *Behaviour* 118, 3/4 (1991): 297–320.

—— "Anthropomorphism and Anthropodenial." *Philosophical Topics* 27, 1 (1999): 255–280.

—— *Primates and Philosophers: How Morality Evolved*. Edited by Josiah Ober and Robert Wright. Princeton, N.J.: Princeton University Press, 2006.

—— "The 'Russian Doll' Model of Empathy and Imitation." In *On Being Moved: From Mirror Neurons to Empathy*, edited by Stein Bråten, 68: 49–69. John Benjamins Publishing, 2007.

—— *The Age of Empathy: Nature's Lessons for a Kinder Society*. New York: Harmony Books, 2009.

De Waal, Frans B.M., and Lesleigh M. Luttrell. "Mechanisms of Social Reciprocity in Three Primate Species: Symmetrical Relationship Characteristics or Cognition?" *Ethology and Sociobiology* 9, 2–4 (1988): 101–118.

De Waal, Frans B.M, and Angeline van Roosmalen. "Reconciliation and Consolation among Chimpanzees." *Behavioral Ecology and Sociobiology* 5, 1 (1979): 55–66.

DeGrazia, David. *Taking Animals Seriously: Mental Life and Moral Status*. Cambridge; New York: Cambridge University Press, 1996.

Dennett, Daniel C. "Beliefs about Beliefs." *Behavioral and Brain Sciences* 1, 04 (1978): 568–570.

—— "Intentional Systems in Cognitive Ethology: The 'Panglossian Paradigm' Defended." *Behavioral and Brain Sciences* 6, 03 (1983): 343–355.

—— *The Intentional Stance*. Cambridge, MA: MIT Press, 1987.

—— "Out of the Armchair and into the Field." *Poetics Today* 9, 1 (1988): 205–221.

—— "Real Patterns." *The Journal of Philosophy* 88 (1991): 27–51.

—— *Kinds of Minds: Toward an Understanding of Consciousness*. New York, NY: Basic Books, 1996.

—— *Brainchildren: Essays on Designing Minds*. Representation and Mind. Cambridge, MA: MIT Press, 1998.

—— "Intentional Systems Theory." In *Oxford Handbook of the Philosophy of Mind*, edited by B. McLaughlin, A. Beckermann, and S. Walter, 339–50. Oxford: Oxford University Press, 2009.

Descartes, René. *Descartes: Philosophical Letters*. Oxford: Clarendon Press, 1970.

—— *A Discourse on the Method for Conducting One's Reason Well and for Seeking the Truth in the Sciences*. In *Philosophical Essays and Correspondence*, edited by Roger Ariew. Cambridge: Hackett Publishing, 2000.

Desrochers, Stéphan, Paul Morissette, and Marcelle Ricard. "Two Perspectives on Pointing in Infancy." In *Joint Attention: Its Origins and Role in Development*, edited by C. Moore and P.J. Dunham, 85–101. New York: Lawrence Erlbaum Associates Inc., 1995.

Di Bitetti, Mario S. "Food-Associated Calls and Audience Effects in Tufted Capuchin Monkeys, Cebus Apella Nigritus." *Animal Behaviour* 69, 4 (2005): 911–919.

Dickinson, Anthony. "Why a Rat Is Not a Beast Machine." In *Frontiers of Consciousness*, edited by Lawrence Weiskrantz and Martin Davies, 275–288. New York: Oxford University Press, 2008.

Donald, Merlin. *Origins of the Modern Mind: Three Stages in the Evolution of Culture and Cognition*. Cambridge, MA: Harvard University Press, 1991.

—— "Precis of Origins of the Modern Mind: Three Stages in the Evolution of Culture and Cognition." *Behavioral and Brain Sciences* 16, 4 (1993): 737–747.

Donaldson, Sue, and Will Kymlicka. *Zoopolis: A Political Theory of Animal Rights*. Oxford: Oxford University Press, 2011.

Dreben, Burton. "Quine and Wittgenstein: The Odd Couple." In *Wittgenstein and Quine*, edited by Robert Arrington and Hans-Johann Glock, 39–61. New York, London: Routledge, 1996.

Dretske, Fred I. *Knowledge and the Flow of Information*. Cambridge, MA: MIT Press, 1981.

—— "The Epistemology of Belief." *Synthese* 55, 1 (1983): 3–19.

—— *Explaining Behavior*. Cambridge, MA: MIT Press, 1988.

—— "Minimal Rationality." In *Rational Animals?*, edited by Susan Hurley and Matthew Nudds, 107–115. Oxford: Oxford University Press, 2006.

Dummett, Michael. *The Seas of Language*. Oxford: Oxford University Press, 1993.

—— *Origins of Analytical Philosophy*. Cambridge, MA: Harvard University Press, 1996.

—— *The Nature and Future of Philosophy*. New York: Columbia University Press, 2010.

Dunbar, Robin. *Gossip, Grooming and the Evolution of Language*. London: Faber and Faber Ltd., 1996.

Dunlop, Rebecca, Sarah Millsopp, and Peter Laming. "Avoidance Learning in Goldfish (Carassius Auratus) and Trout (Oncorhynchus Mykiss) and Implications for Pain Perception." *Applied Animal Behaviour Science* 97, 2–4 (2006): 255–271.

Eales, Lucy A. "Song Learning in Zebra Finches: Some Effects of Song Model Availability on What Is Learnt and When." *Animal Behaviour* 33, 4 (1985): 1293–1300.

Eibl-Eibesfeldt, Irenäus. *Ethology: The Biology of Behavior*. New York: Holt, Rinehart and Winston, 1975.

Ekman, Paul. "An Argument for Basic Emotions." *Cognition & Emotion* 6, 3–4 (1992): 169–200.

Elowson, A. Margaret, Pamela L. Tannenbaum, and Charles T. Snowdon. "Food-Associated Calls Correlate with Food Preferences in Cotton-Top Tamarins." *Animal Behaviour* 42, 6 (1991): 931–937.

Emery, Nathan J., and Nicola S. Clayton. "Effects of Experience and Social Context on Prospective Caching Strategies by Scrub Jays." *Nature* 414, 6862 (2001): 443–446.

Emery, N., N. Clayton, and C. Frith. *Social Intelligence: From Brain to Culture* (1 edn). Oxford, New York: Oxford University Press, 2008.

Endler, John A., Lorna C. Endler, and Natalie R. Doerr. "Great Bowerbirds Create Theaters with Forced Perspective When Seen by Their Audience." *Current Biology* 20, 18 (2010): 1679–1684.

Enfield, Nicholas J. "Lip-Pointing: A Discussion of Form and Function with Reference to Data from Laos." *Gesture* 1, 2 (2001): 185–211.

Erdőhegyi, Ágnes, József Topál, Zsófia Virányi, and Ádám Miklósi. "Dog-Logic: Inferential Reasoning in a Two-Way Choice Task and Its Restricted Use." *Animal Behaviour* 74, 4 (2007): 725–737.

Evans, Christopher S., and Linda Evans. "Chicken Food Calls Are Functionally Referential." *Animal Behaviour* 58, 2 (1999): 307–319.

—— "Representational Signalling in Birds." *Biology Letters* 3, 1 (2007): 8–11.

Evans, Christopher S., and Peter Marler. "Language and Animal Communication: Parallels and Contrasts." *Comparative Approaches to Cognitive Science* (1995): 341–382.

Evans, Christopher S., Linda Evans, and Peter Marler. "On the Meaning of Alarm Calls: Functional Reference in an Avian Vocal System." *Animal Behaviour* 46, 1 (1993): 23–38.

Evans, Gareth. *The Varieties of Reference*. Oxford: Clarendon Press, 1982.

Everett, Daniel. "Cultural Constraints on Grammar and Cognition in Pirahã." *Current Anthropology* 46, 4 (2005): 621–646.

Faragó, Tamás, Péter Pongrácz, Friederike Range, Zsófia Virányi, and Ádám Miklósi. "'The Bone Is Mine': Affective and Referential Aspects of Dog Growls." *Animal Behaviour* 79, 4 (2010): 917–925.

Fehér, Olga, Haibin Wang, Sigal Saar, Partha P. Mitra, and Ofer Tchernichovski. "De Novo Establishment of Wild-Type Song Culture in the Zebra Finch." *Nature* 459, 7246 (2009): 564–568.

Fellner, Wendi, Gordon B. Bauer, and Heidi E. Harley. "Cognitive Implications of Synchrony in Dolphins: A Review." *Aquatic Mammals* 32, 4 (2006): 511–516.

Ferdowsian, Hope R., Debra L. Durham, Charles Kimwele, Godelieve Kranendonk, Emily Otali, Timothy Akugizibwe, J.B. Mulcahy, Lilly Ajarova, and Cassie Meré Johnson. "Signs of Mood and Anxiety Disorders in Chimpanzees." *PLoS ONE* 6, 6 (2011): e19855.

Feyerabend, Paul. "Materialism and the Mind-Body Problem." *The Review of Metaphysics* 17 (1963): 49–66.

Fischer, Julia. "The Myth of Anthropomorphism." In *Interpretation and Explanation in the Study of Animal Behavior: Vol. 1, Interpretation, Intentionality, and Communication*, edited by Marc Bekoff and Dale Jamieson. Boulder: Westview Press, 1990.

Fitch, W. Tecumseh. "The Evolution of Speech: A Comparative Review." *Trends in Cognitive Sciences* 4, 7 (2000): 258–267.

—— "The Evolution of Language: A Comparative Review." *Biology and Philosophy* 20, 2–3 (2005): 193–203.

Fitch, W. Tecumseh, and Marc D. Hauser. "Computational Constraints on Syntactic Processing in a Nonhuman Primate." *Science* 303, 5656 (2004): 377–380.

Flanagan, Owen J. *Consciousness Reconsidered*. Cambridge, MA: MIT Press, 1992.

Flombaum, Jonathan I., and Laurie R. Santos. "Rhesus Monkeys Attribute Perceptions to Others." *Current Biology* 15, 5 (2005): 447–452.

Fodor, Jerry A. *The Language of Thought*. The Language & Thought Series. New York: Crowell, 1975.

Foer, Jonathan Safran. *Eating Animals*. New York: Little, Brown and Company, 2009.

Fogel, Alan. *Developing through Relationships*. Chicago: University of Chicago Press, 1993.

Foote, Allison L., and Jonathon D. Crystal. "Metacognition in the Rat." *Current Biology* 17, 6 (2007): 551–555.

Fouts, Roger S., and Deborah H. Fouts. "Chimpanzees' Use of Sign Language." In *The Great Ape Project*, edited by Paola Cavalieri and Peter Singer, 28–41. New York: St. Martins Press, 1993.

Fouts, Roger S., Alan D. Hirsch, and Deborah H. Fouts. "Cultural Transmission of a Human Language in a Chimpanzee Mother-Infant Relationship." In *Child Nurturance*, 159–193. New York: Springer, 1982.

Franco, Fabia, and George Butterworth. "Pointing and Social Awareness: Declaring and Requesting in the Second Year." *Journal of Child Language* 23 (1996): 307–336.

Freeman, Hani D., and Samuel D. Gosling. "Personality in Nonhuman Primates: A Review and Evaluation of Past Research." *American Journal of Primatology* 72, 8 (2010): 653–671.

Frey, R.G. *Interests and Rights: The Case against Animals*. Oxford: Clarendon Library of Logic and Philosophy, Oxford University Press, 1980.

Fujita, Kazuo. "Metamemory in Tufted Capuchin Monkeys (Cebus Apella)." *Animal Cognition* 12, 4 (2009): 575–585.

Gácsi, Márta, Ádám Miklósi, Orsolya Varga, József Topál, and Vilmos Csányi. "Are Readers of Our Face Readers of Our Minds? Dogs (Canis Familiaris) Show Situation-Dependent Recognition of Human's Attention." *Animal Cognition* 7, 3 (2004): 144–153.

Gagliano, M., M. Renton, M. Depczynski, and S. Mancuso, Experience Teaches Plants to Learn Faster and Forget Slower in Environments Where it Matters. *Oecologia, 175*(1) (2014), 63–72.

Gallese, Vittorio, Luciano Fadiga, Leonardo Fogassi, and Giacomo Rizzolatti. "Action Recognition in the Premotor Cortex." *Brain* 119 (1996): 593–609.

Gallistel, C. R. "Prelinguistic Thought." *Language Learning and Development* 7, 4 (2011): 253–262.

Gallup, G. G. "Self-Recognition in Primates: A Comparative Approach to the Bidirectional Properties of Consciousness." *American Psychologist* 32 (1977): 329–338.

—— "Toward a Comparative Psychology of Self-Awareness: Species Limitations and Cognitive Consequences." In *The Self: Interdisciplinary Approaches*, edited by Jaine Strauss and George R. Goethals, 121–135. New York: Springer, 1991.

—— "Self-Awareness and the Evolution of Social Intelligence." *Behavioral Processes* 42 (1998): 239–247.

Gardner, R. Allen, and Beatrice T. Gardner. "Comparative Psychology and Language Acquisition." *Annals of the New York Academy of Sciences* 309 (1978): 37–76.

Garner, Roberta. *The Joy of Stats: A Short Guide to Introductory Statistics in the Social Sciences*. Ontario: Broadview Press, 2005.

Garson, Justin. *Biological Mind: A Philosophical Introduction*. London: Routledge, 2014.

Gelder, Tim Van. "What Might Cognition Be, If Not Computation?" *The Journal of Philosophy* 92, 7 (1995): 345–381.

Gendler, Tamar Szabó. "Alief and Belief." *Journal of Philosophy* 105, 10 (2008): 634–663.

Gennaro, Rocco J. "Higher-Order Thoughts, Animal Consciousness, and Misrepresentation. A Reply to Carruthers and Levine." In *Higher-Order Theories of Consciousness*, edited by Rocco J. Gennaro. Amsterdam: John Benjamins, 2004.

Gentner, Timothy Q., Kimberly M. Fenn, Daniel Margoliash, and Howard C. Nusbaum. "Recursive Syntactic Pattern Learning by Songbirds." *Nature* 440, 7088 (2006): 1204–1207.

Gergely, György, and Gergely Csibra. "Teleological Reasoning in Infancy: The Naïve Theory of Rational Action." *Trends in Cognitive Sciences* 7, 7 (2003): 287–292.

Gibson, J.J. "The Theory of Affordances." In *Perceiving, Acting, and Knowing. Towards an Ecological Psychology*, edited by Robert Shaw and John Bransford, 127–143. New York: Lawrence Erlbaum Associates, 1977.

Glock, Hans-Johann. "Animals, Thoughts and Concepts." *Synthese* 123 (2000): 35–64.

Glüer, Kathrin, and Peter Pagin. "Meaning Theory and Autistic Speakers." *Mind & Language* 18, 1 (2003): 23–51.

Goldman, Alvin I. *Simulating Minds: The Philosophy, Psychology, and Neuroscience of Mindreading*. Oxford: Oxford University Press, 2006.

Goldman, Alvin I., and Chandra Sekhar Sripada. "Simulationist Models of Face-Based Emotion Recognition." *Cognition* 94, 3 (2005): 193–213.

Gómez, J.C. (2007). "Pointing Behaviours in Apes and Human Infants: A Balanced Interpretation." *Child Development*, 78(3): 729–734.

—— "Embodying Meaning: Insights from Primates, Autism, and Brentano." *Neural Networks* 22, 2 (2009): 190–196.

—— "The Ontogeny of Triadic Cooperative Interactions with Humans in an Infant Gorilla." *Interaction Studies* 11, 3 (2010): 353–379.

Goodenough, Judith, Betty McGuire, and Robert A. Wallace. *Perspectives on Animal Behavior*. New York: J. Wiley, 1993.

Gosling, S.D., and O.P. John. "Personality Dimensions in Dogs, Cats, and Hyenas." In *Annual Meeting of the American Psychological Society*, Washington, DC, 1998.

Gregg, Justin D., Kathleen M. Dudzinski, and Howard V. Smith. "Do Dolphins Eavesdrop on the Echolocation Signals of Conspecifics?" *International Journal of Comparative Psychology* 20, 1 (2007): 65–88.

Grice, H. Paul. "Meaning." *The Philosophical Review* 66 (1957): 377–388.

Griffin, Donald R. *Animal Minds*. Chicago: University of Chicago Press, 1992.

—— "Afterward: What Is It Like?" In *The Cognitive Animal: Empirical and Theoretical Perspectives on Animal Cognition*, edited by Marc Bekoff, Colin Allen, and Gordon M. Burghardt, 471–473. Cambridge, MA: MIT Press, 2002.

Griffith, Coleman R. *Principles of Systematic Psychology*. Illinois: University of Illinois Press, 1943.

Grosenick, Logan, Tricia S. Clement, and Russell D. Fernald. "Fish Can Infer Social Rank by Observation Alone." *Nature* 445, 7126 (2007): 429–432.

Gruen, Lori. *Ethics and Animals: An Introduction*. New York: Cambridge University Press, 2011.

—— "Entangled Empathy." In *The Politics of Species: Reshaping Our Relationships with Other Animals*, edited by Raymond Corbey and Annette Lanjouw, 223–231. Cambridge: Cambridge University Press, 2013.

—— "Should Animals Have Rights?" *The Dodo*, January 20, 2014. https://www.thedodo.com/community/LoriGruen/should-animals-have-rights-396291626.html. Accessed July 25, 2014.

Grüter, Christoph, M. Sol Balbuena, and Walter M. Farina. "Informational Conflicts Created by the Waggle Dance." *Proceedings of the Royal Society B: Biological Sciences* 275, 1640 (2008): 1321–1327.

Guldberg, Helene. "Can Orang-Utans Really Mime?" 2010. http://www.psychologytoday.com/blog/reclaiming-childhood/201008/can-orang-utans-really-mime. Accessed January 27, 2014.

Gunther, York H. *Essays on Nonconceptual Content*. Cambridge, MA: MIT Press, 2003.

Güth, Werner, Rolf Schmittberger, and Bernd Schwarze. "An Experimental Analysis of Ultimatum Bargaining." *Journal of Economic Behavior & Organization* 3, 4 (1982): 367–388.

Haesler, Sebastian, Christelle Rochefort, Benjamin Georgi, Pawel Licznerski, Pavel Osten, and Constance Scharff. "Incomplete and Inaccurate Vocal Imitation after Knockdown of FoxP2 in Songbird Basal Ganglia Nucleus Area X." *PLoS Biology* 5, 12 (2007): e321.

Haffenden, Angela M., and Melvyn A. Goodale. "The Effect of Pictorial Illusion on Prehension and Perception." *Journal of Cognitive Neuroscience* 10, 1 (1998): 122–136.

—— "Independent Effects of Pictorial Displays on Perception and Action." *Vision Research* 40, 10 (2000): 1597–1607.

Haidt, Jonathan. "The Emotional Dog and Its Rational Tail: A Social Intuitionist Approach to Moral Judgment." *Psychological Review* 108, 4 (2001): 814–834.

Haidt, Jonathan, and Craig Joseph. "The Moral Mind: How Five Sets of Innate Intuitions Guide the Development of Many Culture-Specific Virtues, and Perhaps Even Modules." In *The Innate Mind Volume 3: Foundations and the Future*, edited by P. Carruthers, S. Laurence, and S. Stich, 367–391. Evolution and Cognition. Oxford: Oxford University Press, 2008.

Haksar, Vinit. "Moral Agents." In *Routledge Encyclopedia of Philosophy*, edited by E. Craig. London: Routledge, 1998.

Hamm, Alfons O., Almut I. Weike, Harald T. Schupp, Thomas Treig, Alexander Dressel, and Christof Kessler. "Affective Blindsight: Intact Fear Conditioning to a Visual Cue in a Cortically Blind Patient." *Brain* 126, 2 (2003): 267–275.

Hammerschmidt, Kurt, and Julia Fischer. "Constraints in Primate Vocal Production." *The Evolution of Communicative Creativity: From Fixed Signals to Contextual Flexibility* (2008): 93–119.

Hampton, R.R. "Rhesus Monkeys Know When They Remember." *Proceedings of the National Academy of Sciences of the United States of America* 98 (2001): 5359–5362.

—— "Status of Nonhuman Memory Monitoring and Possible Roles in Planning and Decision Making." In *Animal Thinking: Contemporary Issues in Comparative Cognition*, edited by Randolf Menzel and Julia Fischer, 105–120. Cambridge, MA: The MIT Press, 2011.

Hardcastle, Valerie G. "The Why of Consciousness: A Non-Issue for Materialists." *Journal of Consciousness Studies* 3, 1 (1996): 7–13.

Hare, Brian, and Michael Tomasello. "Domestic Dogs (Canis Familiaris) Use Human and Conspecific Social Cues to Locate Hidden Food." *Journal of Comparative Psychology* 113, 2 (1999): 173–177.

Hare, Brian, and Vanessa Woods. *The Genius of Dogs: How Dogs Are Smarter Than You Think*. New York: Dutton, 2013.

Hare, Brian, Michelle Brown, Christina Williamson, and Michael Tomasello. "The Domestication of Social Cognition in Dogs." *Science* 298, 5598 (2002): 1634–1636.

Hare, Brian, Josep Call, and Michael Tomasello. "Communication of Food Location Between Human and Dog (*Canis familiaris*)." *Evolution of Communication* 2, 1 (1998): 137–159.

—— "Do Chimpanzees Know What Conspecifics Know?" *Animal Behaviour* 61 (2001): 139–151.

Harman, Gilbert. "Studying the Chimpanzees' Theory of Mind." *Behavioral and Brain Sciences* 1 (1978): 576–577.

Harriman, Philip Lawrence. *The New Dictionary of Psychology*. New York: Philosophical Library, 1947.

Hassin, Ran R., James S. Uleman, and John A. Bargh (eds). *The New Unconscious*. Oxford Series in Social Cognition and Social Neuroscience. Oxford: Oxford University Press, 2005.

Haug, M., and Richard E. Whalen. *Animal Models of Human Emotion and Cognition*. Washington, DC: American Psychological Association, 1999.

Hauser, Marc D., and Peter Marler. "Food-Associated Calls in Rhesus Macaques (Macaca Mulatta): I. Socioecological Factors." *Behavioral Ecology* 4, 3 (1993): 194–205.

Hauser, Marc D., Noam Chomsky, and W. Tecumseh Fitch. "The Faculty of Language: What Is It, Who Has It, and How Did It Evolve?" *Science* 298, 5598 (2002): 1569–1579.

Hauser, Marc D., Patricia Teixidor, L. Fields, and R. Flaherty. "Food-Elicited Calls in Chimpanzees: Effects of Food Quantity and Divisibility." *Animal Behaviour* 45, 4 (1993): 817–819.

Hauser, Marc D., Fritz Tsao, Patricia Garcia, and Elizabeth S. Spelke. "Evolutionary Foundations of Number: Spontaneous Representation of Numerical Magnitudes by Cotton–top Tamarins." *Proceedings of the Royal Society of London. Series B: Biological Sciences* 270, 1523 (2003): 1441–1446.

Hayes, Catherine. *The Ape in Our House*. Oxford, England: Harper, 1951.

Hebb, D.O. *The Organization of Behavior; a Neuropsychological Theory*. New York: Wiley, 1949.

Henrich, Joseph, Robert Boyd, Samuel Bowles, Colin Camerer, Ernst Fehr, Herbert Gintis, Richard McElreath, et al. "In Cross-Cultural Perspective: Behavioral Experiments in 15 Small-Scale Societies." *Behavioral and Brain Sciences* 28, 06 (2005): 795–815.

Henrich, Joseph, Steven J. Heine, and Ara Norenzayan. "The Weirdest People in the World?" *Behavioral and Brain Sciences* 33, 2–3 (2010): 61–83.

Herman, Louis M. "Cognitive Performance of Dolphins in Visually Guided Tasks." *Sensory Abilities of Cetaceans: Laboratory and Field Evidence* (1990): 455–462.

—— "What Laboratory Research Has Told Us about Dolphin Cognition." *International Journal of Comparative Psychology* 23, 3 (2010): 310–330.

Herman, Louis M., Sheila L. Abichandani, Ali N. Elhajj, Elia YK Herman, Juliana L. Sanchez, and Adam A. Pack. "Dolphins (Tursiops Truncatus) Comprehend the Referential Character of the Human Pointing Gesture." *Journal of Comparative Psychology* 113, 4 (1999): 347–364.

Herman, Louis M., Douglas G. Richards, and James P. Wolz. "Comprehension of Sentences by Bottlenosed Dolphins." *Cognition* 16, 2 (1984): 129–219.

Hermann, Esther, Stefanie Keupp, Brian Hare, Amrisha Vaish, and Michael Tomasello. "Direct and Indirect Reputation Formation in Nonhuman Great Apes (Pan Paniscus, Pan Troglodytes, Gorilla Gorilla, Pongo Pygmaeus) and Human Children (Homo Sapiens)." *Journal of Comparative Psychology* 127, 1 (2013): 63–75.

Herrnstein, R.J., and D.H. Loveland. "Complex Visual Concept in the Pigeon." *Science* 146, 3643 (1964): 549–551.

Hess, Elizabeth. *Nim Chimpsky: The Chimp Who Would Be Human*. New York: Bantam Books, 2008.

Heyes, Cecilia M. "Reflections on Self-Recognition in Primates." *Animal Behaviour* 47 (1994): 909–919.

—— "Theory of Mind in Nonhuman Primates." *Behavioral and Brain Sciences* 21, 1 (1998): 101–114.

—— "Beast Machines? Questions of Animal Consciousness." In *Frontiers of Consciousness*, edited by Lawrence Weiskrantz and Martin Davies, 259–274. New York: Oxford University Press, 2008.

Hinde, Robert A. *Animal Behaviour; a Synthesis of Ethology and Comparative Psychology*. New York: McGraw-Hill, 1970.

Hobaiter, Catherine, David A. Leavens, and Richard W. Byrne. "Deictic Gesturing in Wild Chimpanzees, (Pan Troglodytes)? Some Possible Cases." *Journal of Comparative Psychology* (2013).

Hobson, R. Peter. *Autism and the Development of Mind*. Hillsdale, USA: L. Erlbaum Associates, 1993.

Hockings, Kimberley J., James R. Anderson, and Tetsuro Matsuzawa. "Road Crossing in Chimpanzees: A Risky Business." *Current Biology* 16, 17 (2006): 668–670.

Holland, Peter C. "Occasion Setting in Pavlovian Conditioning." In *Psychology of Learning and Motivation: Advances in Research and Theory*, edited by D.L. Medin, 69–125. San Diego, CA: Academic Press, 1992.

Hood, Lois, Lois Bloom, and Charles J. Brainerd. "What, When, and How about Why: A Longitudinal Study of Early Expressions of Causality." *Monographs of the Society for Research in Child Development* 44, 6 (1979): 1–47.

Hopkins, William D., Jared P. Taglialatela, and David A. Leavens. "Chimpanzees Differentially Produce Novel Vocalizations to Capture the Attention of a Human." *Animal Behaviour* 73, 2 (2007): 281–286.

Hostetter, Autumn B., Monica Cantero, and William D. Hopkins. "Differential Use of Vocal and Gestural Communication by Chimpanzees (Pan Troglodytes) in Response to the Attentional Status of a Human (Homo Sapiens)." *Journal of Comparative Psychology* 115, 4 (2001): 337–343.

Hostetter, Autumn B., Jamie L. Russell, Hani Freeman, and William D. Hopkins. "Now You See Me, Now You Don't: Evidence That Chimpanzees Understand the Role of the Eyes in Attention." *Animal Cognition* 10, 1 (2007): 55–62.

Hubley, P. "The Development of Cooperative Action in Infants." PhD Dissertation, University of Edinburgh, 1983.

Hume, David. *A Treatise of Human Nature*. Edited by David Fate Norton and Mary J. Norton. Oxford: Oxford University Press, 2000.

Humphrey, Nicholas K. "Nature's Psychologists." In *Consciousness and the Physical World*, edited by B.D. Josephson and V.S. Ramachandran, 57–80. Oxford: Pergamon Press, 1980.

Humphrey, Nicholas K., and L. Weiskrantz. "Vision in Monkeys after Removal of the Striate Cortex." *Nature* 215, 5101 (1967): 595–597.

Hunt, Gavin R. "Manufacture and Use of Hook-Tools by New Caledonian Crows." *Nature* 379, 6562 (1996): 249–251.

Hurley, Susan. "Animal Action in the Space of Reasons." *Mind & Language* 18, 3 (2003): 231–257.

Hurley, Susan, and Matthew Nudds. "The Questions of Animal Rationality: Theory and Evidence." In *Rational Animals?* Oxford: Oxford University Press, 2006a.

Hurley, Susan, and Matthew Nudds (eds). *Rational Animals?* Oxford: Oxford University Press, 2006b.

Hursthouse, Rosalind. *Ethics, Humans, and Other Animals: An Introduction with Readings*. New York: Routledge, 2000.

Huxley, Thomas H. "On the Hypothesis That Animals Are Automata, and Its History." *Fortnightly Review* 16 (1874): 555–580.

Imanishi, Kinji. "Social Behavior in Japanese Monkeys, Macaca Fuscata." *Psychologia* 1, 1 (1957): 47–54.

Inoue, Sana, and Tetsuro Matsuzawa. "Working Memory of Numerals in Chimpanzees." *Current Biology* 17, 23 (2007): R1004–R1005.

Itakura, Shoji, Bryan Agnetta, Brian Hare, and Michael Tomasello. "Chimpanzee Use of Human and Conspecific Social Cues to Locate Hidden Food." *Developmental Science* 2, 4 (1999): 448–456.

Jackson, Frank. "What Mary Didn't Know." *The Journal of Philosophy* 83, 5 (1986): 291–295.

James, William. *The Principles of Psychology*. In *The Works of William James*. Cambridge, MA: Harvard University Press, 1981.

Jamieson, Dale. "Science, Knowledge, and Animal Minds." *Proceedings of the Aristotelian Society* 98 (1998): 79–102.

——— "What Do Animals Think?" In *The Philosophy of Animal Minds*, edited by Robert W. Lurz, 15–34. New York: Cambridge University Press, 2009.

Jamieson, Dale, and Marc Bekoff. "Carruthers on Nonconscious Experience." *Analysis* 52 (1992): 23–28.

Janik, Vincent M., Laela S. Sayigh, and R.S. Wells. "Signature Whistle Shape Conveys Identity Information to Bottlenose Dolphins." *Proceedings of the National Academy of Sciences* 103, 21 (2006): 8293–8297.

Jensen, Keith, Josep Call, and Michael Tomasello. "Chimpanzees Are Rational Maximizers in an Ultimatum Game." *Science* 318, 5847 (2007): 107–109.

Jolly, Alison. "Lemur Social Behavior and Primate Intelligence." *Science* 153, 3735 (1966): 501–506.

Kahneman, Daniel, Barbara L. Fredrickson, Charles A. Schreiber, and Donald A. Redelmeier. "When More Pain Is Preferred to Less: Adding a Better End." *Psychological Science* 4, 6 (1993): 401–405.

Kaminski, Juliane, Juliane Brauer, Josep Call, and Michael Tomasello. "Domestic Dogs Are Sensitive to a Human's Perspective." *Behaviour* 146, 7 (2009): 979–998.

Kaminski, Juliane, Josep Call, and Julia Fischer. "Word Learning in a Domestic Dog: Evidence for 'Fast Mapping.'" *Science* 304, 5677 (2004): 1682–1683.

Kano, Fumihiro, Masayuki Tanaka, and Masaki Tomonaga. "Enhanced Recognition of Emotional Stimuli in the Chimpanzee (Pan Troglodytes)." *Animal Cognition* 11, 3 (2008): 517–524.

Kant, Immanuel. *Critique of Pure Reason*. Translated by Paul Guyer and Allen W. Wood. Cambridge: Cambridge University Press, 1998.

Kaufman, Allison B., Erin N. Colbert-White, and Curt Burgess. "Higher-Order Semantic Structures in an African Grey Parrot's Vocalizations: Evidence from the Hyperspace Analog to Language (HAL) Model." *Animal Cognition* (2013): 1–13.

Keagy, Jason, Jean-François Savard, and Gerald Borgia. "Male Satin Bowerbird Problem-Solving Ability Predicts Mating Success." *Animal Behaviour* 78, 4 (2009): 809–817.

Keeley, Brian L. "Anthropomorphism, Primatomorphism, Mammalomorphism: Understanding Cross-Species Comparisons." *Biology and Philosophy* 19, 4 (2004): 521–540.

Kellogg, W.N., and Luella Agger Kellogg. *The Ape and the Child: A Study of Environmental Influence upon Early Behavior*. New York, London: Whittlesey House McGraw-Hill Book Co., 1933.

Kennedy, John S. *The New Anthropomorphism*. Cambridge: Cambridge University Press, 1992.

Kilian, Annette, Sevgi Yaman, Lorenzo von Fersen, and Onur Güntürkün. "A Bottlenose Dolphin Discriminates Visual Stimuli Differing in Numerosity." *Animal Learning & Behavior* 31, 2 (2003): 133–142.

King, Barbara J. *The Dynamic Dance Nonvocal Communication in African Great Apes*. Cambridge, MA: Harvard University Press, 2004.

—— *How Animals Grieve*. Chicago: The University of Chicago Press, 2013.

King, Barbara J., and Stuart G. Shanker. "How Can We Know the Dancer from the Dance? The Dynamic Nature of African Great Ape Social Communication." *Anthropological Theory* 3, 1 (2003): 5–26.

King, Stephanie L., and Vincent M. Janik. "Bottlenose Dolphins Can Use Learned Vocal Labels to Address Each Other." *Proceedings of the National Academy of Sciences* 110, 32 (2013): 13216–13221.

King, Stephanie L., Laela S. Sayigh, Randall S. Wells, Wendi Fellner, and Vincent M. Janik. "Vocal Copying of Individually Distinctive Signature Whistles in Bottlenose Dolphins." *Proceedings of the Royal Society B: Biological Sciences* 280, 1757 (2013): 20130053.

Kirchhofer, Katharina C., Felizitas Zimmermann, Juliane Kaminski, and Michael Tomasello. "Dogs (Canis Familiaris), but Not Chimpanzees (Pan Troglodytes), Understand Imperative Pointing." *PloS One* 7, 2 (2012): e30913.

Kiriazis, Judith, and C.N. Slobodchikoff. "Perceptual Specificity in the Alarm Calls of Gunnison's Prairie Dogs." *Behavioural Processes* 73, 1 (2006): 29–35.

Kitzmann, Carolyn D., and Nancy G. Caine. "Marmoset (Callithrix Geoffroyi) Food-Associated Calls Are Functionally Referential." *Ethology* 115, 5 (2009): 439–448.

Knörnschild, Mirjam, Marion Feifel, and Elisabeth K.V. Kalko. "Mother–offspring Recognition in the Bat Carollia Perspicillata." *Animal Behaviour* 86, 5 (2013): 941–948.

Koch, Christof. *Consciousness: Confessions of a Romantic Reductionist*. Cambridge, MA: MIT Press, 2012.

Kohlberg, Lawrence. *The Philosophy of Moral Development: Moral Stages and the Idea of Justice*. San Francisco: Harper & Row, 1981.

Kohlberg, Lawrence, and Clark Power. "Moral Development, Religious Thinking, and the Question of a Seventh Stage." *Zygon®* 16, 3 (1981): 203–259.

Köhler, Wolfgang. *The Mentality of Apes*. New York: Harcourt, Brace & Co., Inc., 1925.

Korsgaard, Christine. "Morality and the Distinctiveness of Human Action." In *Primates and Philosophers: How Morality Evolved*, edited by S. Macedo and J. Ober. Princeton NJ: Princeton University Press, 2006.

Krachun, Carla, Malinda Carpenter, Josep Call, and Michael Tomasello. "A Competitive Nonverbal False Belief Task for Children and Apes." *Developmental Science* 12, 4 (2009): 521–535.

Krause, Mark A., and Roger S. Fouts. "Chimpanzee (Pan Troglodytes) Pointing: Hand Shapes, Accuracy, and the Role of Eye Gaze." *Journal of Comparative Psychology* 111, 4 (1997): 330–336.

Krebs, John R., and Nicholas B. Davies. *Behavioural Ecology: An Evolutionary Approach*. New York: Wiley, 2009.

Krech, David, Mark R. Rosenzweig, and Edward L. Bennett. "Effects of Environmental Complexity and Training on Brain Chemistry." *Journal of Comparative and Physiological Psychology* 53, 6 (1960): 509–519.

Kruska, D. "Comparative Quantitative Study on Brains of Wild and Laboratory Rats. I. Comparison of Volume of Total Brain and Classical Brain Parts." *Journal Für Hirnforschung* 16, 6 (1975): 469–483.

Kundey, Shannon, Andres De Los Reyes, Chelsea Taglang, Rebecca Allen, Sabrina Molina, Erica Royer, and Rebecca German. "Domesticated Dogs Canis Familiaris React to What Others Can and Cannot Hear." *Applied Animal Behaviour Science* 126, 1 (2010): 45–50.

LaGraize, Stacey C., Christopher J. Labuda, Margaret A. Rutledge, Raymond L. Jackson, and Perry N. Fuchs. "Differential Effect of Anterior Cingulate Cortex Lesion on Mechanical Hypersensitivity and Escape/avoidance Behavior in an Animal Model of Neuropathic Pain." *Experimental Neurology* 188, 1 (2004): 139–148.

Le Roux, Aliza, Noah Snyder-Mackler, Eila K. Roberts, Jacinta C. Beehner, and Thore J. Bergman. "Evidence for Tactical Concealment in a Wild Primate." *Nature Communications* 4 (2013).

Leavens, David A. "The Plight of the Sense-making Ape." In *Enactive Cognition at the Edge of Sense-making*, edited by T. Froese and M. Cappuccio. Basingstoke, UK: Palgrave MacMillan, forthcoming.

Leavens, David A., and William D. Hopkins. "Intentional Communication by Chimpanzees: A Cross-Sectional Study of the Use of Referential Gestures." *Developmental Psychology* 34, 5 (1998): 813–822.

—— "The Whole-Hand Point: The Structure and Function of Pointing from a Comparative Perspective." *Journal of Comparative Psychology* 113, 4 (1999): 417–425.

Leavens, David A., William D. Hopkins, and Kim A. Bard. "Indexical and Referential Pointing in Chimpanzees (Pan Troglodytes)." *Journal of Comparative Psychology* 110, 4 (1996): 346–353.

Leavens, David A., William D. Hopkins, and Roger K. Thomas. "Referential Communication by Chimpanzees (Pan Troglodytes)." *Journal of Comparative Psychology* 118, 1 (2004): 48–57.

Leavens, David A., William D. Hopkins, and Kim A. Bard. "Understanding the Point of Chimpanzee Pointing Epigenesis and Ecological Validity." *Current Directions in Psychological Science* 14, 4 (2005a): 185–189.

Leavens, David A., Jamie L. Russell, and William D. Hopkins. "Intentionality as Measured in the Persistence and Elaboration of Communication by Chimpanzees (Pan Troglodytes)." *Child Development* 76, 1 (2005b): 291–306.

—— "Multimodal Communication by Captive Chimpanzees (Pan Troglodytes)." *Animal Cognition* 13, 1 (2010): 33–40.

Lee, Kisung, Paul E. Kinahan, Jeffrey A. Fessler, Robert S. Miyaoka, Marie Janes, and Tom K. Lewellen. "Pragmatic Fully 3D Image Reconstruction for the MiCES Mouse Imaging PET Scanner." *Physics in Medicine and Biology* 49, 19 (2004): 4563.

Legerstee, Maria, and Yarixa Barillas. "Sharing Attention and Pointing to Objects at 12 Months: Is the Intentional Stance Implied?" *Cognitive Development* 18, 1 (2003): 91–110.

Leslie, Alan M. "Infant Perception of a Manual Pick-up Event." *British Journal of Developmental Psychology* 2, 1 (1984): 19–32.

Lewes, George Henry. *Sea-Side Studies at Ilfracombe, Tenby, the Scilly Isles, and Jersey.* Edinburgh: William Blackwood & Sons, 1860.

Lewis, David. "Psychophysical and Theoretical Identifications." *Australasian Journal of Philosophy* 50, 3 (1972): 249–258.

—— "Lewis, David: Reduction of Mind." In *A Companion to the Philosophy of Mind*, edited by S. Guttenplan. Oxford: Blackwell, 1994.

Liebal, Katja, Josep Call, Michael Tomasello, and Simone Pika. "To Move or Not to Move: How Apes Adjust to the Attentional State of Others." *Interaction Studies* 5, 2 (2004): 199–219.

Lorenz, Konrad. *King Solomon's Ring: New Light on Animal Ways.* New York: Crowell, 1952.

Lurz, Robert W. "In Defense of Wordless Thoughts about Thoughts." *Mind & Language* 22, 3 (2007): 270–296.

—— *The Philosophy of Animal Minds.* New York: Cambridge University Press, 2009.

—— *Mindreading Animals: The Debate over What Animals Know about Other Minds.* Cambridge, MA: MIT Press, 2011.

Lurz, Robert W., and Carla Krachun. "How Could We Know Whether Nonhuman Primates Understand Others' Internal Goals and Intentions? Solving Povinelli's Problem." *Review of Philosophy and Psychology* 2, 3 (2011): 449–481.

MacDermot, Kay D., Elena Bonora, Nuala Sykes, Anne-Marie Coupe, Cecilia S.L. Lai, Sonja C. Vernes, Faraneh Vargha-Khadem, Fiona McKenzie, Robert L. Smith, and Anthony P. Monaco. "Identification of FOXP2 Truncation as a Novel Cause of Developmental Speech and Language Deficits." *The American Journal of Human Genetics* 76, 6 (2005): 1074–1080.

Machery, Edouard. *Doing without Concepts.* New York, Oxford: Oxford University Press, 2011.

MacLean, Evan L., Luke J. Matthews, Brian A. Hare, Charles L. Nunn, Rindy C. Anderson, Filippo Aureli, Elizabeth M. Brannon, et al. "How Does Cognition Evolve? Phylogenetic Comparative Psychology." *Animal Cognition* 15, 2 (2012): 223–238.

MacLean, Evan L., Brian Hare, Charles L. Nunn, Elsa Addessi, Federica Amici, Rindy C. Anderson, Filippo Aureli, et al. "The Evolution of Self-Control." *Proceedings of the National Academy of Sciences* 111, 20 (2014): E2140–E2148.

Maibom, Heidi Lene, (ed.) *Empathy and Morality.* New York: Oxford University Press, 2014.

Manser, Marta B. "The Acoustic Structure of Suricates' Alarm Calls Varies with Predator Type and the Level of Response Urgency." *Proceedings of the Royal Society of London. Series B: Biological Sciences* 268, 1483 (2001): 2315–2324.

Manser, Marta B., Matthew B. Bell, and Lindsay B. Fletcher. "The Information That Receivers Extract from Alarm Calls in Suricates." *Proceedings of the Royal Society of London. Series B: Biological Sciences* 268, 1484 (2001): 2485–2491.

Manser, Marta B., Robert M. Seyfarth, and Dorothy L. Cheney. "Suricate Alarm Calls Signal Predator Class and Urgency." *Trends in Cognitive Sciences* 6, 2 (2002): 55–57.

Marcus, Ruth Barcan. "Some Revisionary Proposals about Belief and Believing." *Philosophy and Phenomenological Research* 50 (1990): 133–153.

Marler, Peter, Alfred Dufty, and Roberta Pickert. "Vocal Communication in the Domestic Chicken: I. Does a Sender Communicate Information about the Quality of a Food Referent to a Receiver?" *Animal Behaviour* 34 (1986): 188–193.

Marler, Peter, Christopher S. Evans, and Marc D. Hauser. "Animal Signals: Motivational, Referential, or Both." *Nonverbal Vocal Communication: Comparative and Developmental Approaches* (1992): 66–86.

Marr, David. *Vision: A Computational Investigation into the Human Representation and Processing of Visual Information*. San Francisco: W.H. Freeman, 1982.

Marsh, Heidi L., and Suzanne E. MacDonald. "Information Seeking by Orangutans: A Generalized Search Strategy?" *Animal Cognition* 15, 3 (2012): 293–304.

Marzluff, John M., and Tony Angell. *Gifts of the Crow: How Perception, Emotion, and Thought Allow Smart Birds to Behave like Humans*. New York: Free Press, 2012.

Marzluff, John M., Robert Miyaoka, Satoshi Minoshima, and Donna J. Cross. "Brain Imaging Reveals Neuronal Circuitry Underlying the Crow's Perception of Human Faces." *Proceedings of the National Academy of Sciences* 109, 39 (2012): 15912–15917.

Mather, Jennifer A., and Roland C. Anderson. "Personalities of Octopuses (Octopus Rubescens)." *Journal of Comparative Psychology* 107, 3 (1993): 336–340.

Matsuzawa, Tetsuro. "Chimpanzee Ai and Her Son Ayumu: An Episode of Education by Master-Apprenticeship." *The Cognitive Animal: Empirical and Theoretical Perspectives on Animal Cognition* (2002): 189–195.

—— "Evolutionary Origins of the Human Mother-Infant Relationship." In *Cognitive Development in Chimpanzees*, edited by Tetsuro Matsuzawa, Masaki Tomonaga, and Masayuki Tanaka, 127–141. New York: Springer, 2006.

Matsuzawa, Tetsuro, Masaki Tomonaga, and Masayuki Tanaka (eds). *Cognitive Development in Chimpanzees*. New York: Springer, 2006.

Matthews, Danielle (ed.). *Pragmatic Development in First Language Acquisition*. Trends in Language Acquisition Research, v. 10. Amsterdam: John Benjamins Publishing Company, 2014.

Maynard-Smith, John, and David Harper. *Animal Signals*. Oxford: Oxford University Press, 2003.

McAninch, Andrew, Grant Goodrich, and Colin Allen. "Animal Communication and Neo-Expressivism." *The Philosophy of Animal Minds* (2009): 128–144.

McGinn, Colin. "Can We Solve the Mind-Body Problem?" *Mind* 98, 391 (1989): 349–366.

McNeill, David (ed.). *Language and Gesture*. Cambridge: Cambridge University Press, 2000.

Mechner, Francis. "Probability Relations within Response Sequences under Ratio Reinforcement." *Journal of the Experimental Analysis of Behavior* 1, 2 (1958): 109–121.

Meketa, Irina. "A Critique of the Principle of Cognitive Simplicity in Comparative Cognition." *Biology & Philosophy*, February 16, 2014, 1–15.

Melis, Alicia P., and Michael Tomasello. "Chimpanzees' (Pan Troglodytes) Strategic Helping in a Collaborative Task." *Biology Letters* 9 (2013): 1–4.

Meltzoff, Andrew N., and M. Keith Moore. "Imitation of Facial and Manual Gestures by Human Neonates." *Science* 198:4312 (1977): 75–58.

Melzack, Ronald, and Patrick D. Wall. *The Challenge of Pain*. New York: Penguin, 2008.

Menzel, Randolf, and Julia Fischer (eds). *Animal Thinking: Contemporary Issues in Comparative Cognition*. Strüngmann Forum Reports. Cambridge, MA: MIT Press, 2012.

Miklósi, Ádam, and Krisztina Soproni. "A Comparative Analysis of Animals' Understanding of the Human Pointing Gesture." *Animal Cognition* 9, 2 (2006): 81–93.

Miklósi, A., J. Topál, and V. Csányi. "Comparative Social Cognition: What Can Dogs Teach Us?" *Animal Behaviour* 67, 6 (2004): 995–1004.

Miles, H. Lyn, Robert W. Mitchell, and Stephen E. Harper. "Simon Says: The Development of Imitation in an Enculturated Orangutan." In *Reaching into Thought: The Minds of the Great Apes*, 278–299. Cambridge: Cambridge University Press, 1996.

Miller, Noam, Simon Garnier, Andrew T. Hartnett, and Iain D. Couzin. "Both Information and Social Cohesion Determine Collective Decisions in Animal Groups." *Proceedings of the National Academy of Sciences* 110, 13 (2013): 5263–5268.

Millikan, Ruth. "Styles of Rationality." In *Rational Animals*, edited by Susan Hurley and Matthew Nudds, 117–126. Oxford: Oxford University Press, 2006.

Mischel, Walter, and Ebbe B. Ebbesen. "Attention in Delay of Gratification." *Journal of Personality and Social Psychology* 16, 2 (1970): 329–337.

Mischel, Walter, Ebbe B. Ebbesen, and Antonette Raskoff Zeiss. "Cognitive and Attentional Mechanisms in Delay of Gratification." *Journal of Personality and Social Psychology* 21, 2 (1972): 204–218.

Mitani, John, and David Watts. "Boundary Patrols and Intergroup Encounters in Wild Chimpanzees." *Behaviour* 138, 3 (2001): 299–327.

Mitchell, Robert W., Nicholas S. Thompson, and H. Lyn Miles (eds). *Anthropomorphism, Anecdotes, and Animals.* SUNY Series in Philosophy and Biology. Albany: State University of New York Press, 1997.

Mohamed, Othman A., Maud Jonnaert, Cassandre Labelle-Dumais, Kazuki Kuroda, Hugh J. Clarke, and Daniel Dufort. "Uterine Wnt/ß-Catenin Signaling Is Required for Implantation." *Proceedings of the National Academy of Sciences of the United States of America* 102, 24 (2005): 8579–8584.

Moll, Henrike, and Michael Tomasello. "Cooperation and Human Cognition: The Vygotskian Intelligence Hypothesis." *Philosophical Transactions of the Royal Society B: Biological Sciences* 362, 1480 (2007): 639–648.

Moore, Richard. "Ontogenetic constraints on Paul Grice's Theory of Communication." In *Pragmatic Development in First Language Acquisition*, edited by Danielle Matthews, 87–104. Amsterdam: John Benjamins, 2014.

Morgan, C. Lloyd. *Animal Life and Intelligence.* London: E. Arnold, 1891. http://archive.org/details/animallifeintell00morguoft. Accessed July 25, 2014.

——— *An Introduction to Comparative Psychology.* London: Walter Scott Publishing Company, 1903.

——— "Autobiography." In *A History of Psychology in Autobiography*, edited by Carl Murchison and Edwin Garrigues Boring. Worcester, MA: Clark University Press, 1930.

Morris, Anne K. "Development of Logical Reasoning: Children's Ability to Verbally Explain the Nature of the Distinction between Logical and Nonlogical Forms of Argument." *Developmental Psychology* 36, 6 (2000): 741–758.

Morton, Adam. *The Importance of Being Understood: Folk Psychology as Ethics.* New York: Routledge, 2003.

Moshman, David. "From Inference to Reasoning: The Construction of Rationality." *Thinking & Reasoning* 10, 2 (2004): 221–239.

Mulcahy, Nicholas J., and Josep Call. "Apes Save Tools for Future Use." *Science* 312, 5776 (2006): 1038–1040.

Murchison, Carl, and Edwin Garrigues Boring. *A History of Psychology in Autobiography.* Worcester, Mass.: Clark University Press, 1930.

Myowa-Yamakoshi, Masako, Masaki Tomonaga, Masayuki Tanaka, and Tetsuro Matsuzawa. "Imitation in Neonatal Chimpanzees (Pan Troglodytes)." *Developmental Science* 7, 4 (2004): 437–442.

Nagel, Thomas. "What Is It Like to Be a Bat?" *The Philosophical Review* 83, 4 (1974): 435–450.

Nakamichi, Masayuki, Eiko Kato, Yasuo Kojima, and Naosuke Itoigawa. "Carrying and Washing of Grass Roots by Free-Ranging Japanese Macaques at Katsuyama." *Folia Primatologica* 69, 1 (1998): 35–40.

Neyman, J., and E.S. Pearson. "On the Use and Interpretation of Certain Test Criteria for Purposes of Statistical Inference. Part 1." In *Joint Statistical Papers*, 1–66. Berkeley: University of California Press, 1967.

—— *Joint Statistical Papers.* Berkeley: University of California Press, 1967.

Nisbett, Richard E., and Timothy D. Wilson. "Telling More than We Can Know: Verbal Reports on Mental Processes." *Psychological Review* 84, 3 (1977): 231–259.

Nonhuman Rights Project. "First-Ever Lawsuits Filed on Behalf of Captive Chimpanzees to Demand Court Grant Them Right to Bodily Liberty (Press Release)," December 2, 2013. http://www.nonhumanrightsproject.org/wp-content/uploads/2013/11/NhRP-Press-Release-Dec-2-2013.pdf. Accessed July 25, 2014.

Nucci, Larry P., and Elliot Turiel. "Social Interactions and the Development of Social Concepts in Preschool Children." *Child Development* (1978): 400–407.

Nussbaum, Martha C. "Beyond the Social Contract: Toward Global Justice." *Tanner Lectures on Human Values* 24 (2004): 413–508.

—— "The Moral Status of Animals." *The Chronicle of Higher Education* 3 (2006). http://www.arcusfoundation.org/images/uploads/downloads/The_Moral_Staus_of_Animals_by_Martha_Nussbaum_2006.pdf. Accessed July 25, 2014.

Okamoto, Sanae, Masaki Tomonaga, Kiyoshi Ishii, Nobuyuki Kawai, Masayuki Tanaka, and Tetsuro Matsuzawa. "An Infant Chimpanzee (Pan Troglodytes) Follows Human Gaze." *Animal Cognition* 5, 2 (2002): 107–114.

Onishi, Kristine H., and Renée Baillargeon. "Do 15-Month-Old Infants Understand False Beliefs?" *Science* 308, 5719 (2005): 255–258.

Osvath, Mathias. "Spontaneous Planning for Future Stone Throwing by a Male Chimpanzee." *Current Biology* 19, 5 (2009): R190–R191.

Osvath, Mathias, and Elin Karvonen. "Spontaneous Innovation for Future Deception in a Male Chimpanzee." *PLoS ONE* 7, 5 (2012): e36782.

Pack, Adam A., and Louis M. Herman. "Sensory Integration in the Bottlenosed Dolphin: Immediate Recognition of Complex Shapes across the Senses of Echolocation and Vision." *The Journal of the Acoustical Society of America* 98, 2 (1995): 722–733.

—— "Dolphin Social Cognition and Joint Attention: Our Current Understanding." *Aquatic Mammals* 32, 4 (2006): 443–460.

Panksepp, Jaak. "Affective Consciousness: Core Emotional Feelings in Animals and Humans." *Consciousness and Cognition* 14, 1 (2005): 30–80.

Panksepp, Jaak, and Jeff Burgdorf. "'Laughing' Rats and the Evolutionary Antecedents of Human Joy?" *Physiology and Behavior* 79 (2003): 533–547.

Parr, Lisa A. "The Discrimination of Faces and Their Emotional Content by Chimpanzees (Pan Troglodytes)." *Annals of the New York Academy of Sciences* 1000, 1 (2003): 56–78.

Parr, Lisa A., Bridget M. Waller, and Jennifer Fugate. "Emotional Communication in Primates: Implications for Neurobiology." *Current Opinion in Neurobiology* 15, 6 (2005): 716–720.

Parr, Lisa A., Bridget M. Waller, Sarah J. Vick, and Kim A. Bard. "Classifying Chimpanzee Facial Expressions Using Muscle Action." *Emotion* 7, 1 (2007): 172–181.

Patterson, Francine G. "The Gestures of a Gorilla: Language Acquisition in Another Pongid." *Brain and Language* 5, 1 (1978): 72–97.

Pavani, F., Irina Boscagli, Francesco Benvenuti, Marco Rabuffetti, and Alessandro Farnè. "Are Perception and Action Affected Differently by the Titchener Circles Illusion?" *Experimental Brain Research* 127, 1 (1999): 95–101.

Pelé, Marie, Valérie Dufour, Bernard Thierry, and Josep Call. "Token Transfers among Great Apes (Gorilla Gorilla, Pongo Pygmaeus, Pan Paniscus, and Pan Troglodytes): Species Differences, Gestural Requests, and Reciprocal Exchange." *Journal of Comparative Psychology* 123, 4 (2009): 375–384.

Penn, Derek C. "How Folk Psychology Ruined Comparative Psychology: And How Scrub Jays Can Save It." In *Animal Thinking: Contemporary Issues in Comparative Cognition*, edited by Randolf Menzel and Julia Fischer, 253–266. Cambridge, MA: MIT Press, 2012.

Pepperberg, I.M. *The Alex Studies: Communication and Cognitive Capacities of an African Grey Parrot.* Cambridge, MA: Harvard University Press, 1999.

Perner, Josef. *Understanding the Representational Mind.* Cambridge, MA: MIT Press, 1991.

Perner, Josef, and Ted Ruffman. "Infants' Insight into the Mind: How Deep." *Science* 308, 5719 (2005): 214–216.

Pika, Simone, and John Mitani. "Referential Gestural Communication in Wild Chimpanzees (Pan Troglodytes)." *Current Biology* 16, 6 (2006): R191–R192.

Pika, Simone, and Thomas Bugnyar. "The Use of Referential Gestures in Ravens (Corvus Corax) in the Wild." *Nature Communications* 2 (2011): 560.

Pilley, John W., and Alliston K. Reid. "Border Collie Comprehends Object Names as Verbal Referents." *Behavioural Processes* 86, 2 (2011): 184–195.

Pillow, B.H. "Epistemological Development in Adolescence and Adulthood: A Multidimensional Framework." *Genetic, Social, and General Psychology Monographs* 125, 4 (1999): 413–432.

Pitt, David, "Mental Representation," *The Stanford Encyclopedia of Philosophy* (Fall 2013 Edition), Edward N. Zalta (ed.). http://plato.stanford.edu/archives/fall2013/entries/mental-representation/. Accessed July 25, 2014.

Ploog, Detlev. "Is the Neural Basis of Vocalization Different in Non-Human Primates and Homo Sapiens?" *The Speciation of Modern Homo Sapiens* 106 (2004): 121–135.

Plooij, F.X. "Some Basic Traits of Language in Wild Chimpanzees." In *Action, Gesture, and Symbol: The Emergence of Language*, edited by A. Lock. New York: Academic Press, 1978.

Plotnik, Joshua M., Frans B.M. de Waal, and Diana Reiss. "Self-Recognition in an Asian Elephant." *Proceedings of the National Academy of Sciences* 103, 45 (2006): 17053–17057.

Pollick, Amy S., and Frans B.M. De Waal. "Ape Gestures and Language Evolution." *Proceedings of the National Academy of Sciences* 104, 19 (2007): 8184–8189.

Poniewozik, James. "Looks like Meerkat Love." *Time Magazine*, November 2, 2007. http://content.time.com/time/magazine/article/0,9171,1680162,00.html. Accessed July 25, 2014.

Poole, Joyce H., and Petter Granli. "Signals, Gestures, and Behavior of African Elephants." In *The Amboseli Elephants: A Long-Term Perspective on a Long-Lived Mammal,* 109–127. Chicago: University of Chicago Press, 2011.

Portavella, M., B. Torres, and C. Salas. "Avoidance Response in Goldfish: Emotional and Temporal Involvement of Medial and Lateral Telencephalic Pallium." *Journal of Neuroscience* 24 (2004): 2335–2342.

Povinelli, Daniel J., and Jennifer Vonk. "Chimpanzee Minds: Suspiciously Human?" *Trends in Cognitive Sciences* 7, 4 (2003): 157–160.

—— "We Don't Need a Microscope to Explore the Chimpanzee's Mind." *Mind & Language* 19, 1 (2004): 1–28.

Povinelli, Daniel J., Timothy J. Eddy, R. Peter Hobson, and Michael Tomasello. "What Young Chimpanzees Know about Seeing." *Monographs of the Society for Research in Child Development* 61, 3 (1996): i–189.

Povinelli, Daniel J., Jesse Bering, and Steve Giambrone. "Chimpanzee 'pointing': Another Error of the Argument by Analogy." *Pointing: Where Language, Culture, and Cognition Meet* (2003): 35–68.

Pratt, Stephen C. "Recruitment and Other Communication Behavior in the Ponerine Ant Ectatomma Ruidum." *Ethology* 81, 4 (1989): 313–331.

Premack, David. "On the Assessment of Language Competence in the Chimpanzee." *Behavior of Nonhuman Primates* 4 (1971): 185–228.

Premack, David, and Guy Woodruff. "Does the Chimpanzee Have a Theory of Mind?" *Behavioral and Brain Sciences* 1, 04 (1978): 515–526.

Prinz, Jesse J. "A Neurofunctional Theory of Consciousness." In *Cognition and the Brain: The Philosophy and Neuroscience Movement*, edited by Andrew Brook, Kathleen Akins, and Steven Davis, 381–396. Cambridge: Cambridge University Press, 2005.

Proctor, Darby, Rebecca A. Williamson, Frans B.M. de Waal, and Sarah F. Brosnan. "Chimpanzees Play the Ultimatum Game." *Proceedings of the National Academy of Sciences* 110, 6 (2013): 2070–2075.

Putnam, Hilary. "Minds and Machines." In *Dimensions of Mind*, edited by Sidney Hook, 148–180. New York: New York University Press, 1960.

—— "Psychological Predicates." In *Art, Mind, and Religion*, edited by W.H. Capitan and D.D. Merrill, 37–48. University of Pittsburgh Press, 1967.

Quine, Willard Van Orman. *Word and Object*. Cambridge, MA: MIT Press, 1960.

Raby, Caroline R., Dean M. Alexis, Anthony Dickinson, and Nicola S. Clayton. "Planning for the Future by Western Scrub-Jays." *Nature* 445, 7130 (2007): 919–921.

Raio, Candace M., David Carmel, Marisa Carrasco, and Elizabeth A. Phelps. "Nonconscious Fear Is Quickly Acquired but Swiftly Forgotten." *Current Biology* 22, 12 (2012): R477–R479.

Regan, Tom. *The Case for Animal Rights*. Berkeley: University of California Press, 2004.

Reiss, Diane L. "Pragmatics of Human–Dolphin Communication." PhD Thesis, Temple University, 1983.

—— *The Dolphin in the Mirror: Exploring Dolphin Minds and Saving Dolphin Lives*. Boston: Houghton Mifflin Harcourt, 2011.

Reiss, D., and L. Marino. "Mirror Self-Recognition in the Bottlenose Dolphin: A Case of Cognitive Convergence." *Proceedings of the National Academy of Sciences* 98 (2001): 5937–42.

Rendall, Drew, and Michael J. Owren. "Animal Vocal Communication: Say What." *The Cognitive Animal* (2002): 307–314.

Rescorla, Michael. "Chrysippus' Dog as a Case Study in Non-Linguistic Cognition." In *The Philosophy of Animal Minds*, edited by Robert W. Lurz, 52–71. Cambridge: Cambridge University Press, 2009a.

—— "Cognitive Maps and the Language of Thought." *The British Journal for the Philosophy of Science* 60, 2 (2009b): 377–407.

Rescorla, Robert A. "Response-Outcome versus Outcome–Response Associations in Instrumental Learning." *Animal Learning & Behavior* 20, 3 (1992): 223–232.

Rilling, Mark, and Colin McDiarmid. "Signal Detection in Fixed-Ratio Schedules." *Science* 148, 3669 (1965): 526–527.

Rizzolatti, Giacomo. "The Mirror Neuron System and Its Function in Humans." *Anatomy and Embryology* 210, 5 (2005): 419–421.

Rizzolatti, Giacomo, and Michael A. Arbib. "Language within Our Grasp." *Trends in Neurosciences* 21, 5 (1998): 188–194.

Rizzolatti, Giacomo, and Laila Craighero. "The Mirror-Neuron System." *Annual Review of Neuroscience* 27, 1 (2004): 169–192.

Rizzolatti, Giacomo, Leonardo Fogassi, and Vittorio Gallese. "Neurophysiological Mechanisms Underlying the Understanding and Imitation of Action." *Nature Reviews Neuroscience* 2, 9 (2001): 661–670.

Romanes, George John. *Animal Intelligence*. New York: Appleton, 1912.

Rorty, Richard. "Mind-Body Identity, Privacy, and Categories." *The Review of Metaphysics* 19, 1 (1965): 24–54.

Rosch, Eleanor. "Natural Categories." *Cognitive Psychology* 4 (1973): 328–350.

—— "Cognitive Representations of Semantic Categories." *Journal of Experimental Psychology: General* 104, 3 (1975): 192–233.

Rose, James D. "The Neurobehavioral Nature of Fishes and the Question of Awareness and Pain." *Reviews in Fisheries Science* 10, 1 (2002): 1–38.

—— "Anthropomorphism and 'Mental Welfare' of Fishes." *Diseases of Aquatic Organisms* 75 (2007): 139–154.

Rowlands, Mark. *The Philosopher and the Wolf: Lessons from the Wild on Love, Death, and Happiness.* New York: Pegasus Books, 2009.

—— *Can Animals Be Moral?* Oxford: Oxford University Press, 2012.

Russon, Anne E., and Kristin Andrews. "Orangutan Pantomime: Elaborating the Message." *Biology Letters* 7, 4 (2011a): 627–630.

—— "Pantomime in Great Apes: Evidence and Implications." *Communicative & Integrative Biology* 4, 3 (2011b): 315–317.

Salas, C., C. Broglio, E. Dúran, A. Gómez, F.M. Ocana, F. Jimenez-Moya, and F. Rodriguez. "Neuropsychology of Learning and Memory in Teleost Fish." *Zebrafish* 3 (2006): 157–171.

Santos, Laurie R., Aaron G. Nissen, and Jonathan A. Ferrugia. "Rhesus Monkeys, Macaca Mulatta, Know What Others Can and Cannot Hear." *Animal Behaviour* 71, 5 (2006): 1175–1181.

Savage-Rumbaugh, E. Sue. *Ape Language: From Conditioned Response to Symbol.* New York: Columbia University Press, 1986.

Savage-Rumbaugh, E. Sue, and Roger Lewin. *Kanzi: The Ape at the Brink of the Human Mind.* New York: Wiley, 1994.

Savage-Rumbaugh, E. Sue, Kelly McDonald, Rose A. Sevcik, William D. Hopkins, and Elizabeth Rubert. "Spontaneous Symbol Acquisition and Communicative Use by Pygmy Chimpanzees (Pan Paniscus)." *Journal of Experimental Psychology: General* 115, 3 (1986): 211–235.

Savage-Rumbaugh, E. Sue, Jeannine Murphy, Rose A. Sevcik, Karen E. Brakke, Shelly L. Williams, Duane M. Rumbaugh, and Elizabeth Bates. "Language Comprehension in Ape and Child." *Monographs of the Society for Research in Child Development* (1993): i–252.

Schechtman, Marya. *The Constitution of Selves.* Cornell University Press, 2007.

Schwartz, Bennett L., Christian A. Meissner, Megan Hoffman, Siân Evans, and Leslie D. Frazier. "Event Memory and Misinformation Effects in a Gorilla (Gorilla Gorilla Gorilla)." *Animal Cognition* 7, 2 (2004): 93–100.

Schwartz, Bennett L., Megan L. Hoffman, and Siân Evans. "Episodic-like Memory in a Gorilla: A Review and New Findings." *Learning and Motivation* 36, 2 (2005): 226–244.

Schwitzgebel, Eric. "A Phenomenal, Dispositional Account of Belief." *Nous* 36, 2 (2002): 249–275.

Searle, John R. "Animal Minds." *Midwest Studies In Philosophy* 19, 1 (1994): 206–219.

See, Adam. "Reevaluating Chimpanzee Vocal Signals: Toward a Multimodal Account of the Origins of Human Communication." In *The Evolution of Social Communication in Primates,* edited by Marco Pina and Nathalie Gontier, 195–215. New York: Springer International Publishing, 2014.

Seed, Amanda, and Richard Byrne. "Animal Tool-Use." *Current Biology* 20, 23 (2010): R1032–R1039.

Seeley, Thomas D. *Honeybee Democracy.* Princeton: Princeton University Press, 2010.

Seeley, Thomas D., and Susannah C. Buhrman. "Nest-Site Selection in Honey Bees: How Well Do Swarms Implement the 'Best-of-N' Decision Rule?" *Behavioral Ecology and Sociobiology* 49, 5 (2001): 416–427.

Seeley, Thomas D., and P. Kirk Visscher. "Choosing a Home: How the Scouts in a Honey Bee Swarm Perceive the Completion of Their Group Decision Making." *Behavioral Ecology and Sociobiology* 54, 5 (2003): 511–520.

Sellars, Wilfred. "Empiricism and the Philosophy of Mind." In *Foundations of Science and the Concepts of Psychology and Psychoanalysis*, edited by Herbert Feigl and Michael Scriven, 253–329. Minnesota Studies in the Philosophy of Science. Minneapolis, MN: Univerisity of Minnesota Press, 1956.

Senghas, Ann, and Marie Coppola. "Children Creating Language: How Nicaraguan Sign Language Acquired a Spatial Grammar." *Psychological Science* 12, 4 (2001): 323–328.

Seyfarth, Robert M., and Dorothy L. Cheney. "Production, Usage, and Comprehension in Animal Vocalizations." *Brain and Language* 115, 1 (2010): 92–100.

Shanker, Stuart G., and Barbara J. King. "The Emergence of a New Paradigm in Ape Language Research: Beyond Interactionism." *Behavioral and Brain Sciences* 25, 05 (2002): 646–651.

Shannon, Claude Elwood, and Warren Weaver. *The Mathematical Theory of Communication.* Urbana: University of Illinois Press, 1949.

Sharpe, Lynda L., Amy Hill, and Michael I. Cherry. "Individual Recognition in a Wild Cooperative Mammal Using Contact Calls." *Animal Behaviour* 86, 5 (2013): 893–900.

Shaw, Robert, and John Bransford. *Perceiving, Acting, and Knowing: Toward an Ecological Psychology.* Hillsdale: New York: Lawrence Erlbaum Associates, 1977.

Shettleworth, Sara J. "Clever Animals and Killjoy Explanations in Comparative Psychology." *Trends in Cognitive Sciences* 14, 11 (2010a): 477–481.

—— *Cognition, Evolution and Behavior.* Oxford: Oxford University Press, 2010b.

—— *Fundamentals of Comparative Cognition.* New York: Oxford University Press, 2013.

Shriver, Adam. "Minding Mammals." *Philosophical Psychology* 19, 4 (2006): 433–442.

Shumaker, Robert W., Ann M. Palkovich, Benjamin B. Beck, Gregory A. Guagnano, and Harold Morowitz. "Spontaneous Use of Magnitude Discrimination and Ordination by the Orangutan (Pongo Pygmaeus)." *Journal of Comparative Psychology* 115, 4 (2001): 385–391.

Silk, Joan B. "Using the 'F'-Word in Primatology." *Behaviour* 139, 2–3 (2002): 421–446.

Singer, Peter. *Animal Liberation.* New York: New York Review of Books; distributed by Random House, 1990.

Slobodchikoff, C.N. "Cognition and Communication in Prairie Dogs." In *The Cognitive Animal, Empirical and Theoretical Perspectives,* 257–264. Cambridge, MA: MIT Press, 2002.

Slobodchikoff, C.N., Andrea Paseka, and Jennifer L. Verdolin. "Prairie Dog Alarm Calls Encode Labels about Predator Colors." *Animal Cognition* 12, 3 (2009): 435–439.

Slocombe, Katie E., and Klaus Zuberbühler. "Functionally Referential Communication in a Chimpanzee." *Current Biology* 15, 19 (2005): 1779–1784.

—— "Food-Associated Calls in Chimpanzees: Responses to Food Types or Food Preferences?" *Animal Behaviour* 72, 5 (2006): 989–999.

Smet, Anna F., and Richard W. Byrne. "African Elephants Can Use Human Pointing Cues to Find Hidden Food." *Current Biology* 23, 20 (2013): 2033–2037.

Smith, J. David. "The Study of Animal Metacognition." *Trends in Cognitive Sciences* 13, 9 (2009): 389–396.

Smith, J. David, Jonathan Schull, Jared Strote, Kelli McGee, Roian Egnor, and Linda Erb. "The Uncertain Response in the Bottlenosed Dolphin (Tursiops Truncatus)." *Journal of Experimental Psychology: General* 124, 4 (1995): 391–408.

Smith, J. David, Wendy E. Shields, Jonathan Schull, and David A. Washburn. "The Uncertain Response in Humans and Animals." *Cognition* 62, 1 (1997): 75–97.

Smith, J. David, Wendy E. Shields, and David A. Washburn. "The Comparative Psychology of Uncertainty Monitoring and Metacognition." *Behavioral and Brain Sciences* 26, 3 (2003): 317–339.

Smith, J. David, Michael J. Beran, Justin J. Couchman, and Mariana V.C. Coutinho. "The Comparative Study of Metacognition: Sharper Paradigms, Safer Inferences." *Psychonomic Bulletin & Review* 15, 4 (2008): 679–691.

Smith, J. David, Justin J. Couchman, and Michael J. Beran. "The Highs and Lows of Theoretical Interpretation in Animal-Metacognition Research." *Philosophical Transactions of the Royal Society B: Biological Sciences* 367, 1594 (2012): 1297–1309.

Sober, Elliott. "Comparative Psychology Meets Evolutionary Biology." In *Thinking with Animals*, edited by Lorraine Daston and Gregg Mitman, 85–99. New York: Columbia University Press, 2005.

—— "Anthropomorphism, Parsimony, and Common Ancestry." *Mind & Language* 27, 3 (2012): 229–238.

Solms, Mark. "Dreaming and REM Sleep Are Controlled by Different Brain Mechanisms." *Behavioral and Brain Sciences* 23 (2000): 793–1121.

Spelke, Elizabeth S. "Principles of Object Perception." *Cognitive Science* 14, 1 (1990): 29–56.

Spelke, Elizabeth S., and Gretchen Van de Walle. "Perceiving and Reasoning about Objects: Insights from Infants." *Spatial Representation: Problems in Philosophy and Psychology* (1993): 132–161.

Spelke, Elizabeth S., Claes von Hofsten, and Roberta Kestenbaum. "Object Perception in Infancy: Interaction of Spatial and Kinetic Information for Object Boundaries." *Developmental Psychology* 25, 2 (1989): 185–196.

Sperber, Dan, and Deirdre Wilson. *Relevance: Communication and Cognition*. Cambridge, MA: Harvard University Press, 1986.

Stegmann, Ulrich. *Animal Communication Theory: Information and Influence*. Cambridge: Cambridge University Press, 2013.

Stich, Stephen P. "Do Animals Have Beliefs?" *Australasian Journal of Philosophy* 57 (1979): 15–28.

—— *From Folk Psychology to Cognitive Science: The Case against Belief*. Cambridge, MA: MIT Press, 1983.

Stoerig, Petra. "Blindsight, Conscious Vision, and the Role of Primary Visual Cortex." *Progress in Brain Research* 155 (2006): 217–234.

Stokoe, William C. *Language in Hand: Why Sign Came Before Speech*. Washington DC: Gallaudet University Press, 2001.

Strack, Fritz, Leonard L. Martin, and Sabine Stepper. "Inhibiting and Facilitating Conditions of the Human Smile: A Nonobtrusive Test of the Facial Feedback Hypothesis." *Journal of Personality and Social Psychology* 54, 5 (1988): 768–777.

Strawson, Galen. *Real Materialism: And Other Essays*. Oxford: Oxford University Press, 2008.

Subiaul, Francys, Jennifer Vonk, Sanae Okamoto-Barth, and Jochen Barth. "Do Chimpanzees Learn Reputation by Observation? Evidence from Direct and Indirect Experience with Generous and Selfish Strangers." *Animal Cognition* 11, 4 (2008): 611–623.

Suddendorf, Thomas, and David L. Butler. "The Nature of Visual Self-Recognition." *Trends in Cognitive Sciences* 17, 3 (2013): 121–127.

Suddendorf, Thomas, and Michael C. Corballis. "Mental Time Travel and the Evolution of the Human Mind." *Genetic, Social, and General Psychology Monographs* 123, 2 (1997): 133–167.

—— "The Evolution of Foresight: What Is Mental Time Travel, and Is It Unique to Humans?" *Behavioral and Brain Sciences* 30, 3 (2007): 299–312.

—— "Behavioural Evidence for Mental Time Travel in Nonhuman Animals." *Behavioural Brain Research* 215, 2 (2010): 292–298.

Suddendorf, Thomas, and Andrew Whiten. "Mental Evolution and Development: Evidence for Secondary Representation in Children, Great Apes, and Other Animals." *Psychological Bulletin* 127, 5 (2001): 629–650.

Taglialatela, Jared P., Jamie L. Russell, Jennifer A. Schaeffer, and William D. Hopkins. "Chimpanzee Vocal Signaling Points to a Multimodal Origin of Human Language." *PLoS ONE* 6, 4 (2011): e18852.

Taglialatela, Jared P., Lisa Reamer, Steven J. Schapiro, and William D. Hopkins. "Social Learning of a Communicative Signal in Captive Chimpanzees." *Biology Letters* 8, 4 (2012): 498–501.

Tan, Shaun. *The Arrival*. New York: Arthur A. Levine Books, 2007.

Tanner, Joanne E. "Gestural Phrases and Gestural Exchanges by a Pair of Zoo-Living Lowland Gorillas." *Gesture* 4, 1 (2004): 1–24.

Tanner, Joanne E., Francine G. Patterson, and Richard W. Byrne. "The Development of Spontaneous Gestures in Zoo-Living Gorillas and Sign-Taught Gorillas: From Action and Location to Object Representation." *Journal of Developmental Processes* 1 (2006): 69–103.

Terrace, Herbert S, and Janet Metcalfe. *The Missing Link in Cognition: Origins of Self-Reflective Consciousness*. Oxford: Oxford University Press, 2005.

Terrace, Herbert S., Laura-Ann Petitto, Richard J. Sanders, and Thomas G. Bever. "Can an Ape Create a Sentence?" *Science* 206, 4421 (1979): 891–902.

The Stanford Encyclopedia of Philosophy, edited by Edward N. Zalta, published by The Metaphysics Research Lab. http://plato.stanford.edu/ Accessed July 25, 2014.

Thelen, Esther, and Linda Smith. *A Dynamic Systems Approach to the Development of Cognition and Action*. Cambridge, MA: MIT Press, 1996.

Thelen, Esther, Gregor Schoner, Christian Scheier, and Linda B. Smith. "The Dynamics of Embodiment: A Field Theory of Infant Perseverative Reaching." *Behavioral and Brain Sciences* 24, 1 (2001): 1–34.

Thompson, Evan. *Mind in Life: Biology, Phenomenology, and the Sciences of Mind*. Cambridge, MA: Harvard University Press, 2007.

Thorndike, Edward L. *Individuality*. Boston: Houghton, Mifflin, 1911.

Tibbetts, Elizabeth A., and James Dale. "Individual Recognition: It Is Good to Be Different." *Trends in Ecology & Evolution* 22, 10 (2007): 529–537.

Tinbergen, Niko. *The Study of Instinct.* Oxford: Clarendon Press, 1951.

—— *Curious Naturalists*. New York: Basic Books, 1958.

—— "On Aims and Methods of Ethology." *Zeitschrift Für Tierpsychologie* 20, 4 (1963): 410–433.

Tinbergen, N., and A.C. Perdeck. "On the Stimulus Situation Releasing the Begging Response in the Newly Hatched Herring Gull Chick (Larus Argentatus Argentatus Pont.)." *Behaviour* 3, 1 (1950): 1–39.

Tolman, Edward C., B.F. Ritchie, and D. Kalish. "Studies in Spatial Learning. II. Place Learning versus Response Learning." *Journal of Experimental Psychology* 36, 3 (1946): 221–229.

—— "Studies in Spatial Learning. V. Response Learning vs. Place Learning by the Non-Correction Method." *Journal of Experimental Psychology* 37, 4 (1947): 285–292.

Tomasello, Michael. *Origins of Human Communication*. Cambridge, MA: MIT Press, 2008.

Tomasello, Michael, and Klaus Zuberbühler. "Primate Vocal and Gestural Communication." In *The Cognitive Animal: Empirical and Theoretical Perspectives on Animal Cognition*, edited by M. Bekoff, C. Allen, and G.M. Burghardt, 293–299. Cambridge, MA: MIT Press, 2002.

Tomasello, M., M. Davis-Dasilva, L. Camak, and K. Bard. "Observational Learning of Tool-Use by Young Chimpanzees." *Human Evolution* 2, 2 (1987): 175–183.

Tomasello, Michael, Malinda Carpenter, and Ulf Liszkowski. "A New Look at Infant Pointing." *Child Development* 78, 3 (2007): 705–722.

Trevarthen, Colwyn. "Descriptive Analyses of Infant Communicative Behavior." In *Studies in Mother–Infant Interaction*, edited by H.R. Schaffer, 227–270. London, UK: Academic Press, 1977.

—— "Communication and Co-Operation in Early Infancy: A Description of Primary Intersubjectivity." In *Before Speech*, edited by M. Bullowa, 321–347. Cambridge: Cambridge University Press, 1979.

Trevarthen, Colwyn, and Penelope Hubley. "Secondary Intersubjectivity: Confidence, Confiding and Acts of Meaning in the First Year." *Action, Gesture and Symbol: The Emergence of Language* (1978): 183–229.

Tschudin, Alain, Josep Call, R.I.M. Dunbar, Gabrielle Harris, and Charmaine van der Elst. "Comprehension of Signs by Dolphins (Tursiops Truncatus)." *Journal of Comparative Psychology* 115, 1 (2001): 100–105.

Tulving, Endel. *Elements of Episodic Memory.* Oxford: Clarendon Press, 1983.

—— "Episodic Memory and Autonoesis: Uniquely Human?" In *The Missing Link in Cognition: Origins of Self-Reflective Consciousness,* edited by Herbert S. Terrace and Janet Metcalfe, 3–56. New York: Oxford University Press, 2005.

Twain, Mark. *Tom Sawyer and Huckleberry Finn.* Ware: Wordsworth Classics, 1992.

Tye, Michael. "The Problem of Simple Minds: Is There Anything It Is like to Be a Honey Bee?" *Philosophical Studies* 88 (1997): 289–317.

Udell, Monique A.R., Nicole R. Dorey, and Clive D.L. Wynne. "Wolves Outperform Dogs in Following Human Social Cues." *Animal Behaviour* 76, 6 (2008): 1767–1773.

—— "Can Your Dog Read Your Mind? Understanding the Causes of Canine Perspective Taking." *Learning & Behavior* 39, 4 (2011): 289–302.

Udell, Monique A.R., Jessica M. Spencer, Nicole R. Dorey, and Clive D.L. Wynne. "Human-Socialized Wolves Follow Diverse Human Gestures and They May Not Be Alone." *International Journal of Comparative Psychology,* 25 (2012): 97–117.

Uller, Claudia. "Disposition to Recognize Goals in Infant Chimpanzees." *Animal Cognition* 7 (2004): 154–161.

Van Gelder, Tim. "What Might Cognition Be, If Not Computation?" *The Journal of Philosophy* 92, 7 (1995): 345–381.

Varner, Gary E. *Personhood, Ethics, and Animal Cognition: Situating Animals in Hare's Two Level Utilitarianism.* Oxford: Oxford University Press, 2012.

Vasconcelos, Marco. "Transitive Inference in Non-Human Animals: An Empirical and Theoretical Analysis." *Behavioural Processes* 78, 3 (2008): 313–334.

Veà, Joaquim, and Jordi Sabater-Pi. "Spontaneous Pointing Behaviour in the Wild Pygmy Chimpanzee (Pan Paniscus)." *Folia Primatologica* 69, 5 (1998): 289–290.

Vigo, Ronaldo, and Colin Allen. "How to Reason without Words: Inference as Categorization." *Cognitive Processing* 10, 1 (2009): 77–88.

Vinden, Penelope G. "Children's Understanding of Mind and Emotion: A Multi-Culture Study." *Cognition & Emotion* 13, 1 (1999): 19–48.

Voltaire. *Philosophical Dictionary.* Translated by H.I. Woolf. New York: A.A. Knopf, 1929.

Von Frisch, Karl. *The Dance Language and Orientation of Bees.* Cambridge: Harvard University Press, 1967.

von Rohr, Claudia Rudolf, Judith M. Burkart, and Carel P. van Schaik. "Evolutionary Precursors of Social Norms in Chimpanzees: A New Approach." *Biology & Philosophy* 26, 1 (2011): 1–30.

von Rohr, Claudia Rudolf, Sonja E. Koski, Judith M. Burkart, Clare Caws, Orlaith N. Fraser, Angela Ziltener, and Carel P. van Schaik. "Impartial Third-Party Interventions in Captive Chimpanzees: A Reflection of Community Concern." Edited by Mark Briffa. *PLoS ONE* 7, 3 (2012): e32494.

Warneken, Felix, and Michael Tomasello. "Altruistic Helping in Human Infants and Young Chimpanzees." *Science* 311, 5765 (2006): 1301–1303.

Watson, John B. "Psychology as the Behaviorist Views It." *Psychological Review* 20, 2 (1913): 158–177.

Watumull, Jeffrey, Marc D. Hauser, Ian G. Roberts, and Norbert Hornstein. "On Recursion." *Frontiers in Psychology* 4 (2014).

Watwood, Stephanie L., Peter L. Tyack, and Randall S. Wells. "Whistle Sharing in Paired Male Bottlenose Dolphins, Tursiops Truncatus." *Behavioral Ecology and Sociobiology* 55, 6 (2004): 531–543.

Wegner, Daniel M. *The Illusion of Conscious Will*. Cambridge, MA: MIT Press, 2002.

Weisbuch, Max, Kristin Pauker, and Nalini Ambady. "The Subtle Transmission of Race Bias via Televised Nonverbal Behavior." *Science* 326, 5960 (2009): 1711–1714.

Weiss, Alexander, James E. King, and Lori Perkins. "Personality and Subjective Well-Being in Orangutans (Pongo Pygmaeus and Pongo Abelii)." *Journal of Personality and Social Psychology* 90, 3 (2006): 501–511.

Wellman, Henry M., David Cross, and Julanne Watson. "Meta-Analysis of Theory-of-Mind Development: The Truth about False Belief." *Child Development* 72, 3 (2001): 655–684.

Wheeler, Brandon C. "Production and Perception of Situationally Variable Alarm Calls in Wild Tufted Capuchin Monkeys (Cebus Apella Nigritus)." *Behavioral Ecology and Sociobiology* 64, 6 (2010): 989–1000.

Wheeler, Brandon C., W.A. Searcy, M.H. Christiansen, M.C. Corballis, J. Fischer, C. Grüter, D. Margoliash, et al. "Communication." In *Animal Thinking: Contemporary Issues in Comparative Cognition*, edited by R. Menzel and J. Fischer, 187–205. Cambridge, MA: MIT Press, 2011.

White, Thomas. *In Defense of Dolphins: The New Moral Frontier*. New York: John Wiley & Sons, 2007.

Whiten, Andrew. "Primate Culture and Social Learning." *Cognitive Science* 24, 3 (2000): 477–508.

Whiten, Andrew, and Richard W. Byrne. *Machiavellian Intelligence II: Extensions and Evaluations*. Cambridge; New York: Cambridge University Press, 1997.

Whiten, Andrew, and Byrne, Richard. "The Machiavellian Intellect hypotheses." In *Machiavellian Intelligence*, edited by R. W. Byrne & A. Whiten, 1–9. Oxford: Oxford University Press, 1988.

Wilson, Timothy D. *Strangers to Ourselves: Discovering the Adaptive Unconscious*. Cambridge, MA: Belknap Press of Harvard University Press, 2002.

Wimmer, Heinz, and Josef Perner. "Beliefs about Beliefs: Representation and Constraining Function of Wrong Beliefs in Young Children's Understanding of Deception." *Cognition* 13, 1 (1983): 103–128.

Wit, Sanne de, and Anthony Dickinson. "Associative Theories of Goal-Directed Behaviour: A Case for Animal–human Translational Models." *Psychological Research PRPF* 73, 4 (2009): 463–476.

Wozniak, Robert. "Conwy Lloyd Morgan, Mental Evolution, and The Introduction to Comparative Psychology," 1997. http://www.brynmawr.edu/psychology/rwozniak/morgan.html#5. Accessed July 25, 2014.

Wynne, Clive D.L. *Do Animals Think?* Princeton: Princeton University Press, 2004.

Wynne, Clive D.L, and Monique A.R Udell. *Animal Cognition: Evolution, Behavior and Cognition*. New York: Palgrave Macmillan, 2013.

Xu, Fei, and Elizabeth S. Spelke. "Large Number Discrimination in 6-Month-Old Infants." *Cognition* 74, 1 (2000): B1–B11.

Yazdi, Amir Amin, Tim P. German, Margaret Anne Defeyter, and Michael Siegal. "Competence and Performance in Belief–Desire Reasoning across Two Cultures: The Truth, the Whole Truth and Nothing but the Truth about False Belief?" *Cognition* 100, 2 (2006): 343–368.

Zentall, Thomas R., Tricia S. Clement, Ramesh S. Bhatt, and Jessica Allen. "Episodic-like Memory in Pigeons." *Psychonomic Bulletin & Review* 8, 4 (2001): 685–690.

Index